HISTORY OF THE UNITED STATES FROM 1865 TO THE PRESENT

DOUBLEDAY COLLEGE COURSE GUIDES

Analytic Geometry	*William L. Schaaf*	U1	$1.95
The Calculus	*William L. Schaaf*	U5	$1.95
Essentials of Zoology	*Leon Augustus Hausman*	U3	$1.75
Fundamentals of Speech	*George W. Hibbitt*	U8	$1.45
History of English Literature to 1660	*Martin S. Day*	U10	$1.95
History of English Literature 1660 to 1837	*Martin S. Day*	U12	$1.95
History of the United States to 1865	*James P. Shenton*	U4	$1.75
Introduction to American Education	*S. E. Frost, Jr.*	U2	$1.75
Introduction to American Government	*James Tracy Crown*	U11	$1.75
An Introduction to Psychology	*John F. Hahn*	U7	$1.45
An Outline of English Composition	*Alan B. Howes*	U6	$1.45
Principles of Accounting	*R. Dean White and Floyd W. White*	U9	$1.75

HISTORY OF THE UNITED STATES FROM 1865 TO THE PRESENT

James P. Shenton, *Ph.D.*

Associate Professor of History

Columbia University

A COLLEGE COURSE GUIDE

DOUBLEDAY & COMPANY, INC., GARDEN CITY, NEW YORK

1964

To

Henry and Julia Ebel

Excerpt from *The Crack-Up* by F. Scott Fitzgerald. Copyright 1945 by New Directions. Reprinted by permission of New Directions.

Library of Congress Catalog Card Number 64–11740

Printed in the United States of America
First Edition

Preface

The Civil War was a major turning point in American history: a new tradition had to be established, new values had to be found, new directions charted. Throughout the century that has elapsed since the Civil War, it has been the continuing quest of the citizens of the United States, and of their leaders, to achieve a workable and satisfactory national identity, philosophy, and objective. This book tells the story of that hundred-year quest.

The text has been written to explain American history since 1865 in all its dimensions. Beginning with the chaos and conflict of the post-war period, it examines the nation's growth in material terms and the nation's progress in ideological terms. Detailed attention is given to the specific personalities and events of the past hundred years. And this factual material is expanded and enriched by discussion of the major historical movements and themes which have influenced or resulted from American growth: urbanization, industrialization, corruption and reform, physical expansion, the swelling of the population by immigrants, the decline of agriculture, the increasing interaction and interdependence with the other nations of the world. America, a nation that in 1865 was economically wracked, militarily depleted, and concerned almost exclusively with her domestic tensions and needs, has become, in 1964, a nation of supreme material wealth and military power, whose every move is of potential international consequence.

A companion volume to *History of the United States to 1865,* this text is broad and inclusive in its coverage so as to meet the varying needs of individuals in their study of American history. Intended to provide the fundamentals of a general introductory college course in American history, suitable both for study and for review, the text aims to be clear and understandable in plan and detail. A reader who wishes to use it for home study may well do so.

The book is divided into four parts: The Reunited Republic, The Industrial Republic, The Progressive Republic, and The New Republic. A number of maps, graphs, and charts depict various significant aspects of American history. The tables of Presidents and political parties at the back of the book are designed for helpful and efficient use as reference tools; and the comprehensive index should prove a convenient guide.

Faced with a world in which man possesses power so vast that it can finally either liberate him or consume him, the American people still seek to define the national purpose. No better beginning exists for such a search than a re-examination of the past, for it is from there that we have emerged. As F. Scott Fitzgerald, America's great writer of the golden twenties, reminds us: "So we beat on, boats against the current, borne back ceaselessly into the past."

I wish to acknowledge my deep indebtedness to Henry Ebel of Columbia University, for his generous and artful criticism; to Lewy Olfson and Lawrence W. Lamm of Copeland & Lamm, Inc., for their careful editorial work; to my mother, for her infinite patience with the cluttering of her home made necessary by the writing of this book; and to Max Teninbaum, who was a source of endless moral support and friendly guidance.

J.P.S.

Contents

PART TWO

The Industrial Republic

PART THREE

The Progressive Republic

PART FOUR

The New Republic

List of Maps, Graphs, and Charts

Part One

THE REUNITED REPUBLIC

Chapter 1

Reconstruction in the South

April 9, 1865: the Civil War was over; the peace had not yet begun. Grant and Sherman had revolutionized the conduct of war, leaving much of the South in rubble; and there were men in Washington who were determined that when the South was rebuilt, it would be along new social and political lines.

THE COST OF THE CIVIL WAR

The loss of life in the four years of conflict had been staggering. Altogether, 359,528 soldiers are known to have died for the Union; for the Confederacy, whose records are incomplete, the estimated deaths totaled 258,000. The number of wounded on both sides ran into the hundreds of thousands, and no one is certain how many of these men were permanently maimed. The scale of loss in the South is suggested by the fact that, in those Southern counties where the necessary records have survived, more than half of the white female population after the war consisted of widows. It had cost the federal government more than $3,400,000,000 to carry on the war. The cost of federal pensions after the war exceeded $8,200,000,000. If similar costs are estimated for the Confederacy, the direct and indirect charges of the war approach $20,000,000,000. And yet, even this figure does not include the staggering cost of cities wholly or partly destroyed; of the ruined plantations and farms of the South; of the twisted rail routes and burned bridges that marked the paths of the advancing armies. And no accountant could estimate in dollars the cost of the psychological scars that accompanied this devastation. After the war, Sherman could write:

> Look to the South, and you who went with me through that land can best say if they too have not been fearfully punished. Mourning in every household, desolation written in broad characters across the whole face of their country, cities in ashes and fields laid waste, their commerce gone, their system of labor annihilated and destroyed. Ruin, poverty, and distress everywhere, and now pestilence adding the very cap sheaf to their stack of misery; her proud men begging for pardon and appealing for permission to raise food for their children; her five million of slaves free, and their value lost to their former masters forever.

Though the Northerner had his own bitter reflections—Andersonville and its 15,000 starved corpses haunted and horrified the memory and imagination—he returned, at least, to the relative stability of an intact home and an economy which had flourished in the hot-house stimulation of war financing. For the Southern veteran returning to Columbia or Charleston, journey's end was "a wilderness of ruins . . . a mass of blackened chimneys and crumbling walls." Endless sacrifice had earned the South nothing but the wreck of a civilization and the right to despair. A rebellion begun in pride and defiance had ended in the ultimate ignominy of military occupation.

OPPOSING ATTITUDES TOWARD RECONSTRUCTION

When Lincoln made the Northern object of the war the restoration of the Union, the South was given official warning that the war could end in either the defeat of the federal forces or the destruction of the Confederacy, but nowhere in between. Lincoln had embraced the Buchanan doctrine that the framers of the Constitution "never intended to implant in its bosom the seeds of its own destruction, nor were they at its creation guilty of the absurdity of providing for its own dissolution"; he had specifically rejected the legal possibility of secession. In the course of fighting the war, the preservation of the Union had remained the paramount objective of the North. Even the issuance of the Emancipation Proclamation was not contrary to this primary objective, since Lincoln justified it as a "military necessity." Now, if Lincoln held to a literal interpretation of this position, the moment the fighting ceased the Confederate states were entitled to return—with their rights intact—to a full participation in the federal government. Yet no one could deny that these states had been in a state of rebellion. To restore the South without exacting consequences for her effort to disrupt the Union struck many Northerners as rewarding the wicked. It was also necessary to face the unpleasant truth that although secession was not a *de jure* possibility, it had been a *de facto* occurrence. Normal political communications between the sections had broken down. There had to be some interregnum method of providing for the transition from illegal secessionhood to political restoration. It was upon this issue that Lincoln and the radical faction of the Republican party disagreed, thereby opening a bitter dispute that would long survive the war.

Presidential Theories of Reconstruction. Lincoln viewed the task of reconstruction as an executive function. Using the war powers vested in the President, he proceeded to establish provisional governments in the occupied areas of the South. In a proclamation issued on December 8, 1863, Lincoln set up a system whereby presidential pardons would be extended to most supporters of the Confederacy who agreed to take an oath supporting "the Constitution of the United States and the Union of the states thereunder." When, in any Southern state, the equivalent of a tenth of the number of voters who had cast their vote in 1860 swore their allegiance to the Union and established a state government abolishing slavery, that government would receive executive recognition as the legitimate state authority. This plan was implemented in Tennessee, Louisiana, Arkansas, and Virginia. Since portions of these states were still under Confederate control, hostile members of Congress could charge that the elections held were irregular. Efforts to elect federal and state officers for Louisiana in 1864 were challenged by members of Congress as invalid under state law. On June 29, 1864, the United States Senate refused to seat the newly elected senators from Arkansas. Lincoln had no better success with Tennessee and Virginia, the former being denied readmission until 1866, even though Andrew Johnson, a Tennessean, sat in the White House.

Congressional Theories of Reconstruction. Under the leadership of such radicals as Henry Winter Davis, Benjamin Wade, Zachariah Chandler, George W. Julian, Thaddeus Stevens, and Charles S. Sumner, the Republican 38th Congress challenged a Republican President for control of reconstruction. On July 2, 1864, Congress sent Lincoln the stringent Wade-Davis Bill. This provided that in each reconquered Southern state the President would appoint a provisional governor—with senatorial approval. The governor would then be assigned the task of enrolling white male citizens—Negroes, it must be remembered, though free, were not citizens, and therefore were ineligible for the franchise—and once a majority of the enrolled took an oath of allegiance, "the loyal people of the state" would be permitted to organize a new government. But the Wade-Davis Bill specifically denied to anyone who had served in the Confederate government or armed forces the right to participate in the organization of the new government. Before Congress would accept the legitimacy of such a state government it would have to prohibit slavery, repudiate "rebel" debts, and exclude from office and the franchise most Confederate officeholders. Congress' position was clearly incompatible with that of Lincoln.

The Veto of the Wade-Davis Bill. Lincoln chose a peculiar method of expressing his distrust of the Wade-Davis proposal. He received the bill an hour before the adjournment of Congress and simply exercised a pocket veto to prevent it from becoming law. Unfortunately for the tranquillity of his party, however, he decided to issue a statement explaining his failure to sign the bill. In it he declared that while "unprepared by a formal approval of this bill to be inflexibly committed to any single plan of restoration, . . . nevertheless I am fully satisfied with the system for restoration contained in the bill as one very proper plan for the loyal people of any State choosing to adopt it." Thus, Lincoln seemed to be offering a compromise to Congress: he would accept the congressional plan of reconstruction as at least potentially of equal merit with his own. But, as he slyly noted, he would leave it to "the loyal people of any State" to decide whether to inflict upon themselves executive leniency or legislative harshness.

Publication of the Wade-Davis Manifesto. Benjamin Wade and Henry Winter Davis, both endowed with lively tempers, responded with a joint manifesto published in the New York *Tribune* on August 5, 1864. In it they charged—with "indignation"—that Lincoln had manipulated reconstruction for his personal political advancement, and that he planned to use the electoral votes of the states reconstructed under his authority in order to secure his re-election in 1864. They had supported Lincoln hitherto, they declared, out of necessity; but they had no intention of following him blindly now that war had ended. Wade and Davis succinctly defined the radical position:

> . . . he must understand that our support is of a cause and not of a man; that the authority of Congress is paramount and must be respected; that the whole body of the Union men of Congress will not submit to be impeached by him of rash and unconstitutional legislation; and if he wishes our support, he must confine himself to

his executive duties—to obey and execute, not make the laws—to suppress by arms armed rebellion, and leave political reorganization to Congress.

Lincoln and Flexible Reconstruction. The intensely politic Lincoln moved cautiously in his subsequent relations with Congress whenever the issue of reconstruction was raised. He never formally surrendered presidential authority over reconstruction; but he showed an increasing disposition to share control with Congress. Only three days before his assassination he publicly reaffirmed that he was prepared to consider alternative methods of reconstruction. But he firmly dismissed as "utterly immaterial" the question of whether or not the Southern states had seceded. The issue, as Lincoln understood it, was that "the seceded States, so called, are out of their proper practical relation with the Union." It was imperative that these relations be restored as soon as possible. The conditions for the restoration of each state should be tailored to meet its particular needs.

Thoroughly aware that legal precedent carries heavy weight among Americans, Lincoln pushed, although with little success, for the quick reorganization of Louisiana. Had he succeeded in this, it is likely that a more lenient version of reconstruction would have prevailed. But throughout the developing debate over the nature of reconstruction, Lincoln took care to avoid identifying himself with an inflexible plan of presidential reconstruction, understanding that the art of politics is accommodation. What would have happened had Lincoln not been assassinated is conjectural; but the evidence suggests that he would have pursued a flexible policy which would have permitted compromise. The tragedy of his successor Andrew Johnson was that he converted a policy of accommodation into an inflexible plan, and made the war between executive and legislature inescapable.

THE AFTERMATH OF DEFEAT

The Economic Plight of the South. The concept of "reconstruction" can only be understood in terms of the conditions which prevailed in the defeated South. The catastrophic human and material losses in the area have already been indicated. The possibilities of recovery were set even further back by the massive social dislocations that followed the emancipation of the slaves. During the last months of the war, freedmen left the plantations by the hundreds of thousands and poured into the towns and cities of the South. Without means of support, subsisting from day to day, they faced the threats of famine and plague.

The plight of untold thousands of destitute whites was only slightly less fearsome. The simplest elements of daily existence presented an endless struggle. Poverty was everywhere. The typical Southern family made do with broken furniture, miscellaneous items of crockery and cutlery, and clocks and watches that rarely worked. Such elementary items as hairbrushes, toothbrushes, combs, pins, needles, and thread were almost unobtainable; tea, coffee, sugar, spices, and candles had entirely disappeared. Formerly wealthy planters now ate corn bread and cow peas—food which, before the war, had been considered fit only for cattle and slaves. Most plantations were encumbered with mortgage and debt; and many planters, unable to meet their obligations, saw their remaining lands pass into the hands of strangers. The South Carolinian writer William Gilmore Simms described his own situation—and his was paralleled throughout the South—thus:

> I have lost everything but my lands. I have barely a sufficiency of clothes—chiefly homespun—for decency; and with 9 persons to support, my whole income is but $10 per week. . . . Nearly all my hogs & cattle have been destroyed. . . . My son, just recovering from typhoid, comes home to me naked. . . . Of 16 Bedsteads, I have 1 left; so, in proportion of matresses & feather beds. We have not a chair or a table. Not a knife or fork; hardly a cup or plate or tumbler. And such things we cannot buy. Our basins for washing are of tin, made out of tin saved amid the ruins of Columbia. We have literally nothing left us. . . . Alas! Alas! We are cherry stones in the hands of Fate who delights in flinging!

Southern Morale after the War. For ordinary folk the aftermath of defeat was even more acute. Thousands were homeless, many of them widows with children; often they survived by going from door to door begging their daily bread. In the counties surrounding Atlanta, no less than 35,000 men, women, and children were dependent upon the federal government for rations. One contemporary traveler described most Southern towns when he wrote: "A city of ruins, of desolation, of vacant houses, of widowed women, of rotting wharves, of deserted warehouses, of weed-wild gardens, of miles of grass-grown streets, of acres of pitiful and voiceful barrenness,—that is Charleston." Where towns remained intact, human morale had been so utterly crushed that living men resembled corpses in their inertia and passivity. Somehow out of this grim reality a normal existence had to be restored to the South. Reconstruction involved, therefore, not only the question of the proper relationship of the defeated states to the Union, but also the future of some ten million people, black and white. For them reconstruction was not a set of abstract principles but a question of survival, a point Whitelaw Reid, later editor of the New York *Tribune,* made graphically when he wrote, "The problem which the South has to solve [is] not how to be comfortable, . . . but how to live at all."

Railroads in the Defeated South. Conditions in the countryside were no less dismaying than those in the cities. One English traveler noted that "between Chattanooga and Atlanta I do not remember to have seen a smile upon a single human face." Rail travel was utterly disrupted. With bridges down, long stretches of track torn up, stations destroyed or gutted, and rolling stock dilapidated, only the rudiments of service remained. Passengers were fortunate if they found themselves traveling at ten miles an hour, and with only an occasional transfer to wagons where the tracks had been torn up. Few railway coaches still had glass in their windows; thin boards served to protect the rider from the elements. And whole areas of the South were deprived of rail service altogether. Between Pocahontas, Tennessee, and Decatur, Alabama, for instance, the entire line of almost 114 miles of railroad was in ruins. The railroads could only be restored through extensive capital investment; but capital barely existed in the South.

THE PROBLEM OF THE FREEDMAN

The Freedman and Economic Dislocation. In the midst of devastation the institution of slavery was brought to an end, and the first condition of Negro equality was achieved. But the *de facto* achievement of full civil rights for the Negro was to be an agonizingly slow process, one that remains uncompleted to this day. The relationship that existed between the races until 1865 made it unlikely that the social revolution implicit in emancipation would be carried through smoothly or easily. Many Southern planters welcomed the labor of Negro freedmen with ill grace; one Alabaman protested:

> As to this thing of free negro labor, I do not believe in it, but I will give it a fair trial. I have a plantation and am going to make contracts with my hands, and then I want a real Yankee to run the machine for me; not one of our New Yorkers or Pennsylvanians, but the genuine article from Massachusetts or Vermont—one who can not only farm, but sing psalms and pray, and teach school—a real abolitionist, who believes in the thing just as I don't believe in it. If he does not succeed, I shall consider it proof conclusive that you are wrong and I am right.

Though the freeing of the Negro had profound social implications, its most immediate effects were economic. The labor system of the South had been inextricably bound up with slavery; now, no matter how grudgingly, Southerners had to establish a workable substitute.

The circumstances could not have been more unfavorable. Slaves by the tens of thousands had deserted the plantations in the wake of the federal forces. Many had served in the Union army and had by their service convinced Lincoln that Negro veterans, at least, ought to possess the franchise. Along the southeastern seaboard and along the Mississippi River, Negro refugees in vast numbers were dependent on government charity. Many planters had removed their slaves into the interior of the South as the Union armies advanced, thus causing further dislocations. When the war ended, the slaves remaining on plantations began a wholesale flight as they became convinced that their liberation was an actual, irrevocable fact. To the burden of war was added the incalculable derangement of the traditional labor supply.

White Views of the Freedman. For many white Southerners, the restoration of dependable Negro labor seemed incompatible with the idea of Negro equality. The irresponsible behavior of some Negro freedmen was, for the whites, an irrefutable proof of Negro inferiority, and of the need for white domination if order was to be restored in the South. On the basis of his own observations, Carl Schurz conceded that most Negroes were "perfect children" who "in their abject ignorance . . . have been led to believe that their freedom means unrestraint—license to work as they please and do as they please, regardless of contracts or other legal obligations." But Schurz added that "these characteristics . . . are the result of their former, rather than their present, relations, and only need kindness, patience, education, and good faith to overcome." All too few Southerners were capable of so sympathetic (and yet hardheaded) an understanding of the Negro plight.

Indeed, white antipathy for the Negro was often expressed with brutal vehemence; and the most bitter hatred for Negroes was often expressed by those who had owned few or no slaves. The poor whites had felt small sympathy for the Negro before the war; the prospect of having to accept former slaves as equals often led them to perpetrate contemptible persecutions against inoffensive Negroes. Under such circumstances the future of the freedman hardly seemed auspicious. A long-term program of Negro education and rehabilitation by the federal government might have made a difference. But this was not to be; and as the gifted ex-slave Frederick Douglass wrote:

> The government had left the freedmen in a [bad] condition. . . . It felt it had done enough for him. It had made him free, and henceforth he must make his own way in the world. Yet he had none of the conditions of self-preservation or self-protection. He was free from the individual master, but the slave of society. He had neither money, property, nor friends. He was free from the old plantation, but he had nothing but the dusty road under his feet. He was free from the old quarter that once gave him shelter, but a slave to the rains of summer and to the frosts of winter. He was . . . turned loose, naked, hungry, and destitute to the open sky.

The ultimate tragedy of emancipation was the failure of Americans to realize that the freedman carried into liberty the disabling legacy of slavery.

The Founding of the Freedmen's Bureau. As the war drew to an end, it became evident to the North that emergency aid would have to be provided for displaced freedmen. The War and Treasury Departments had hitherto cared for the slaves who fled behind the Union lines (and nearly 200,000 of whom enlisted in the Union forces, thus providing sorely-needed labor, services, and infantry to the hard-pressed North). In various parts of the occupied South, like the Sea Islands of South Carolina, Negroes had been settled on confiscated Southern property. By 1865, many of the freedmen had come to expect land from the federal authority. To the problem of the Negro was added that of tens of thousands of whites who had lost everything in the debacle which overtook the Confederacy. To provide necessary relief, Congress, on March 3, 1865, established the Bureau of Freedmen, Refugees, and Abandoned Lands. Its purpose was to issue provisions, clothing, and fuel to "destitute and suffering refugees and freedmen." It also provided for the leasing of confiscated land to freedmen and loyal refugees—but no more than forty acres per person.

Johnson and the Freedmen's Bureau. The Bureau's influence quickly expanded. It undertook to encourage the establishment of Negro education, and to assure justice to the freedman in the courts. Under the vigorous leadership of General O. O. Howard, Bureau officials intervened to modify Southern state legislation which endangered Negro rights. The life of the Bureau had originally been limited to one year, which was to expire in the late winter of 1866. Congress met this event by voting on February 19, 1866, to extend the Bureau's life for an additional year; but Andrew Johnson vetoed the measure. From that moment the legislative and executive branches were locked in a struggle that culminated in Johnson's impeachment.

The "Black Codes." Congress' decision to extend the life of the Freedmen's Bureau was a response to the institution by Southern states of special laws governing the Negro. These "black codes" stirred up the fear that Southerners would do everything possible to maintain the spirit of slavery even after the fact of slavery had been eliminated. The exact motives behind these codes are hard to ascertain, though Southerners usually justified them by the doctrine of Negro irresponsibility. This was said to manifest itself in the failure of former slaves to abide by labor contracts, and in instances of Negro disorder. Needless to say, the many instances in which freedmen worked conscientiously and well for planters were ignored, as was the fact that open disorder among Negroes was rather the exception than the rule. In justifying his conviction that Negroes needed disciplinary agencies to insure their good behavior, the Southern white chose his instances selectively.

Southern treatment of Negro freedmen before the war offered little hope for the way in which the South would treat its former slaves after they had been emancipated by force of arms. Since Negro freedmen had traditionally been denied even the most elementary rights, it was scarcely surprising that many of the "black codes" were brutally harsh. But it is also true that the codes included legislation necessary to cover the altered condition of the freedmen, and that the codes were not equally punitive. They were harshest in South Carolina, Louisiana, and Mississippi, where the Negro population exceeded the white, and where any direct extension of the suffrage would bring the former slaves to power.

The Mississippi "Black Code." The Mississippi Code was especially limiting. Although it granted the Negro the right to sue and to be sued, to own property, and to dispose of it as he saw fit, it severely limited his right to rent or lease real property. The code also legalized Negro marriages contracted under slavery, but (and this was a common feature of all the codes) made it a criminal offense to contract an interracial marriage. In Mississippi, intermarriage was punishable by life imprisonment. Strong restrictions were placed on the negotiating of labor contracts. Though they limited the jurisdiction of the employer, they obliged Negro workers to forfeit their wages if they left without good cause before the contract had expired. Even more severe was the provision that such workers would be returned to their employers by the civil authorities. A Mississippi Apprentice Law permitted state and local authorities to bind Negroes between the ages of eighteen and twenty-one to an employer who would possess almost complete power over them until their twenty-first birthday was reached. Similar laws, supposedly dealing with "vagrancy," granted the courts the power to imprison or to farm out any Negro who did not possess a steady job. A similar fate awaited any whites who associated with blacks "on terms of equality."

The Judicial Rights of Southern Negroes. The judicial rights of the Negro varied from state to state. In Alabama, the code denied them the right to testify in cases involving whites; but in South Carolina such testimony was accepted. Louisiana provided severe penalties for employers who inflicted cruel punishment on their black employees. In North Carolina, the ordinary criminal code was extended to the Negro, but with the amendment that rape of a white woman by a Negro would be treated as a capital offense. Punishment for lesser crimes was altered in most instances elsewhere in the South to make "hard labor" the usual penalty instead of the "whipping and branding" that had been prescribed before the war. Colored persons were defined in Tennessee as any persons "having any African blood in their veins," while in Virginia anyone with more than one-fourth Negro blood was deemed colored.

Congressional Response to the "Black Codes." Whether the codes were wholly justified, partly justified, or unjustified, it was only too clear that they were often excessively cruel. They left the impression that a disguised slavery was being reinstituted in the South; and this motivated Congress, now able to override a presidential veto, to extend the life of the Freedmen's Bureau. To the original functions of the Bureau was added the power to defend the civil rights of citizens where the ordinary courts seemed incapable of doing so. Cases of discrimination on the basis of color or previous condition of servitude were to be tried by military courts made up of Bureau officers and agents. Supplementing this legislation was the Civil Rights Bill, which confirmed the Negro in his rights of citizenship, and in his equality before the law. To insure full protection of Negro rights, the Civil Rights Bill granted the federal district courts jurisdiction over any violation of its provisions.

Johnson's Civil Rights Veto. The federal government had taken a gigantic step toward securing Negro rights. President Johnson moved swiftly to veto the program. Johnson was strongly opposed to the extension of federal power at the expense of the states, and convinced that the freedmen were not yet prepared to exercise the full rights of citizenship. While acknowledging the legacy of slavery, Johnson denied the federal government any power to redress the wrong. His simultaneous insistence that the Southern states be fully restored to the Union gave the impression that he was prepared to leave the problem of Negro rights to the very states that had passed the "black codes."

THE CONGRESSIONAL ELECTION OF 1866

The Fight for Control over Reconstruction. Johnson's vetoes of the Freedmen's Bureau and the Civil Rights Bill precipitated a schism in the Republican party. It also brought to a head the struggle between the executive and legislative branches for control of reconstruction. What had been, under Lincoln, a subject for negotiation, had become a struggle in which no quarter was given. Under the leadership of William Pitt Fessenden, senator from Maine, the Republicans succeeded in passing the Civil Rights Bill over the presidential veto by a narrow margin. Taking a lesson from this experience, the Republican congressional majority then decided to secure the legal power that would enable them to override presidential vetoes with impunity. Their immediate intention was, however, to incorporate the legislative version of reconstruction into the Constitution by amendment.

The Fourteenth Amendment. Under the guidance of the Joint Committee on Reconstruction, the Fourteenth Amendment was formulated. It provided full citizenship for "all persons born or naturalized in the United States" and secured them their civil rights. Though the rights of citizens to vote were not guaranteed, those states that limited the franchise were to be penalized by a reduction of their congressional representation. Further limitations were imposed upon future office-holding by former Confederate leaders without the sanction of two-thirds of Congress. Finally, the amendment upheld the legitimacy of the public debts incurred by the United States government in order to prosecute the late war, while repudiating those contracted by the Confederacy. The passage of the proposed amendment on June 13, 1866, provided Congress with its ultimate weapon against the South. The congressional Republicans were determined not to readmit a single Southern state unless each first ratified the amendment.

The New Orleans Riot. With an awesome stubbornness, Andrew Johnson undertook to oppose Congress' position at the polls, and thus made reconstruction the central issue of the 1866 election for Congress. (The next presidential election would not occur until 1868.) This allowed his congressional opponents to exploit the festering memories of the four-year struggle. Zachariah Chandler, the dour senator from Michigan, set the tone when he warned, "The so-called policy of

Andrew Johnson . . . is not his policy; it is the policy of the rebels to get back into this government to overthrow the government, and Andrew Johnson is merely a tool in the hands of the rebels to accomplish their new rebellion." The theory of the unrepentant South seemed confirmed when bloody riots shook the cities of New Orleans and Memphis. In New Orleans the city police fired on radical Republicans trapped by a besieging mob. Northern newspapers declared that "The hands of the Rebels are again red with loyal blood," and mourned "brothers and friends . . . . butchered by a Rebel mob." Johnson and his policy were held responsible.

The Philadelphia Convention. The rising chorus of anti-Johnson sentiment was helped immeasurably by Johnson's own political incompetence. Chosen in 1864 to provide a Democratic counterbalance to the Republican Lincoln on the Union ticket, he had succeeded not only to the presidency but to the nominal leadership of a party of which he was not a member. Had he vigorously appealed to the conservative and moderate membership of the Republican party, he might well have checked the radical coterie of Thaddeus Stevens, Charles Sumner, Benjamin Wade, and Zachariah Chandler. Had he exploited Western economic grievances, he might have divided the Republicans fatally along sectional lines. Instead, he fostered the Philadelphia Convention which met on August 14, 1866, and which attempted to form a moderate third party.

There was only one flaw in Johnson's reasoning: this new political force could not be brought into being without the destruction of the Republican party; and the moderate Republicans, who constituted his one remaining source of potential support, were not willing to see their party destroyed. They preferred to work within it, maneuvering against the radicals, and trying to secure party control for their own purposes. Johnson had crawled to the end of the limb, and had systematically sawed it through behind himself.

The Radical Attack on Johnson. The Republican press subjected Johnson to misrepresentation and ridicule. Stories of his habitual drunkenness were circulated; they could be substantiated with his behavior at the 1865 inaugural, when he had clearly been inebriated, and had delivered a long, rambling speech. Johnson, meanwhile, was using the political tactic he knew best: he was appealing directly to the public. During late August and September he made a "Swing 'round the Circle," preaching moderation, conciliation, and respect for the Constitution. But he found his audiences packed with radical hecklers, and he made the fatal mistake of replying in kind to their taunts and insults. The result was to demean the dignity of the presidential office, and to convert his tour into a spectacle in which insult replaced discussion. The nation read in its newspapers of the presidential lapse from grace, and of the fact that he delivered the same speech again and again. The reporters were not slow to conclude that Johnson had disgraced his office.

Republican Success in 1866. In September the Republicans gained an overwhelming victory in Maine, and the rest of New England followed suit. The radicals gained a more narrow victory in the Middle Western states. Deliberate disenfranchisement of Democrats in Missouri added to Republican gains. In the strategically placed state of Pennsylvania the Republicans won a narrow victory, partly because the Democrats had chosen as their candidate Heister Clymer, a vehement Peace Democrat. The Democrats made a similar blunder when they nominated for the New York governorship one John T. Hoffman, a Tammany hack who had opposed the war. The result was a further loss, narrow but emphatic. Thus the electorate signaled their approval of the congressional version of reconstruction. Andrew Johnson could acquiesce in its decision, or he could fight a hopeless delaying action. He chose the latter course.

THE TRIUMPH OF RADICAL RECONSTRUCTION

The Republicans had carried every contested governorship; they were in control of every state legislature in the North; and they dominated every delegation to Congress. Had the Southern states agreed to accept as the minimal condition of their readmission to the Union ratification of the Fourteenth Amendment, it is likely that restoration would have been swiftly completed. Johnson, however, stubbornly refused to urge the South to accept the price demanded; instead, he threw the weight of his office behind continued Southern opposition to ratification. The radicals seized the opportunity thus offered them and, under the leadership of the harsh and unyielding Thaddeus Stevens, they shaped a program that would bring about the utter humiliation of the South. At any other time their vengefulness might have found little or no echo in the Northern states. But from the South came a growing stream of appeals from Negroes and Unionists pleading for protection from attacks and oppression. Stories of assault and murder in the South filled the Northern journals and slowly reawakened the passions that had led to war. An intransigent President and a seemingly defiant South were helping to bring into existence the culminating stage of reconstruction.

Military Occupation of the South. Under the guidance of John Sherman and Thaddeus Stevens, a Reconstruction Act was passed on March 2, 1867. It provided for the creation of five military districts made up of the ten unreconstructed states, in which military authority would take precedence over civil authority. To prevent the President from frustrating this control, his authority as commander-in-chief was qualified. Congress decreed that all military orders from the President or Secretary of the War would be issued by the General of the Army from a Washington headquarters. (The radicals assumed, rightly, that the incumbent General of the Army, Ulysses S. Grant, would favor their point of view.) Congress then passed another act, this one limiting the appellate functions of the Supreme Court, thereby preventing any judicial interference with the proposed military reconstruction. The Court took the hint, and declined to hear the appeal of either Mississippi or Georgia for an injunction against executive enforcement of reconstruction.

The Supplementary Reconstruction Act. The radicals had trapped the South at last; restoration could be achieved only by accepting Negro equality through the confirmation of the Fourteenth Amendment. Though Johnson vetoed the Reconstruction Act of 1867, Congress promptly overrode his veto. When the white Southerners refused to organize conventions to amend their state governments, Congress passed a Supplementary Reconstruction Act (March 23, 1867) which gave the responsibility for organizing these conventions to the federal military commanders. Again Johnson fired off his futile veto; again Congress overrode him.

Military Rule in the South. The direction of military rule was now firmly established. John M. Schofield commanded in Virginia; Daniel E. Sickles in North and South Carolina; John Pope in Georgia, Alabama, and Florida; Edward O. C. Ord in Mississippi and Arkansas; and Philip Henry Sheridan in Texas and Louisiana. Southerners were especially outraged at the appointments of Sheridan (who had scourged the Shenandoah Valley) and Pope. Sheridan's repressive rule in Louisiana, where he forcibly registered Negro voters while disenfranchising whites, simultaneously removing state and city officials, finally created such a turmoil that he had to be replaced by Winfield S. Hancock.

The Third Reconstruction Act. As President, Johnson was expected to enforce the reconstruction plans of Congress. Following the advice of his Attorney General, Henry Stanbery, he directed the military

MILITARY DISTRICTS OF THE RECONSTRUCTION ACT OF 1867

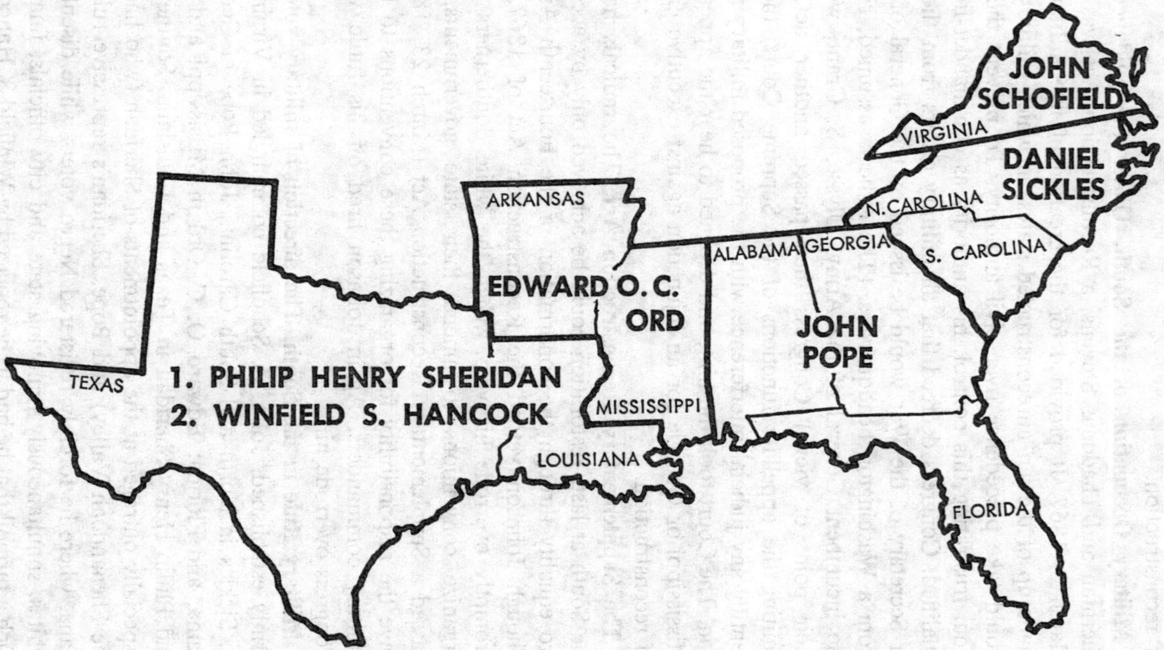

commanders to work with, rather than replace, the established civil authorities. Congress promptly reassembled and passed the Third Reconstruction Act on July 19, 1867, which placed full and final authority in the hands of the military. The Southerners themselves made a last-ditch stand; in Alabama, conservatives succeeded in rejecting a constitution drawn up at a military convention by simply refusing to vote. Since approval required a majority of the registered voters, the 70,000 votes cast in favor of the constitution proved inadequate. Congress parried this new defense by passing a Fourth Reconstruction Act which made ratification of a new constitution contingent on approval by a majority of the votes cast. With their last defense gone, white Southerners could begin to believe that they had been placed wholly at the mercy of Negroes, Southern scalawags, and Northern carpetbaggers. Many of the Southern feelings about reconstruction had their origins in this phase of *military* reconstruction, a phase that lasted for less than two years.

THE IMPEACHMENT OF ANDREW JOHNSON

The Resolution to Investigate Johnson. In the rumbling controversy between legislature and executive, Congress increasingly contemplated the drastic act of impeachment. As early as January 7, 1867, the House passed a resolution, proposed by James M. Ashley of Ohio, which ordered an investigation of Johnson as a preliminary to impeachment. Subsequently the House judiciary committee investigated not only such acts of Johnson as his pardoning and restoring property to Southerners, but also absurd sensational rumors that he had conspired in the assassination of Lincoln. Although the committee, by a narrow margin, recommended Johnson's impeachment, the House strongly rejected such a motion on December 7, 1867. But the controversy was only momentarily stilled.

The Dismissal of Stanton. The radicals now turned their attention to Johnson's action in removing Edwin M. Stanton as Secretary of War on August 12, 1867. Under the Tenure of Office Act passed by Congress on March 2, 1867, cabinet officers could not be removed without the consent of the Senate; but they could be suspended by the President while Congress was out of session. Thus Johnson, in eliminating Stanton during the summer recess, had conformed to the act; and he had apparently gone on to strengthen his position by appointing Ulysses S. Grant as acting Secretary of War. Johnson's intent was to force a court test of the act, and he expected Grant's prestige to carry him through to victory. It seemed very unlikely that the Republicans would directly challenge the "Victor of Appomattox."

But Johnson had misread his appointee's character, for when the Senate refused to uphold Stanton's removal, Grant promptly surrendered his office. Johnson then pleaded with William Tecumseh Sherman to take Grant's place, but without success. Finally Johnson persuaded General Lorenzo Thomas to accept the office. On February 21, 1868, Johnson summarily dismissed the restored Stanton, but the deposed Secretary of War barricaded himself in his offices and continued to function in the post. The House now invoked that part of the Tenure Act which made it illegal for the President to remove a cabinet officer without senatorial consent. On February 24, 1868, the House voted 126–47 to impeach Johnson for "high crimes and misdemeanors in office." Although no specific charges had been drawn against the President, a committee of two congressmen, on the motion of Thaddeus Stevens, was directed to impeach Johnson at the bar of the Senate. To draw up an indictment, a committee of seven was formed "to declare Articles of Impeachment against the President of the United States." Since all seven had voted to impeach, the result was never in doubt. Such vigorous radicals as Thaddeus Stevens, George S. Boutwell, John A. Logan, and George W. Julian seemed equal to the task of drawing up charges with which to "safely go to the Senate and the country for the final judgment of guilty against the person accused." Nonetheless, so severe was the disorder governing these proceedings that it was not until March 3 that the House drew up a specific bill indicting the President.

The Articles of Impeachment. Nine of the eleven charges leveled against Johnson dealt with his attempted removal of Stanton. For all practical purposes, these accused him of violating the Tenure of Office Act. Since there was considerable doubt about the act's constitutionality—a doubt which the Supreme Court finally laid to rest in 1926, when it substantially upheld Johnson's position in Meyers *v.* United States—there was a distinct possibility that the executive might be convicted on unconstitutional grounds. The tenth charge indicted Johnson for attempting "to bring into disgrace, ridicule, hatred, contempt, and reproach the Congress of the United States." The eleventh article was a synopsis of charges that had preceded it, but also included the threatening charge that Johnson had described Congress as the legislature for only a part of the country, thus implying that he was not obliged to enforce legislation passed by it. The final struggle between legislature and executive had been joined.

The Trial. Once the House had drawn up its charges, the Senate had to prepare the trial. (The radicals had made intensive efforts to increase Republican strength in the Senate, and thus fortify their power, but they were only partially successful. Johnson's attempt to halt the admission of Nebraska to statehood was not upheld, and the two new senators ultimately voted for impeachment, as the radicals had hoped. But Johnson's veto of the admission of Colorado to statehood *was* upheld by the Supreme Court, thus eliminating the possibility of two more new senators voting against him.) The Senate drew up a set of twenty-five rules to govern the trial, and Chief Justice Salmon P. Chase worked to formulate a judicial procedure. A smoldering dispute developed between the crusty Supreme Court Chief, with his insistence on complete legality, and the radicals, who thought of the proceedings as political rather than legal. The sentiments of those most bent on conviction were summed up by Charles Sumner when he charged: "Andrew Johnson is the impersonation of the tyrannical slave power." For such men, the expulsion of the Tennessean from the White House would justify the sacrifices of war.

The Executive Defense. The senatorial managers of the proceedings against Johnson agreed that the executive presence at the trial would not be required. They declared at the outset that Johnson had not been governed by corrupt motives but was guilty (in Thaddeus Stevens' words) of "official violations of law." This was meant to forestall the defense's argument that Johnson had only violated the Tenure of Office Act in order to force a court hearing on its constitutionality. But William M. Evarts, one of the executive lawyers, insisted that the intent of Congress was to overthrow the checks and balances system and concentrate all power in the legislature; and that the impeachment proceedings were in fact the culmination of the political rivalry between executive and legislature. (Indeed, more than one observer of the trial noted that the radicals were ready to bring down the very system in whose defense the late war had been fought; and that if they had their way, the result would have been more revolutionary than the triumph of the Confederacy would have been.)

The Failure of Impeachment. An awesomely slim minority of the Senate forestalled the ambition of the radicals. On May 16, and again on May 26, 1868, voting separately on each of the eleven articles, the Senate failed by one vote to give the necessary two-thirds support to conviction. There were twelve Democrats and seven Republicans in the crucial faction that saved Johnson; and in the end, it was the single vote of Edmund G. Ross of Kansas—whose sentiments were in doubt until the last moments of the trial—that prevented Johnson's conviction. Ross, like the other six Republicans who deserted the radical cause, paid for his action with his political career.

The exonerated President and his accusers now turned their attention to the oncoming presidential elections. The crisis of the struggle over reconstruction had passed.

THE FACTS AND MYTHS OF SOUTHERN RECONSTRUCTION

Few issues in American history have stirred up more furious emotions than Southern reconstruction. For white Southerners the memory of reconstruction is one of catastrophic humiliation; of a time when they were brutally exploited, denied the most elementary rights, and subjected to the fantastically incompetent rule of the Negro. The South's resistance to reconstruction was, according to this view, a mighty struggle by Southerners to regain their legitimate identity as Americans.

The New View of Reconstruction. When Northerners were still certain that their victory at Appomattox had been divinely ordained, they accepted reconstruction as an attempt to fulfill the purpose of the Civil War—the establishment of a more perfect Union; but during most of the twentieth century they have tended to surrender the reconstruction period to its Southern interpreters. Only recently, as a consequence of the fight to extend civil rights, has an attempt been made to re-evaluate the Southern time of tribulations. In the process, the "southern catastrophe" has come to be seen within the context of the society that had been overturned by total war. A slave society was turned into a free society by proclamation, amid the ruins of the most devastating conflict that the world then knew. When we keep this in mind, the dislocations of the reconstruction period are seen to be the logical consequences of preceding events, rather than malignant acts of sabotage by a vindictive North.

The Radical Case. For Lincoln the Civil War had been a struggle to save the Union; for his radical supporters it was a crusade to destroy the slave power that had brought the Union to its ultimate crisis. But the radicals were to find that emancipation was only the first step toward solving the racial problem. Everywhere in the nation—not in the South alone—the Negro's status was ambiguous. Except for New York and five New England states, the North denied Negroes the right to vote. In the autumn of 1865, Connecticut, Wisconsin, and Minnesota voted overwhelmingly against extending the franchise to Negroes. No one should have been surprised, therefore, when the South took an even dimmer view of such an eventuality. The radicals, having failed to make angels of their own constituents, turned their attentions to the South, determined that there, at any rate, virtue would triumph. They chose to vest in the federal government the power to achieve the equality praised in the Declaration of Independence. The Fourteenth Amendment incorporated this aim into the Constitution. White Southerners accused the radicals (and still accuse them) of rank hypocrisy. But the onus falls rather on their fellow Americans, Southern and Northern, than on the radicals themselves. They strove against all the dragons of human nature to make America live up to her own pretensions, and as such they were in the mainstream of American Democracy.

Carpetbaggers, Scalawags, and "Black Domination." Radical reconstruction has been commonly dubbed "black reconstruction." Widely accepted myths have it that during this time a coalition of ignorant Negroes and self-seeking whites misruled the South. From the institution of military rule in 1867 until its end in 1877, the story goes, Southern whites were strangers in their own homeland; and it was only when reconstruction finally ended that a numb and looted South began its fearful struggle toward restoration. There were too many instances of corruption for this picture to be completely without substance, but it still has the fault of being lopsided. In its hunger for grievances, it neglects the vital advances that occurred during the reconstruction period; it exaggerates the scope of the abuses that actually occurred; and it fails to acknowledge the reason behind the ready (and apparently gullible) Southern acceptance of these distortions. In fact, the Southern version of the history of reconstruction seeks to establish the legitimacy of discrimination against the Negro, who is declared to have demonstrated his incapacity at government when the South was "in his power."

The Scope of Military Reconstruction. The Southern portrait of this crucial period has it that the Negro was kept in power with federal bayonets; but with the exception of Virginia, Texas, and Mississippi, military rule had ended in all the Southern states by 1868. By 1870 military rule had ceased throughout the South. When Georgia, after its readmission in 1868, tried to ignore the Fourteenth Amendment by denying Negroes their seats in the legislature while permitting former Confederates (disqualified by law) to sit, Congress renewed military rule there until 1870. The "bayonets" used to enforce military rule never exceeded 20,000, and of these more than one-third were concentrated in Louisiana and Texas. Though the federal authority could easily have used troops to maintain order thereafter, it only did so once. In 1871, after a careful investigation by the Attorney General, Congress authorized the sending of troops into nine South Carolina counties to suppress violence against Negroes. Enforcement acts were passed to meet this crisis, but in the prosecutions that followed fewer than a quarter of those indicted were convicted. Generally, therefore, Southern rights were maintained so long as Negro rights were respected.

The Scope of White Disenfranchisement. Southerners have also contended that the enfranchisement of the incompetent Negro was paralleled by the disenfranchisement of the persecuted white. This argument supplies some basis for the conclusion that the Negro dominated Southern politics. But it is probable that no more than 150,000 or so Southern whites were denied the ballot during the brief phase of military reconstruction. Once a state had been readmitted into the Union these disabilities were swiftly eliminated, so that by 1872 fewer than 750 Southern whites were so deprived. Even when disenfranchisement was at its peak, no less than 630,000 whites were registered, and untold thousands chose as a protest not to register. In most instances, conventions erected under military rule were surprisingly easy in their suffrage and officeholding restrictions, and only Louisiana, Arkansas, and Alabama ever enforced restrictions of this kind. In 1868, white voters outnumbered Negro voters in Virginia, North Carolina, Texas, and Georgia; and at no time did Negroes completely control a single state.

The Scope of "Black Reconstruction." Another myth that persists is that Negroes in the postwar South held many major offices. Actually, no Negro ever achieved the status of governor; there were only two Negro senators; and only a handful became congressmen. Only in Louisiana and South Carolina, where Negroes were an absolute majority of the population, were the legislatures ever under partial Negro control. And in both of those states there were countless instances in which Negro legislators took severe exception to vindictive treatment of whites, or any attempt to exact revenge for the degradations of slavery. It is true that some Negro officeholders were ignorant of the most elementary legislative procedures, and that these individuals made a gaudy spectacle of themselves as they debated matters of which they had no knowledge. But the surprising fact, given their recent condition of servitude, was that most Negroes acquitted themselves well in dealing with the catastrophic conditions that existed in the South after the war.

Positive legacies were left to the South as a result of reconstruction. The constitutions composed under radical rule were considerably more democratic than those they replaced. No single innovation was more meaningful than the establishment of public education. Before the war the idea of such a system was viewed by the aristocratic Southerner as a useless experiment; the status quo insured that ignorance which in turn insured aristocratic domination of the South. Though public education had been extended to whites throughout most of the South by the legislatures established before radical reconstruction, efforts to establish parallel accommodations for Negroes were often met with violence. By 1867, however, the Freedmen's Bureau had established some 4,000 primary schools, 61 industrial schools, and 74 teacher preparatory schools. If the slave heritage had made Negro enfranchisement an act of doubtful wisdom, the effort to provide Negroes with the facilities to compensate for their educational deficiencies mitigated the fault.

The Cost of Southern Reconstruction. The establishment of a public school system, and the restoration of ruined public edifices and roads, brought a heavy increase in tax burdens throughout the South. The weight of this burden was compounded by the poverty which prevailed throughout the region. This provides little basis, however, for the idea that these increased expenditures were an index of wholesale governmental corruption, and for the school of interpretation which has tried to make radical rule synonymous with bad government. In states like South Carolina and Louisiana spectacular examples of corruption occurred. The establishment of the Louisiana Lottery in 1868 was made possible by wholesale bribing of the legislature. It put into private hands the charter privilege of operating a lottery that grossed more than $28,000,000 a year, in return for which New Orleans received an annual contribution of $40,000 for a hospital. But it is worth noting that Southerners no less illustrious than P. G. T. Beauregard and Jubal Early lent their prestige to the enterprise for a tidy fee; and that when Louisiana passed into conservative hands in 1877, the lottery's charter was renewed. In Virginia, where radical rule ended with military reconstruction, the conservative government proved as proficient in contracting debts as any radical government. Nowhere did the overthrow of radical rule, and its replacement by conservative Democrats, insure honesty. In Alabama, Virginia, Mississippi, Louisiana, Georgia, and Tennessee major scandals continued to shake the state governments.

The mistake has been to see corruption in government after the war as a sectional rather than a national phenomenon. Beside the looting of New York City by the Tweed Ring, corruption in the South pales into insignificance. The question is not why Southern radicals were sometimes dishonest but why the nation as a whole experienced a collapse of moral restraint after the war. The answer may lie in the war itself.

Chapter 2

The Aftermath of War in the North

Walt Whitman had sung the praises of democracy before the Civil War; when peace was restored, he despaired of democracy's future. The steady deterioration of traditional restraints in social behavior was marked on every hand. Henry Adams wrote scornfully of democracy; and it provided Mark Twain with ample material for satire in his *The Gilded Age*. Sensitive men everywhere agreed with Whitman's diagnosis of society in the postwar era as "canker'd, crude, superstitious, and rotten." Preoccupied with material growth, America seemed destined to exercise her superiority on a scale unparalleled since the time of ancient Rome; but it was widely feared by men of sensibility that the price of such material superiority would be high—that it might, in fact, cost America her soul.

AN INDUSTRIAL AMERICA

The Civil War had demanded of every man an unprecedented expenditure of energy. When the war was over, the energy which had been one of the greatest resources at the North's command sought new channels in which to expend itself, and found them in the relentless pursuit of money. Factories sprang up everywhere. Railroads expanded, crisscrossing the vast expanses of the republic with an ever-growing network of tracks. Whole forests were leveled to meet the needs of the cities that were mushrooming everywhere. The ransacking of America's mineral wealth began. The industrial expansion, which had been encouraged during the war by extensive federal subsidies, now became the nation's dominating concern; it propelled the North out of its agrarian past, and brought a new federal republic into being. The postwar tide also threw up a new class of exploiters and entrepreneurs, whose activities (although occasionally paralleled before the war) were a painful spectacle to men who had known an older America. It was less obvious that out of the ruthless self-aggrandizement of these men, and the economic chaos in which they built their personal empires, America would emerge as the world's mightiest power.

The Republican Program. As the United States fought to survive as a nation, and then to forge a lasting peace, the Republican Congress chose to institute a vast program of reform. This program was partly designed to meet the staggering costs of the war, but it also sought to resolve the major issues which had arisen during the 1850s as a result of sectional rivalries. The secession of the South had assured the Republicans a working congressional majority. They had quickly exploited this advantage to pass laws dealing with tariffs, banking, land, and transcontinental railroads. The cumulative effect of these laws was to establish a firm alliance between the federal government and the business community, a political arrangement that dominated politics until the end of the nineteenth century. But this result was not fully foreseen.

Lincoln and Congress. When Fort Sumter was attacked, Lincoln was forced to act in the absence of Congress; but he issued a call for a special session of the legislature to meet on July 4, 1861. As it became clear that the war would last much longer than the originally expected three months, Lincoln took increasing pains to maintain friendly relations with Congress. He was aware that without consistent legislative support he would be unable to teach the secessionists "that when ballots have fairly and constitutionally decided, there can be no successful appeal back to bullets." His consummate political tact was evident when the special session of Congress approved all the actions he had already undertaken without its approval.

The Acts for Confiscation. The Union defeat at Bull Run, on July 21, 1861, converted Congress to Lincoln's view that the war would be a long one. In a quick succession of acts passed during late July, Congress provided for the enlistment of 500,000 volunteers for three years, a time span that was subsequently extended to cover the duration of the war. On August 6, 1861, a Confiscation Act was passed which provided for the seizure of property used to aid the rebellion; but as the war grew, demands for more drastic measures increased. Congress responded with a Second Confiscation Act (July 1862) that provided for the punishment by fine and imprisonment—or death—of anyone guilty of treason; for the immediate confiscation of all property under Northern jurisdiction which belonged to Confederate officials; and, after a sixty-day period, for the seizure of all property belonging to anyone guilty of aiding the rebellion. By implication, it also provided for the emancipation of those slaves who were being used for the Confederate war effort. Though the vast scope of the act was never fully implemented, it did lay the foundation for the North's most important act of confiscation: the emancipation of the slaves.

The Radical Republicans. With the confiscation acts, Congress indicated its determination to prosecute the war vigorously. Indeed, Congress showed itself—the Second Confiscation Act was an example—more fiercely radical than Lincoln himself in the desire to push the war forward. The Republicans, led by Thaddeus Stevens, Owen Lovejoy, George W. Julian, Henry Winter Davis, and John Covode in the House, and by Benjamin F. Wade, Charles Sumner, Zachariah Chandler, William Pitt Fessenden, and Jacob Collamer in the Senate, gave Lincoln all the support he could have wished—and sometimes more than he wanted. Where Lincoln fought to preserve the Union, they were fighting to re-order it substantially or altogether. It was unlikely that a Confederate surrender, and the reintegration of the South into the political structure of the nation, would suffice to quiet their ambitions.

The Protective Tariff. Between 1846 and 1861, the tariff policy of the United States seemed directed toward establishing free trade. The Republicans, however, had pledged in their platform to adjust the tariff schedule in order "to encourage the development of the industrial interests of the . . . country." On February 20, 1861, when the withdrawal of Southern delegations left them in control of Congress, the Republicans promptly passed the Morrill Tariff, which returned the low tariff rates of 1857 to the considerably higher rates of 1846. The result was a precipitous decline in tariff revenue at precisely the time when government expenditures were sharply increasing. Confronted with a growing fiscal crisis, the Republicans simply raised the tariff again. On August 5, 1861, heavy duties were placed on coffee, tea, sugar, spices, and rubber (among other products). Since these commodities were not produced in the North, the duty was equivalent to a tax on imported necessities. On July 14, 1862, Congress passed an openly protective tariff which secured American products from competition by applying "compensatory" duties, that is, duties which were intended to compensate American industrialists for the heavy internal taxes to which they were now subject. By June 30, 1864, the compensatory principle dominated tariff legislation. Industrialists had thus obtained protection as their reward for supporting the war effort. The average rate increase of forty-seven per cent between 1861 and 1864 did not, however, close the American market to foreign goods. Between 1865 and 1869, merchandise imports exceeded similar exports by $466,799,000. Despite the help given by protectionist tariffs, American industry had not yet achieved the efficiency or scope to undersell European producers. But the Republicans had established themselves in the eyes of American manufacturers as friends of industry.

The Homestead Law. Freed from effective opposition of any kind, the Republicans set to work fulfilling their platform pledges. They had promised to support homestead legislation which would open public lands to settlement free of cost; they redeemed their pledge by passing a Homestead Act on May 20, 1862. It was virtually identical to an act vetoed in 1860 by President Buchanan, who had doubted its constitutionality, and who had described it as legislation that discriminated in favor of the farmer. Under the new law, a settler could obtain title to 160 acres after a nominal payment, provided he had lived on the land for at least five years. Though large numbers of legitimate settlers were thus enabled to take up homesteads, vast tracts of land were channeled into the hands of speculators. Without quite intending to do so, Congress had given an enormous boost to free enterprise, throwing open to settlement a domain that could be described, at least in terms of size, as an empire.

The Morrill Land Grant Act. Of equal significance was the passage on July 2, 1862, of the Morrill Land Grant Act. This legislation was the fulfillment of the dream of Professor Jonathan B. Turner of Illinois College, who had fought during the 1850s for the establishment of mechanical and agricultural colleges which would be subsidized with land grants from the federal government. Each state was now entitled to receive 30,000 acres of public lands for each senator and representative in its congressional delegation. This federal largesse provided the basis for what has since become the state university system. Ultimately, more than 20,000 square miles of public lands were used for subsidies of this kind.

The Transcontinental Railroad. Few subjects had triggered sharper controversy before the war than the construction of railroads linking the Atlantic and Pacific seaboards. In 1853 Congress authorized a survey of various possible routes, but the issue became hopelessly bogged down by sectional rivalries. Then, on July 1, 1862, Congress took advantage of the Southern secession to authorize a northern route. They authorized the construction of the Union Pacific Railroad. To insure it the maximum chance for success, Congress provided the company with a basic subsidy of 15,500,000 acres of land. Congress further encouraged the project by agreeing to give the company $16,000 in United States bonds for each level mile of road constructed, $32,000 for each hilly mile, and $48,000 for each mountainous mile. These bonds were to be secured by the equivalent of a first mortgage on the railroad's property. Two years later, the land subsidy was increased by nearly 31,000,000 acres, and instead of the first mortgage originally given to secure the bond issuances, a second mortgage was accepted. All told, the company received a land grant of 45,000,000 acres—an area larger than New England—and $60,000,000 in federal bonds. A grand fusion had been effected between federal subsidy and private enterprise.

Financing the War. The prosecution of the war effort posed an ever increasing problem for the government. Congressmen accustomed to the expenditure of millions of dollars per year now found themselves spending hundreds of millions. In 1864 and 1865 alone, Congress would authorize appropriations exceeding the grand total of all the appropriations made between 1789 and 1860. The available money supply was strained to the breaking point. The Lincoln government, which had inherited a public debt of almost $75,000,000, was faced simultaneously with a severe decline in income, a deteriorating state of public confidence that left few investors willing to accept government obligations at par, and a drastic increase in expenditures. As the secession crisis worsened, the Treasury Department had to accept staggering interest rates, reaching as high as twelve per cent in some cases. A good deal of government energy would be directed toward resolving this problem.

Salmon P. Chase. Salmon P. Chase, Lincoln's shrewd, self-confident, and inordinately ambitious Secretary of the Treasury, proved eminently capable in his new duties. Although he grossly underestimated the ultimate cost of the war, he supplied a leadership vigorous enough to conceal the fact that he had failed to propose a comprehensive program of taxation at the very outset of the war. In July and August of 1861, Congress gave Chase the power to borrow up to $250,000,000 against government securities. With the cooperation of the bankers of New York, Philadelphia, and Boston, Chase successfully obtained the needed funds, but as disbursements were made from the Treasury he realized that expenditures for the fiscal year ending June 30, 1862, would exceed his original estimates by almost $214,000,000. The crisis was worsened by the fact that the public, which now began to appreciate the serious dimensions of the war, revealed a disinclination to invest in government securities. The drain upon specie that resulted, as people sought to convert their assets into hard currency, finally compelled the nation's banks to cease specie payments.

The Legal Tender Act. Mounting pressure was now brought to bear on the government to expand the currency supply, and especially to find a means other than specie with which to meet government obligations. Under the guidance of Representative Elbridge G. Spalding, the House Ways and Means Committee authorized the issuance of $100,000,000 in non-interest bearing Treasury notes, and the conversion of some $50,000,000 worth of outstanding Treasury notes into "lawful money, and a legal tender in payment of all debts, public and private." Despite opposition from the banking community, the Legal Tender bill became law in February 1862. As the urgency of the war grew, Congress authorized the issuance of an additional $300,000,000 in legal tender (March 1863).

Greenbacks. As a result of specie suspension, greenbacks (as the legal-tender notes were called) became the accepted standard of value. For all practical purposes, gold was reduced to the status of a commodity, one primarily needed for the payment of foreign imports and customs duties. During and after the war, gold commanded a premium in greenbacks—that is, it took more than a dollar in greenbacks to purchase a dollar in gold; as war inflation wracked the national economy, the value of this premium spiraled upward, until in 1864 it took almost three dollars in greenbacks to purchase a single dollar in gold. Simultaneously, as the economy strained to maintain the war effort, prices almost doubled between 1861 and 1864, as a result of the vast expansion of the national currency and extensive foreign and domestic borrowing by the government. Despite these difficulties, the Union was able to finance its war successfully. But when the war ended, inflation persisted. Hugh McCulloch, Secretary of the Treasury from 1864 to 1869, worked strenuously to reduce it. His efforts to remove the greenbacks from circulation after the war inaugurated the currency disputes that agitated the nation until 1896.

The National Banking Acts. When the war began in 1861, more than $200,000,000 in state bank currency was in circulation. Since the federal government refused to accept such money in payment of obligations, it clearly lacked the stature of a federal currency. In December of 1861, Secretary of the Treasury Chase proposed that the federal government issue a national currency secured "by the pledge of the United States stock, and an adequate provision of specie." From this proposal sprang the National Banking System, formulated in 1863 and completed in 1864. When finally passed on June 3, 1864, the National Banking Act put responsibility for the supervision of the new system in the hands of a Comptroller of the Treasury, who would be appointed for a five-year term.

The Comptroller was responsible for supervising the practices of the national banks authorized by the act. Each bank could be organized by no less than five people, with a combined minimum capital of $50,000; each had to deposit with the government registered United States bonds valued at no less than $30,000, or one-third of the capital stock paid in. For these deposits the banks received circulating currency equivalent to ninety per cent of their bond deposit value. The new currency was limited to $300,000,000, but it did not achieve wide circulation until Congress, on March 3, 1865, placed a punitive tax of ten per cent on state bank notes. To secure the new system, reserve requirements were established for three different categories of banks. The "country banks," located in small towns, had to maintain reserves equivalent to fifteen per cent of their notes in circulation and their deposits. Of this amount, three-fifths could be placed on deposit in one of the seventeen reserve cities. (These reserve cities were Baltimore, Cleveland, Cincinnati, Chicago, Albany, Boston, New York, Philadelphia, Milwaukee, Detroit, Pittsburgh, Louisville, St. Louis, New Orleans, Washington, Leavenworth, and San Francisco. After the war had ended, Charleston and Richmond were added to the roster.) The banks in these cities were, in turn, required to maintain a reserve of twenty-five per cent, one half of which could be kept on reserve at a reserve bank in the central reserve city of New York.

Weaknesses of the National Banking System. Though an immeasurable improvement over the previous banking system, the National Banking Act had a major inherent weakness. It created a pyramid structure which made the nation's banking subject to the vagaries of the New York money market. Heavy calls for money during harvest time frequently sparked large withdrawals of money by the country banks, resulting in sharp contractions throughout the system, especially in loans to brokers, with consequent plummeting of stock values. A further complication resulted from the uneven distribution of the $300,000,000 authorized under the act. More than $170,000,000 of the total was allotted to New York and New England, providing a per capita circulation in that region of $33.30, as opposed to $6.36 in the Middle West, and $1.70 in the South. This disparity makes it evident that the frequent agitations over money in the West and South were the result of a genuine currency shortage. This shortage accentuated the dependence of Westerners and Southerners on Eastern banks, and made their running complaints of poverty a simple statement of fact. It also gave a factual basis to their conviction that they were the exploited victims of the East.

In spite of these obvious weaknesses, however, the National Banking Act remained the basis of the nation's financial system until the passage of the Federal Reserve Act in 1913.

The Scope of Reform. The reforms which have been discussed, though not completely adequate, were comprehensive in their scope and in their effect. The tariffs, homesteads, railroad subsidies, and banking reforms had all involved a tacit encouragement to individual enterprise. Though marginal benefits were derived by other elements of the population, the chief beneficiaries were businessmen, especially those who were eager to exploit the resources of the nation. The tariff gave very poor protection to those manufacturers who had to import raw materials from abroad, or who were dependent on foreign markets for consumption of their products. The movement for contraction of the currency, and especially for the withdrawal of greenbacks from circulation, gained a ready assent from Eastern financiers with large capital reserves, but it sent a chill of horror through those industrialists who had contracted large debts in expanding their plants. Any tightening of the currency, with its consequent deflation, would make it far more difficult for these businessmen to redeem their indebtedness.

Business and Politics. It soon became evident that the alliance between "business" and the Republican party, which was consummated between 1861 and 1865, was an imperfect one. Some businessmen gained—but often at the expense of others. The vast sums granted to railway entrepreneurs by the federal government, for instance, brought little security for the investor in railroads; they simply enabled management to extract huge profits from the actual construction of a line, with little concern for its future as a sustaining enterprise. The vast numbers of businessmen who thus bore the brunt of federal taxation, and who were yet denied a corresponding helping of federal gravy, could only have recourse to the Democratic party. As a result, the Republicans gradually lost their image as a "businessman's party," though different kinds of businessmen were represented in each.

THE POLITICAL BACKGROUND OF NORTHERN RECONSTRUCTION

The Republican Dilemma. The Republican party comprised, at best, an odd alliance of frequently conflicting interests. Former Whigs, eager for more government assistance to private enterprise; dissident Democrats, driven into opposition as the Southern element gained the upper hand during the fifties; Free-Soilers, resisting the expansion of slavery; and outright abolitionists—all these combined to form a party whose only binding purpose seemed to be the closing of the Western territories to slavery. Ironically, the Civil War, by settling the issue of slavery, threatened to deprive the Republicans of their one unifying objective. Rather than cast about for a new political *raison d'être,* the postwar Republicans tried to capitalize on their role in the recent conflict: they presented themselves as "the party of Union." In doing this they took a calculated risk, since such a stance, as long as it was maintained, could only keep the passions and hatreds of the war alive, especially insofar as it cast the South in a permanently secessionist role. They also took the risk of reducing their own party, and the Democratic opposition, to sectional rather than national forces.

The Union Party of 1864. The intention of the Republicans to embrace the issue of union first became evident in 1864, when they abandoned the Republican label and ran Lincoln and Johnson as Union party candidates. The obvious objective of this move was to permit "War Democrats" to join the Republicans, since the "Peace Democrats" had committed their party to overt opposition to the war effort. Congressman Clement L. Vallandigham, an Ohio Democrat, whose active fight against continuing the war had made him the most notorious "copperhead"—the term used in the North during the war to describe Northerners who were sympathetic to the South—was identified by the Republicans as the symbol of the Democratic opposition. In a real sense, the Republicans were raising the "bloody flag of rebellion" as a vote-getting issue.

But the Republicans had not abandoned hopes of winning Southern support. Lincoln, in advocating a generous peace, hoped to make it possible for former Southern Whigs to join the Republican party. The radical Republicans went even further, and hoped to secure the South through a complex program which involved allying (a) the newly enfranchised Negroes with Southern Unionists and (b) disenfranchising Southern whites who had aided the Confederacy. This objective was summed up by Thaddeus Stevens in January 1866, when he declared before the House of Representatives: "I do not want [the South] to have the right of suffrage before this Congress has done the great work of regenerating the Constitution and the laws of this country according to the principles of the Declaration of Independence." He anticipated that enfranchisement of the Negro "would assure the ascendancy of the Union party" which he believed necessary to "the safety of this great nation."

A Minority Party. In 1864 a powerful wave of opposition within the Republican party sought to deny Lincoln a second nomination. At the core of this opposition was Salmon P. Chase, Secretary of the Treasury. His retention in the cabinet had been a strategic maneuver by Lincoln, who thought it best to keep his enemies in positions where they would have to bear some responsibility for the conduct of the administration. In February 1864, Senator S. C. Pomeroy of Kansas circulated a memorandum which declared Lincoln's re-election improbable, and called for the nomination of Chase. Lincoln ignored the challenge. On May 31, 1864, a rump convention of radicals led by Wendell Phillips nominated John C. Frémont. Frémont launched a violent denunciation of Lincoln and his administration, but despite this evidence of localized disenchantment with the incumbent, the Republicans renominated Lincoln early in June, with Andrew Johnson as a running mate. Thus, the ticket of the so-called Union party had the benefit of combining with Lincoln an articulate war Democrat who was also a Southerner.

Chase's Resignation. Once the nomination had been secured, Lincoln took the first opportunity to remove Chase from the cabinet. When the Treasury chief (who had previously submitted his resignation unsuccessfully) once again attempted to resign on June 29, 1864, in a fit of pique, Lincoln surprised him by promptly accepting, observing at the same time that their relationship had "reached a point of mutual embarrassment . . . which it seems cannot be overcome or longer sustained consistently with public service."

The Election of 1864. Meanwhile, the Democrats had shrewdly combined their nomination of George B. McClellan with a platform demand that hostilities end forthwith, and that "the Federal Union of the States" be restored. Such a platform accentuated the differences between the two parties and seemed to give the Democrats a potent appeal in the war-weary North—an appeal so potent that Lincoln himself lost heart. The war had ground to a stalemate; Grant seemed unable to make any headway against Lee; Lincoln could only resign himself to defeat at the polls. But when Sherman won a signal victory at Atlanta in early September, the Northern gloom began to lift. On September 2, 1864, Horace Greeley issued a call for a new Republican convention to replace Lincoln with another candidate; but Sherman's triumph in the field and a Lincoln victory at the Maine polls checkmated his efforts. On September 22, Frémont withdrew as a presidential candidate, and the schism within the Republican party came to an end. Lincoln now moved to placate his opponents within the party by permitting Montgomery Blair to retire from the Postmaster Generalship, thus removing the leading conservative from his cabinet.

Lincoln's Re-election. Lincoln won a solid victory at the November polls with a majority of more than 400,000 votes. In such strategic states as New York, Connecticut, and Pennsylvania, however, victory margins had been exceedingly close. In Maryland and Indiana, the use of troops, who voted themselves while preventing Democrats from voting, had probably carried those states. All in all, the Democrats had done surprisingly well—well enough to raise the serious possibility that in a restored Union, with solid Southern support, they would emerge as the dominant party.

Andrew Johnson. The inherent weakness of the Republican party was made even more obvious by the decision to make Andrew Johnson, a War Democrat, Lincoln's running mate. When John Wilkes Booth's bullet catapulted Johnson into the presidency, the Republicans soon learned that there existed a fundamental gap between themselves and the new President. Johnson's background had left him with a deep loathing for Southern aristocrats; at the same time, he shared the common Southern conviction that Negroes were generically and irredeemably inferior to whites. That Johnson would ever share the radical enthusiasm for Negro enfranchisement was, to say the least, unlikely. Indeed, as time went on, he tended to identify himself more and more with the Democratic party. The Blair brothers, Montgomery and Francis, both of whom had practically returned to the Democratic party, systematically cultivated the President, while from all sides he received assurances that the Democratic party was, in fact, "a Johnson party." At the same time, Democratic newspapers and Democratic leaders made it quite clear that their party looked to the South for their real regenerative power. As it was, Johnson never made the full return to the Democratic party. His aim seems to have been the establishment of a conservative coalition dedicated to the restoration of the political *status quo ante bellum,* and he apparently pursued it without ever realizing that it boded ill for the emancipated slaves, and that it would, if successful, doom the Republican party to permanent minority status.

The Republican Response to Johnson. Confronted with what they regarded as the catastrophe of Andrew Johnson, the Republicans first tried to oust him, and when that failed, cast about desperately for a new image and permanent status. Much of the history of reconstruction can be understood in the light of this quest. It ended in 1868, when the Republicans gave their presidential nomination to Ulysses S. Grant, and presented themselves to the nation as "the party of union." They had found the folk hero who was to be their political salvation.

GRANT'S FIRST TERM

The Temper of the Times. No era in American history seems quite so thoroughly tarnished—so devoid of taste and principle—as the two terms of Ulysses S. Grant. The Victor of Appomattox presided at what has been succinctly called by the twentieth century critic Vernon L. Parrington "the Great Barbecue," a cookout which enabled a select (though unsavory) few to dine on the wealth of the United States. It seems in retrospect to have been the very triumph of corruption and vulgarity—a time when the flamboyant Jim Fisk could say of his acknowledged railroad frauds that he had "lost nothing save honor," a time when Roscoe Conkling, Republican master of the Senate, could dismiss questions about corruption within his party's ranks with the contemptuous statement: "Parties are not built up by deportment, or by ladies' magazines, or gush!"

The Nadir of Public Morality. That Grant's presidency was marked by an almost total eclipse of public morality is abundantly clear. Why the eclipse took place at precisely that time in history is less certain. Much can, no doubt, be attributed to the long, bitter, and ultimately disillusioning war that ended in 1865. Moreover, the war had created a dynamic economy whose growth was not paralleled by an adjustment in the nation's political institutions. The Jacksonian idea that government should play only a marginal role survived the war. All effort to move beyond a policy of *laisser faire* would raise the deeply rooted American suspicion of public power. As Charles Francis Adams, Jr., grandson of John Quincy Adams, put it:

> Government supervision among Anglo-Saxons is apt to degenerate into jobbery. In America, particularly, the whole instinct of the people leads them to circumscribe rather than to enlarge the province of

> government. This policy is founded in wisdom. Government by the people is apt at all times to degenerate into government by the politicians and the caucus; and the people, if wise, will keep the province of the government within reasonable limits. The spoils of victory are large enough already.

The reformers of the later nineteenth century were forced to swim against the current. Much of their energy was dissipated in the attempt to convince Americans that all government action was not, by definition, bad. But the belated triumph of Jacksonian principles under Grant did trigger a reaction, and the twentieth century was launched with a massive program of reform.

Grant as President. In political terms, the Republican decision to nominate Grant proved eminently wise. He won a narrow but decisive victory over Horatio Seymour. The result could hardly have been the same if the Republican candidate had been a regular politician, or if it had seemed less obvious to the nation that Grant was the man to heal the split between the executive and the legislature. The Republicans were helped still more by the fact that the South had not been fully restored, and that many Democratic voters were thus disqualified.

As President, Grant revealed a disinclination to participate openly in political decisions. Accustomed by his military training to follow the lead of civilian politicians, he was content to reign rather than rule. He viewed himself as a man chosen to supervise the faithful administration of routine governmental procedures: the honest collection and honest disbursement of public funds, and the dispassionate enforcement of the laws of the land. Above all, he was determined to be "in sympathy with Congress."

Grant the Politician. Grant's innocence of politics was complemented by a reticence that made his contemporaries think of him as a "strong, silent soldier." Only his closest friends knew that he was a man so gnawed by self-doubt, so chronically unsure of his own capacities, that he had seemed doomed, before the war, to a life of quiet and ignominious desperation. With the suddenness of fate the war had revealed him as a truly great general, and had propelled him to international fame. But the stamp of poverty was still upon him; Grant never lost his awe of the wealthy, and was always pathetically grateful for their gifts. It seems not to have entered his mind that those who gave him gifts of houses and money might expect reward; he never lost the sense that the rich man was, after all, a success, and one whose advice was to be sought. In such a context Grant's real and deep-seated virtues became vices: he was incapable of abandoning men who had befriended him, refusing to desert them even when there was irrefutable evidence that they had callously betrayed him. Grant was an admirably decent, though woefully simple, man who had the grave misfortune to be elected President of the United States. The reputation he had earned on the battlefield was dissipated in the White House.

Grant's First Experiences. Grant's bland ignorance of politics was revealed as soon as he began to form his cabinet. Consulting no one—not even the prospective appointees—Grant made a series of hallucinatory choices that stunned the nation. As Secretary of the Treasury, for example, he chose A. T. Stewart, a wealthy New York merchant whose major qualification seemed to be the lavish gifts he had bestowed on the President. Congress responded by promptly resurrecting an almost forgotten law of 1789 which disqualified anyone engaged in commerce from service in the cabinet. Contritely, Grant accepted as a replacement for Stewart one George S. Boutwell, a radical who was devoted to Republican patronage and policies. The ineptitude of Grant's original cabinet was so manifest that he was compelled to reshuffle it even as he assumed the presidency.

The Tenure of Office Act. Grant's political naïveté was further illustrated when he attempted to force repeal of the Tenure of Office Act, which forbade removal of executive officers by the President without approval of the Senate. The Republican leadership immediately threatened him with an open break. Slowly it dawned on Grant that the very instrument he had helped to wield against Johnson was now being held in reserve against him. Had he been a shrewder politician, he might have mobilized his vast prestige to force a showdown with Congress; instead, he capitulated. The net effect of his action—or, more precisely, inaction—was to eliminate all executive control over legislative behavior.

The Spoils System. The spoils system had once been a secondary matter in government. By Grant's time it had acquired primary importance. So vast were the numbers of party-faithful seeking patronage that it had become customary to demand a large fee for an appointment. Prices ranged from $4,000 for a seat in Congress to $15,000 for a judgeship. The money thus obtained was used to subsidize party expenses. As the price of an appointment rose, the office itself became an opportunity for recouping the expenditure necessary for obtaining it. Since tenure was indefinite in most instances, an appointment had to be milked as quickly as possible; the ratio of corruption went up accordingly. Grant and subsequent Presidents gradually discovered that Congress viewed the spoils system as its own peculiar prerogative, in return for which it was prepared to deliver legislation required by the President. "In ordinary affairs a President who will not so purchase help," Rutherford B. Hayes discovered, "will find his recommendations treated with slight respect, or even ostentatiously overruled." Grant adjusted himself to the system, and paved the way for the series of scandals that was to shake his administration.

Corruption under Grant. In a sense, reconstruction and corruption frequently went hand in hand. But the depredations to which the treasuries of defeated Southern states were subjected pale into insignificance beside the raids upon the federal coffers. A venal alliance between marauding entrepreneurs and public officials permitted both groups to emerge from the Great Barbecue with substantial rewards. The floor of Congress became a gladiatorial pit in which wealthy tycoons fought each other for congressional land grants and charters. Jay Cooke, for instance, a Philadelphia banker, received more than 47,000,000 acres of public land to subsidize construction of the Northern Pacific Railroad. Like many other entrepreneurs he was a product of the war, and had gained access to the inner circles of Republican power by selling government bonds in vast quantities. To Oakes Ames, a Massachusetts congressman with a questionable reputation, went the contract to build the eastern half of the Union Pacific Railroad. His congressional brethren, whose motives in getting him the contract were somewhat less than altruistic, expected a substantial slice of the pie. To meet their demands, Ames organized the Credit Mobilier, ostensibly a joint stock company for the construction of the railroad. Its history provides a typical example of postwar corruption.

The Credit Mobilier. The Credit Mobilier originated amid the tumult and confusion of the Civil War. As an inadequately staffed government strove to manage a military enterprise that dwarfed all previous federal endeavors, and one that involved the expenditure of staggering sums of money, many politicians found it a relatively easy matter to advance their own economic well-being. In this atmosphere the Credit Mobilier was born. Its ostensible purpose was to obtain construction contracts for the Union Pacific; in actuality, the moneys collected were used to pay huge dividends to a select group of major stockholders. These consisted largely of congressmen who had been permitted to purchase their stock at a substantially reduced cost. Oakes Ames made it clear that these stock sales had been designed to "make friends" for the Union Pacific in Congress. Though the total amount distributed to the stockholders may not have exceeded $65,000, the men who had shared it included former Vice-President Schuyler Colfax, and the current Vice-President, Henry Wilson. The Credit Mobilier was finally investigated during the presidency of James Garfield. Garfield himself became entangled in a mass of contradictory evidence as he tried to protect his fellow Republicans. When the investigating committee had completed its work, it recommended the expulsion from Congress of Ames, of Democratic Representative James Brooks of New York, and of Senator James W. Patterson of New Hampshire. But Congress, fully aware that members guilty of far more heinous offenses had escaped retribution, settled for censure rather than expulsion.

The Salary Grab Act. Even as the nation shuddered in dismay at the revelations concerning the Credit Mobilier, Congress callously passed a bill that became popularly known as the "Salary Grab Act" (March 3, 1873). It raised the salaries of members of Congress from $5,000 to $7,500 per year, with a retroactive bonus of $5,000 for each member. In order to assure Grant's approval, the presidential salary was simultaneously increased from $25,000 to $50,000. This was one outrage too many for a public that could, after all, inflict retribution at the polls. In the elections of 1874 the Republicans suffered heavily, and Congress saw the wisdom of reinstating its former system of stipends.

The Spread of Corrupt Practices. It should not be thought, however, that corruption was a peculiarly congressional characteristic. Secretary of War William W. Belknap, responsible for the maintenance of the Indian reservations, gave his wife a post tradership which she turned over to a New York contractor. The incumbent trader then agreed to pay the new appointee $12,000 a year for the privilege of retaining his appointment. Of this amount, $6,000 a year was to be paid to Mrs. Belknap. Unfortunately, she died after receiving only $1,500, but her husband managed to conquer his grief to the extent of continuing to accept payments. Moreover, Belknap had made similar arrangements for a number of his friends, who could thus obtain "salaries" ranging up to $100,000 without the inconvenience of actually having to work. In March of 1876, the House Committee on Expenditures in the War Department moved to impeach the Secretary of War for gross malfeasance in office. But Belknap had been forewarned, and he rushed to Grant with his resignation. Grant accepted it "with great regret"; but Congress refused to stop impeachment proceedings, and although Belknap was ultimately acquitted because the impeachment failed of a two-thirds vote, no one doubted his guilt.

The Democratically controlled House elected in 1874, having struck pay dirt in its scrutiny of the War Department, now turned its attention to the Department of the Navy. Here it discovered that between 1869 and 1876 the Secretary, George M. Robeson, had made personal bank deposits totaling $300,000 more than he had earned. His connection with a Philadelphia grain, feed, and flour company had made this firm the channel through which naval purchases of such items were directed. All suppliers to the Navy had been forced to pay a percentage to the company, and they in turn had paid Robeson *his* percentage. Similar charges were leveled, though not pressed, against the men responsible for the management and supply of naval yards.

Nor did the Attorney General's office escape investigation. It turned out that Attorney General George H. Williams, who had been nominated to the Chief Justiceship upon the death of Salmon P. Chase in 1873, had used contingent funds of the Department of Justice to purchase a carriage and livery, and to pay the wages of two personal servants. It was further revealed that Williams, during the Panic of 1873, had used government funds to meet his personal expenses. Although the Senate Judiciary Committee recommended his nomination as Chief Justice, the Senate thought otherwise, and Grant was compelled to withdraw the nomination. Williams remained in the Justice Department for an additional two years, since Grant concluded that he had not done "anything corrupt or illegal."

The Sanborn Contracts. In 1874, a further scandal involving the Treasury Department was revealed. Some two years earlier, Congress had repealed the revenue laws which provided for the payment of informers in cases of tax dodging, but it had subsequently added to an appropriation act a rider which permitted the Secretary of the Treasury to appoint not more than three persons to seek out such delinquencies. One appointment went to John Sanborn, a protégé of the erratic Civil War general Benjamin Butler. After some success in locating tax delinquencies, Sanborn obtained under questionable circumstances a contract to investigate 592 railroad companies, representing almost the entire railway system of the United States.

In the investigation which he then conducted, Sanborn collected $427,000, of which he himself pocketed $213,500. The House Ways and Means Committee subsequently noted that under normal circumstances the same amount would have been collected by the Internal Revenue Service without incurring the heavy fee paid to Sanborn. When Congress sought to discover who was responsible, both William A. Richardson, Secretary of the Treasury, and his Assistant Secretary, Frederick A. Sawyer, disclaimed all knowledge of the affair, though the department solicitor claimed both men had been fully aware of Sanborn's activities. Subsequently, all the principals in the case resigned, but the President astonished the nation by appointing Richardson to the Court of Claims.

The Whiskey Ring. The removal of Richardson from the Treasury left Grant with the task of finding a new Secretary. On June 4, 1874, Benjamin H. Bristow, a Kentucky Republican, received the appointment, inheriting at the same time a seething host of rumors about corruption among the collectors of internal revenue taxes on distilleries. For nearly eight years, distillers had been protesting that certain of their competitors were receiving unfair advantages from the fact that they were not obliged to pay their full tax. Bristow heard their complaints and launched an investigation which revealed the truth of the distillers' complaints and ultimately implicated not only the collectors of internal revenue at St. Louis, Chicago, Milwaukee, and San Francisco, but also the chief clerk of the Washington internal revenue division of the Treasury, numerous Treasury employees, and General Orville E. Babcock, Grant's private secretary. So pervasive was the so-called Whiskey Ring's influence in the Treasury that Bristow found he could trust only the department's solicitor, Bluford Wilson.

Operating under the strictest secrecy, Bristow, Wilson, and a handful of agents obtained evidence that permitted the indictment of forty-seven distillers, sixty rectifiers, ten wholesale dealers, and eighty-six internal revenue field agents. More than one hundred of the two hundred and three men indicted pleaded guilty, and twelve fled the country, but fewer than twelve were finally convicted, and among those acquitted was General Babcock. Grant, who viewed the prosecution of his private secretary as part of a covert campaign to gain Bristow the Republican nomination in 1876, gave Babcock a favorable deposition, and, upon his acquittal made him inspector of lighthouses. Grant then proceeded to drive home his peculiarly myopic view of politics by forcing the resignation of Bristow, removing Wilson, and firing the Treasury agents who had been most instrumental in revealing the full dimensions of the whiskey scandal. The unyielding stubbornness that had made Grant so admirable when he faced Lee before Richmond now showed its darker side—a blind, senseless devotion to men whose behavior cried for rebuke but whom he rewarded instead with positions of public responsibility and trust. By 1876 the Victor of Appomattox had nearly bankrupted his fund of good will; the breeze of reform was turning into a high wind.

THE ELECTION OF 1872

The Liberal Republicans. The Republican party in the postwar period was a peculiar amalgam of flagrant politics and impassioned morality. The anti-slavery sentiment of 1860 had developed, by 1867, into an intense determination to grant the Negro equal rights; by 1870 the "moral" elements in the party were convinced that only deep-seated institutional reforms could secure responsible government. The flagrant misuse of patronage focused reform sentiment on a demand for the establishment of a civil service. The pressure grew until, in December 1870, Grant was compelled to call for reform of the patronage, a demand that was acceded to on March 3, 1861, when Congress authorized the President to establish rules and regulations for a civil service. Grant, in a surprising reversal of his customary political form, appointed a Civil Service Commission headed by the reformer George William Curtis. Using a system of competitive examinations, the commission set to work creating an apolitical civil service, but their efforts were to run afoul of a growing rift in the Republican party.

The tide of reform was clearly rising among Republicans. New England manufacturers, who were adversely affected by high tariffs, threw themselves behind the free trade agitation led by Edward Atkinson of Boston and David A. Wells of Connecticut. The center of this activity became the Taxpayers' Union established at Washington in December 1871. But reform agitation within the Republican party was weakened by the fact that it had no central focus, and—what was more important—it never reached the Republican rank and file.

Reform in the South. In 1870, an underlying political ferment in the South finally erupted. In the Missouri state legislature, a coalition of Democrats and dissident Republicans forced through amnesty provisions for Missourians who had aided the Confederate cause. When Carl Schurz of Missouri tried to push a nationwide amnesty bill through Congress he was rebuffed, and the Republican congressional leadership, intent upon holding its Southern strength, passed a Ku Klux Klan Act, the intent of which was not so much to suppress that organization as to permit continued interference in the affairs of Southern states.

The Liberal Republican Program. In January 1872 the Missouri reformers Carl Schurz and B. Gratz Brown launched a national reform movement. Their program was a shrewd blend of American dissatisfactions, and included a reduction in the tariff, civil service reform, a general amnesty for former Confederates, and the protection of state rights. At a convention of interested Republicans, held in Cincinnati, their program drew a broad base of support which included not only conventional reform elements but such conservative Republicans as Gideon Welles, Salmon P. Chase, and former Governor Andrew Curtin of Pennsylvania as well. The program naturally received the support of Democrats, who saw in the reform movement an opportunity to break the power of the Republican radicals. These oddly assorted interests combined to form the political party which provided the major challenge to Grant in 1872. It took the name Liberal Republican.

Reform Candidates in 1872. Unfortunately, the reform movement also attracted disgruntled office seekers and those with personal grievances against Grant. Horace Greeley, for instance, a lifetime advocate of protectionism with an incorrigible craving for public office, suddenly announced his support of the reformers. The movement began to reveal fundamental contradictions as disgruntled Republicans tried to reconcile their detestation of its principles with their appreciation of its political possibilities. A welter of candidates, some active and some indifferent, complicated still further the efforts to establish a well-defined party program. Salmon P. Chase and Charles Sumner were mentioned as possible candidates, but their function in the new party was more ornamental than utilitarian. The presidential candidate could only come from the ranks of the party's effective leaders: Governor B. Gratz Brown of Missouri; Judge David Davis (who had considerable backing in democratic ranks); Lyman Trumble; Charles Francis Adams, son of John Quincy Adams; and Horace Greeley. There was considerable support for Adams but he did little to encourage it, and even took the position that he would accept the nomination only if it were to come to him unsolicited and uncommitted. The contemptuous arrogance implicit in Adams's stand may well have cost him the nomination, which went instead to the quixotic Greeley, who had energetically campaigned for it. But the choice of Greeley demoralized many Liberal Republicans, whose free trade sentiments made it impossible for them to accept the lead of an overt protectionist. When B. Gratz Brown was given the vice-presidential nomination, it was charged that he was being paid off for his previous support of Greeley. The Democrats, though cramped at the prospect of supporting their long-time enemy of the newspaper wars, swallowed their doubts and subscribed to the Liberal Republican designation.

Grant's Re-election. Grant, who had not yet been tarred by the brush of corruption, proved far too popular for the inept Greeley. In addition, the campaign was savage, and Greeley's inconsistencies were so systematically dredged up that he was finally left wondering whether he was running for "the White House or the penitentiary." When the votes were counted, Grant had a 763,000 popular majority; he had swept every state but Missouri, Tennessee, Texas, Georgia, Kentucky, and Maryland. Riding high on a wave of jubilation, Grant's supporters unwisely concluded that the electorate had given them *carte blanche* to be corrupt. Their caution was whisked to the winds; they gave way to an arrogance and a recklessness that would force the Republican party to fight the next election with its back to the wall.

FOREIGN POLICY AFTER THE WAR

Floundering in domestic corruption, the nation struggled to regain dominance in the Western Hemisphere after having temporarily relinquished enforcement of the Monroe Doctrine during the war. In the conduct of foreign policy under Johnson and Grant, the United States revealed a wavering endorsement of manifest destiny, flashes of belligerency often squelched by public indifference, and an extension of corrupt practices from the domestic to the foreign arena. At least, the nation's diplomacy was colorfully inept; at most, it was a national disgrace.

American Intervention in Mexico. The nation that emerged from the Civil War found that the Monroe Doctrine was undergoing a severe test. Taking advantage of the American conflict, Louis Napoleon of France sent his army into Mexico City in 1863 to establish an empire to be ruled over by the Hapsburg Emperor Maximilian. The French invasion provoked a desperate war of liberation under Benito Juarez, and Mexico was on the brink of collapse at the time the Civil War ended. The American State Department now brought increasing pressure to bear on Louis Napoleon to withdraw his army from North America. Finally, in 1867, a threat of direct intervention ended the French adventure in Mexico. As the French withdrew from Mexico, the United States was well advanced upon a renewed career of territorial expansion.

The Purchase of Alaska. During the 1850s, the Russian government, increasingly doubtful as to whether its occupation of Alaska could be made profitable, began to explore the possibility of selling the territory to the United States. The crescendo of American sectional strife precluded serious talks at that time, but in the winter of 1867 the Russian minister to Washington, Baron Stoeckl, reopened negotiations. The commercial interests of the Northwest had already brought pressure to bear on Secretary of State Seward to assure their trading rights in Alaska. When Seward learned from the Russian government that such rights would not be granted, he determined on the purchase of the area. On March 30, 1867, a treaty was signed whereby the United States agree to pay $7,200,000 for Alaska, and a week later the Senate approved the transfer. It was not until July 27, 1868, that Congress appropriated the necessary funds; the House leadership could not resist the opportunity to embarrass the Johnson administration by refusing to originate the necessary appropriation.

The sum at stake had also whetted some of the greedier congressional appetites. Baron Stoeckl spent about $135,000 to persuade certain congressmen to reduce their opposition to the purchase, though the exact distribution of his largesse remains uncertain. Some $60,000 in gold passed into the hands of John Forney and Robert J. Walker, the former an editor of several jingoistic newspapers, the latter a protean advocate of expansionism whose career reached back to the annexation of Texas. Both men were active lobbyists for the bill at the capital. Andrew Johnson believed that $8,000 had been paid to Representative N. P. Banks, chairman of the Committee on Foreign Affairs, and that $10,000 had gone to Thaddeus Stevens. The purchase of Alaska provides further evidence—if further evidence is needed—that the corruption of the postwar period was already well advanced under Johnson. What is more important is that by mid-summer of 1868 a vast northern territory had been added to the American domain, radically extending this country's occupation of the North American continent. A good many Americans were left with the impression that the expulsion of the British from Canada was imminent.

The Fenian Invasion of Canada. Two conditions served to worsen relations between Great Britain and the United States for several years after the Civil War. One was the aggressive action taken by the Fenian Brotherhood, an Irish-American society which launched an abortive invasion of Canada from Buffalo in the late spring of 1866. The Fenians intended to donate their conquest to the United States in return for American help in liberating Ireland from British rule. The British suspected that the Fenians had had the encouragement of Seward, who had already made his feelings clear by terminating the British-American reciprocal trade agreement of 1854. Nor was British and Canadian unease lessened when Congressman Nathaniel P. Banks presented the House with a bill admitting the "states" of East and West Canada, New Brunswick, and Nova Scotia into the Union. American aggressive designs against Canada were permanently checked, however, when the British gave their territory Dominion status in 1867.

The Alabama, Florida, and Shenandoah. Canada was not the only source of tension between the United States and Great Britain. Many Northerners still held the angry memory that British shipyards had constructed three Confederate cruisers—the *Alabama,* the *Florida,* and the *Shenandoah*—which had inflicted heavy losses on Northern shipping. The *Florida* alone had seized almost fifty prizes before she was captured in a neutral Brazilian port. The *Alabama* had a similarly effective career, sinking no less than fifty-seven ships before she was sunk off Cherbourg, France. The *Shenandoah* had the strangest career of all. She sank much of the New England whaling fleet while prowling the South Pacific, reaching her apogee of destruction only after the war was over, as it was not until August 1865 that her captain learned of the Confederate surrender.

The careers of these cruisers and their less famous sister ships were bitterly attributed, in the North, to flagrant violations of neutrality on the part of the British. Many Northerners felt that only full compensation by Great Britain for all losses caused by British-built shipping could assuage their grievance; and others, like Charles Sumner, felt that nothing less than the acquisition of Canada would suffice.

The Alabama Arbitration. As soon as the war was over, Charles Francis Adams, the American Minister to London, tried to obtain an international adjudication of the issue; but he was rebuffed by Earl Russell, the British foreign minister. An ominous note entered the quarrel when a number of congressmen declared their intention to aid all present and future enemies of Great Britain. By 1869 a new British government had accepted the principle of international arbitration, but an irate Senate, insistent upon full compensation and no compromise, rejected the British overture as inadequate. The harshness of this viewpoint was to be attributed in large part to Charles Sumner, chairman of the Foreign Relations Committee, who had convinced his colleagues that the issue was not one of shipping losses only but of British sympathy for the Confederacy. Sumner and others claimed that British aid to the enemy had prolonged the war for two years, and that the British therefore owed the United States "full compensation" to the tune of $2,125,000,000—half the total cost of the war.

Such was the impasse inherited by Grant, who had no sooner taken office than he indicated that he was ready to go to war in order to settle the issue. Only the steady influence of Secretary of State Hamilton Fish prevented rash action. Two years of informal negotiations culminated in the establishment of a joint high commission, consisting of five American and five British arbitrators, which negotiated the Treaty of Washington (May 8, 1871). The treaty consigned the *Alabama* claims to international arbitration, and was accompanied by an official expression of regret on the part of Her Majesty's Government for damages inflicted on the United States. The final tribunal of arbitration consisted of five persons, one each to be selected by the President of the United States, the Queen of England, the Emperor of Brazil, the King of Italy, and the President of Switzerland. From the outset the American case received a favorable hearing, and under the skillful guidance of America's delegate, Charles Francis Adams, the issue was focused on direct rather than indirect claims. In the resulting decisions, Britain was held liable for claims arising from the depredations of the *Alabama, Florida,* and *Shenandoah.* Damages of $15,500,000 were awarded the United States. The findings also confirmed the fifty-year-old tradition whereby Britain and America settled their differences by arbitration and negotiation.

Grant and Santo Domingo. Less successful in its outcome was the ill-fated scheme to annex Santo Domingo, a scheme in which Grant permitted himself to become the agent of a freebooting adventurer. The effort to annex the Caribbean republic had its origins in an earlier effort by Seward to obtain an American naval base at Samana Bay, in the northeastern part of Santo Domingo. Buenaventura Baez and Jose Maria Cabral, who alternated in the office of Dominican President, sought to lease or sell the region. Then Baez, encouraged by two American speculators, William L. Cazneau and Joseph W. Fabens, both of whom had large land holdings and extensive mineral rights in the country, made a spectacular new offer to allow the United States to annex the entire country. Though Johnson and Seward viewed the proposal with some favor, the House of Representatives turned it down by an emphatic majority.

The energetic Fabens turned his attention to the new administration. He was rebuffed by Secretary of State Hamilton Fish, but warmly received by Grant, who delegated his private secretary, Orville E. Babcock, to visit Santo Domingo and determine the feasibility of the proposed annexation. Fabens, Cazneau, and Baez found the young and unscrupulous Babcock to be a man of their own ilk. Without authority, he signed an agreement committing the United States to annex the country by paying its $1,500,000 external debt, or, failing that, to purchase Samana Bay for $2,000,000. He also pledged the private influence of the President to secure congressional acceptance of annexation. Grant, far from disturbed by his secretary's precipitous action, gave Babcock the diplomatic power to negotiate a treaty absorbing the Caribbean republic into the United States. Baez arranged a plebiscite in which his countrymen gave a massive vote of approval for annexation. But in the United States, strenuous objections were being raised. Hamilton Fish viewed with profoundest distaste the manner in which his department had been circumvented during the negotiations. He notified the President of the dubious character of any transaction involving Cazneau and Fabens, but Grant continued to press the matter forward until he ran into the obdurate resistance of Senator Sumner, chairman of the Committee on Foreign Relations. Though efforts were made to undo the senatorial veto by obtaining a favorable report on the treaty from a reputable investigating committee, annexation remained a dead issue. Grant, disgruntled at this rebuff and settling on Sumner as the culprit in the affair, threw his full weight behind the *Alabama* claims negotiations, a proposal he knew Sumner bitterly opposed. In this way, at least, the exceedingly dubious Santo Domingo affair was of some benefit to the nation, though the benefit derived more from malice than forethought.

In the America of President Grant corruption had a Midas touch. Its effects were visible in every agency of government, in business, in foreign affairs. As an apparently endless chain of scandals was dredged up from the mire, it became evident that the disease was breeding its own antidote. The stirrings of the reform movement in 1872 were only a prelude. It was becoming increasingly apparent to many Republicans that drastic steps were needed to save their party from repudiation at the polls. The Democrats, long out of office, saw in the issue of corruption their key to success. By 1876 both parties were in the throes of a campaign for reform—one which would end, ironically, in a corrupt bargain for the presidency.

Chapter 3

The End of Reconstruction

However terrible a war has been, when peace returns the combatants must learn to live with one another; not in friendship, necessarily, but in a relationship essentially of respectful cordiality. Such a relationship can most easily be established when the antagonists are separate nations, and the procedures of diplomatic accommodation can be used to effect a *rapprochement*. The situation is immensely more complicated in the aftermath of a civil war, when both victor and vanquished must live together in a single country.

The Civil War had prevented a permanent separation between North and South, but had erected a profound psychological gulf between the two sections. Southerners who still hoped for victory in the bleakest hours of the war had no choice after the surrender at Appomattox but to accept that for them, as one Confederate officer put it, "there would be no dawn." They would have to live within a republic they had done their best to destroy. In the humiliation of such a defeat, each act of the postwar reconstruction seemed a handful of salt cruelly and gratuitously rubbed into a gaping wound. For Northerners, the grievances of the war were muted by the very totality of their triumph. The North's insistence on penance and retribution, which left so indelible a scar on Southern sensibilities, was only a postwar episode; Northern energies were already beginning the plunge into an absorbing frenzy of industrialization. Lulled by the rattle of its machines, the North would not feel called upon to analyze the catastrophe that had almost destroyed it; and this indifference would permit Southerners to undo the worst consequences of their defeat. In 1877, with the end of radical reconstruction, America began the roundabout, frustrating, often retrograde journey toward a reconciliation which still eludes us today.

FINANCIAL FAILURE AND GRAFT

The Panic of 1873. A seemingly endless prosperity came to America after the war. Occasional setbacks occurred, but the general trend of the economy was one of constant upsurge; vast new railroads and huge factories sprang up everywhere, and the country's natural resources were the target of rampant exploitation on a staggering scale. Businessmen in increasing numbers complained that Republican misrule in the South was impoverishing potential Southern customers; others viewed with growing alarm the heavy cost inflicted upon the business community by government corruption. But prosperity kept the sharpest complaints in check, for the flow of gold was sufficient to permit both tidy profits and the expenses of corruption.

The Failure of Jay Cooke. On September 18, 1873, the illusion was shattered. Jay Cooke & Company, a banking firm that had gained national stature by managing the sale of federal bonds during the war, and which had also become deeply involved in Republican politics, suddenly failed. The root of Cooke's difficulties was his heavy investment in the incomplete Northern Pacific Railroad. Heavy overdrafts and a mounting deficit had convinced him by 1872 that only with the aid of a re-elected Grant could he survive until the Northern Pacific began to show a profit. His lavish contributions to the Republican campaign had been the act of a desperate man. But his gamble had not paid off, and the business community was not slow to draw its conclusions. If the firm of Jay Cooke could go under, no firm was safe. Companies suspected of instability were swept away in the ensuing panic. Even the presence of Grant at a conference of financiers and businessmen in New York provided no relief. Although Grant entertained the idea of using federal funds to subsidize public projects, thus providing work for the unemployed, he was dissuaded with the argument "that the true remedy for the finances at present was economy and retrenchment, until business restored itself." But Grant was no longer in the White House by the time these traditional maxims had had their restorative effect.

Samuel Tilden and the Tweed Ring. Even before the panic sharpened the discontent of American businessmen with political corruption, New York City had witnessed a political upheaval which ended with the imprisonment of Tammany's Boss Tweed. In the process, it was revealed that the so-called "Tweed Ring" had looted the city of no less than $100,000,000 during the previous decade. On September 4, 1871, a mass meeting of the city's leading businessmen elected a Committee of Seventy, headed by Samuel J. Tilden, a prominent New York lawyer, to check further depredations on the municipal treasury. Since both Tilden and his chief associate, August Belmont, were Democrats, and members of the Tammany organization to boot, the nation was treated to the unusual spectacle of Democrats actively engaged in cleaning up Democratic corruption.

None of the men who were most active in the taming of Tweed made any bones about the fact that they favored good municipal government because it was profitable. Their goals were lower taxes and more efficient (and hence cheaper) service. Tilden, a grimly ambitious and coldly calculating man, had the further purpose of using the prosecutions for political advantage. They catapulted him into the governorship of New York State in 1874, and brought him within a hair-breadth of the presidency in 1876. Above all, Tilden succeeded in establishing the Democrats as the party of reform, a party eager to undo the grasping control of industry by the favored classes as a result of the demoralization of war.

THE DISPUTED ELECTION OF 1876

Faced with a revitalized Democratic party which was succeeding in the exploitation of a dynamic issue, the Republicans, meeting at Cincinnati, had no choice but to meet the reform challenge. But in choosing a presidential candidate they found themselves in a quandary: a straight-out politician of the Blaine or Conkling sort would drive reform-minded Republicans into the Tilden camp, while the nomination of an energetic reformer like Benjamin H. Bristow would drive the party's shrewdest politicians into revolt. Fearing a split, they nominated the relatively unknown Rutherford B. Hayes of Ohio. He had the multiple advantage of having dutifully supported reconstruction measures; of advocating a return to hard money; of having supported Bristow's candidacy; and of having refused to run on a ticket headed by Blaine. Hayes, though not quite a dark horse, was at least suitably gray.

The Democratic Nomination. At St. Louis, the Democrats subscribed to a platform of reform and reconciliation. As Tilden's running-mate they nominated Senator Thomas A. Hendricks of Indiana, a stubborn and consistent opponent of the excesses of reconstruction. Under the shrewd guidance of the Democratic chairman, Abram S. Hewitt, the Democrats contrasted Grant's record of corruption with Tilden's cleanup of New York City and New York State. They drove home the fact that Tilden had not only prosecuted Boss Tweed, but that, as governor, he had exposed wholesale looting of the state treasury through fraudulent public works contracts. Hewitt's call for a return to "the spirit of reformation . . . when to be summoned into the public service was a priceless honor and not an opportunity for private gain" struck a responsive chord. It also created an inherent contradiction in Democratic goals. While Tilden promised limited constitutional government based on principles of Jeffersonian economy, regular Democratic politicians saw in his prospective victory a chance to gain the rewards so long denied them. It was obvious to a few men at least that both aims could not be gratified. But the fact remained that amid continuing hard times Tilden's call for economy had its attractions.

The Democratic Upsurge. As the drift toward the Democrats became increasingly apparent, the Republicans were driven to a desperate waving of the bloody flag. A Republican orator declared that "every man [who] tried to destroy this nation was a Democrat." In response to the call from South Carolina's Republican governor, Grant sent federal troops into that state in mid-October to suppress riots. A wave of arrests to forestall supposed intimidation of Negro voters followed. The situation in South Carolina, Florida, and Louisiana was obscured as Republican state officials labored to secure each for their national slate. The groundwork had been laid for the most controversial election in American history.

Tilden at the Edge of Victory. On the night of November 7, 1876, Tilden, having safely carried New York, New Jersey, Connecticut, and Indiana, was conceded to have won the election. He held a plurality of more than 250,000 over Hayes, and a clear majority of 160,000 over his combined opponents; only a single electoral vote was needed, and the Democrats could begin to divide up the offices for which they hungered. But it was a vote that Tilden would never receive. On November 8, the Republicans, aware that the election results in South Carolina, Louisiana, and Florida were uncertain, moved swiftly to throw the outcome in those states even further into doubt. Their aim was to force a canvass in which enough Democratic votes would be thrown out to secure a Republican majority in the electoral college. They had set themselves a prodigious task, since Tilden had an estimated majority of 9,000 votes in Louisiana alone; and most historians who have investigated the matter have concluded that Florida actually gave him her electoral vote, a vote that would have sufficed to win him the presidency. But Republican canvassing boards in the three states submitted new totals turning the electoral vote over to Hayes. The Democrats counterattacked by having their officials in the three states submit a set of returns favoring Tilden. They also claimed an electoral vote in Oregon on the grounds that one of the Republican electors was a federal officeholder and therefore ineligible. Congress was left with the task of determining how the votes at issue should be divided.

The Compromise of 1877. No ready solution was provided either by experience or by the Constitution, and the issue was stalemated between a heavily Democratic House and a Republican Senate. The country seemed to be drifting toward a new civil war as Democratic war veterans throughout the nation prepared to resist by force any effort to relieve Tilden of his victory. But the crucial fact in this increasingly tense situation was that many Southern Democrats with Whig backgrounds viewed the idea of a renewed civil conflict with undisguised dismay. These Southern ex-Whigs were the very men Lincoln had thought would move into the Republican party after the war, and who had been diverted into the Democratic party by the activities of the radicals. They were now prepared to negotiate a sensible solution with the Republicans. Under the guidance of Colonel Andrew J. Kellar of Memphis, a conservative Democrat, and General Henry Van Ness Boynton, a widely known journalist, the Republicans made a direct appeal to the former Whigs among the Southern Democrats. This group now held the key to continued Republican dominance in the South. It seemed very possible too that a revitalized Whig coalition in both parties would secure the dominance of big business in American life.

But it was clear that before the Southern ex-Whigs could be drawn into such a coalition the old radical program for the South would have to be abandoned. This would involve the destruction of the remaining carpetbagger governments and the relegation of the Negro to a permanent position of inferiority. These aims could be achieved under the Democrat Tilden; but his pledge to restore economy in government grated harshly on Southern ears. Struggling to recover from the maiming consequences of the war, crushed by the depression that followed the Panic of 1873, Southerners hoped for large federal subsidies to restore their harbors, complete their rail system, and rebuild their economy. The Republicans took advantage of this breach between the

Northern and Southern Democratic outlooks by offering to trade an extension of federal subsidies for the election of Hayes.

The Electoral Commission. The Republicans received a further boost when a special Electoral Commission, formed by a bi-partisan coalition in Congress to count the electoral vote, decided eight to seven in favor of Hayes. Northern Democrats in the House of Representatives countered with a filibuster which they hoped would halt the count of the electoral vote until after Inauguration Day. Since the success of this maneuver required the steady support of all Southern Democrats, Hayes promptly assured the latter that he would live up to any bargain reached between his party and the South. This maneuver broke the wavering Democratic ranks. In the compromise that was finally reached, the South traded the presidency for federal funds to subsidize internal improvements; for the promise of a subsidy to construct the Texas and Pacific Railroad linking New Orleans to the Pacific coast, (a promise, incidentally, that was never kept); and for the appointment of Tennessee's Senator David Key as Postmaster General. The Southern Democrats also promised to elect the Republican James A. Garfield to Speaker of the House, but they reneged on this part of the bargain. Hayes agreed to withdraw the remaining federal troops from South Carolina and Louisiana, thus bringing carpetbag rule of the South to an end. To prevent any further use of federal troops in the South, the House of Representatives refused to approve an army appropriation bill, leaving Hayes unable to meet the army payroll.

On March 4, 1877, Rutherford B. Hayes was inaugurated as President. Rising from the ashes of reconstruction, the South regained her full political stature in the republic she had deserted seventeen years before.

REALIGNMENT OF SOUTHERN POLITICAL POSITIONS

The Southern Redeemers. The Compromise of 1877 did not mark the end of sectional politics; instead, it confirmed the transformation of the South into a Democratic preserve, and the establishment of the North as an almost equally secure Republican preserve. The political shifts that occurred thereafter were largely due to political shifts in the West and in those Northern states that remained marginal. But this division of the nation meant little ideologically. The Southern Democracy was a contradictory alliance of old Whigs and Democrats. The former had entered into the arrangement in reaction against the acts of the radical Republicans during reconstruction. Yet the Democratic label was so objectionable to the new Whig membership that the joint ticket in various states was designated as "Conservative" or "Redeemer." The radical, freewheeling, individualistic Democrat of former times had his more colorful inclinations checked by his Whig collaborators. As one Southern Democrat protested, "In principle [I am] an Old Line Whig, but, under existing circumstances, in practice and from necessity, a Southern Democrat."

The Southern Bourbons. Under the circumstances, it was not surprising to find many of these new Democrats involved in the encouragement of Southern industrial growth. Two-term Governor James D. Porter of Tennessee, for instance, had been an ante-bellum Whig; he switched his allegiance to the Democrats and completed his career as president of the Nashville, Chattanooga, and St. Louis Railroad. In Kentucky, Henry Watterson of the Louisville *Courier-Journal* called for a drive to obtain Eastern capital for industrial expansion. The powerful Louisville and Nashville Railroad, though dominated by Northern and foreign capital, and controlled by Northerners August Belmont, Jay Gould, Thomas Fortune Ryan, and Jacob Schiff, managed to identify itself with Southern aspirations. In return it obtained such inestimable advantages as the chance to exploit the vast deposits of Alabama iron ore. The railroad strongly identified itself with the efforts of the conservative Democrats, known as "Southern Bourbons," to restore white supremacy in the election of 1874. For the remainder of the nineteenth century, only those Democrats approved by the Louisville and Nashville had much chance of gaining office in Alabama.

The New South. By 1880 the campaign to build a New South was in full swing. It had two aims—the inclusion of the South in the national movement toward industrialization and urbanization, and the securing of white supremacy. For Henry W. Grady, editor of the Atlanta *Constitution* and high priest of the New South, restoration meant a "rapid diversification of crops and diversification of industries" throughout the South, and its "clear and unmistakable domination [by] the white race." The latter need precluded the division of Southern white opinion "on economic or moral questions as interest or belief demands." For to do that would be to give the Negroes the balance of power, and the ability to dictate once more to the whites. As such views crystallized, Southerners moved ever more swiftly toward the establishment of a system of Jim Crow laws that would segregate the Negro at every level of Southern life.

THE NEGRO AS A SOUTHERN DILEMMA

The disappearance of moral fervor from Republican ranks was practically complete by 1880. Much of the enthusiasm that had found its focus in the cause of the Negro now passed into agitation for institutional reforms. Those who were striving to complete the reconciliation of North and South began to make pugnacious appeals to the inherent superiority of the white race. "It is not a sectional issue," harangued one border state newspaper. "It speaks in Ohio, and in Georgia. It speaks wherever the Anglo-Saxon touches an alien race." Southerners indirectly suggested that their program to exclude the Negro from full citizenship had the approval of the nation as a whole. Nor was their suggestion without a basis in fact. Few Northerners took time to criticize the Southern decision, since most assumed an air of generous tolerance as the South resolved its own destiny. It had, in effect, been conceded that the Negro was a Southern, rather than an American, dilemma. The resulting system of Jim Crowism must therefore be viewed as a Southern solution that received national assent.

Postwar Status of Negroes. The end of reconstruction was not synonymous with segregation. It was still possible for Negroes to ride in unsegregated street- and rail-cars. In that citadel of Southernism, Columbia, South Carolina, Negroes were freely admitted to entertainments and were served in bars and ice-cream parlors—though not elsewhere as a general rule. Negro policemen helped maintain law and order in many Southern cities; in Mississippi, restaurants frequently served both races in the same rooms; and Negroes were served food in railroad-station restaurants while sitting at the same tables as whites. The intermingling of the races that had characterized the South under slavery continued. White infants were still suckled by Negro wet-nurses, whites and Negroes lived in close proximity, and an easy camaraderie often prevailed between the races. Violence of the lynching order occurred, but there was no system of deliberate exclusion. The relationship of white to Negro was that of superior to inferior, but it had not been embedded in, or harshened by, the force of law.

Southern Racial Relations. At the core of the postwar relationship between the races was the conviction of Southern conservatives, who were prepared to accept Negro political rights so long as they were used to buttress conservative political domination, that the Negro had to be elevated lest he drag the white down to his depressed status. This was hardly the sentiment of the poorer whites, who had seen their own condition worsened by the economic exploitation that followed the war, and whose hostility toward the Negro had intensified accordingly. In addition, the pathetic ignorance of the poor whites, compounded by illiteracy, made them especially susceptible to the appeals of Negro-baiting organizations like the Ku Klux Klan. The courts trying cases of K.K.K. atrocities in the early 1870s soon discovered that most of the defendants were illiterates, whose hatred of the Negro was an assertion of their own one redeeming condition—the possession of white skin. The upper-class Southerners, many of them members of the old slaveowning aristocracy, generally identified themselves with the protection of Negro rights. They energetically approved Booker T. Washington's program of Negro self-help through industrial education. They entertained the idea of a gradual integration of educated Negroes into the aristocratic ruling class. For the moment, they formed an alliance with the Negro political leadership to secure the support of the Negro voters.

The alliance was helped by the fact that Negroes were acutely aware of the hatred felt for them by poor Southern whites, and they turned to the upper class for protection. Since the disenfranchisement of the Negro did not take place until almost the end of the nineteenth century, their electoral power was potent. As a result, it was not uncommon for Negroes to hold political office even in Mississippi, where Senators Lucius Q. C. Lamar and J. Z. George provided patronage for Negroes in return for their political backing. The effectiveness of this alliance between white conservatives and the Negro electorate was evident when Grover Cleveland appointed a good many Negroes to federal office in the South at the behest of Southern congressmen.

The Redneck Revolt. For all its pragmatic value, however, the interracial alliance bore heavily on the poorer whites, known as a class by the label "rednecks." Southern conservatives could keep this class in check with the threat that a divided white vote would permit the return of complete Negro dominance. At the same time, poor whites could never overcome their hatred for the Negro to the point of cooperating politically with men whose status was virtually identical to their own but whose skins were black. Between their racial pride and the political weight of a still enfranchised Negro population the poor whites were helplessly caught; and their ineffectiveness was a certain guarantee of conservative white domination. But the effective Populist challenge in the 1890s, followed in turn by the usual conservative threat that a divided white vote would admit the Negro to dominance, culminated in an effort to reconcile the warring whites by excluding the Negro from the franchise. In this compromise the conservatives tacitly admitted that their domination of the Democratic party in the South had ended. The spokesman for Mississippi was no longer Senator Lamar, but the strident racist James K. Vardaman, who proudly dubbed himself "the Great White Father"; in South Carolina, Wade Hampton was followed as Senator by "Pitchfork" Ben Tillman. In Georgia, Tom Watson, who had appealed for racial cooperation in the 1890s, surrendered to the *Zeitgeist* and espoused a virulent racism that bordered on the psychotic.

Negro Disenfranchisement. Disenfranchisement of the Negro began in Mississippi in 1890, and spread rapidly: to South Carolina in 1895, to Louisiana in 1898, to North Carolina in 1900, to Alabama in 1901, to Virginia in 1902, and to Georgia in 1908. In the other four states of the Old Confederacy the poll tax was used to achieve a like result. To insure Negro exclusion, the white primary was established. All opposition was howled down in a hysterical campaign of vilification. The reconstruction period was redrawn in luridly exaggerated colors, and audiences throughout the South learned that they were being saved from a second reconstruction that would have been even more horrible than the first. As the campaign took fire, Negroes were lynched and subjected to other brutalities in New Orleans, Atlanta, and lesser Southern towns.

Jim Crow. A system of segregation was now extended into almost every aspect of daily life. By 1900, Negroes were compelled to ride in segregated rail coaches; ten years later railway waiting rooms had joined the list. In the same decade segregation was extended to street cars, steamboats, theaters, ticket windows, toilets, parks, and water fountains. In factories, hospitals, restaurants, prisons, and circuses the pattern was the same. Wholesale rezoning split cities into white and Negro sections. Once the campaign was fully underway, no indignity seemed too harsh, no humiliation too cruel, for the Negro; South Carolina carried the logic of segregation to its final extreme by setting up separate school systems for white, Negro, and mulatto children. The pattern was adopted in the other states of the chronically poor South, and the level of Southern education was thus comprehensively and permanently lowered. Even so, white children fared better; only minimal training was provided for colored children, who, it was believed, scarcely needed much education to live in a ghetto with sealed exits.

The Federal Government and the Negro. The culminating phase of segregation came with its official incorporation into the federal employment system under Woodrow Wilson. Only bitter protests from

Northern Negroes and progressive leaders prevented its complete application to the employment practices of the United States government. In Washington, D.C., the mark of segregation was everywhere—an appropriate outward manifestation, since in a very real sense segregation had been born in the nation's capital. In a series of momentous decisions, the Supreme Court established the legality of a system that, more than half a century later, it would struggle to undo.

The Supreme Court and Civil Liberties. On March 1, 1875, Congress passed the Civil Rights Act. It secured to all persons the right to equal use of such facilities as inns, hotels, public transportation on land and sea, theaters, and other places of public amusement. If upheld, it would have erased the possibility of a comprehensive system of segregation such as was introduced in the South in the first decade of the twentieth century. Five cases charging discrimination against Negroes in the use of public facilities reached the Supreme Court in 1883. The Court, which was made up of eight Republicans and one Democrat, rendered an eight-to-one decision against the complainants. The Court concluded that the Negro's status as a "freeman" remained uncompromised even if he was not "admitted to all the privileges enjoyed by white citizens, or [if] he was subjected to discriminations in the enjoyment of accommodations in inns, public conveyances and places of amusement." Against "mere discriminations," as Justice Bradley expressed it, the Negro was defenseless.

Plessy v. Ferguson. Thirteen years later, the Court rendered an important decision in the case of Plessy *v.* Ferguson. Plessy, who was only one-eighth Negro, had refused to sit in a Louisiana railroad coach assigned to colored people. He was arrested and jailed for violating a Louisiana segregation statute of 1890. The Court found against Plessy, and declared that he had made the fallacious assumption "that the enforced separation of the two races stamps the colored race with a badge of inferiority." The Court reasoned that segregation was admissible as long as the two races were provided with "separate but equal" facilities. Justice John Marshall Harlan, a Kentucky Republican and former slaveholder, warned in a prophetic dissent that the decision would foster "race hate," and that it would cast into the shade America's pretensions as the home of liberty. "We boast of the freedom enjoyed by our people above all other peoples," Harlan declared. "But it is difficult to reconcile that boast with a state of the law which . . . puts the brand of servitude and degradation upon a large class of our fellow citizens." Sooner or later, he predicted, Americans would be compelled to recognize that "our Constitution is color blind, and neither knows nor tolerates classes among citizens." But, for the time being at least, and for many years ahead, the Court had put its mark of approval upon segregation.

The Nadir of Negro Rights. The Court's action signaled the national acceptance of Jim Crow. Northerners were prepared to allow the South its own solution. They were hardly in a position to protest after the Congress of the United States passed measures "requiring separate schools for colored children in the District of Columbia." Thus the American Negro reached his nadir of freedom, and began to fill that ledger of suffering, suppression, and injustice against which the so-called savagery of radical reconstruction must be measured. In the light of subsequent history, it seems at least possible that the radical Republican insistence on implementing the rights of Negroes with the threat of force contained a wisdom which has still to be acknowledged.

Part Two

THE INDUSTRIAL REPUBLIC

Chapter 4

The Web of Industry

When American historian Brooks Adams contemplated the accelerating speed of change at the end of the nineteenth century in which he lived, he concluded that the industrial revolution was destined to confront man with an increasingly incomprehensible world. But others took a less gloomy view, realizing that the explosion of American industrial growth was shifting the seat of western empire to the New World. The twentieth century seemed destined to be as fully the "American" century as the nineteenth had been the "British" century. The steel industry, which had not existed in 1860, produced almost 20,000 tons of steel in 1867, and more than 10,000,000 tons in 1900. Pig iron production that barely reached 800,000 tons in 1860 exceeded 14,000,000 tons in 1900. During the same time period, coal production soared from less than 3,500,000 tons a year to 244,000,000 tons at the end of the century. Annual industrial production increased at the rate of 5.2 per cent annually between 1885 and 1914. So vast was this industrial revolution that by 1914 the United States' industrial production exceeded that of Europe, and totaled thirty-five per cent of the world's manufacturing.

THE NATIONAL RAIL SYSTEM

The Growth of Railroads. The industrial expansion meant that industry could no longer remain a sectional activity, but must now take on continental proportions. And effective exploitation of the continent could be achieved only by developing improved systems of transportation, so that raw materials from one part of the nation could be quickly and economically moved to factories located elsewhere, and the resulting manufactured goods could be transported as readily to the many widely separated markets. Railroads were the obvious answer to the need.

Well before the Civil War, the rudiments of a national rail system had been laid, and even war itself had not halted its expansion. In the North, the war years saw growth and improvement in the form of standardization of gauge, the beginnings of a transcontinental system, the conversion from iron to steel rails, and the change in fuel from wood to coal. Keeping pace with the swift growth demonstrated by the other industries, railroads expanded at a phenomenally rapid rate. Rail mileage increased from less than 31,000 miles in 1860 to more than 240,000 by 1910; capital investment in railroads, which had been just more than $1,000,000,000 in 1860, had grown more than tenfold by 1890; and tonnage carried increased from thirty-nine million tons (1882) to seventy-nine million tons (1890)—though the cost per ton mile decreased by one quarter during the same period. So dynamic was postwar railroad construction that a system which reached scarcely halfway across the continent in 1865 had spanned it by 1869. The entire western half of the United States, which had been consigned to the status of "Great American Desert" before the war, was swiftly settled in the wake of this movement; indeed, it may be justly claimed that each of the twelve states admitted to the Union between 1867 and 1912 was actually brought into it by the railroads. The great eastern and western trunk lines had become steel arteries uniting the vast reaches of the republic.

Government and the Railroads. During the 1850s, the government had been prevented by sectional rivalries from pursuing major railroad construction. The delay was more than compensated for, however, during the 1860s, when the government authorized construction of the Union Pacific Railroad (1862) and the Northern Pacific Railroad (1864). The government further encouraged the railroad boom with vast land subsidies. Most of the 131,350,534 acres granted for railroad construction were located west of the Mississippi, but 15,436,000 acres were located in Alabama, Mississippi, Florida, Michigan, Illinois, and Wisconsin. More than twenty-three per cent of North Dakota's total acreage was disposed of in this fashion. In addition to grants made by the federal government, various states also gave railroads a total of 48,883,327 acres on their own authority, bringing the combined federal-state grants to the equivalent of an area larger than the state of Texas. The railroads ultimately sold the lands they had thus received for amounts totaling in excess of $500,000,000; but the government was repaid for its largesse. It is estimated that the federal government saved about $900,000,000 in the reduced rates it paid to the lines. Moreover, for the nearly $65,000,000 in credit which the government had advanced to the Union Pacific-Central Pacific enterprise after the Civil War, it received a settlement of $168,000,000 in 1898–99. In spite of many abuses by private developers, therefore, the arrangement was reciprocally beneficial. It permitted private individuals to make large personal profits by diverting especially valuable lands to subsidiaries; it allowed the emergence of a vast property interest under private control; it guaranteed that the men who controlled the huge railway networks would wield an enormous power answerable to no public agency. But the railroads were built, and the nation bound together, in an inconceivably short time. And insofar as they represented a threat to the maintenance of an equalitarian democracy because they had created a fabulously powerful and wealthy clique of developers and managers, the railroads would soon be challenged by the rising tide of reform.

The Great Railroad Barons. The granting of huge tracks of land for railroad development quickly attracted a number of entrepreneurs, who saw in the government's eagerness to establish an efficient transportation system an opportunity for accumulating great personal fortunes. And in spite of the fact that the government compelled the railroads to provide it with rail services at reduced rates, a few men were indeed able to reap a golden harvest in the boom. Typical were four California merchants—Leland Stanford, Collis P. Huntington, Mark Hopkins, and Charles Crocker—who invested heavily in the western half of the first continental system, the Central Pacific; then, using construction companies which were under their own management, they negotiated contracts with the Central Pacific—that is, with themselves. When efforts were finally made to investigate the details of this arrangement, a convenient fire burned the Central Pacific's books.

One of the most famous of the era's railroad maneuverings was that involving Commodore Cornelius Vanderbilt and Jay Gould. Vanderbilt and his son William, who had made a huge family fortune by constructing the New York Central during the Civil War, tried to wrest control of the competing Erie Railroad from the financial trio consisting of Gould, Jim Fisk, and Daniel Drew. The Vanderbilts were badly burned in the attempt: Gould, Fisk, and Drew issued millions of dollars of worthless Erie stock which the Vanderbilts promptly bought in the mistaken notion that they were buying control of the line. After seemingly endless litigation, the Vanderbilts were finally forced to withdraw, leaving Gould and Fisk to complete the looting of the line which came to be known as the "Harlot of Wall Street." Having drained the Erie, Gould went on to loot the Union Pacific, the Wabash, the Missouri Pacific, and the Texas Pacific. When he died, his estate was valued in excess of $80,000,000.

In 1878, Henry Villard, a Bavarian immigrant who had secured control of the Oregon Central Railroad and the Oregon Steamship Company, turned his attention to the incomplete Northern Pacific. Using a fund of $8,000,000 raised among his New York friends, Villard gained control of the line; and five years later, the Northern Pacific had united with the Oregon Central. Villard subsequently established another connecting line into Seattle.

A similar adventure was launched in 1878 when James J. Hill and some Canadian associates took over the bankrupt St. Paul and Pacific Railroad. Hill slowly and methodically constructed his Great Northern Railroad, sending a spur from St. Paul to Winnipeg and the main line westward until it entered Seattle in 1893. Careful construction, fair settlements with farmers along the route (who then became primary users of the Great Northern's services), conservative financing, and energetic management made the Great Northern a model of railroading. By the end of the century, Hill had also succeeded in bringing the Northern Pacific under his control.

Farther south, the 1870s and 1880s saw a tumultuous struggle between the Atchison, Topeka, and Santa Fe and the Denver and Rio Grande, as the two companies struggled to secure the few mountain passes through the southern Rockies. In the end, it turned out that there was room enough for both of them.

The Central Pacific's Big Four—Stanford, Huntington, Hopkins, and Crocker—turned their attention to the construction of the Southern Pacific, and, remembering the lucrative profits of the Central Pacific, organized the Western Development Company in order to award themselves construction contracts. After obtaining the covert support of President Hayes and his cabinet, the Southern Pacific coalition completed the road to El Paso, where it joined Jay Gould's Texas Pacific. Thus by 1890 five transcontinental railroads were in existence. A complex net of lines crisscrossed the farm states of the Great Plains. They carried vast harvests of wheat and herds of cattle to the great processing centers of Chicago, Kansas City, Omaha, Sioux City, Minneapolis, and St. Paul—and, incidentally, made a handful of men very, very rich.

Southern Railroads. Though the postwar years saw incredible railroad development in the North, the situation was less promising in the South. The destruction inflicted on Southern railroads during the war forced them to seek capital for reconstruction under the most disadvantageous conditions. Moreover, many Southern state politicians found the railroad boom an easy target for graft. Issuing fraudulent railway bonds in large amounts (in Georgia alone they totaled $40,000,000), they lined their pockets with moneys ostensibly destined for the rebuilding or extension of railroads. In spite of such disabilities, however, railroads expanded in the South at a steady rate; in the fifty years following the war, they had grown sevenfold. However, the fiscal instability of many Southern systems made them easy prey for consolidation by Northern capital. J. P. Morgan, for example, created the six-thousand-mile-long Southern Railroad in 1894; and other Northern interests were quick to follow Morgan's lead in taking over dominance of the Southern railroads.

The Rate Wars. As consolidation of the rail lines progressed, the railroads engaged in desperate struggles for freight. *Laisser faire* principles prevailed as competing roads sought to drive each other out of business by reducing rates. The lines had no illusions about the enduring value and glory of the competitive market; each line sought to achieve an effective monopoly, one which would permit it to recoup the losses sustained in rate wars. In the course of these battles rates fluctuated so violently that weekly changes were commonplace, and shippers were often unable to predict their charges. Competitive reduction of passenger rates allowed travelers to make the trip from New York to California for less than $30.00 in 1886. Further complications resulted when bankrupt lines reduced their rates to a pittance, hoping thus to force their competitors into a pool in which they would obtain a favorable division of the traffic. The situation was hardly encouraging to investors, who watched this cutthroat competition in horror, waited in vain for dividend checks, and (ultimately) refused to invest further in railroads until their investments were given some semblance of stability.

REGULATION OF THE RAILROADS

Morgan and Railroad Management. In the absence of effective regulation of railroads by the government, J. P. Morgan willingly took it upon himself to assume the role of disciplinary agent. As early as 1885 he managed negotiations between the New York Central and the Pennsylvania railroads, bringing to an end the ruinous rate war that had been going on between them. Following this success, Morgan energetically set to work reorganizing the corporate structure of numerous other roads. His aim was to eliminate profitless competition; to secure predictable dividends; and to prove that there was more profit in cooperation than in competition. His efforts took on particular significance when, in the middle of 1894, one quarter of the nation's railroads, with nearly 45,000 miles of track and capitalization of two and a half billion dollars, went bankrupt. Under the skillful management of Morgan and the banking firm of Kuhn, Loeb and Company, all but a third of the rail systems were concentrated under the control of seven groups: the Vanderbilt roads (23,000 miles); the Pennsylvania lines (20,000 miles); the Morgan combination (18,000 miles); the Gould roads (17,000 miles), located largely in the Southwest; the Rock Island (15,000 miles), concentrated in the Mississippi Valley; the Hill lines (21,000 miles); and the Harriman lines (21,000 miles). The size of these combinations made any conflict between them frightening to contemplate; their mismanagement would have been a national calamity. The managers of these lines held in their own hands a power that dwarfed the imagination. This fact was driven home in the first five years of the twentieth century when William H. Moore, a Chicago adventurer, used $5,000,000 in borrowed money to gain control of the billion-and-a-half dollar Rock Island enterprise. When he was finally compelled to surrender the property, its stockholders discovered that their property had been thoroughly looted, and there was little they could do to recoup their losses.

The Demand for Regulation. The abuses perpetrated on the public by the railroads could not continue long unopposed. Demands for regulation swelled toward the end of the nineteenth century until they could no longer be denied. The nation was, after all, dependent on the services that the lines provided, since there existed as yet no alternative to railway transportation. Although shippers and passengers might derive occasional benefits from rate wars, they hardly profited when cutthroat competition led to a deterioration in service. Moreover, the lines compensated for the lower rates they were forced to charge in competitive circumstances by gouging the consumer whenever and wherever no competition existed. Thus it was not unusual for farmers or businessmen located a bare hundred miles from New York City to pay three times as much for rail services to the metropolis as a man located a thousand miles away. In addition, arrangements were made under which certain large shippers—most notoriously Rockefeller's Standard Oil—were given special rates and rebates. They thus gained a crucial advantage which provoked resentment among their less fortunate competitors. In this way the railroads, whose control was being concentrated more and more in the hands of a few men, assisted the movement toward consolidation in the major industries of the country.

Consumers demanded in turn that railroad practices and railroad management be supervised by public regulatory agencies. There was already a precedent for the demand: a number of state railroad commissions had been established before and after the war to make certain that the roads complied with their charters. None of these agencies had possessed effective power, but the railroads had accepted the principle of regulation.

State Railroad Regulation. During the depression of the 1870s, the anti-railroad grievances of the farmers of the Midwest culminated in the Granger movement. Originally designed as a social agency to elevate the farmer, it increasingly directed its efforts toward lobbying in state legislatures for effective railroad regulation. Between 1871 and 1873 the Illinois legislature established a Board of Railroad and Warehouse Commissioners, authorized to regulate maximum passenger fares and to enforce freight rates based on distance covered. This latter provision was expanded in 1873 to give the commissioners the right to determine reasonable maximum freight charges. In quick succession, Minnesota, Iowa, Wisconsin, Nebraska, Kansas, Missouri, Georgia, and California instituted similar regulations; and in most instances, compliance was enforced with legal penalties.

The railroads responded with court battles and the bribing of state legislators. The latter course of action persuaded some legislatures to soften the law. In Wisconsin, the railroads simply provided poor service until the legislature repealed the offending regulations. But the court battles ended with a painful repulse for the railways when, in 1876, the Supreme Court delivered a series of decisions upholding the so-called Granger Laws. In Munn *v.* Illinois, the Court upheld the right of Illinois to regulate the maximum rates charged for grain storage in railroad grain elevators. In Peik *v.* Chicago & North Western R.R., and again in Chicago, Burlington & Quincy R.R. *v.* Iowa, the Court upheld the right of states to fix maximum passenger and freight charges, and also decreed that in the absence of federal legislation these rates could apply to interstate commerce. These decisions gave a powerful boost to the demand for national regulation of the railroads. Reformers insisted that the dimensions of the problem were greater than any single state could manage.

Federal Railroad Regulation. Token regulation of the railroads had been proposed in Congress as early as 1871, but it was not until 1878 that positive action was taken. In that year, the House of Representatives approved a bill proposed by Congressman John H. Reagan of Texas which established equal rates and forbade the giving of rebates, and which made provision for the rectifying of several other glaring railroad malpractices; enforcement of the proposed act was left to the courts. The Senate, however, declined to concur. After 1880, the accelerating consolidation of railroads could no longer be ignored. In his 1883 annual message, President Chester A. Arthur declared that "Congress should protect the people at large in their interstate traffic against acts of injustice which the State governments are powerless to prevent." Two years later a Senate committee under Shelby M. Cullom of Illinois investigated railroad practices; in January, 1886, they delivered a scathing indictment of such practices as rate discrimination; watered stock; rebates; free railroad passes; and wasteful management. The committee recommended the establishment of a federal supervisory commission on railroads.

The debate over whether the state or federal governments could most effectively regulate railroads ended abruptly in October 1886 when the Supreme Court reversed its previous stand. In the case of the Wabash, St. Louis and Pacific Railways *v.* Illinois, the Court denied to the states the power to regulate rates on shipments moving in interstate commerce. Such regulation, it concluded, "must be of . . . national character" and established "by the Congress of the United States under the commerce clause of the Constitution." The pressure for federal regulation was now irresistible.

The Interstate Commerce Act. On February 4, 1887, President Grover Cleveland signed the Interstate Commerce Act, after it had obtained overwhelming congressional approval. It forbade discriminations of any sort, long haul-short haul variations on the same line, and traffic pools; it provided for uniform accounting methods; and it required that railroads make their rate schedules available to the public. To supervise the carrying out of these requirements a five-man Interstate Commerce Commission, free of railroad connections, was established. The railroads accepted the new law placidly. They knew that such vague wordings in the law as "reasonable and just [rates]" would permit lengthy litigation. They knew, too, that although the commission could order violators to cease and desist on pain of a $5,000 fine, it had to appeal to the federal courts for enforcement of its decisions. The result would be extended court proceedings—during which the violator could continue his illegal profitmaking.

The immediate impact of the creation of the commission was thus anything but detrimental to the railroads. Cleveland's Attorney General, Richard Olney, could explain to a railroad owner protesting the commission's acts that it "satisfies the popular clamor for a government supervision of railroads, at the same time that that supervision is almost entirely nominal." But this ineffectiveness should not conceal from us the inherent gain represented by the Interstate Commerce Act. Federal regulatory power had, after long dispute, been confirmed; the proposition that business could act with no regard for the public welfare had been severely qualified. Moreover, the inadequacy of the regulatory powers granted to the I.C.C. was to prove the incentive for further expansion of the federal authority. The first major step had been taken in a campaign for reform that would continue well into the twentieth century. The Interstate Commerce Act signaled the beginning of the national repudiation of *laisser faire*.

TRUSTS AND THE CONSOLIDATION OF INDUSTRY

Technological innovation, in the form of new machinery and the development and utilization of electric power, resulted in a swift expansion of industrial output, as well as in the reduction of the manpower needed to achieve this result. In fact, production often so far exceeded immediate demand that industry was compelled to resort to drastic measures. Pools in which major producers agreed to limit output to profitable levels quickly became common in such diverse industries as salt, cordage, and wallpaper. Such collusion, of course, drove all but the strongest producers out of business. As American industry developed, a few mammoth corporations increasingly dominated most of the nation's industries, creating oligopolistic control under the banner of "free enterprise."

Rockefeller and Standard Oil. Nowhere were the tendencies toward concentration more quickly evident than in the petroleum industry, where, beginning in 1872, the Standard Oil Company asserted its dominance. By combining the advantages of its location in Cleveland (where a number of routes were available for transporting oil to market) with an emphasis on the refining rather than the mere production of oil, John D. Rockefeller's company was soon able to manipulate both the original producer and the railway. Rockefeller repudiated competition, with its waste and disorder. He recognized that profits were most secure in a market where stable prices existed and where production was regulated to meet the demand. Rockefeller was so successful in his operations that he convinced the independent refiners of Cleveland to unite under himself, submerging their identity in a huge corporation with the understanding that by submerging they would become fabulously rich.

Rockefeller's control of the refineries was supplemented with control of the pipe lines which carried oil from the wells to railheads and storage tanks. Thus, he could force the oil drillers to accept regulation of their production by simply refusing to transmit, store, or refine their oil. In addition, he could obtain beneficial rates from railroads by promising them his business—a promise that came to mean more and more, as in a period of six years Standard Oil's share of the petroleum business rose to more than ninety per cent of the nation's total output. But Rockefeller was still irritated at the fact that the Standard combination was made up of many firms, the result of which was a wasteful duplication of functions and overlapping management. Seeking a more efficient device for Standard's organization, he originated the first "trust." It was adopted in 1879 and improved in 1882. Under this system, a board of nine trustees was assigned all the capital stock of the member companies, while the stockholders received "trust certificates." Management was thus stabilized, effective control was put in the hands of a few men, and Rockefeller was assured that a single policy would govern the affairs of the entire Standard combination. There was a danger in this course as well: the trust was to some extent more vulnerable to legal attack, since the agreements upon which it was built were matters of public record. This was to give an opening to the trust-busting reformers in later years.

The size of the Standard Oil trust permitted it to seize control of the pipe lines which transported crude oil from the production fields to eastern refineries. Munificent profits gave it a secure flow of capital with which to buy up storage tanks, refineries, and the patents on technological advances; at the same time, the trust launched fleets of ocean tankers to ship its production abroad. Rockefeller, always preoccupied with efficiency, saw it was cheaper to refine oil near the market of consumption than at a central refinery, and Standard Oil therefore decentralized its facilities. As the company extended its marketing facilities at home and abroad, Rockefeller was in control of the industry from the moment the oil appeared above ground to the moment when the profits clinked into the Standard Oil coffers.

Carnegie and the Steel Industry. Iron and steel were at the heart of American industrialization in the nineteenth and twentieth centuries, providing the basis for everything from locomotives to the kitchen stove. As in the case of railroads and oil, the iron and steel industry's postwar growth was monumental in scope. Between 1870 and 1890, annual production rose from a bare 30,000 tons to almost 2,000,000 tons. A crucial turning point for the industry came when, in the 1870s, it moved from the East to the Great Lakes region. The move was spurred by the discovery of vast iron deposits in the Mesabi Range of northern Minnesota; by the opening up of equally vast deposits of bituminous coal in western Pennsylvania, West Virginia, and Illinois; and by the growing use of the network of water transportation of the Great Lakes. Of equal importance to the growth of the industry was the eagerness with which the American managers adopted English and German technological advances. The American industrialist, although he displayed little interest in subsidizing theoretical research, did not hesitate to apply such discoveries to his own production when they were made elsewhere. The result was that the American steel industry soon outstripped its European competitors. By the end of the nineteenth century, the great industrialist Andrew Carnegie was convinced that American steel could undersell its competitors anywhere in the world.

The acute competitive struggle within the industry, made even more fierce by the need to provide vast sums of money for expansion and improvement of techniques, drove out the small and inefficient producer. At the same time, the responsibility for success shifted from the producer to the manager.

Andrew Carnegie was unique in his ability to hire talented men who would devote all of their energies to the advance of his steel plant. The canny Scot also took care to secure his raw material supplies; in 1882, he amalgamated with the H. C. Frick Company, which controlled eighty per cent of the nation's coke supply. Carnegie, whose geniality and warmth had made him a national figure, remained the company's public spokesman; Frick brought to it a cold shrewdness typified by his use of thousands of laborers from southern and eastern Europe, and by his grim opposition to unionism. By 1892, the Carnegie Steel Company, Limited, capitalized at $25,000,000, was a world-wide operation. In 1900 alone it produced a profit of $40,000,000 for its managers. The rewards for industrial achievement in America were no less spectacular than the achievement itself.

Morgan and U. S. Steel. As the number of competitors declined, a few producers dominated whole segments of the American economy. The inherent logic of the development of a national economy seemed to be toward the establishment of comprehensive, centralized control. Diversification of ownership through stock distribution accelerated the secondary process whereby real control was shifted to the manager. Preoccupation with profits, coupled with a consuming concern for efficiency, was bringing the *laisser faire* ideal into a steady decline. The final step in the inevitable process was reached when the company managers themselves were subjected to the control of a single man—J. P. Morgan.

The processes of consolidation, first employed by the railroads, were rapidly extended throughout the economy as the nineteenth century drew to an end. The climax came in 1901, with the establishment of the United States Steel Corporation. Morgan was the key to its formation—the only man who could, by common assent, "swing the deal."

Morgan was already deeply involved in the processing of crude steel when he became aware that Carnegie was eager to dispose of his own vast holdings in the production of crude steel. When the Rockefellers, who controlled the vast Mesabi iron deposits, indicated their interest in participating in a consolidation of all steel production, Morgan set to work organizing a vast combination. The cost alone was staggering: Carnegie exacted $447,000,000 in cash and United States Steel stocks and bonds for his holdings; and the Rockefellers were paid $80,000,000 for their Mesabi mines. Thus, in April 1901, the United States Steel Corporation, capitalized at $1,400,000,000, was launched. Through a system of interlocking directorates, the House of Morgan, the Rockefellers, and the major banks controlled more than sixty per cent of the nation's steel industry. Against an estimated true value of $793,000,000, Morgan distributed almost $1,500,000,000 in securities. But U. S. Steel owned 112 ore vessels, a railroad of more than 1,000 track miles, and more than 700,000,000 tons in iron ore reserves—and with such unprecedented resources to back it, the new corporation's stock was not likely to suffer because it overissued by a mere $100,000,000. The size of U. S. Steel had one drawback, however; it called attention to the need for effective regulation of trusts, and spurred reformers to demand that teeth be added to existing antitrust legislation.

EFFORTS AT TRUST REGULATION

Incorporation laws were as various as states were numerous. Restrictions which severely limited corporate practices in one state were often altogether unknown in another. Delaware, West Virginia, and New Jersey—the latter known as "the mother of trusts"—were notorious for their generosity to corporations. Since state comity required that corporations authorized by one state be respected by another, it was obvious that corporations would tend to incorporate where restrictions were least inhibiting. But as the number of trusts increased, Congress moved to provide national control over the process.

The Sherman Anti-Trust Act. One of the first legislators to step into the arena against railroads, Congressman Reagan of Texas again took the initiative. In 1888 he submitted an anti-trust bill to the House of Representatives. In the same year, both political parties included a call for trust regulation in their platforms. On December 4, 1889, Senator John Sherman of Ohio introduced a bill "to declare unlawful trusts and combinations in the restraint of trade and production." The "Sherman Act" that resulted was largely the work of Senators Edward Hoar of Massachusetts and George Edmunds of Vermont. Since both men had long careers behind them as legal advisers to combinations, pools, and trusts, the final act was a masterpiece of obscurity. It did not define the terms "trust" and "monopoly," and it left the meaning of the term "restraint" to the courts. When the bill was finally passed, on July 2, 1890, after three months of agitated debate in Congress, its vagueness justified the conclusion of Senator Orville Platt of Connecticut, who felt that the whole effort of the Senate had been directed not at getting an effective law, but merely at obtaining "some bill headed: 'A Bill to Punish Trusts' with which to go to the country."

Failure of the Sherman Act. Of course, the Sherman Act proved ineffective. When, shortly after its passage, the Harrison administration moved against the whiskey combination, it turned out that the combination had disbanded and re-formed itself as an Illinois corporation, with trust certificates exchanged for stock. The federal district court found no cause for action. Again, when the E. C. Knight Company, a Philadelphia sugar refinery, joined the American Sugar Refining Company, it completed the establishment of a nationwide trust controlling over ninety per cent of the nation's sugar industry; but government action against the trust was halted in 1894 when the Supreme Court ruled that the purchase of the E. C. Knight Company was not illegal *even though it might complete a monopoly.* Since the Sherman Act only prohibited restraint of trade in interstate commerce, and since "the contracts and acts of the defendants related exclusively to the acquisition of the Philadelphia refineries and the business of sugar refining in Pennsylvania," the act was found nonapplicable.

Not only was the Sherman Act ineffective against existing trusts, it did not even impede the formation of new ones. Almost twice as many combinations came into being between 1891 and 1895 as had been formed during the previous decade. By a final irony, the act was successfully used against labor unions. In 1893 the Court applied its provisions in upholding an injunction against striking draymen in New Orleans. The following year, Eugene Debs was sentenced to prison during the Pullman strike for violating a Supreme Court injunction authorized by the Sherman Act. For the first decade of its life, the chief victims of the Sherman Act were workers. A minor consolation is that the act, though ineffective, had established the principle that business combinations were answerable to the law. The problem was now to make the law effective, and this Congress began to do in the first decades of the twentieth century.

THE IDEOLOGY OF FREE ENTERPRISE

As we have seen, free enterprise was replaced in the later nineteenth century by oligopolistic control, in which a few large producers dominated each segment of the nation's economy. The process inevitably provoked demands for effective federal regulation. The extension of federal power through regulatory activities makes it true that big business was the father to big government. There is less truth in the very common assumption that nineteenth-century *laisser faire* gave the rugged individualist of the lower classes the opportunity to accumulate a vast fortune. Such energetic entrepreneurs as Carnegie, Vanderbilt, Gould, Rockefeller, Ford, Armour, and Guggenheim did indeed spring from the ranks of the underprivileged; but several recent studies indicate that the successful underdog was the exception rather than the rule. Most of those who made fortunes in *laisser faire* America were scions of the upper or upper-middle classes who grew up in a business atmosphere, had good educations, accepted social deference as their due, and had an insatiable appetite for wealth and work.

The correlation of work and wealth was natural in a Protestant society, bred on the Calvinistic notion that divine election manifests itself in the possession of worldly goods. Here religion ended. A characteristic common to all the successful entrepreneurs was a total absence of scrupulous methods. They aimed to achieve monopoly, and were perfectly willing to use the arguments in favor of free enterprise to justify both their methods and their successes. When they were attacked for running monopolies they replied that to interfere with their gains was to deprive them of the fruits of their industry, obtained as a result of superior enterprise—and that a just God would surely note such a violation of His free enterprise doctrines. Noteworthy too is the passion with which men like Rockefeller and Morgan fought to bring order into the economy. To tame the wild beast was a *raison d'être* in itself, and success was as fulfilling as the moment of truth in a bullring.

Though great fortunes passed into relatively few hands during this period, there was a marked increase in the size of the middle class. By 1900, more than 4,400,000 Americans owned shares of stock; countless young men—and even some women—were being absorbed into the management of the large corporations; and the relentless migration to the cities of America continued. The virtues of rural life had lost their attraction; the young turned to urban America for fulfillment. Whatever else industrialization had accomplished in its brief period of spectacular and unlimited flowering, it provided an alternative to agriculture, thus completely reordering the bases of American life.

But industry's success was, in many respects, only temporary, for it had created a power which, if allowed to grow unchecked, threatened the survival of American democracy; a power that staggered the world's imagination, and which subjected American institutions to their profoundest test after the Civil War.

Chapter 5

The Rise of the City

No single phenomenon was more momentous in the last third of the nineteenth century than the urbanization of the American people. In 1860, only one fifth of the population lived in cities; by 1900, the number had doubled, and two out of every five Americans lived in urban centers. This migration constituted a massive repudiation of rural America. It also drove home the great irony of American agriculture: technological progress brought abundance, abundance drove down prices, and the farmer found it increasingly difficult to lead "the good life." The city lured the surplus young, allowing those who remained behind to maintain at least a semblance of prosperity.

The great factories around which the cities grew cast their shadows not only upon rural America, but into the isolated peasant hamlets of eastern and southern Europe as well. The promise of work and wealth brought 25,000,000 Europeans across the ocean between 1880 and 1920. So vast an external and internal migration was to create severe problems of adjustment for urban dwellers. The demands of collective living on which a city is based went counter to rural values. A great many Americans still shared either Jefferson's dictum that cities were "ulcers on the body politic," or the naïve idea of William Jennings Bryan that "the great cities rest upon our broad and fertile prairies." Within the accepted scheme of American values, the city was seen as a pernicious evil, its inhabitants as inferior in citizenship to the farmer. The American nation was not as yet psychologically equipped to cope with the challenge of urban life.

THE URBAN EXPLOSION

Between 1880 and 1890, 101 cities with an original population of 8,000 or more doubled in size. Kansas City (Missouri) boomed from 60,000 to nearly 133,000; Minneapolis, from 47,000 to 164,000; Omaha, from 30,500 to 140,000; Denver, from 35,000 to nearly 110,000. Towns that had hardly existed in 1880 grew at a staggering rate. Typical were Tacoma, which recorded a population of 1,100 in 1880 and one of 36,000 in 1890, and Spokane, which expanded similarly from 350 to 20,000. The decline of rural townships proceeded simultaneously. Nearly thirty-nine per cent of the nation's 25,746 townships reported declines, but the proportion was even higher in the Middle Western "bread basket," where more than fifty per cent of the rural townships lost population, though the statewide populations increased. In the swiftly urbanizing East, seventy per cent of such townships reported population declines. Deserted farmsteads and abandoned villages dotted the Eastern landscape, while once fertile fields went to thistle and weed. And swelling urban populations pushed their way out beyond normal city boundaries, until Census Bureau administrators were forced to create a new designation: "The Metropolitan Districts."

Within the first decade of the twentieth century, close to one out of every four Americans lived in a metropolitan area. New York City steadily engulfed northern New Jersey, Long Island, and Westchester. Chicago expanded along its lakefront until it stretched from the Indiana line almost to that of Wisconsin. As the city grew industrially, so did its suburbs. New York had its booming clothing industry, and its near neighbors, Passaic and Paterson, produced finished woolens and silks. Philadelphia's shipping industry overlapped into Camden and Chester. A vast steel industry grew up at Gary, Calumet, and the other eastern suburbs of Chicago. The traveler entering Pittsburgh at night passed miles of belching chimneys and furnaces in its surrounding towns. But swift expansion carried a correspondingly heavy price: American cities were malodorous, dirty, and dreary. Visitors could barely distinguish between them. Except for New York, New Orleans, San Francisco, and a few others, American cities were succinctly summed up by Lord Bryce when he said that they differed from one another "only herein, that some of them are built more with brick than with wood, and others more with wood than brick."

PROBLEMS OF MUNICIPAL GROWTH

American individualism at the turn of the century had many virtues and a single serious drawback: it would have made urban life impossible. The nature of the city makes collective living and cooperative planning inescapable. The free American was ill-equipped to meet such demands. But aside from the problem of social order, municipal governments were faced with the overwhelming difficulty of providing necessary services in cities whose mushroom growth made all arrangements perpetually obsolete. American cities were, as a result, studies in contradiction.

River Pollution. The swiftly flowing Delaware was a crystalline stream above Trenton; in its passage through the New Jersey capital it became an open sewer. Philadelphia emptied its wastes into the Delaware while simultaneously drawing its water supply from it. The average Philadelphian held his nose as he drank his free beverage. Dozens of slop wagons dumped the waste of Indianapolis into its White River, while the urban complexes stretched along the Missouri dumped so much debris into the mighty stream that visitors to St. Louis claimed you could smell your way to its banks. It was not unusual for a metropolis as great as Baltimore to have almost no sewers, and to be virtually wholly dependent on wells for its water supply. Those who viewed the city as alien to the American way of life did not have to look far for horrors which would substantiate their claims.

The Absence of Urban Planning. Urban planning was minimal. The vast stockyards immediately outside Chicago gave the city an atmosphere that was truly unique. Rudyard Kipling summed up the attitude of most visitors to the Midwestern metropolis when he exclaimed: "Having seen it, I urgently desire never to see it again." Parks were everywhere the exception rather than the rule. Though New York had its magnificent Central Park, planned by Frederick Law Olmstead, the entire West Side of the city, from 42nd Street to 110th Street, was a shanty town in which man and pig lived side by side. New Orleans, with a population of nearly 220,000 in 1880, had little more than a fifth of its streets paved. In summer, stifling dust infiltrated nearly every building in the Louisiana metropolis, and when the rains came, whole sections of the city were isolated as the streets turned into quagmires. Where paved streets did exist, little or no effort was made to keep them clean.

Urban Slums. Housing conditions in the burgeoning cities were often appalling, American slums having the unenviable reputation of being as bad as any found in the Orient. Tenements in New York were of the "dumbbell" type, in which only slight indentations midway in the building's sides separated it from its neighbors and provided an air shaft. By 1879, New York tenements numbered 21,000 and housed over 500,000 people; ten years later another 11,000 tenements had been added, and over 1,000,000 people lived a crowded, cheerless, sunless existence. It was not unusual to find a hundred people forced to use a single privy, and as many as twenty people living in a single room. Disease and vice were hidden visitors in these homes. Typhoid fever was a common affliction in Philadelphia and Chicago, where the water supply was scarcely more than strained sewage. Cholera and yellow fever frequently swept through cities during the summer. Infant mortality often claimed a third of all children born, and childbirth ranked among the top killers of women. Tuberculosis, respiratory infections, diphtheria, and scarlet fever were omnipresent afflictions.

Urban Crime. With this as a background, it is hardly surprising that American cities were seedbeds of crime. Between 1881 and 1898, the annual murder rate in the United States increased from 1,266 to 7,840. Juvenile crime flourished in the slums, where gang warfare was a basic fact of life, and the police exercised only the loosest control. Public safety departments were usually understaffed and underpaid. They sought to keep the illusion of law and order, undertaking active enforcement only during sporadic outbreaks of public indignation. Often, too, official laxity was merely an indication of how hopelessly urban life was intertwined with corrupt politics. Local officials viewed municipal employment as a source of patronage with which to reward the faithful wardheeler. Competence played a poor second to prior political service.

Urban Corruption. The Tweed Ring had been only the most spectacular manifestation of a common American condition. Almost every city had its machine, a political combination that both exploited the city folk and supplied them with necessary services. Rudimentary police and health protection and the absence of adequate welfare services gave the machines their opening. Another source of urban political corruption was the fact that in a free enterprise system public transportation and public utilities automatically passed into private hands. To obtain control of these services, entrepreneurs were prepared to fight hard for the necessary franchises; and the result was often wholesale bribing of municipal officials. Like his colleagues in the trusts, the urban businessman was prepared to subsidize corruption in the expectation of profits to come. Still, corruption would not have flourished as it did had it not been for an indifferent public, which accepted graft as an inevitable consequence of urban life, and which protested only when the charge became monstrously excessive.

In the daily life of the urban citizenry, collisions with the law—and circumventions of it—were a regular occurrence. The law might forbid a grocer to use a portion of the sidewalk to display his wares, but a well-placed police bribe would insure nonenforcement of the ordinance. City prisons and hospitals required foodstuffs in quantity; a supplier anxious to obtain the contract would smooth the way with an under-the-table payment. Officials responsible for supervising public institutions accepted as a perquisite of their employment the diversion of foodstuffs to their own larders. Tax assessments were open to manipulation, and the beneficiary was prepared to divide his saving with the assessor. Any tradesman or businessman who needed a license to conduct his business found it expeditious to advance a gratuity. Obtaining payment for services rendered to the city government was often a cumbersome business; it could be simplified by a gift to the fiscal agent responsible for disbursements. The construction of public buildings was a recognized ladder to large and easy wealth. Vice and crime were also sources of income for the corrupt public servant. In this way the municipal citizenry paid a vast secret tax to obtain relief from the law.

But it is wrong to assume that these payments benefited only the recipient; this would leave unexplained the massive majorities rung up at the polls by the Tammany Ring in New York and the "gas ring" in Philadelphia. In fact, corruption was mutually beneficial. Those who paid bribes did so because they thought they were receiving commensurate value for their money, and a large part of this money went, in turn, to subsidize the expenses of the machine. The machine commanded the loyalty of the tenement voter by supplying him with services that government was not ready or able to provide. The daily work of a local district leader might include sending a Christmas basket of food to an impoverished family or a gift of cash to a family whose breadwinner was sick; seeing to it that a boy who had run afoul of the law received a suspended sentence; and supplying coal to the shivering inhabitants of a tenement. A constituent who learned that the local politician was extensively involved in crooked dealings might remember the personal favor he had himself received from the man, multiply it by thousands, and exclaim: "Let him have his graft!" The result, as Lincoln Steffens later discovered, was municipal corruption so pervasive and deep-rooted that genuine reform was all but impossible. Men of good will were in favor of reform until they learned that it would cost them their little privilege, their little gratuity. Corruption seemed inevitable in a democracy; and in this light the possibility began to suggest itself that democracy was perhaps unworkable.

LABOR PROBLEMS OF THE URBAN ERA

The Increase in Urban Manpower. In 1860, less than two million workers were employed in manufacturing and construction. Forty years later, the same activity commanded the industry of nearly eight million men. More than six of every ten workers were engaged in agriculture in 1860; barely one in three was similarly employed in 1900. The lure of the factory had precipitated this vast shift of labor, and the increase in numbers was only part of the story. Productivity maintained a constant, spectacular rise. Although the number of plants

NUMBER OF FARM WORKERS AND NON-FARM WORKERS COMPARED (1870-1930)

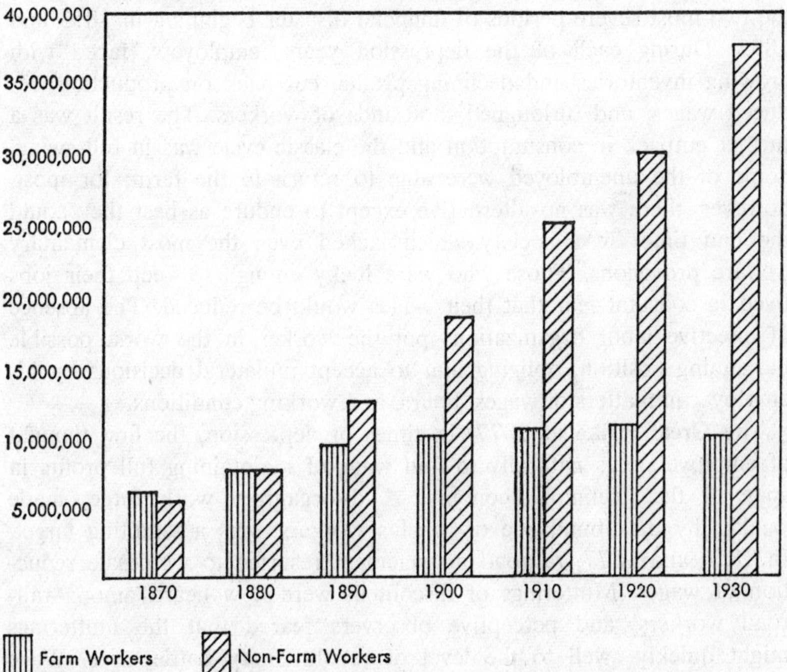

manufacturing farm implements fell by one half in the latter decades of the nineteenth century, total productivity in the industry increased by 3,300 per cent. The number of plants manufacturing cotton textiles remained constant; production increased by over 600 per cent. Comparable developments were noted in all phases of industry. At the same time, the work day was slowly being shortened, from an average of eleven hours in 1860 to ten hours thirty years later. Wages rose an average of sixty per cent in the same period, with skilled workers earning slightly more than twenty-one cents an hour and unskilled workers slightly less than fifteen cents an hour in 1890. During the same period, prices, though subject to inflationary pressures during and immediately after the Civil War, increased by only about ten per cent. Basically, the worker had experienced a steady improvement in his condition. But he was still at the mercy of an unpredictable economy, afflicted with frequent depressions and even more frequent recessions.

Major Economic Depressions. The overexpansion of the economy which inevitably resulted from the swift upswing in production and income ultimately precipitated several severe depressions. Between 1870 and 1910, approximately thirteen years were "depression years," the two most severe periods of financial disaster beginning in 1873 and 1893. During each of the depression years, employers, faced with growing inventories and declining profits, cut back on production, reduced wages, and furloughed thousands of workers. The result was a further cutback in consumption and the classic cycle was in full swing. Some of the unemployed were able to return to the farm; for most, however, there was no alternative except to endure as best they could the bad times in a society which lacked even the most elementary welfare provisions. Those who were lucky enough to keep their jobs lived in constant fear that their wages would be reduced. The absence of effective labor organizations put the worker in the worst possible bargaining position, obliging him to accept unilateral decisions by his employer in matters of wages, hours, and working conditions.

The Great Strike of 1877. In times of depression, the first thought of employers was naturally to find ways of maintaining full profits in spite of the declining economy. A disorganized work force, made weaker by the abundance of surplus workers, was a tempting target. In 1876 and 1877, railroad management resorted to wholesale reduction of wages. Mutterings of discontent were now heard among railroad workers, and perceptive observers feared that the mutterings might quickly swell to the level of revolutionary battle cries. Wage cuts averaging ten per cent to fifteen per cent on daily wages which ranged from $1.00 to $2.15 for a twelve-hour day were, from the point of view of railway management, an economy measure; for employees, such cuts could be matters of life and death. In July 1877, a railroad strike began to spread slowly across the East. Concurrently, riots erupted in Baltimore, Martinsburg, Altoona, East St. Louis, and countless other railroad towns. Under the urgent pressure of railroad management and state officials, President Hayes ordered federal troops to restore order. But matters were moving too swiftly, and Hayes's action came too late to halt what was to become a bloody nationwide strike. On July 18 the strike reached Pittsburgh, and two days later a violent battle raged there between state militia and an inflamed worker force. When the news spread that an undetermined number of workers had been killed, the entire population of Pittsburgh rose up in a savage explosion that forced the state militia to fight their way to safety outside the city. Before the uprising had finally spent itself three days later, a good part of the city had been put to the torch. For the remainder of July, the nation was rocked by similar outbursts which subsided only when federal troops occupied the major centers of discontent and arrested strike leaders. In the future, business would look to government to protect it from attack.

Response to Labor Violence. The violence of the labor uprising convinced some business leaders that their employees had real grievances which were worthy of consideration, and they agreed to try to mitigate the most offensive of the abuses. Others, however—and they were in the majority—agreed with President Grant's dictum that strikes should be "put down with a strong hand and so summarily as to prevent a like occurrence for a generation." To the middle class, bred on the doctrines of Social Darwinism, it was easy to assume that the poor must suffer the misfortunes of their inherent inferiority, while the rich were justifiably left free to reap the fruits of their superior wisdom; and it seemed natural to conclude, as had young Theodore Roosevelt, that "if the club of the policeman, knocking out the brains of the rioter, will answer, then well and good; but if it does not promptly meet the exigency, then bullets and bayonets, canister and grape . . . constitute the one remedy. . . . Napoleon was right when he said the way to deal with a mob is to exterminate it." A yawning gulf had opened between the American worker and his middle-class employers; it would have to be bridged if the nation were to escape a class conflict that might tear it apart.

The Pullman Strike. The violence of the great strike of 1877 was to be repeated in 1894, when the Pullman strike precipitated a stoppage of rail service, ultimately spreading to twenty-seven states. Violence shook the nation, and a Democratic President (Cleveland) took a leaf from his Republican predecessor (Hayes) in dealing with the situation: federal troops dispersed the strikers and jailed their leaders. Ironically, Eugene Debs, the strike leader, was sent to prison for violating (of all things) the Sherman Anti-Trust Act. It was one blow among many, as labor was beaten again and again in its struggle to secure a place among American institutions. It was difficult to believe that business would ever reign less than supreme in the United States. But labor continued to struggle, and began to make slow but perceptible progress.

THE STRUGGLE FOR UNIONIZATION

Problems of Labor Organization. Before the Civil War, labor unions had rarely extended beyond municipal boundaries. The development of a national economy, however, had made such local unions hopelessly outmoded. Skilled workers responded by organizing national craft unions, thirty of which had been established by 1870 with a combined membership of more than 290,000. At the same time, however, technological innovation was rapidly eliminating the need for skilled labor; more and more industrial functions were being assigned to semiskilled or unskilled workers. Dispensable laborers now found themselves confronted by vast impersonal corporations, in which their "freedom" was tenaciously defended against efforts at collective bargaining. The old industrial relationship, in which the employee dealt directly with his employer, was superseded by a remote authority, whose decrees had all the impersonal arbitrariness of Fate. Employers accepted as divinely ordained the grindings of a *laisser faire* economy which assured the survival of the fittest. They were not well disposed toward unionists who violated the principle of an open market—indeed, they took pains not to employ such pernicious malcontents.

The maintenance of a labor organization, difficult in the best of times, became an almost insuperable task during depressions. At such times, the savage competition of workers for jobs gave the employers an even greater advantage. Scarcely 50,000 men remained in the ranks of the labor movement after 1876; and, seeking to retain its small toehold, organized labor instructed its members to avoid provoking management. For the unemployed, who probably numbered one out of every four workers in the 1870s, there remained only the hopeless existence of the soup kitchen and the open road. No visible symbol of labor's weakness was needed beyond the thousands of tramps and vagrants who drifted across the country in the 1870s.

The Knights of Labor. Bred in a tradition that emphasized individual responsibility and the equality of mankind, the American worker was not equipped to understand the complexities posed for him by the rise of industrialism. Moreover, the fact that the workers considered themselves as part of a nation in which opportunity and social mobility were available to all made them less susceptible to labor organization, less militant than European laborers, and much slower in organizing themselves for their own protection. When the laborer pondered his plight, he tended to think of himself as a member of a single class with common aspirations and grievances. The subtle differentiations arising from the fragmentation of the industrial process escaped him, as they escaped most of his leaders. At the same time, the generalized emphasis of union leaders on fraternity, worker unity, and "self-sacrifice beneficial to one's fellow-workers" antagonized businessmen who viewed labor as a commodity subject to the whims of the free market.

Operating in a system whose larger operations they did not understand, and which was profoundly hostile to their existence, American unions tended to be conservative and timid. They were in no way connected with the outbreaks of violence that marked the recurrent depressions, and they had as little use as J. P. Morgan for the red flag. These qualities were fully revealed in the history of the Noble Order of the Knights of Labor, organized in 1869, which attained a membership of more than 700,000 in the mid-1880s. It accepted all workers as members without discrimination by sex or race, but excluded bankers, lawyers, physicians, and liquor dealers. Its major aim was to create a system of worker-owned factories which would eliminate the worker-employer division. In effect, the Knights advocated a return to an earlier and simpler industrial condition; they waged a quixotic but unremitting war against an industrial system which fostered an "unjust accumulation" of wealth, leading invariably "to the pauperization and hopeless degradation of the toiling masses."

For all their timidity, however, the Knights made a strong appeal to both the prevalent Protestant morality and the qualitarian impulse of American democracy. "An injury to one is the concern of all" summed up their view of the workingman as a member of a single class. They repudiated the notion that the titans of industry were an index of national worth, arguing, instead, that "moral worth, not wealth, [was] the true standard of individual and national greatness." Their program included demands for a more equitable distribution of wealth; the substitution of arbitration for strikes; the eight-hour day; and government ownership of railroads, telephones, and telegraphs. They insisted on the efficacy of local political action, although they maintained a legislative lobby in Washington, and simultaneously conducted a temperance drive in which they received pledges of abstinence from 100,000 workers.

Perhaps the most radical aspect of the Knights' program was their flat refusal to distinguish between skilled and unskilled workers. The union's leaders felt that the distinction was being eliminated by labor-saving machinery which brought "the machinist down to the level of a day laborer," and that only a fully comprehensive labor organization could accomplish very much. As a result, skilled workers were reluctant to join the union. Further division resulted from the Knights' participation in political action. Invariably, a decision to support a candidate of one party precipitated the secession of those members who belonged to the other party. Moreover, the Knights were bitterly hostile to the wage system—which meant that they were *ipso facto* hostile to the established industrial order—and yet they were unwilling to embrace an overtly revolutionary program. Internal dissension, worker hostility, and the worsening economic outlook after 1888 brought the Knights to a swift demise. From a membership of more than 1,000,000 in 1887, they had declined a decade later to scarcely 100,000. But even in failure, they were able to teach many lessons that would be invaluable to later labor organizations.

The American Federation of Labor. The Knights of Labor were torn apart by contradiction. Their decline revealed, among other things, the weakness of a union that organized on a comprehensive rather than a restrictive basis, and suggested, too, that the effectiveness of a labor union was proportional to its control of the entire labor force of an industry, or to its control of strategic stages of production. Such control could be achieved only through the organization of skilled workers. The American Federation of Labor profited from this lesson.

The A.F.L. focused its activities on the organization of craft unions, with an almost exclusive emphasis on skilled workers. Founded in 1881, it quickly revealed its conservative bias. It accepted the industrial system as it was, and sought exclusively to improve its members' wages by all available peaceful means; these included strikes, secondary boycotts, slowdowns, and nonpartisan political action. It asked for higher dues than any other labor organization, realizing that a union's financial resources were vital in enabling it to survive prolonged strikes. The Federation's most important move was the setting up of an effective central authority, capable of preventing strikes, of transferring surplus funds from strong to weak branches, and of insuring coordinated action. To encourage full worker loyalty, the Federation sponsored insurance programs against sickness, disability, and death.

The A.F.L. techniques had been previously proven workable by Samuel Gompers, a leader of the Cigarmakers' International Union who was to become the president of the A.F.L. in 1882. Taking an intensely pragmatic view of labor's aims, Gompers insisted that the labor movement should direct its attention to nothing except the improvement of wages, hours, and general working conditions, an emphasis that was popularly known as "bread and butter" unionism. He repudiated the idea that the average worker could "escape" his condition, and contended, therefore, that the laborer's self-interest dictated an unremitting concentration on efforts to improve his working environment. Though avoiding any suggestion that might lead to the establishment of a labor party, the A.F.L. used political action to obtain better working conditions. Having accepted the wage system as inevitable, it also accepted the innate divergence of interest between employer and employee. Rather than sponsor class war, however, the Federation advocated a policy of slow attrition whereby relations between the owning and working classes would gradually be equalized.

The Federation carefully avoided the futile and disruptive attempt to create a common worker identity. Each craft adjusted its practices to the peculiar needs of its workers. Although membership in the A.F.L. reached only 278,000 in the first decade of its existence, this result had been achieved during the trying years of a depression, and therefore it may be considered a remarkable achievement—a sign that organizing skill could triumph even over periods of economic dislocation. The return of economic stability in 1898 brought a swift upsurge in membership, and by 1904, 1,676,000 unionists marched beneath the American Federation of Labor's banner. But growth was to precipitate a hostile response among employers.

The I.W.W. A unique development in the history of American labor organization was the Industrial Workers of the World, known popularly as the I.W.W. or the "Wobblies." This radical, left-wing movement was founded in 1905 by a group of Socialists, Communists, and other extremists, and it urged that the workers of the world, organized as a class, should unite, and wrest control of industry and business, abolishing the wage system entirely, and making use of tactics of violence such as sabotage. Because American laborers were bred in a democratic tradition, few of them felt oppressed as a group; and the class stratification implied by the I.W.W.'s program did not coincide with the experiences of workmen who had grown up in an essentially classless society. Therefore, whatever appeal the Industrial Workers of the World had was largely among foreign-born laborers, and the organization's influence—only marginal at best—soon became negligible. By the early 1920s the group had virtually disappeared.

The National Association of Manufacturers. In 1902, the National Association of Manufacturers, under the vigorous leadership of David Parry, opened a campaign to cripple organized labor. Throughout the Middle West, local employer associations worked openly to drive out unions, while an Anti-Boycott Association subsidized prosecutions against them under the Sherman Anti-Trust Act. By 1909, union membership had declined by 276,000. The truth of Gompers' argument—that the interests of worker and employer were innately divergent—had been amply demonstrated.

THE TIDAL WAVE OF IMMIGRATION

The Character of the New Immigrants. The flood tide of immigration into the United States reached a climax between 1880 and 1920. In those four decades, almost 25,000,000 persons made the long journey into the unfamiliar American environment. Unlike those who had come to America during the earlier mass migrations, which had originated largely in Britain, Ireland, Scandinavia, and western Germany, the new immigrants came from the Mediterranean basin and the plains of eastern Europe. Into a society that was largely Protestant and western European in its outlook, there now poured: displaced peasants from remote Carpathian villages, where the values of individual liberty were most noticeable by their absence; the hopeless poor of Calabria, born to a life of serfdom, who found even the grinding labor of an American factory an enormous improvement; and the harassed, persecuted Jews of the Polish and Russian ghettos. Driven abroad in a desperate effort to escape the traditional poverty and degradation of their European lives, ignorant of all but the outlines of the country and future they embraced, these immigrants constituted for the American nation a massive challenge.

The Role of the New Immigrants. It was by no means certain that the United States could or would absorb these millions, transmuting them into American citizens who would subscribe to the traditional system of American values. With each new immigrant, the gnawing fears of native Americans found fuller and more violent expression. The outlandish customs of the newcomer; his timid retreat into ghettos; his ignorance of American mores—all these were cited as proof that these newcomers would destroy the American way of life. Equally emphatic, though no more charitable, were those who saw in the immigrant an invaluable asset, a source of cheap labor for the construction of railroads, the mining of minerals, the manning of factories. They could point to the fact that while immigrants constituted scarcely thirteen per cent of the total population in 1880, they provided well over thirty per cent of the nation's industrial labor. Consisting predominantly of able-bodied men who were accustomed to hard work and conditioned to obedience by their past political experience, the immigrants were often recruited from their native villages by agents of American employers. In effect, they gave America a mature labor force whose training in the ability to do hard, dirty work had been subsidized by their European homelands.

Precisely because they were unskilled, they provided the kinds of workers that the labor-saving machines of the mushrooming factories required: men able to endure the repetitive and boring assembly-line methods of modern times. In addition, they took over all those dirty chores of society which native Americans were increasingly unwilling to perform—a perennial immigrant pattern. The hostility of the American worker who believed he was being driven from his job by the foreign-born competitors ignored the important advantage he derived from the presence of immigrants; they boosted the native worker up the social and economic ladder to the more secure semiskilled, skilled, and managerial jobs. In the coal and steel industries, white-collar positions were occupied by native Americans or older immigrants and their children, while the southern and eastern Europeans were confined to unskilled common labor. The low-paying textile and clothing industries looked upon immigrant labor as a godsend. As skilled labor became increasingly expensive and hard to get, the cheap availability of immigrant workers was also an immense stimulus to mechanization; they could easily be trained to perform the simple manual tasks required in operating machinery.

Social Consequences of the New Immigration. Since more than seventy per cent of the new immigrants were men, either unmarried or with families in Europe, many of them were working to bring families or wives across the Atlantic (a plan first pursued in the middle of the nineteenth century by the Irish) or to earn enough to return home and buy a European farmstead. When women and children accompanied the men, the low prevailing wages forced them into factory and sweat-shop jobs to augment the family income. The primary motive for emigration was unquestionably economic; studies of the Atlantic economy have noted that the number of immigrants declined sharply during depression periods. Thus, in 1895 only 258,536 immigrants entered the country as opposed to 579,663 in 1892.

The immigrants, entering on the lowest rung of the American economic ladder, poured into the rundown areas of the cities. Seeking low rents and proximity to their places of employment, they accepted life in the tenement. Two hundred people might live in a tenement each of whose six floors averaged 20′×90′, with rooms as small as 8′×7′. A single city block might house 4,000 people. Immigrants brought with them the strong family ties of peasant life, and often accentuated the misery of their housing by extending hospitality to an even more recently arrived brother, cousin, or niece. Products of a rural environment, accustomed to the open air, these former peasants now lived amid the dirt, discomfort, and unfamiliarity of the city. The absence of even the most elementary sanitation facilities in the great cities turned thoroughfares into rubbish heaps where rodents foraged. Primitive drainage and sewage systems added to the misery of the packed tenements, in which the immigrant struggled to retain some semblance of normality and dignity.

Crucially hampered by their inability to spend time obtaining an education—unable, therefore, to acclimatize themselves to the world beyond their ghettos—immigrants could only try to recapture some semblance of the familiar past. They presented the American churches with the most significant problem these religious bodies had ever faced in the New World. Poles, Italians, and Hungarians of the Roman Catholic faith insisted upon hearing the rites (such as marriage and baptism) and the sermons in their own languages, on celebrating their particular feast days in the traditional fashion, and on providing their children with a parochial education which would teach them not only doctrinal Catholicism but also the mother tongue. At first, the powerful Irish contingent in the Church struggled to make it a wholly American institution; then the ethnic principle was accepted on the parish level (though not on the level of the diocese). Thus the swiftly expanding Church was able to maintain a semblance of unanimity in its hierarchy—which was heavily Irish, with a sizable German representation—while the flock was directly ministered to by a parish priest who spoke its own language and maintained the ancient cultural values. No less tenacious were the efforts of the Jewish immigrant, of the German and Scandinavian Lutheran, and of countless other religious sectarians to maintain their faiths, their traditions, and their cultural heritages. In the depraving existence of the slum, the churches were a last sanctuary of moral and ethical values.

The Native Response. The high proportion of adult males among the immigrants and their concentration in the great urban centers profoundly affected American politics. The Irish had progressively entrenched themselves in control of urban politics; they were accustomed to serving as brokers for the discontented urban masses, as providers of charity, protection, and even as interpreters who would guide the newcomer through the maze of American life. As payment they demanded nothing except the immigrant's vote. As they performed their indispensable functions, the urban Democratic party became a political home for the immigrant, while most urban, middle class, native Americans, appalled at "the rule of the uncultivated Irish Catholics," wedded themselves to the Republican party. A subtler explanation for this phenomenon was the traditional receptivity of the Democratic party to religious, ethnic, and social diversity, and the strong Protestant and nativistic biases of the original Republican party. Native reformers traced the source of urban political corruption to "the ignorant, lawless, idle and dangerous overflow of all other countries." Abram S. Hewitt, the reform Mayor of New York, told his Irish Board of Aldermen that "America should be governed by Americans"; and the economist Henry George bemoaned the fact that "our human garbage can vote."

The association of immigrants with corruption in the minds of many native Americans was quickly complemented by a virulent outbreak of anti-Catholicism. The Catholic priesthood, which had been the focal point of earlier attacks, was now joined by the immigrant, whom the native saw as providing the mass support for a conspiracy to subvert American life. Anti-Catholic nationalist societies sprang up throughout the land, with names like "The Red, White, and Blue" and "The Loyal Men of American Liberty." The Catholic threat was lumped together with "anarchists and all that class of heartless and revolutionary agitators [who] terrorize the community and . . . exalt the red flag of the commune above the Stars and Stripes." The Chicago Haymarket Affair of 1886, in which a policeman and several others were killed by a bomb during an anarchist riot, triggered an upsurge of native outrage. "These people are not Americans," charged one newspaper, "but the very scum and offal of Europe." The immigrant, no matter what his religious or political inclination, was denounced as a potential threat to the essential bases of the American ideal.

The American Protective Association. The growing antagonism between employer and employee was traced by some apologists to Catholic labor leaders who were reputed to be fomenting an upheaval at the instigation of "red priests." More outrage was generated by the supposed threat of parochial education to public schools. The specifically anti-Catholic societies were joined in this attack by the secret quasi-political organizations, but it remained for Henry F. Bowers, a passionate anti-Catholic, to organize the American Protective Association, which after 1887 proved the most active instrument of nativist agitation. It pledged its members never to vote for Catholics, never to employ them, and never to join with them in collective labor action. The economic dislocations following the depression of 1893 emphasized the strong appeal that the A.P.A. had for native American workers. From a membership of little more than 70,000, located largely in the upper Middle West, the organization spread rapidly eastward until Buffalo and Pittsburgh each claimed a membership of 16,000. A similar expansion in the West brought the organization a total membership of well over half a million by 1894. The A.P.A. charged that the depression was a Catholic conspiracy, and the first step in preparing for a Catholic seizure of power. Supporting temperance efforts, the A.P.A. denounced the liquor interests as tools of a Papist plot to undermine the moral fiber of America. And insidious rumors spread among credulous Protestants that Catholics were planning a St. Bartholomew's Day massacre in various cities.

For the A.P.A. to have maintained its program of agitation successfully would have required overt action by Catholic immigrants. But most of these were too preoccupied eking out a bare existence to notice the attacks, let alone respond to them. The appeal of the A.P.A. declined almost as quickly as it had risen. Immigrants were subjected to discrimination, attacks in native journals, and denunciation from Protestant pulpits—even to ugly acts of violence like the lynching of eleven Italians in New Orleans in 1891—but this activity was sporadic rather than organized. Advocates of the "melting pot" were already sounding their characteristic note, and although they often dismissed too easily the difficulties of eliminating traditional antipathies and ancient antagonisms, they still saw more clearly than the hatemongers the ultimate destiny of America. "The strong stomach of American civilization must, and doubtless will, digest and assimilate ultimately this unsavory throng," one journal editorialized. "In time they catch the spirit of the country and form an element of decided worth." There was a pronounced element of noxious condescension in statements like these, but it was interfused with hope. Out of many, America would ultimately weave a single people.

Chapter 6

Politics, Business, and Money

American politics between 1876 and 1896 was dominated by men who paid hieratic reverence to established institutions and traditions, men who were certain that they lived in the best of all possible worlds. A good deal of protest managed to make itself heard, but it was deftly turned aside by politicians who preferred the semblance rather than the substance of remedial legislation. In rejecting the demand for reform, these politicians reflected the sentiments of a middle class whose primary concern lay with the protection of property rights. The leveling impulse of democracy had run into the formidable bulwark of the property-conscious Constitution. Few Americans doubted that it was, in the words of one cynical politician, a "Magic Parchment" serving as the "Guardian of Mankind."

With scarcely a quibble, middle class Americans also accepted the elementary proposition that the successful man survived because he was "fittest." The natural order of things, in which the rich were secure and the poor content with their fate, was justified as a natural consequence of immutable laws. Though few had read *The Origin of Species,* everyone knew that Darwin had demonstrated—scientifically—the true nature of the human species, and many people accepted the transmutation of Darwin's biological laws into social "laws" by Herbert Spencer. The cosmic processes of biological evolution, with their underlying principle of the survival of the fittest, were paralleled, according to Spencer, in society. Existing institutions had demonstrated their superiority by surviving. The successful man had demonstrated the superiority of his talent. Though social maladjustments existed, only the gradual and almost imperceptible processes of evolution could correct them. Set against the laws of nature, legislation was as ineffective as King Canute's ordering back of the waves. A free nation—in which each man was equally free to find his proper and deserved level—was obliged to accept the inequality of property distribution. To protest was to hurl dust to the winds. The average man's belief in this concept was articulated by the Reverend Henry Ward Beecher: "God has intended the great to be great and the little to be little."

THE ABUSIVE POWER OF CONGRESS

The Political Voice of the Business Interests. With Olympian blandness, Senator George Hearst of California informed his fellow survivors of the high estate they had achieved by membership in that most exclusive of clubs, the United States Senate: "I do not know much about books; I have not read very much; but I have traveled a good deal and observed men and things, and I have made up my mind after all my experience that the members of the Senate are the survival of the fittest." The "Millionaire's Club," as the Senate was called between 1880 and 1900, no longer reflected geographical entities alone; it had broadened its outlook, and now took in the representatives of such economic interests as lumbering, railroads, mining, and manufacturing. From Rhode Island came the patrician Senator Nelson Aldrich and from Wisconsin the semiliterate lumber king Philetus Sawyer. Nevada provided John P. Jones, the silver tycoon and friend of the British aristocracy. Ohio sent, first, the Democrat H. B. Payne, spokesman for Standard Oil, and later, Mark Hanna, steel magnate and President-maker. Under the skilled guidance of Aldrich, both Houses of Congress revealed a profound deference to the aspirations of business. The successful few, the survivors of Nature's mighty struggle, were the constituents to whom the legislator bent his ear. To condemn such legislators is easy; but we should remember that legislators are chosen to represent their constituents, that the constituents they actually represent are those with the loudest voices, and that in the last third of the nineteenth century the loudest voice was that of business.

The Decline of Executive Power. Congress had failed in its attempt to expel Andrew Johnson from the presidency. But it had asserted legislative supremacy over the executive, and had almost succeeded in fracturing the system of checks and balances. As Henry Adams shrewdly noted, "The mere repeal of the Tenure-of-Office Bill cannot at once restore [presidential] prestige, or wrest from Congress the initiative which Congress is now accustomed to exercise." For the remainder of the century, the Executive power operated in the shadow of the legislature. Though Grant obtained a modification of the Tenure-of-Office Act whereby the President no longer had to report to the Senate his reasons for removing an executive appointment, he had failed to obtain the act's repeal. And Grant subsequently admitted that "the President very rarely appoints, he merely registers the appointments [made by] members of Congress."

Hayes Opposed to Congress. Two successive Presidents—Johnson and Grant—saw the presidency humiliated and its powers reduced. It remained for Rutherford B. Hayes, by the nature of his election, to compromise its moral integrity. For millions of Americans Hayes was "His Fraudulency"; his express intention to serve for only one term was a tacit admission that he could never win re-election. Committed as he was to reform, Hayes could not escape the nagging fact that his own election was as corrupt as any scandal revealed under Grant.

Hayes was nevertheless determined to redeem the blot of his election, and he laid the foundations upon which the executive would reassert its equality with Congress. Ignoring the congressional view that congressmen were the dispensers and brokers of patronage, Hayes appointed a singularly competent and nonpolitical cabinet. The Senate's attempt to refuse confirmation of the presidential nominations was overridden by public protests, and the executive department won its first victory over Congress since the Civil War. Hayes now pressed for reform in the New York Customshouse. After an investigating commission had conclusively established corrupt mismanagement of the customshouse, Hayes attempted to remove its collector, Chester A. Arthur, and its naval officer, Alonzo B. Cornell. Both men refused to resign. The President now appointed their replacements, Edwin A. Merritt and Silas W. Burt, and sent them to the Senate for confirmation. They were rejected amid hoots of derision. After the Senate had adjourned in the summer of 1878, Hayes summarily removed Arthur and Cornell, made interim appointments, and submitted them for confirmation in December 1878. A coalition of Democrats and minority Republicans confirmed the appointments on February 3, 1879.

Burdened with the responsibility of office, haunted by "the heartbreaking sufferings which we can't relieve, the ever-present danger of scandals and crimes among those we are compelled to trust," Hayes concluded that he "could advance the reform of the civil service in no way so effectively as by rescuing the power of appointing to office from the congressional leaders." And he had settled for a single term in office convinced that it would free him from the temptation to use the patronage of his office to promote his own re-election.

THE ELECTION OF 1880

The "Stalwart" Republicans. In the early winter of 1879, Secretary of the Interior Carl Schurz called for "a healthy movement not only to prevent Grant's nomination but that of any candidate whose record is not clean." Schurz expressed a growing fear that a forgetful public, rhapsodic as it greeted Ulysses S. Grant upon his return from a leisurely trip around the world, would elect the Hero of Appomattox to a third term. In fact the "Stalwart" wing—the machine politicians—of the Republican party, deeply resentful of the treatment they had been accorded by the reformer Hayes, did persuade Grant to make a third try for the presidential nomination. For them the party was a machine for attaining power, with patronage as its fuel. Legislation was a marketable commodity, and competence was less important in an appointee than his willingness to pay for office either in services or in cash. Public office being, for the Stalwarts, a short-cut to wealth, "Stalwart" and "corruption" soon became synonymous terms.

The "Half-Breed" Republicans. The prospect of a third term for Grant stimulated counteraction in the Republican party not only from the reformer Schurz, but from James G. Blaine and his "Half-Breed" faction, as opponents of a third term for Grant were called. Blaine was a shrewd and subtle politician who sensed the importance of the reform agitation which had nearly deprived the Republicans of the presidency in 1876. Although he had been involved in every one of the major scandals that had rocked the Grant administration, he now dissociated himself from Conkling and the Stalwarts. At the same time, he was careful not to identify himself too openly with the anti-Grant reform faction. In this way, he gradually emerged as the leader who would provide business with the services it expected from the Republican party—but at a moderate cost, with none of the fantastic overhead of the Stalwarts. When Blaine realized that his opposition was necessary to forestall Grant and the renewed domination of the party by Senator Conkling of New York he put himself forward as a candidate. The Republican party seethed with discontent as the 1880 convention was called to order.

The Nomination of Garfield. Though Grant led the pack on the first ballot, it was immediately evident that he could not win renomination. Fearful that a deadlock would tear the party apart, the Half-Breeds combined with the Hayes element to nominate a reluctant James A. Garfield, who had had a responsible if undistinguished career in Congress. To assuage the beaten Stalwarts, Chester A. Arthur, the deposed New York Collector of Customs, was nominated as Vice-President. Over the opposition of Conkling, who was apparently bent on a "rule or ruin" policy, Arthur accepted the nomination. Garfield, a vigorous forty-eight, proved a popular choice among Republicans.

The Election. The Democrats gave their nominations (on the second ballot) to General Winfield S. Scott and Congressman William H. English. The ensuing campaign was tepid, with neither side developing a major issue. Its significance lay in the rather unattractive fact that it inaugurated an era in which both parties accepted the pre-eminence of business. The voter had a choice between Tweedledum and Tweedledee. The only basic difference between the parties was that the Democrats had not controlled the presidency for two decades and their patronage appetites were correspondingly whetted. Alas, civil service reform would have been instituted by the time they finally gained their victory. Garfield was elected with a tidy electoral margin of 59 votes, but with a bare plurality of less than 10,000.

Garfield's Brief Administration. The newly elected President promptly revealed his Half-Breed sentiments by appointing Blaine to head the State Department. He declined to appoint the Stalwart banker Levi P. Morton to be Secretary of the Treasury, a subtle move which carried out his dictum that the Stalwarts "must have their throats cut with a feather." At the same time, Garfield was careful not to push the Conkling faction too far: he left the disposal of patronage in New York in Stalwart hands. Few Republicans understood that Garfield meant to maintain a balance within the party, and to build up what would be in effect a personal machine.

Thus, Garfield appointed William H. Robertson, a Blaine supporter and a bitter foe of Conkling, to Collector of Customs for the port of New York. An enraged Conkling, unable to prevent his Republican colleagues from confirming the presidential appointment, resigned from the Senate with his new colleague from New York, Thomas C. Platt. They intended to discipline Garfield for not being "square, nor honorable, nor truthful with Conkling," and sought vindication of their stand through re-election by the New York State legislature. But two unforeseen incidents terminated their campaign. First, Platt was caught in a compromising situation with a lady of easy virtue. And then, on

July 2, 1881, as Garfield strode with Blaine through Washington's Union Station, Charles J. Guiteau, an unbalanced office seeker, fired a bullet into the President's back, exclaiming: "I am a Stalwart and Arthur is President now." On September 19, Garfield succumbed. A shocked nation, now made fully aware of office seeking abuses, insisted upon patronage reform. Conkling, the unregenerate spoilsman, was retired to the private practice of law.

THE ADMINISTRATION OF CHESTER A. ARTHUR

Arthur's Unexpected Position. Guiteau's bullet had catapulted a Stalwart into the presidency. The prospect of Chester A. Arthur in the executive mansion sent a chill of horror down many a reformer's spine. His decision to dispense with James G. Blaine as Secretary of State seemed a tacit admission that Half-Breeds would not be tolerated. But his decision to retain Robertson in the New York Customshouse made it equally clear that he intended no classic purge of the patronage. Instead, the President, whose magnificent wardrobe and genuine delight in good food brought a touch of sophistication to the White House, showed intelligence, tact, and shrewd political sense. He had no intention of making himself the tool of the rapidly dissolving Stalwart faction. Conkling was relegated to the limbo of defeated politicians; Arthur proved an excellent administrator and an independent executive. Before the end of his term, he had won respect and even a measure of affection from the public.

Reform of Civil Service. With the assassination of Garfield, the agitation for a civil service free of political strings reached proportions that could no longer be ignored. Aroused by newspaper editorials, the public demanded checks upon the spoils system. Less than four months after Garfield's death, the Civil Service Act of 1883, also known as the Pendleton Act, received overwhelming congressional approval and was signed into law. It created a bipartisan Civil Service Commission consisting of three members appointed by the President. They had to be approved by the Senate, and they would hold office indefinitely until removed by the President. The commissioners were vested with control of civil service examinations, and with the power to investigate the enforcement of rules governing appointments. An open competitive examination was established, with appointment going to those who earned the highest grades. Appointments were distributed among the states in proportion to their populations. Civil servants who successfully served a probationary period were put on a classified list of officeholders who were then protected from political pressure. The various departments were called upon to draw up such classified lists of employees who could not be removed, a practice that was subsequently extended to both the customshouse and the post office. And the President was vested with the power to extend these lists.

The Extension of Non-Partisan Civil Service. Although civil service coverage extended originally to only 13,780 out of 131,208 federal offices, it was steadily extended until, in 1910, 222,278 out of 384,088 posts were covered. The new act specifically protected civil servants from attempts to make them pay for their posts. Although ways were discovered of circumventing this restriction, the heyday of spoils politics had passed. A politically neutral civil service had been created, whose members would not be heaved out of office with every change of administration. Deprived of their assessment income, politicians turned increasingly to businessmen for contributions to meet their expenses, and in the process they were considerably tamed. Finally, the establishment of a civil service was the first step in a pattern of reform which was to move from humble beginnings to progressively greater effectiveness.

The Star Route Frauds. Arthur's vigorous support of civil service reform was a climactic irony: a former patron of the spoils system was working energetically against it. Even more surprising was his insistence upon a full prosecution of the Star Route Frauds. Garfield's Postmaster General, Thomas L. James, had discovered that a number of mail contractors servicing special mail routes in the Southwest, commonly designated the Star Routes, with the connivance of S. W. Dorsey, the Secretary of the Republican National Committee, and Thomas W. Brady, an Assistant Postmaster General, had been exacting special fees from the government for nonexistent services. Brady was dismissed, and he retaliated by publishing a letter which indicated that Garfield had looked to him in 1880 to raise campaign funds through officeholder assessments, the implication being that funds raised from among mail contractors in the present instance had been used for a similar purpose. When Garfield was assassinated it was uncertain whether the frauds would be prosecuted; many reformers harbored the suspicion that Garfield intended to preach rather than press reform.

At first, Arthur seemed even more unlikely to prosecute the Star Route Frauds with vigor. But despite his party's embarrassment, he ordered his Attorney General to press the case. At the resulting trial of Dorsey, Brady, and six postal officers and contractors, the defendants had the potent legal aid of such lawyers as Conkling and Robert

Ingersoll. These counsels attacked the original indictment as prejudiced and politically motivated. The jury were offered bribes; they were asked to determine the validity of repudiated confessions; and they were expected to ascertain the motives of government witnesses who no longer could recollect their role in the frauds. The result was a hung jury. A second, even more farcical trial ended with the defendants acquitted. But although the guilty went unpunished, the trial had given Arthur an opportunity to put attention to his duty before partisan loyalties.

Economic Policies of the Arthur Administration. Faced with a swollen Treasury into which taxes poured faster than they could be distributed, Congress had appropriated increases in veterans' pensions and an expansion of the public works programs; but Arthur revealed a surprising independence when, in 1882, he vetoed an $18,700,000 Rivers and Harbors Bill. Congress overrode his veto, but he had made his stand for economy in government. At the same time, he tried to relieve the excess of funds pouring into the government chests by maneuvering to lower the tariff; but Congress ignored the tariff commission which recommended substantial reductions and produced, instead, the high Tariff of 1883, the product of a lame duck Congress dominated by Republicans who had been crushingly defeated the previous November.

THE ELECTION OF 1884

After the election of 1882, 197 Democrats faced 118 Republicans in the House. In New York State, the Democratic reform Mayor of Buffalo, Grover Cleveland, had been swept to an avalanche victory in the gubernatorial race. The Democratic victory of 1884 was in the offing.

The Nominations. The Republican convention of 1884 met in Chicago. At what E. L. Godkin, the skeptical editor of the *Nation,* called "a mass meeting of maniacs," James G. Blaine gained the nomination. The Mugwump (or good government) faction of the Republican party was responsible for this result; their insistence upon reform led them to withhold their support from Arthur, and they refused also to accept Blaine, whom they viewed as incorrigibly corrupt. Instead, they turned to the Democrats to give them a candidate they could support.

The Democrats scented victory over their divided opponents at last, and nominated Cleveland, the aforementioned reform Governor of New York who had endeared himself to businessmen by vetoing a bill reducing transit fares in New York City on the grounds that it constituted an illicit confiscation of property. Despite Tammany opposition, he won the nomination on the second ballot, with the venerable Senator Hendricks of Indiana as his running mate.

The Campaign of 1884. The campaign that ensued had all the elements of a low comedy. By cleverly leaving their tariff plank ambiguous—they pledged to provide reform "in a spirit of fairness to all interests" and to insure that any reductions would not "injure any domestic industries, but rather . . . promote their healthy growth"—the Democrats had short-circuited the very issue Blaine had hoped to exploit. At the same time, they laid heavy emphasis on Blaine's dubious past. Cleveland mobilized to his support the New York City boss Daniel Manning, Wall Street magnate William C. Whitney, and Senator Arthur P. Gorman of Maryland—all consummate politicians—as well as the fiery reform element led by Carl Schurz. In addition, Cleveland had on his side an ample campaign fund, President Charles W. Eliot of Harvard University, the Harvard faculty, Henry Ward Beecher, E. L. Godkin, *Harper's Weekly,* the *Nation,* and the New York *Times.* Such earnest Republican reformers as Henry Cabot Lodge, Theodore Roosevelt, and Senator George F. Edmunds of Vermont were able to support Blaine only after much hard soul-searching. It remained for Roscoe Conkling to seal the indictment against his old rival. When asked to support Blaine, he declined, noting, "I do not engage in criminal practice."

The Mulligan Letters. Blaine was held up to public ridicule by the great political cartoonist Gillam, of *Puck,* who depicted him as a Roman Senator standing naked before his colleagues, his body tattooed with the names of the scandals in which he had been involved. Blaine's cause was further battered—and more seriously—by the so-called Mulligan letters, which revealed that he had sold worthless bonds of a defunct Arkansas railroad to the Union Pacific at a handsome price. In Blaine's favor it could be said that he had done so to protect his clients from loss when the original project in which they had invested failed, but the effect was undeniably damaging. The letters first came to public attention when a bookkeeper, James Mulligan, turned them over to a Democratic-controlled House committee in 1876. Blaine, with unusual aplomb, managed to get the letters into his own hands—and then refused to return them, though he did present an edited version of their contents to the House. In 1884 the issue was revived with added material, including a letter in Blaine's handwriting in which he asked a Boston broker who had handled the bonds to copy a letter exonerating him from wrongdoing. His request that the broker burn the letter had not been honored.

Cleveland's Paternity Scandal. The Republicans responded in kind to the scandalous baiting of Blaine. They revealed that Cleveland was the admitted father of an illegitimate child born in 1874 to a widow, Maria Halpin. Cleveland, as matters turned out, had made financial provision for the boy and had placed him in an orphanage when his mother continued her scarlet ways. (The child was subsequently adopted by a respectable family.) In thus accepting responsibility, Cleveland had also shielded several married men who had had relations with Mrs. Halpin. When the story broke in July of 1884, Cleveland acknowledged the accuracy of the story and offered no excuses. Thunderous denunciations poured from the pulpits of the nation, but a male electorate appreciated Cleveland's straightforward frankness. The fact that Cleveland was still a bachelor at this time, with no wife to be offended or forced into taking a public "stand" on the scandal, also probably helped to mitigate his guilt in the public's eye.

"Rum, Romanism, and Rebellion." Cleveland's strained relations with Tammany and Blaine's Irish origin—his mother was a Roman Catholic—threatened a wholesale defection of the Irish vote to the Republicans. But six days before the election a Presbyterian minister, Samuel D. Burchard, greeted Blaine with a sentence which belongs in the roll of words that should never have been spoken: "We are Republicans," he declared, "and don't propose to leave our party and identify ourselves with the party whose antecedents have been rum, Romanism, and rebellion." A weary Blaine missed the remark, failed to repudiate it, and gave the Democratic managers a chance to remind the Irish of their ancient allegiance.

Cleveland's Election. When the election returns were finally in, Cleveland had won with a plurality of 23,000 votes and a margin of 37 electoral votes. The state of New York, where Cleveland had a margin of only 1,149 votes, clinched the electoral majority. Cleveland's narrow margin remains a matter of dispute. The Reverend Burchard's remark may have swayed some Irish votes, but it is not improbable that Democratic exploitation of the remark may have swayed Protestants in the opposite direction. The revelations about Cleveland's illegitimate child must have had some effect, and heavy rainstorms in upstate New York had held down the Democratic farm vote. Cleveland might easily have lost if a great many Republican votes—25,016 in New York—had not been siphoned off by a prohibition ticket. Whatever the ultimate explanation, however, Cleveland became the first Democratic President in twenty-four years.

THE ADMINISTRATION OF GROVER CLEVELAND

Cleveland the Incorruptible. "No harm shall come to any business interest as the result of administrative policy so long as I am President," Cleveland had assured the nation. He added that "a transfer of executive control from one party to another does not mean any serious disturbance of existing conditions." Cleveland was as straightforward in his sentiments as he was bulky in size and ponderous in his movements; he had the courage of his convictions, though they were largely negative in their intent and result. He maneuvered with difficulty between the demands of old-line Democrats, who lusted for the rewards of patronage, and the reformers, who insisted that only those Republican appointees who revealed active incompetence be removed. Finally, he acceded to the removal and replacement of more than 40,000 out of nearly 53,000 minor postmasters. But he retained some Republicans in office, and extended the classified civil service list until 27,000 posts were covered. He also forced the Senate to repeal the last restraints imposed by the Tenure of Office Act, and thus regained for the executive the power to remove officeholders without restriction.

Laisser Faire Government. Although Cleveland reasserted the independence of the President, he insisted upon maintaining a strict separation between the branches of government. "I believe the most important benefit that I can confer on the country by my Presidency," he declared after a year in the White House, "is to insist upon the entire independence of the Executive and legislative branches of the government, and to compel the members of the legislative branches to see that they have responsibilities of their own." The idea that the President should provide dynamic leadership to Congress was utterly alien to his spirit. Nor did he think that government should take an active role in alleviating public want. In 1887, when Congress had the temerity to appropriate $10,000 so that drought sufferers could buy new grain seed, Cleveland unhesitatingly vetoed the item, declaring that "though the people support the Government the Government should not support the people." For him, *laisser faire* economics were ordained by nature, which power also decreed the godliness of hard money and the righteousness of small government. To the business community he came as a revelation: here was a politician who would give the business interests gratis those benefits for which others had always exacted a stiff price.

Major Acts of Cleveland's Administration. Though Cleveland made an impressive popular reputation by his ready veto of veteran pensions and of bills designed to aid veteran dependents, he did approve two major pieces of legislation. One, the Interstate Commerce Act of 1887, confirmed the principle that private enterprise had public obligations. Although it proved largely ineffective, it joined the earlier Civil Service Act as evidence that government had the right to regulate in the public interest. Now the task for the future was no longer to establish the power to reform, but to draw up legislation that would prove effective. In the same year Cleveland signed the Dawes General Allotment Act, which attempted to resolve the problem of the Indians by integrating them into American life. The act authorized the President to terminate tribal government and to divide reservation lands among individual Indians. Heads of families received 160 acres, single adults or orphans 80 acres, and dependents 40 acres. Surplus acreage could be bought by the government for subsequent sale to white settlers, and the proceeds of these sales were placed in a government fund for the education of the Indians. Those Indians who received land were forbidden to sell it for twenty-five years. Although those who were concerned for the welfare of the Indian described the act as "the end of a century of dishonor," its immediate effect was to throw open vast acreages for white settlement. The most important of these territories was the state of Oklahoma. Aside from this, the immediate impact of the reform was small; but again, the federal government had committed itself to a genuine effort to resolve a painful problem.

The Tariff Dispute. The ambiguous tariff plank of the Democratic party in 1884 reflected its divided sentiments. Efforts to obtain a moderate reduction in 1886 were beaten in the Democratic-controlled House, where Samuel J. Randall of Pennsylvania led a bloc of protection-minded Democrats to victory. But Cleveland was now confronted with the prospect of a Treasury surplus of $140,000,000, nearly one-third of the nation's circulating currency, and within the same year he decided to act. In his annual message of 1887, he warned that if the surplus continued to grow Congress might be tempted to undertake extravagant expenditures which would lead to a radical deflation. "The public Treasury, which should only exist as a conduit conveying the people's tribute to its legitimate objects of expenditure," Cleveland protested, "becomes a hoarding place for money needlessly withdrawn from trade and the people's use, thus crippling our national energies, . . . and inviting schemes of public plunder. . . ." Public necessity dictated action, and the President saw little gain in "dwelling upon the theories of protection and free trade." Solemnly he declared, "It is a *condition* which confronts us now, not a theory."

Cleveland now made ruthless use of the patronage to compel the Democratic House to bring forth a reduced tariff. Under the guidance of Representative Roger Mills of Texas, Chairman of the Ways and Means Committee, the House passed a bill which provided for an *ad valorem* reduction averaging seven per cent on finished goods, and sought to create a free market for raw materials like wool, lumber, and flax. To assuage Pennsylvania Democrats, little was done to alter the tariff on coal or iron. But the Republican-controlled Senate prepared an alternative tariff, highly protective, in time for the election of 1888. They thus succeeded in making the election primarily a national referendum on the tariff.

THE ELECTION OF 1888

The Nominations. When Cleveland had first broached the tariff issue, he had been warned by members of his party that it could be used to defeat him in 1888. But he had persisted, convinced that his office was not worth holding if he could not take a firm stand on major issues. There was never any doubt that Cleveland would be renominated; and the nomination of Allen G. Thurman for the Vice-President's slot satisfied the cheap-money agrarian wing of the party. The Republicans thought at first that they would renominate Blaine, but he stepped aside, leaving a number of favorite sons, the foremost of whom was John Sherman of Ohio. In a convention characterized by devious intrigues and bargains, the Republicans finally settled for Benjamin Harrison (grandson of William Henry Harrison) of Indiana and Levi P. Morton, the New York banker.

The Republican Platform. In their platform the Republicans came out strongly not only for a protective tariff, but also for the regulation of trusts, and for bi-metalism, that is, currency backed by both gold and silver. For the first time, prominent businessmen took an active part in the campaign. The chairman of the Republican finance committee was John Wanamaker, who was reputed to have raised a campaign chest of $3,000,000—several times the sum at Cleveland's disposal. In the Middle West, Mark Hanna, an Ohio steel magnate, cleverly exploited the popularity of Blaine, while Harrison himself proved to be a surprisingly effective orator who campaigned from his front porch. Although the attack on the trusts was an appeal to the farm and small business votes, the key issue was protection, and industrialists who wanted protection swelled Harrison's campaign funds. The Republican party had wedded itself to big business. To a large extent, the most energetic supporters of Cleveland were members of the American Free Trade League and the American Tariff Reform League. Intellectuals like William Graham Sumner, Henry George, and E. L. Godkin added to the aura of thoughtful reform that surrounded Cleveland.

A Corrupt Election. Although Cleveland won a plurality of more than 100,000 votes, he lost electorally to Harrison. In New York and Indiana, rumors of deals and bribery circulated. David Hill was re-elected Democratic Governor of the Empire State by a majority of more than 19,000, though Harrison carried the state by almost 13,000; some observers traced this peculiar variation to the refusal of German Republicans to support a Republican gubernatorial candidate who was also a prohibitionist, while others accounted for it by the defection of Irishmen who were outraged when the British minister, Sir Lionel Sackville-West, was lured into writing a letter supporting Cleveland over Harrison. In Indiana, which went Republican by little more than 2,000 votes, wholesale purchases of "floater" votes had determined the outcome. So comprehensive were the frauds that when the newly elected Harrison informed Matthew Quay, the Republican National Chairman, that "Providence has given us the victory," Quay subsequently exclaimed: "Think of that man! He ought to know that Providence hadn't a damn thing to do with it." He observed further that Harrison "would never know how close a number of men were compelled to approach the gates of the penitentiary to make him President."

THE ADMINISTRATION OF BENJAMIN HARRISON

Harrison's Personality. Harrison labored under something like the dark cloud that had marred the presidency of Hayes. He was not the popular choice, rumors of fraud surrounding his election; and it was soon apparent that he had an essentially repulsive personality. "During and after an interview, if one could secure it," Boss Platt of New York complained, "one felt even in torrid weather like pulling on . . . winter flannels, galoshes, overcoats, mitts, and earlaps." Harrison's frigidity, which often approached open rudeness, alienated everyone exposed to him.

Reform under Harrison. Harrison surrendered the State Department to Blaine with an obvious reluctance that provoked the Maine politician's legion of friends. Wanamaker got the Post Office, and civil service reformers were dismayed at the flagrant distribution of spoils over which he presided. Wanamaker could not redeem himself even when he later revitalized the Civil Service Commission—charged with administering civil service reform—by appointing Theodore Roosevelt to it. The merit system was then extended anew, but its immediate effect was to secure tenure for Republican appointees.

The results of 1888 had put the Republicans in command not only of the White House but of both houses of Congress as well. Under the skillful and ruthless management of Speaker Thomas B. Reed, the small Republican majority was kept intact, and a flood of legislation passed into law. Committed to reform of the trusts, the Republicans passed the Sherman Anti-Trust Act, which provided (as we have seen) the rudiments rather than the substance of effective reform. Under the vigorous direction of William McKinley, the Republicans forged a high tariff which had as its true aim not protection but the elimination of any competitive challenge to American industry. When it was argued that lower tariffs would mean lower consumer prices, McKinley replied angrily: "Cheap is not a word of hope; it is not a word of inspiration! It is the badge of poverty; it is the signal of distress." In the Democratic ranks, a young, eloquent Congressman from Nebraska, William Jennings Bryan, denounced the new tariff and its author. Already the shadows of the '96 campaign were being cast.

The Spending of Federal Funds. To dispose of the Treasury surplus that had plagued Cleveland, the Republicans passed a flood of bills increasing expenditures for veteran pensions and defense. And unlike previous tariffs, the McKinley Tariff did not augment the flow of money into the Treasury. Quite the contrary: it was so high that imports dwindled, and with them, the surplus duty payments which had caused Cleveland so much difficulty. The "spend and elect" program of the Republicans permitted the thrifty Democrats to label their opponents as members of a "billion dollar Congress." Steadily deteriorating farm prices, the effects of which were aggravated by drought conditions and the heavy fixed costs involved in farm management, provoked increasing agricultural discontent; meanwhile, rising consumer prices angered urban dwellers and laborers.

The Election of 1890. The public disaffection with Republican spending was to make itself sharply felt. The off-year election of 1890 decimated Republican ranks in the House; only 88 Republicans remained to face 235 Democrats and 9 Farmers' Alliance men, (the latter group being the forerunner of the Populist party). William McKinley departed, victim of a gerrymander. A Democratic resurgence seemed to be in the offing as the heated currency problem moved slowly to the center of the stage.

CALLS FOR MONETARY REFORM

Gold versus Silver. The currency issue which agitated the nation in the last four decades of the nineteenth century was essentially a debate as to whether the government ought to support inflation or deflation. An expanding economy called for an expanded currency, but creditors naturally viewed any inflation of the circulating medium as endangering the value of the obligations due them. Important too was the widespread feeling that the United States had to conform to the accepted system of world value—gold. But the possibility of inflation seemed like a godsend to the debt-encumbered farmers of the Midwest. Expansion of the currency would raise their produce prices, and would permit many of them to finally retire their indebtedness. Few seemed to realize that inflation would also affect the prices of the goods they had to buy. The most striking characteristic of the currency debate was that neither side showed any awareness of the subtle factors that actually determined the value of money; both were convinced that they had a panacea which would make America financially paradisiacal.

Greenbacks and Greenbackers. The Supreme Court followed an erratic course in determining the value of paper currency. In 1869 it decided, in the case of Hepburn *v.* Griswold, that Congress could not assign value to paper currency unless it had gold backing. Two years later, in the Legal Tender cases, it reversed its stand and allowed Congress to declare an unbacked paper currency legal tender. During the depression of 1873, public agitation to expand greenback circulation to $400,000,000 was frustrated by Grant's veto. By the Resumption Act of 1875, Congress voted to redeem paper currency with specie on demand, and also directed the government to reduce greenback circulation, beginning on January 1, 1879, until the amount outstanding did not exceed $300,000,000. Farm agitation for increased currency finally led to the establishment of the Greenback party. "Inflate the currency, and you raise the price of my steers," summed up its supporters' expectations. In 1876 the Greenback ticket, headed by the octogenarian philanthropist Peter Cooper, polled almost 82,000 votes—primarily in the four states of Iowa, Indiana, Illinois, and Michigan. Two years later the party polled well over a million votes and elected fifteen Congressmen. Improvement of economic conditions during the next two years reduced the party's strength, and its candidate for the presidency in 1880, James B. Weaver, won only a little over 308,000 votes. The party subsequently dwindled into insignificance, but it had set the tone for other protest movements during the remainder of the century. As the two major parties became increasingly identified with business interests, third parties provided a refuge for the discontented elements of the Gilded Age.

The Crime of 1873. Even during the heyday of Greenbackism, agitation for monetary reform was already shifting to demands for the minting of silver. In 1834, Congress had established a 16–to–1 ratio in the value of silver to gold. A silver dollar therefore contained sixteen times as much silver as a gold dollar contained gold. The increased availability of gold after 1849 resulted in an increase in the relative value of silver to gold. Instead of putting it into coins, silver owners preferred to obtain the higher price prevailing on the commercial market. In 1873, Congress, confronted with the fact that silver currency was no longer in circulation, terminated the minting of silver dollars. But a sharp decline in the price of silver during the depression of 1873, combined with the discovery of new silver sources and improved refining methods, meant that the old 16–to–1 ratio would once again make the minting of silver a profitable venture. Agrarian inflationists and owners of silver mines now pressed for the resumption of silver coinage. The absent-minded congressional decision of 1873 to stop minting silver dollars became, for them, "The Crime of 1873."

The Bland-Allison Act. The hard-money proclivities of President Hayes led to an ambitious refunding program. Under the direction of Secretary of the Treasury John Sherman, some $235,000,000 in government obligations was converted into lower four per cent loans. Everything pointed toward a reduction of the circulating medium, but in Congress moves were made to restore silver to free circulation. Richard "Silver Dick" Bland, a Missouri congressman, proposed a bill which would permit unlimited coinage of silver at 16–to–1. It passed the House by an overwhelming vote, but in the Senate, under the astute management of Senator William Allison of Iowa, the bill was modified to permit a limited monthly silver coinage of no less than

$2,000,000 and no more than $4,000,000. To secure the stability of silver currency, it was made redeemable in gold. The presence of nearly $200,000,000 in gold at the Treasury stabilized the value of all circulating media, since public confidence in the government's ability to redeem in gold was complete. The fiscal reforms of the Hayes regime stabilized the currency system for twelve years.

The Sherman Silver Purchase Act. Increasing discontent with the Bland-Allison Act among conservatives led Presidents Arthur and Cleveland to urge its repeal, but neither had pressed his request very strongly. Although in the act's twelve years of life the Treasury put $378,166,000 in silver dollars into circulation, and though silver in 1889 held a value of only 72 cents as compared to the gold dollar, the gold standard was secure. It hardly seemed likely that silver would soon become a major issue. But William Windom, Secretary of the Treasury under Harrison, changed all that when he proposed in his first annual report that the government purchase the nation's total silver production each year. Harrison seems to have been taken by surprise; he merely acknowledged that he had always favored the use of silver in the currency. Windom's motive was to secure for his party the support of inflationists and of the silver-mining states.

The silver interests, faced with mounting inventories of their product, made it apparent that they would support the McKinley Tariff only if they were given concessions. On July 14, 1890, over unanimous Democratic opposition, the Sherman Silver Purchase Act was passed. It provided for the monthly purchase of 4,500,000 ounces of silver by the government, to be paid for with legal tender treasury notes redeemable in either gold or silver. A compromise measure, it pleased no one. Sherman, its author, later admitted: "The day it became law, I was ready to repeal it, if repeal could be had without substituting in its place absolute free coinage." Congress had made a concession to the demand for increased circulation, but it had left unsettled an issue which would grow in importance: the demand for free and unlimited conversion of silver into currency. In January 1891, the Senate, with heavy Democratic support, passed a free silver bill. Grover Cleveland promptly dissociated himself from the proposal, warning that "if in the present situation we enter upon the dangerous and reckless experiment of free, unlimited and independent silver coinage" the nation would be courting disaster. His stand inaugurated a split within the Democratic party which would shatter it in 1896. The era of political stalemate was fast ending; the domination of business in the national life would now be subjected to a powerful challenge.

Chapter 7

The Agrarian Revolt

An American in the years before the Civil War lived in a continent half subdued. On maps of the United States the area west of the Missouri River, stretching to the Sierra Nevada and the Cascade ranges of the Pacific coast, and covering almost a million and a half square miles, was called the Great American Desert. The expeditions of Lewis and Clark and Major Stephen Long in the early nineteenth century, and the reports of many Western travelers, served only to establish the idea that this vast region must forever remain the preserve of the nomadic Indians. In this semiarid, treeless plain, and in the massive mountain ranges that surrounded it, the retreat of the red man would end; here he could dwell for a bit longer, secure from the threat of white encroachment.

THE OPENING OF THE GREAT WEST

In the middle of the nineteenth century, the discovery of gold in California and the lure of fertile valleys in the Oregon Territory sent thousands of Americans journeying along the Santa Fe, Overland, Oregon, and Bozeman Trails. Trains of covered wagons lumbered westward, surrounded by a sea of grass that seemed to stretch into infinity. To deviate from the wagon tracks was to invite being lost in a world without distinctive features, and the vast grazing herds of buffalo and antelope stirred awe and fear. In the endless solitude of the rolling plain, broken only by an occasional wind-scarred butte, there seemed to exist a subdued power, ready to devour anyone with the temerity to linger.

Beyond the Great Plains, the migrants came to a twisted, ravaged world, torn asunder by the thrusting peaks of the Rockies, the Grand Tetons, the Sangre de Cristo; clefted with endless canyons; shimmering with the baked heat of salt deserts. To an eye accustomed to limited horizons and the familiar woods and streams of the East, the Great West seemed a forbidding wilderness. Yet within thirty years after the end of the Civil War the region had been converted into the breadbasket of the nation. Millions of acres of wheat covered land once given over to brown grass; where buffalo and antelope had grazed, endless herds of cattle and sheep were fattened for Eastern markets; cities boomed where only an occasional Indian village or early mining camp had given proof that human life could be sustained; and the eerie silence across which the pioneer wagons had lumbered and creaked was broken by the periodic wail of the locomotive. On what had once been called a desert, American agriculture achieved the epitome of its success, and gave birth to an abundance that would ultimately prove a nightmare. A republic dedicated by Jefferson to "cultivators of the earth, . . . the most vigorous, the most independent, the most virtuous, the most valuable citizens," would discover that in the lush Western harvests there lay not profit but the poverty of surplus.

Settlement of the Plains. In 1893, the historian Frederick Jackson Turner, having read with care the census returns of 1890, observed that the contiguous frontier, "the meeting point between savagery and civilization," no longer existed. An epoch in American history had ended. The dawdling pace of the westward movement, which had settled only half the continent in 1850, had spurted forward to encompass the remaining half in less than three decades. This speed was all the more surprising in that the western half of America presented the settler with problems unlike any he had previously met.

The Lack of Water. West of the ninety-eighth meridian, the average annual rainfall rarely exceeded twenty inches, hardly enough to encourage traditional agriculture. As John Wesley Powell, the great geologist and explorer, noted in 1879, "All the present and future agriculture of more than four-tenths of the area of the United States is dependent upon irrigation, and practically all values for agricultural industries inhere, not in the lands, but in the water. . . ." To ignore this elemental problem was, as many Americans were to discover, to invite the agony of drought, the disaster of a dust bowl. Without water, the lushest of fields would wither, leaving only dry dust to be blown across the parched earth.

The Lack of Lumber. The treeless plains posed the further problem of obtaining building materials for both houses and fencing. Many settlers made their first home in a sodhouse. Built of "bricks" cut from the matted soil of the plain, it provided protection both from the blazing heat of summer, when temperatures of 100° and more were not uncommon, and from the Arctic blasts that blanketed the plain with a frozen white covering in winter. But the rains of spring and summer turned the house into a soggy mass of mud. Some families preferred to burrow into a hillside; others camped in a parked covered wagon or pitched a wigwam. All dreamed of the day when they could import the lumber with which to build proper homesteads.

The Need for Fences. The building of fences was no less important, for without fences the limits of ownership could not be defined. "Cheap and durable fences are imperatively demanded on our broad Texas prairies," said an early settler, and his summation obtained common assent. Driven by necessity, farmers invented a radical solution to the timber problem—barbed wire. Within a short time it had become a major industry, providing the farmer with a fence that had the advantages of resisting high winds, occupying no appreciable room, shading no vegetation, making no snowdrifts, and being both durable and cheap. A machine-made product thus began the conquest of the desolate land; other inventions would complete it. In a real sense, the American West was made subject to man by the industrial revolution; the toughest of nature's nuts was finally cracked by American ingenuity. But before that ingenuity could make itself felt there were many natural obstacles that had to be removed, as well as one human obstacle—the Indian.

THE AMERICAN INDIAN

The Indian Way of Life. The Plains Indians were a ferociously proud nomadic people who derived their livelihood from the buffalo and their transportation from the horse. They swept unimpeded across the vast reaches of the plains, and provided the most formidable of the many challenges to white settlement. Ruthless fighters at all times, they fought all the more ruthlessly for what was their own. Surrender was alien to them; they expected no mercy if captured and extended none to their captives. "Cruelty," wrote Colonel Richard Dodge, historian of the Great West, was to the Indian "both an amusement and a study." Those who met him in battle quickly learned that savagery was an accepted part of his warfare. He moved swiftly, struck suddenly, and disappeared into the vast grasslands.

Indian Weapons. The chief weapon of the Plains Indian was a small bow which the warrior used with facility as his war horse galloped at full speed. Arrows were tipped with bone or flint, later with steel, and were of two sorts: one made to pierce and kill buffalo, the other meant for human enemies. The latter had barbs that remained within the wound when the shaft was withdrawn. A formidable shield of buffalo hide permitted the Indian to deflect enemy arrows. Spears enabled him to joust with his opponent and to kill his game with a single thrust. Later the Indian would add guns to his armament and would thus become an even more formidable enemy. Unlike the Eastern tribes who had been driven steadily westward through the forests by the oncoming white man, the Plains Indian had no choice but to stand and fight. The Great Plains were his last frontier; there could be no further retreat.

The Buffalo Herds. For his survival, the Plains Indian depended completely on the buffalo. It was not unusual for a single herd to number a half million. Somewhere between 10,000,000 and 15,000,000 buffalo were probably grazing on the Western plains in 1850, providing thirty-one tribes with food, fuel, clothing, shelter, and weapons. But the buffalo obviously could not be tolerated if white settlers were to build a successful agriculture on the plains; no crop could sustain the beat of their hoofs. The problem began to be solved after 1860, when the demand for hides by the growing leather industry sent dozens of buffalo hunters into the plains. These men would nonchalantly slaughter the leader of a herd, and then proceed to massacre his milling and disorganized followers. The great herds were decimated with astonishing speed until, by 1890, less than 100,000 head of buffalo remained. The conquest of the Plains Indians proceeded concurrently.

Indian Policy. The tragedy of the American Indian had been foreshadowed in the widely held opinion that the best Indian is a dead Indian. Systematically deprived of his lands, driven to desperate and futile resistance, the Indian's successive defeats were used to justify his expulsion westward, and sometimes his outright massacre. The record of American treatment of the Indian was hardly inspiring; and, especially after the publication in 1881 of Helen Hunt Jackson's *A Century of Dishonor,* some Americans thought it a national disgrace. As the edge of white settlement pushed across the plains, the government was called upon to establish a policy that would terminate the Indian "menace." Such events as the great Sioux Uprising of 1862 had resulted in the massacre of dozens of settlers in Minnesota and the Dakotas. Congress was under irresistible pressure to supply both immediate protection and a final solution.

In 1871 Congress terminated the treaty policy by which the Indians had been negotiated with as independent nations. The Indians now became pensioners of the government, under the jurisdiction of the Indian Agency. Within fourteen years, almost the entire population of Indians in the United States had been confined to 171 reservations covering an area about equal to the size of Texas. The United States Army devoted much of its energy to subduing recalcitrant tribes and insuring that those on the reservation would stay put. Deprived of his self-respect, the ward of a government that permitted unscrupulous agents and traders to rob him of his due, the Indian succumbed to disease and despair.

The Dawes and Burke Acts. In the decades following his subjugation, the Indian's numbers steadily declined, until barely 237,000 remained in 1900. Tentative efforts were made by some Americans in the 1870s to provide Indians with educational facilities. Some 4,000 Indian children were registered at reservation schools in 1878. But at the same time, mounting pressure was exerted to expel Indians from the more valuable reservation lands. The Dawes Act of 1887 ostensibly provided Indians with the opportunity to achieve an independent agricultural existence, but actually deprived them of eighty per cent of their reservation land. Often unaccustomed to agriculture, further demoralized by the disappearance of tribal authority, the Indian was now the victim of an indifferent society which saw in his demoralization proof of his inferiority. The Dawes Act made him a citizen, but his "rights" amounted in practice to the privilege of drinking freely the liquor he had never learned to manage, and which was so assiduously supplied to him by white purveyors. Crime and immorality skyrocketed, until the "savage" Indian gave place to the "thieving" Indian as a stereotype. In 1906, the Burke Act deferred full citizenship for a probationary twenty-five-year period, except in individual cases. Not until the New Deal, under the guidance of Indian Commissioner John Collier, was an effort made to restore tribal life, and a people forced to repudiate their old ways were finally permitted to salvage some semblance of their past. During the past few years, increasing attention has been paid to the traditions, languages, customs, beliefs, and mores of the various Indian cultures, and in many parts of the West—particularly in New Mexico—there has been a renaissance in traditional

AMERICAN INDIAN POPULATION, 1950

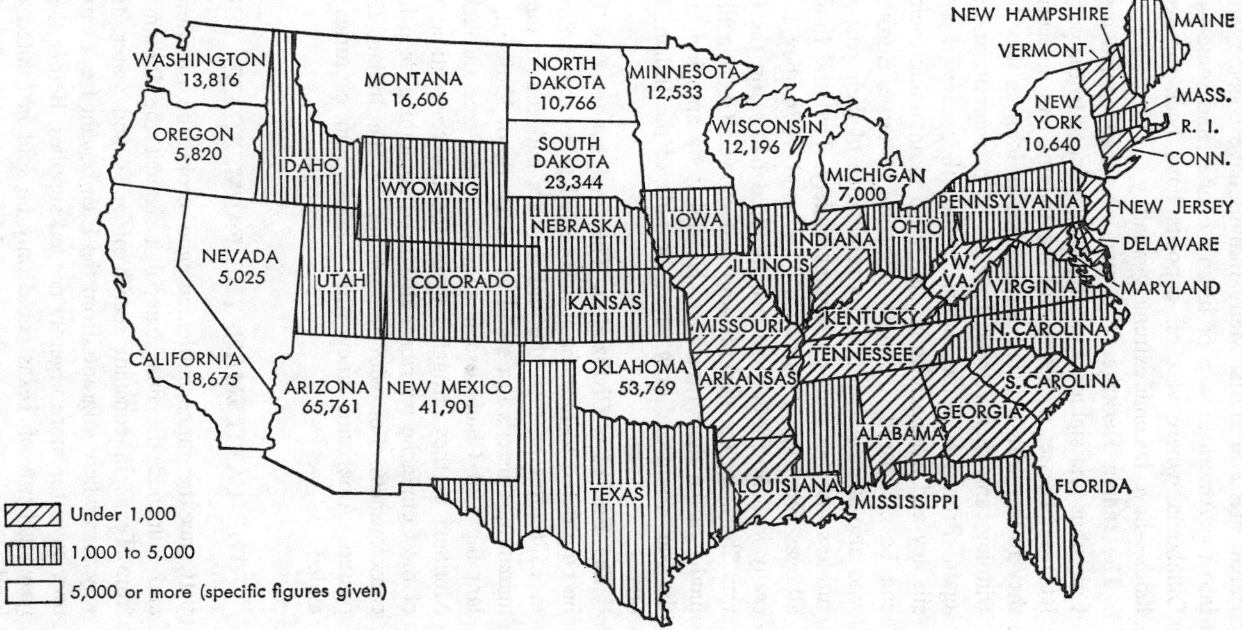

Indian arts and crafts. Many Indians have become wholly assimilated into the American way of life, of course, and some—most notably in Oklahoma, where vast oil deposits have been discovered on Indian lands—have become extremely wealthy.

The Indian Heritage. The men who had owned a continent when Columbus first sighted America were reduced to the possession of desolate wildernesses by 1900. But the Indians had not surrendered easily; they fought with a crazy desperation as long as they had a chance of winning, and then retreated westward to regroup and stand and fight again. Primitive, fierce, brave, proud, they showed a remarkable resiliency and a tenacious insistence on maintaining their identity. They can be compared, in some respects, to those European immigrants who also struggled to retain a semblance of their past in the face of a ruthless and booming Protestant society. That the Indians survived at all was remarkable. Between 1869 and 1876 they fought, and generally lost, no fewer than two hundred battles on the Great Plains. It was Sherman, the general who had mowed Georgia like a lawn, who finally broke their resistance. He did it by applying his principle that the war would end only when the bulk of the Indians had been killed off.

The End of a Civilization. The final conquest of the Indians can be considered to have been accomplished by the capture of Geronimo in 1886. But by then the Indian wars had caught the American imagination. Custer's last stand at the Battle of Little Big Horn; the gallant flight of Chief Joseph and the Nez Perce through the snows of Montana as they struggled to escape the reservation; the war whoop of the Comanche warrior—all stirred something deep in the American consciousness. For with the passing of the Indian, the frontier had passed. Americans knew that almost four centuries of history had ended.

THE CATTLEMAN, THE FARMER, AND THE MINER

It was the range cattlemen who broke the isolation of the plains and launched the final campaign against the Indian. Moving north from Texas in constant search of grass and water, they established waystops where migrants from the East bought fresh cattle or sold their own cows for more urgently needed supplies. Before the Civil War the growing herds of Texas could only be sold in limited markets of this kind. During the war the trans-Mississippi West, isolated from the rest of the Confederacy and deprived of any outlet for its cattle, saw its herds grow at a speed that left cattle worthless. Huge numbers of unbranded longhorns wandered wild across the plains of Texas and were sometimes spoken of as "game."

The Cattle Drive. In the aftermath of war, destitute Texans organized "cow hunts," and slowly built up private herds. In 1866, they organized the first great cattle drive, moving 260,000 head into the feeding areas of Iowa, Kansas, and Missouri. Encouraged by the willingness of Iowa farmers to pay as much as $35 a head when the going price in Texas was $3 or $4, they organized a second, much smaller drive in 1867 up the Chisholm Trail to the Abilene railhead of the Kansas Pacific. The great cattle drive thereafter became an institution, and buyers flocked regularly to the cowtowns of Sedalia, Dodge City, and Abilene. From there, trains carried the cattle into the Middle West for corn fattening, and finally they arrived at the booming slaughterhouses of Chicago, St. Louis, Kansas City, and Cincinnati.

The Cowboy. Out of the great cattle drives emerged a gallant figure—the cowboy. It was he who rode pell-mell through the streets of Abilene and the other cowtowns, raising holy hell after the long trip north. The lurid hotels, the noisy dance halls, the violent saloons, the painted dancing girls, the fancy man—the sum and substance of every American's vision of the West—were all, in effect, his creation. At the end of the drive came payday, providing a momentary escape from the grueling existence of the saddle.

The cowboy's life was not an easy one. From the moment the drive north began, the tension mounted. Andy Adams, in his *Log of a Cowboy,* recalled:

> Sometimes the demands were so urgent that a man's boots would not be taken off his feet for an entire week. The nerves of the men usually became wrought up to such a tension that no man was to be touched by another when he was asleep until after he had been spoken to. The man who suddenly aroused a sleeper was liable to be shot, as all were thoroughly armed and understood the instant use of the revolver or the rifle.

An eighteen-hour day, riding the herd, keeping it moving northward, rounding up stragglers, keeping a wary eye out for the marauding Indian or the rustler, searching always for the water that would mean the difference between a successful journey and a disastrous failure—this was the lot of the cowboy. Behind the romance was back-breaking work.

Cattleman-Farmer Rivalry. The cattle industry also laid the foundations for a bitter rivalry between rancher and farmer. The usual 160 acres provided for under the Homestead Act proved uneconomic on the Great Plains. The cost of machinery, irrigation, and fencing alone precluded success with so little land. The Timber Culture Act of 1873, the Desert Land Act of 1877, and the Timber and Stone Act of 1878, all of which were designed to encourage farmers in tree-planting and irrigation by giving them land bonuses, made it possible for a single farmer to accumulate as much as two "sections," the equivalent of two square miles. The sole effect of these laws was to make it possible for cattle kings, speculators, and land barons to obtain control of vast acreages through "dummy" claimants. The problem of irrigation on the high, semiarid plains was still not solved, however. Only in 1902, when the federal government, under the Newlands Act, assumed direct responsibility for providing irrigation facilities, did farming in semiarid regions become feasible. Meanwhile, in the 1870s and 1880s, the cattlemen were left to rule the high plains unimpeded.

Single herds of 25,000 and more were not uncommon. No less than 5,713,976 cattle were driven to Northern markets between 1866 and 1885. As railroads penetrated into Texas, additional hundreds of thousands were shipped directly to the Middle Western meat-packing centers. The development of refrigerated cars made it possible to consolidate meat packing, and to ship the dressed carcasses to the booming urban centers of the East and later even to Europe. As the demand grew, prices spurted from $7 or $8 a head in 1878 to $12 in 1881. The following year, $30 to $35 was the going price. Formidable profits, often ranging up to three hundred per cent, persuaded investors as far afield as Scotland and England to invest in Texas cattle lands. Then, a combination of hard winters, droughts, and overstocking sent prices plummeting. The steady movement of farmers into range country, enclosing land and water holes as they moved, completed the debacle. One cattleman complained bitterly:

> These fellows from Ohio, Indiana, and other northern and western states—the "bone and sinew of the country," as politicians call them—have made farms, enclosed pastures, and fenced in water holes until you can't rest; and I say, Damn such bone and sinew! They are the ruin of the country, and have everlastingly, eternally, now and forever, destroyed the best grazing-land in the world.

By 1886, after two short decades, the cowboy and the cattle drive had both passed into legend.

The Great Western Mines. As the cattleman brought the taming hand of civilization to the Great Plains, so the miner subdued the mountains. The lure of gold had initiated a massive march to the Pacific. In January 1849, an itinerant carpenter, James Marshall, while constructing a sawmill for John A. Sutter, a Sacramento farmer, discovered gold. Although Sutter struggled to keep the discovery a secret, it leaked out, and soon a stampede of gold seekers surged into the region. The first great gold rush was on, destined to make a handful rich, and to populate California with the less fortunate. When gold was discovered near Pike's Peak in 1859, approximately 50,000 men pushed their way to Colorado and disappointment, because the ore proved too refractory for known methods of mining. Only the introduction of Guggenheim capital in the 1880s, and the technological advances it made possible, finally cracked Colorado's mineral wealth. The mining camp of Denver survived and expanded, serving ultimately as a railroad terminal and service center for a swiftly growing agriculture.

The discovery of the Comstock lode in 1858 sent 25,000 people pouring into Nevada. The mining camps of Carson City and Virginia City spawned a lusty life, with the familiar dance hall and saloon standing next to the belching chimneys and clanging machinery of the mines. Mansions, theaters, schools, and the shoddier attributes of civilization were erected in what had been, only a few years before, a desolate wilderness. Fortunes were made and lost, more often through speculation in mining companies than through pick-and-shovel work. It was not unusual for stock prices to increase by 2,000 per cent in a four-month period. One can hardly disagree with the diagnosis of the Federal Commissioner of Mining Statistics who wrote of Nevada speculations: "It would confirm the mischievous feeling that mining is half grab and half gamble; that the only way to make money at it is to dig out what rich ore you can get and then find a fool to buy the property; or failing that to make a fool of that collective individual, the public, and to 'unload' yourself of your stock." The boom died as fast as it had been born; Nevada mining stocks, which had been valued at $393,000,000 in 1875, commanded only $7,000,000 five years later.

Some mining towns—Virginia City was an example—sank into the obscurity of ghost towns; others, like Coeur d'Alene, Reno, and Butte, became flourishing cattle towns on a par with Laramie and Cheyenne. Even as the gold boom faded, other metals entered their heyday. The discovery of gold along the tributaries of the South Platte had brought an influx of prospectors and settlers into the Colorado territory as early as 1858; but with the discovery of huge deposits of silver ore in 1879, a major development of the area was undertaken. Such mining cities as Leadville, Cripple Creek, Silverton, and Creed transformed Colorado from a wilderness inhabited primarily by Cheyenne and Arapahoe Indians into a group of thriving, burgeoning mining centers. In Montana, the vast copper deposits around Butte provided the foundation of the Anaconda Copper Mining Company. Under the shrewd leadership of William A. Clark and Marcus Daly, the company's influence became paramount throughout the state. Banks, newspapers, power plants, lumber stands, and coal mines were but a few of its related interests. Western Montana's dependence upon mining was typical of the region. As a result, the whole vast Rocky Mountain region was peculiarly susceptible to the vagaries of world prices. In a real sense it had a one-crop economy, and the rugged topography and forbidding climate kept its population small. Something of the original vastness of America was retained in the western rim of the great valley that stretched to the Appalachians.

Utah and the Mormons. One of the reasons for a number of the important settlements in the thirteen colonies had been the desire felt by various religious sects to escape persecution for their beliefs and the need to find a haven of freedom. Similar needs and goals were responsible for the much later settlement of part of the American West, the territory that was one day to become the state of Utah. The Mormons, forced to embark upon a westward migration to escape religious persecution in the East, reached the Great Salt Lake Valley on July 24, 1847. There, under the leadership of Brigham Young, they established their colony. Although the early years of the Mormon settlement were difficult, a flourishing community was established, its economy based on agriculture—the Mormons were the first Americans to practice irrigation on a major scale—and its government dominated primarily by the church. Mormon colonists expanded the community's influence in the area, establishing settlements in the Ogden valley, the Sampete valley, the Utah valley, and the valley of Little Salt Lake. In addition to agriculture, mining became a major occupation of the Mormons, and the territory soon became a model of industry and productivity; and when Utah entered the Union on January 4, 1896, she could point with considerable pride to the wealth and security of the Mormons, who had truly brought about a flowering in the desert.

CHANGING PATTERNS OF AGRICULTURE

The American ideal was the family farm; in the placid valleys and plains of the East and Middle West, the farmstead was as typical a landmark as the tenement in the city. But farm conditions were slowly —sometimes almost imperceptibly—changing. During the nineteenth century, the center of staple agriculture shifted steadily westward. Throughout the Northeast and the upper Middle West, abandoned farms were common. The emphasis on grains gave way to dairy and truck farming as the swiftly growing urban centers provided an insatiable market for perishables. In the lower Middle West, the farmer not only raised corn but also fattened hogs and cattle for the packing houses. By 1880, millions of farmers had become cogs in a far-flung industrial enterprise that processed food for the domestic and world market. Nevertheless, most farmers retained the naïve confidence that they were most truly and centrally the American people.

The Decline of Eastern Farming. In some sections of the country agriculture had already ceased to play a predominant role by the later nineteenth century. On the stony soil of New England the farmer could fight only a mocking and futile battle. He had long ago learned, in the words of a New England editor, that he could not "compete in cereals with the West; in fruits and vegetables with Delaware and New Jersey; . . . in butter with Nebraska and Iowa; in dressed beef with the Armour sydicate. . . ." The flight to the mill town which had begun in the 1820s went on unimpeded. Thus, the Yankee farmer was the first to surrender the illusion that the promise of American life was necessarily a promise for him. The New Englanders who remained on the soil were those whose Yankee shrewdness enabled them to see the significance of the growing urban market for perishables. In fact, that market gave Eastern agriculturists a new lease on life. But a subtle change had occurred: the Eastern farmer, who often transported his own produce to market, now took increasing note of his business role. By the end of the nineteenth century he thought completely in terms of profit and loss, and had in fact become an agricultural entrepreneur.

The Two Agricultures. Without anyone quite realizing it, two distinct farm communities had come into being by 1890. One was oriented around the consumer needs of urban populations. It had the security of a certain market; and it generally had the good fortune not to rely on a single staple crop. In short, it hedged its bet. The other was the staple crop agriculture that prevailed in the South, the remoter regions of the Middle West, and the Great Plains. For them the dilemma was increasingly that of an ever more successful production and ever declining prices. Particularly acute was the problem of the South, which still labored under the impoverishment of the Civil War, and of the Great Plains, where successful farming demanded large capital investment. Both regions were forced to borrow heavily; each year the task of retiring indebtedness became more burdensome. The average Southern and Western farmer gradually awoke to the realization that he had borrowed more than money; he had borrowed time, and by 1890 it had almost run out.

The Wheat Farmer. The plowing of the Great Plains proceeded at a reckless pace during the 1880s. Vast crops of the amber grain poured onto the world market, but they commanded a notoriously unstable price. A production of 405,886,000 bushels sold for $1.20 per bushel in 1881; four years later, a harvest of 399,931,000 bushels brought only 77¢ per bushel. To farmers encumbered with debt—one out of every two Kansas and North Dakota farmers labored under a mortgage, and one out of every three in Minnesota, Nebraska, and South Dakota were similarly strapped—the obvious solution was to increase production. By 1889 production had expanded to 504,370,000 bushels, and the price per bushel had declined to 69¢. In a decade, the wheat farmer had increased his production by one quarter while his income had declined thirty per cent; the faster he ran, the further behind he fell in the race.

The Drought. The vagaries of climate also accentuated farm difficulties on the Great Plains. During the years of settlement in the western reaches of Kansas, Nebraska, and the Dakotas, and in the eastern plains of Montana and Colorado, an annual rainfall of 21.63 inches was recorded. It was adequate to insure good crops of both wheat and corn. Nevertheless, water supplements were required to permit staple agriculture. Farmers resorted to drilling wells, though these were generally so deep that artificial assistance was needed to raise the water. Soon the Western landscape was dotted with the windmills that had already been proved successful by the transcontinental railroads and cattlemen. Dry farming, which involved quickly covering rainfall with a layer of earth to prevent evaporation, also minimized the water scarcity. Thus the first settlers, lulled by the seemingly endless water supply, made no provisions to supplement rainfall with irrigation. In the drought years after 1887, the rickety structure of Western agriculture collapsed. The wheat farmer suddenly awoke to the fact that the Great Plains was a region of periodic famine.

The reminiscences of a young man who had abandoned farming described how, where the water supply had once seemed ample, steady, endless, the farmer now watched as "the rain clouds forming day after day disappear under the horizon, and weeks lengthen into months without a drop of moisture." The day of the locust had arrived; even the strongest men finally despaired. Slowly and ruthlessly, nature was reclaiming her own. A Western editor described it thus:

> The grasses wither, the herds wander wearily over the plains in search of water holes, the crops wilt and languish, yielding not even the seed for another year. . . . Another and perhaps another season of drought occurs, the settlers depart with such of their household furniture as can be drawn away by the enfeebled draft animals, the herds disappear, and this beautiful land, once so fruitful, is now dry and brown and given over to the prairie wolf.

The Depression of the 1890s. Two years of ample rainfall, 1891 and 1892, temporarily broke the pattern. Production soared to more than 677,000,000 bushels in the first year, at a price of more than 83¢ per bushel. In the second year the drought was already resurgent in the westernmost reaches of the Great Plains; production dropped by nearly 66,000,000 bushels while prices dropped to little more than 62¢ per bushel. The drought reached its apogee in 1894, destroying crops in sixty-one of Nebraska's ninety-one counties. Conditions were no better in Kansas and the Dakotas. As production declined to little more than 500,000,000 bushels, depression prices governed the wheat market—in 1894, they sank to less than 49¢ per bushel. Conditions were no better in the corn market, where prices declined from nearly 63¢ per bushel in 1881 to little more than 21¢ in 1896, even as production rose from a staggering 1,244,000,000 bushels to an astronomical 2,671,000,000.

The great mass of small farmers and speculators who had rushed westward in the land boom of the 1880s, and had converted Kansas (in the succinct words of a contemporary) into "a vast insane asylum," now began a reverse migration. At least 18,000 prairie schooners passed eastward through Omaha in a single season, and 179,884 persons left Kansas between 1887 and 1891. The young man who had heeded the injunction given three decades earlier, and had "gone West," now went East with a vengeance.

The Southern Farmer. No less numbing was the plight of the Southern farmer. "Apart from the New South, by which I mean the country around the region of the rapidly developing iron industries," reported one traveler, "the same wretched poverty prevails among the Southern people . . . twenty-two years after the war." The 2,757,000 bales of cotton produced in 1871 earned 18¢ per pound; but the 10,026,000 bales of 1894 sold for scarcely 4½¢ the pound. Tobacco followed the same startling pattern: huge crops and no profits.

Tenantry, sharecropping, and crop liens were the hallmarks of the New South's agriculture. Superficially, statistics of land distribution in all the formerly Confederate states except Florida and Virginia imply an abandonment of the plantation system. The average farm of 347 acres in 1860 had been reduced to 156 acres in 1880; the total number of farms had increased, in the same period, from 449,936 to 1,110,294. These figures alone, however, present a misleading picture.

The Plantation System. By 1880, the plantation system, far from having perished, had merely undergone a revolution in its labor system. Instead of gangs of slaves working the fields, the land was now parceled out to families who produced cotton in return for a share of the crop. Since 1860, the total number of such sharecroppers had risen from practically none to 301,738. Ownership was as concentrated as ever, often in the form of tenant plantations, but more often than not the old planter aristocrat had surrendered his fief to Northern land corporations, commission merchants, and banks, who drew the bulk of profits from Southern agriculture after the war. The transferral of ownership had been accelerated by the lien system, which committed the poverty-stricken farmer to a curious form of bondage. Commission merchants would advance credit against future crops, providing the farmer with supplies—food, farm implements, clothing—in return for a pledge to deliver his crop as payment. The commission merchant ordinarily dictated the size of the crop, and included a penalty in the contract in case it was not produced. To protect himself against risk, he also tacked an extra interest charge on the price of any goods given on credit. (This charge was rarely less than thirty per cent, and often reached as high as seventy per cent.) As a rule, the farmer was obliged to sell his crop to the merchant at "inside" prices, sufficiently low to insure him against loss. If the farmer failed to redeem his obligation—which was not unlikely—he was compelled by the terms of contract to renew his lien for the following year with the same merchant. Critical observers dubbed the victims of this system "The Peons of the South." Lest we make the commission merchant a mere villain reaping exorbitant profits, however, we must consider the risks he took. To obtain credit, he had to agree to pay high interest rates to factors, who in turn paid their tribute to Northern bankers. The margin of profit was painfully narrow, since cotton had to sell at 8¢ per pound to bring a profit, and could not sell for less than 7¢ per pound without incurring a loss. Between 1885 and 1890, the average margin of profit was scarcely ½¢; between 1891 and 1899, with the exception of 1892, cotton sold for 7¢ or less. It is doubtful whether either the cotton grower or the commission merchant made money under such circumstances. By 1890 the cotton farmers of the South, like staple crop growers throughout the rest of the nation, had reached a fundamental crisis.

THE FARMERS' ALLIANCES

John Wesley Powell noted in 1890 that on the Great Plains there was a strong tendency toward domination of agriculture by "a few capitalists, employing labor on a large scale, as is done in the great mines and manufactories of the United States." On these "bonanza" farms, covering thousands of acres, a single management prevailed. "The aim of some of the great 'bonanza farms' of Dakota," Senator William A. Pfeffer of Kansas complained, "has been to apply machinery so effectually that the cultivation of one full section, or six hundred and forty acres, shall represent one year's work of only one man." A pattern which had already been enacted in industry now reappeared: bonanza farmers obtained favorable rates from the railroads, while the small farmer, with his shipments of a few hundred bushels at most, paid rates that drove him close to bankruptcy. Similarly, the small livestock raiser found himself unable to compete with ranchmen whose vast spreads supported tens of thousands of cattle. The American citadel—the family farm—was being submerged by corporate agriculture.

The Early Alliances. Small Western and Southern farmers were at last driven to collective action to meet the challenge of the big organizations. Sometime around 1875, the Southern Farmers' Alliance was formed in the frontier county of Lampasas, Texas. Its purpose was to protect farmers against cattlemen and foreign-owned land syndicates. Though it did not survive, it provided the pattern for the formation, in 1880, of the more durable (but still restricted to Texas) Farmers' State Alliance. The Alliance was soon agitating for collective action to force better credit from Southern merchants. A similar Alliance had been formed in New York, in March 1877, to press for Granger reforms. In April 1880, a Chicago editor, Milton George, founded a central agency to organize similar groups throughout the country. The movement spread rapidly, denouncing the evils of railroads and the concentration of wealth. Though not specifically political, the Alliances agitated for reform of rail and storage rates and urged the farmers to practice collective buying of machinery, supplies, and even nonessentials. The general drift of their thinking was toward cooperatives. To match the power of corporate agriculture, they advocated the setting-up of a countervailing organization which would give small farmers the strength of unity.

"Unity" was the rallying cry of Alliances, but it soon became only a catchword. Many members of the rank-and-file were already looking to state and federal governments for practical aid. In 1886 the Texas Alliance, meeting at Cleburne, issued a set of resolutions which demanded prohibition of alien land ownership, higher taxes on lands purchased for speculative purposes, abolition of speculation in staple crop futures prices, heavier taxation of railroads, interstate commerce legislation, and inflation of the currency. Steps were taken to present these demands at Austin and Washington. But—and this was the first sign of what was to be a continuing weakness in the Alliances—the demand for political action threatened to split the organization. Only the fortuitous intervention of C. W. Macune, the new chairman of the Texas Alliance's executive committee, closed up the rift.

Macune and Southern Alliances. In January 1887, Macune launched an effort to unite the cotton farmers of the South into a regional alliance. He sent teams of organizers throughout the South, and their evangelical zeal swept hundreds of thousands of farmers into a regional alliance. Within a short time other farm organizations, like the Agricultural Wheel, united with the Alliance. By 1889, the organization encompassed somewhere between a million and a half and three million white members; its subsidiary, the Colored Farmers' National Alliance and Co-operative Union, numbered a million and a quarter. Although the color line had been drawn, the Southern Alliance accepted the proposition that the plight of the white farmer could not be alleviated without parallel relief for the Negro farmer.

Limited Appeal of the Alliances. A similar growth was noted in the Alliances of the Great Plains, but the Alliance movement generally succeeded better in the South, where membership was two or three times that of the North. The highly centralized administration of the Southern Alliance proved immeasurably more effective than the decentralized state organizations of the North; but, what was more significant, the Alliances seemed to have an extremely limited appeal to Northern farmers. Only staple crop farmers joined in large numbers. In Minnesota, Wisconsin, and the Dakotas, Yankee farmers rather than German, Bohemian, or Scandinavian farmers joined the movement. As one moved eastward, the appeal of the Alliances declined precipitously. There were two prime circumstances which prevented the Alliances from attracting much support among the farmers of the Northeast. First, the existing political channels were organized so much more efficiently there than elsewhere, and the farmers had for so long found them open to his influence, that most Eastern agriculturists believed that whatever changes were desirable could be brought about through proper use of existing political parties, institutions, and facilities. Second, unlike his Western and Southern brothers, the farmer of the Northeast combined his agricultural pursuits with more commercial activities. As we have seen, the Eastern farmer was now an agricultural entrepreneur. He was, therefore, less at the mercy of purely antiagricultural interests and influences, and the causes espoused by the Alliances did not affect the Eastern farmer to the same degree that they did the farmers of the South and West. This lack of effectiveness in the North boded ill for any farm movement that resorted to independent political action, for it precluded it from obtaining anything like the support of farmers nation-wide.

The Alliance Programs. In a world that seemed to demand endless work for the farmer without a commensurate reward, the Alliances provided tentative counteraction. Their purpose was to obtain justice for the farmer. They traced the root of his difficulty to the existence of "combination among all the members of other callings until competition became unknown." To meet such realities, only farmer combination would suffice. Under the guidance of Macune, the Farmers' Alliance Exchange was organized; its purpose was to provide the farmer with an exchange in which to sell his cotton with minimal middleman charges, and with an agency able to reduce the costs of farm necessities by buying in volume. When efforts were made to raise the price of jute, which was used in the baling of cotton, the Exchange organized a boycott which proved so successful that the "jute trust" collapsed. The Alliance also urged the construction of factories that would supply the equipment distributed through its Exchanges, but the lack of sufficient capital thwarted these ambitious plans. In 1889, Macune, eager to resolve this weakness, proposed the establishment of the "subtreasury plan." This would involve the creation of storage facilities such as warehouses and elevators, and would require a subtreasury office in every county which sold at least $500,000 worth of farm produce annually. The farmer would be permitted to store nonperishable crops, such as grains and cotton, in these warehouses, in return for certificates of deposit. These certificates could be converted into a one-year loan representing eighty per cent of the market value of the stored crops. The cost to the farmer would be one per cent and nominal fees, and it was argued that the credit thus obtained would permit him to hold his crops until prices improved. The overweening concern of the Southern Alliance, as suggested by the subtreasury plan, was credit. The Northern Alliances expressed greater concern for railroad regulation, demanding government ownership if necessary, and an end to the excessive land holdings of both railroads and "aliens."

The Alliances and Political Action. The demands of the Alliances carried an implicit threat of political action. In December 1889, at St. Louis, the Northern and Southern Alliances joined with the Knights of Labor to allow "the legislative committee of both organizations [to] act in concert before Congress for the purpose of securing the enactment of laws in harmony with the demands mutually agreed [upon]." Macune noted: "Whatever else this movement may be, a third-party movement it is not"; but he added that it intended "to exert a more decisive influence in the primaries of *both parties*." In 1890 the Alliances took an active part in Southern Democratic conventions, insisting that nominees pledge themselves to support their demands. A parallel development in Kansas found county Alliance leaders resolving "that we will no longer divide on party lines, and will only cast our votes for candidates of the people, by the people, and for the people." (A Northern flavor was obvious in this Lincolnesque phrasing.) In the summer of 1890, the State Alliance in Nebraska took independent political action, nominating a People's Independent ticket headed by its president. Similar uprisings resulted in the nomination of independent slates in the Dakotas, Minnesota, Michigan, and Indiana. They frankly called for a revolt of "farmers, prohibitionists, and friends of reform" against "political bosses and ring masters." Macune's prediction about a third-party movement was being disproved; the first steps in the organization of the Populist Party were being taken.

THE POPULIST PARTY

The new party, the Populists, gave vent to the gathered frustrations of the American farmer. Trapped by the anonymous and impersonal machinations of an industrial society, he flocked to the rural hustings to hear impassioned Populist orators preach the gospel of "less corn and more hell." Mary Elizabeth Lease, a lawyer and mother of four children, rushed across the plains, making no less than a hundred and sixty speeches in a single year, entrancing audiences as she warned: "The people are at bay, let the blood-hounds of money who have dogged us thus far beware." Jerry "Sockless" Simpson pounded away at the thesis that "man must have access to the land or he is a slave." Ignatius Donnelly, a prairie author whose lectures arguing Baconian authorship of Shakespeare's plays had earned him a spice of notoriety, and who had gained political experience in a succession of third-party movements, threw in his lot with the Populists. The staid Iowa reformer James B. Weaver added his serenity and prestige, providing a balance to the erratic vivacity which made Populism so colorful. The movement was an explosion of secularized fundamentalism. Its vivid indignation, its self-righteous sense of grievance, shook the nation. "It was a religious revival, a crusade, a pentecost of politics," one contemporary recalled, "in which a tongue of flame sat upon every man, and each spake as the spirit gave him utterance."

Political Success. The power of Populism demonstrated itself at the polls in 1890. In the South, where the Populists avoided organizing a third party, but pledged their support to any politician who supported their aims, the movement compelled obeisance from the traditional parties. (The Democratic party was so solidly entrenched in the South that any candidate who did not march beneath the Democratic standard—nominally, at least—had not the remotest chance of securing election.) In North Carolina, eight congressmen were Populists, as were all the Democratic state officials and half the Republican contingent in the legislature. Nearly two-thirds of Alabama's state legislature was deemed friendly to the cause, while in neighboring Georgia six congressmen, the governor, and more than three-quarters of the legislature were considered Alliance men. In Tennessee the governor and almost half the legislature shared the faith, and in Florida a senator and more than half the legislature owed their election to the Alliance. Incumbents elsewhere took the hint. In Virginia and Kentucky it was believed that nine congressmen were prepared to assist Alliance programs. Many Southern Alliance men concluded that they had taken possession of the Democratic party. No less emphatic was the Alliance success in the Great Plains. In Kansas the State Assembly had an overwhelming membership of Populists, and the movement could also claim five congressmen and Senator William A. Pfeffer. In Nebraska both houses of the legislature were solidly held, while a Populist-inclined Democrat won the governorship, and the Republicans lost all the state's congressional seats to either Democrats or a fusion ticket. Less successful in Minnesota and South Dakota, the Populists nevertheless held the balance of power in the state legislatures, and secured the election of a friendly senator in South Dakota. In North Dakota, Iowa, Illinois, Indiana, Michigan, and Colorado, the Populist ticket undermined Republican strength, permitting a large-scale Democratic congressional victory. As the scope of the movement's success became manifest, the

Populist evangelion began to take on apocalyptic overtones. Members of the established order read with deep unease such party pronouncements as:

> We send the plutocrats a grim warning. . . . The twin of this oppression is rebellion—rebellion that will seek revenge with justice, that will bring in its Pandora's box fire, rapine, and blood. Unless there is a change and a remedy found, this day is as inevitable as that God reigns, and it will be soon.

The Populists looked forward to a national triumph in 1892.

The Populists and the Election of 1892. "In the elections of 1890" the *Nation* editorialized, "the agrarian revolt went far beyond what we or anybody anticipated." Neither of the two major parties could quite estimate the impact of the burgeoning Populist movement on their own fortunes. The immediate victim seemed likely to be the Republican party, which faced the threat of wholesale defections of Western Populists, while Southern Populists had chosen to remain within the Democratic organization. In December 1890, at Ocala, Florida, the Alliances debated the advisability of a third party, but agreed to suspend a final decision until February 1892. But they were increasingly unable to exercise effective control over legislators or congressmen pledged to Alliance principles, a fact which made their decision for them. At the February 1892 meeting they agreed to support a national Populist ticket. The nomination of Cleveland, who was viewed by Southern Populists as a spokesman of Eastern privilege, in June 1892 insured uniform action by the Alliances in the South. But neither party entered the election of 1892 with any certainty of victory.

Nominations of the Three Parties. It had been a foregone conclusion when the Democrats met at Chicago that Cleveland would head the ticket. After retiring from the presidency, he had energetically resumed his legal practice, seeming to forget all political aspirations. But in 1890, outraged by the McKinley tariff and encouraged by the heavy Democratic gains in the off-year elections, Cleveland permitted himself to be "pulled and hauled" back into politics. His opposition to "reckless experiments" in free silver and his insistence on economy in government attracted increasing favor in business circles. Only the opposition of Senator David Hill of New York threatened to obstruct Cleveland's path to the presidential nomination. The shrewd guidance of William C. Whitney, a New York traction tycoon, threw the support of a large body of conservative businessmen behind Cleveland. When Tammany, under growing pressure, pledged organization support if he were renominated, the choice of Cleveland was settled and he was chosen on the first ballot, with Adlai E. Stevenson, an advocate of silver, as a running mate.

The Republicans renominated Harrison, although there was a deep undercurrent of hostility toward him; the choice was ultimately dictated by the absence of a formidable opponent and by the genuine pessimism of Republicans as to their chances. "Well, perhaps he is as good a man to get licked with as anybody," Thomas B. Reed concluded.

A journalist described how, in Omaha, the Populists, convening in July 1892, met amid scenes in which "cheers and yells . . . rose like a tornado . . . during which women shrieked and wept, men embraced and kissed their neighbors, locked arms . . . leaped upon tables and chairs in the ecstasy of their delirium." Only the sudden death of Leonidas Polk, president of the Southern Alliance, cast a flicker of gloom on the gathering, for it deprived the Populists of their first candidate. When Walter Q. Gresham declined the nomination, they fastened upon James B. Weaver, a former Union General, and James G. Field, a Confederate veteran.

The Populist Platform. It was the Populist platform, a product of Ignatius Donnelly's prolific pen, rather than the candidates, that attracted major attention to the party. Its preamble contained a scathing denunciation of a state of affairs in which "corruption dominates the ballot-box, the Legislatures, the Congress, and touches even the ermine of the bench." It denounced the concentration of wealth and the importation of "pauperized labor" to beat down native wages, and concluded that "the same prolific womb of governmental injustice [bred] two great classes—tramps and millionaires." It demanded free and unlimited coinage of silver and gold at the legal ratio of 16–to–1, and a currency "speedily increased to not less than $50 per capita." It pressed for postal savings banks; the secret ballot; initiative and referendum; the direct election of senators; and a single presidential term. A graduated income tax and government ownership of railroads, telegraph, and telephone services commanded its approbation. It demanded an end to alien ownership of land, and the confiscation of all lands held by corporations and railroads in excess of their actual needs. Having thus demanded the extension of governmental responsibility on a massive scale, the Populist platform insisted upon the extension of civil service "to prevent the increase of the power of the national administration," and urged that "all State and national revenues shall be limited to the necessary expenses of the government, economically and honestly administered." Even as the Populists agitated for the most significant program of reform proposed in the nineteenth century, they revealed their ties with the past. The old Jeffersonian fear of big government was still with them; they demanded additional power for federal authority and simultaneously demanded that it be carefully restrained. The vehement language of the Omaha platform, however, was not carried into the campaign. The two major parties presented a stance of dignity and decorum, confirming the Populist argument that there was no greater dispute between them than over who would obtain the power to plunder. The Republicans found themselves condemned again by the Populists for the McKinley Tariff.

The Homestead Strike. While the campaign was in progress, a strike erupted at the Carnegie plant in Homestead, Pennsylvania. Pitched battles took place between strikers and Pinkerton detectives hired by management, and ended in the complete defeat of the strikers. While Republican leaders pleaded unavailingly with the Carnegie Company to recognize the union, the Democrats insisted that the root of labor troubles lay in the McKinley Tariff. The use of state militia at Homestead, and the subsequent use of federal and state troops in strikes of railway switchmen in Buffalo, silver miners in Coeur d'Alene, Idaho, and coal miners in Tennessee, reminded workers of Hayes's strike-breaking tactics in 1877 and did the Republicans much damage. At the same time, William Whitney was carefully mending fences in New York, assuming that in a narrow squeeze the Empire State's electoral votes would be crucial.

Cleveland's Election. The result of the election was a heavy plurality for Cleveland. He outpolled Harrison by almost 400,000 popular and 132 electoral votes. For the first time in decades the Democrats carried Illinois and Wisconsin, and they missed Ohio by hardly 1,000 votes. The Populists polled more than 1,000,000 votes, carrying Kansas, Colorado, North Dakota, Idaho and Nevada, and revealing substantial support in the remainder of the Great Plains and in the Mountain States. But in the South, in a campaign characterized by violence, economic intimidation, and mass bribery, Populist strength proved disappointing. Nonetheless, the Populists had elected five senators, ten representatives, and three governors, and many Populist sympathizers had found their way into office under the Democratic and Republican labels. In the South, especially, Populist sentiment was rife among Democrats. 1892 had revealed a bubbling cauldron of discontent, but the semblance of normality had been temporarily retained. Cleveland, as most businessmen realized, did not intend to rock the boat. Andrew Carnegie noted: "We have nothing to fear."

CLEVELAND'S SECOND ADMINISTRATION

The Depression of 1893. Even as Cleveland entered the White House for a second time, there was ample evidence that the national economy was shaky. Though Harrison's farewell address emphasized prosperity, the Philadelphia and Reading Railroad went bankrupt on February 23, 1893; by the end of the year it had been joined by the Erie, the Northern Pacific, the Union Pacific, and the Atchison, Topeka and Santa Fe. They were joined by no less than 500 banks and well over 15,000 other businesses. Unemployment first reached into the hundreds of thousands, and then, during the winter of 1893–94, probably exceeded 2,500,000—nearly a fifth of the work force. Though prices declined by ten per cent, wages suffered an even more precipitous drop. The demand for consumer goods fell by twenty-five per cent; industrial expansion was off by nearly sixty per cent. "The convulsion of 1893 left its victims dead-water," Henry Adams recalled. "While the country braced itself . . . the individual crawled as he best could, through the wreck, and found many values of life upset. . . . Much that had made life pleasant between 1870 and 1890 perished in the ruin."

Probable Causes of the Depression. Blame for the debacle was freely distributed. Conservatives indicted Populists and labor agitators for having undermined national confidence. Labor and farm radicals saw it as the culmination of capitalistic greed, and added the charge that free minting of silver would have averted the worst. Democrats blamed Republicans, who naturally blamed Democrats. Few bothered to note that an economy which had been nationalized would breed depression of national scope. The long farm depression had steadily sapped the resources of the agrarian consumer, thus driving much of the rural professional and business class into active Populist agitation. The centralization of banking power in New York made any instability in the banking system evident throughout the nation. Railroad bankruptcy forced contraction of steel purchases, and steel responded by reducing production. The intertwining of the domestic and international economies had been revealed in 1890 with the failure of the British investment house of Baring Brothers. European investors began a steady withdrawal of their assets from the American economy, selling well over $400,000,000 in American securities between 1890 and 1896.

Cleveland's Position. Cleveland traced everything to the nation's failure to maintain the gold standard rigidly. But still holding to the idea of minimal government interference in the economy, he reluctantly succumbed to Wall Street pressure and convened Congress in special session on August 7, 1893, asking it to repeal the Sherman Silver Purchase Act of 1890. Though the Democrats possessed healthy congressional majorities, they now split along sectional lines. Eastern Republicans joined Eastern Democrats to answer the charge of Republican and Democratic agrarians from the West and South that a financial conspiracy was sapping the heart of American democracy. After a bruising fight, Cleveland finally had his way, and on October 30, 1893, the Silver Act was repealed.

The Gold Standard. No one doubted that Cleveland had won a major victory. But his emphatic endorsement of repeal carried with it a heavy responsibility; if a return to the gold standard did not bring prosperity, he would be held personally responsible. In fact, the nation's gold reserves had declined steadily as banks pressed for Treasury redemption of government obligations in gold. By early January 1894, gold reserves in the Treasury totaled less than $62,000,000, well below the $100,000,000 thought necessary for minimal safety. Only urgent presidential pressure, and a conference of bankers in New York convoked by Secretary of the Treasury John G. Carlisle, enabled the government to sell a loan of $50,000,000 in ten-year gold bonds yielding five per cent interest. Cleveland's insistence on redeeming all government obligations in gold now enmeshed him in an open alliance with Eastern financiers. Outraged silverites, Populists, and other monetary radicals protested as the Treasury continued to float gold loans, only to have gold leave almost as fast as it was deposited. When Congress refused to allow Cleveland the power to negotiate short-term notes or to permit further contractions of the currency, and when, on February 8, 1895, the gold reserve slipped to $42,000,000, the administration entered into further bond sales. This time however, rather than sell the bonds publicly, Cleveland, under an old Civil War law, allowed J. P. Morgan and August Belmont to give the government cash and to receive bonds as payment. In the resulting transaction, which was justified by Morgan's argument that only a private syndicate could persuade Europeans to part with their gold, the Morgan syndicate made profits variously estimated as between $1,534,516 and $16,000,000, while the government obtained slightly more than $65,000,000 in gold.

The government's obvious dependence on private bankers to maintain its credit supplied the agrarian radicals with proof positive that their charges of government-banker collusion were valid. A former Nebraska congressman, swept out in the heavy defeat sustained by the Democrats in the off-year elections of 1894, concluded that the American people owed Cleveland the gratitude "which a passenger feels toward the trainman who has opened a switch and precipitated a wreck." William Jennings Bryan was already contemplating the election of 1896. As for Cleveland, he viewed his association with Morgan and Belmont "with satisfaction and self-congratulation," and deemed it an appropriate time to make money through judicious investments.

Cleveland: a Profile in Stubbornness. Grover Cleveland, stolid and stubborn, revealed a profound indifference to popularity. Economic catastrophe, he believed, had to solve itself through the natural workings of economic law. Sooner or later, prosperity would return. When the Pullman workers attempted to alleviate their difficulties with a strike, the President dispatched federal troops to Chicago—in spite of the vehement protests of Democratic Governor Peter Altgeld of Illinois, who insisted that the state authorities could maintain order, and the petitions of the mayors of Chicago and Detroit that Pullman negotiate with his workers. But as in the Homestead affair, management wanted only to destroy the unions, and the government stood ready to help. Cleveland defended the breaking of the strike with federal bayonets and the subsequent jailing of the strike leaders as the action of responsible authority "to restore obedience and law and to protect life and property." A Democratic President had shown himself no less reluctant than his Republican predecessors to use federal power in order to protect—or overprotect—private property. Once again, radical charges had been substantiated: there was no fundamental difference between the two major parties. Cleveland dug his heels in for a last ditch defense of the established order, but the tide of events was already lapping at his supports. When Cleveland left the White House, only his stubbornness was intact. His influence and his popularity were nonexistent.

The Election of 1894. The dissatisfaction with Cleveland the man carried over to the Democratic party. In 1894, the Republicans gained an overwhelming majority of 140 in the House of Representatives. The Democratic party was reduced, for all practical purposes, to its Southern contingent; in twenty-four Northern states, not a single Democrat was returned, and even the border states went Republican. Although the Populists added well over 400,000 votes to their 1892 totals, their political representation declined to a mere four senators and four representatives. But their votes suggested to the anti-Cleveland wing of the Democratic party that a shift to more radical stances on the currency and other issues might lure the Populists into the Democratic ranks. Such an accession of strength would secure for the Democrats majority political status.

The Wilson-Gorman Tariff. The decline of Cleveland's influence was manifest when the Wilson-Gorman Tariff, the fulfillment of his pledge to lower import duties, established rates only slightly lower than the McKinley Tariff. It set the seal on a second term which had proven an unrelieved record of failure. A slight recovery in late 1894 and early 1895 was followed by renewed unemployment and ever more acute signs of farm depression. The nadir of American confidence had been reached.

THE ELECTION OF 1896

Free Silver. By the time the conventions gathered in 1896, the Western and Southern crescendo in favor of free silver made it seem evident that the currency question would be the central issue of the campaign. On the Republican side Mark Hanna, determined to elect his protégé William McKinley to the presidency, assented to the inclusion in the Republican platform of a pledge to maintain the gold standard. In return he expected unquestioning support of his candidate, whose personal bias toward bi-metalism made orthodox Republicans uneasy. When Senator Henry M. Teller of Colorado proposed Republican endorsement of "the use of both gold and silver as an equal standard money," the convention overwhelmingly voted him down. Teller, three other senators, and twenty-two silver delegates withdrew from the gathering. The remainder of the Republican convention was listless and hollow. It adjourned with a ticket consisting of McKinley and Garret A. Hobart.

William Jennings Bryan. The Democrats gathered at Chicago in a state of seething—uncertain whom to nominate, but not in a pacific mood. The result was a fiery display in which the order of the day was "No compromise on the currency issue." The platform which emerged from the pen of Peter Altgeld was a savage indictment of Cleveland's administration. It denounced the unrelenting gold policy, bond deals, and "trafficking with bank syndicates," and "arbitrary interference by Federal authorities in local affairs." It demanded the implementation of effective power for the Interstate Commerce Commission, stricter enforcement of the Sherman Anti-Trust Act, establishment of a revenue tariff, and free coinage of silver. The Eastern Democrats who had the temerity to offer palliating amendments were savagely castigated; the repudiation of Cleveland extended to the Cleveland wing of the party. It was difficult to believe that the incumbent President was a member of the assembled party. As the debate grew ever more heated, the thirty-six-year-old William Jennings Bryan made his way to the rostrum, with a speech that he had been rehearsing for two years. His soaring tones, his angry challenge, his determination to make the forthcoming election a time of fundamental choice, made Bryan's speech a classic. He swept his audience along to roaring acclamation; and when he reached the defiant peroration, "You shall not press down upon the brow of labor the crown of thorns, you shall not crucify mankind upon a cross of gold," the convention had its candidate. Altgeld, who was precluded from the nomination by his German birth, thought it took "more than speeches to win real victories," but Bryan's very simplicity swept all before him. He was chosen on the fifth ballot, together with the silverite banker Arthur Sewall. Amid thunderous acclamation, the Democrats had repudiated their immediate past and had re-embraced their old commitment to agrarian democracy. To their more conservative members they seemed embarked on "revolution," trumpeting the rights of man over the rights of property. The "goldbug" Democrats retreated, and either pledged their support to McKinley, or settled for a schismatic National Democratic ticket consisting of Senator John M. Palmer of Illinois and General Simon B. Buckner.

The Populist Endorsement of Bryan. The Populists awoke to the realization that the Democrats had usurped their program. When they assembled at St. Louis, it was a foregone conclusion that a fusion ticket would be supported in which Bryan would run, but with Thomas E. Watson, a Georgia Populist, as his running mate. In the campaign that followed, the Democrats invoked straight-out, old-fashioned Jacksonian democracy, with a strong flavor of evangelical Christianity. While McKinley remained at home in Canton, Ohio, receiving delegations on his front porch, Bryan traveled 18,000 miles in twenty-one states, made well over 600 speeches, and addressed a probable total of 5,000,000 people. His energy, supplemented by a campaign fund of $300,000, was the sum of the Democratic campaign. Unshakably convinced of his own rightness, he hardly noticed the vast flood of denunciation that followed him, financed by a Republican campaign fund that totaled at least $3,500,000 and was perhaps as high as $16,000,000.

McKinley's Election. In the East and in the industrial Middle West, the Hanna campaign took effect. From far-off Europe, Henry Adams "went home in October, with every one else, to elect McKinley President and to start the world anew." A coalition consisting of workers, the middle class, men of wealth, and those farmers who were in fact rural businessmen—all apathetic or hostile toward Bryan's vision of an agrarian paradise lost—swept McKinley into office. Until October the matter was still in doubt, but a rise in farm prices seems to have swung doubtful farm states into the Republican column. When the results were counted, McKinley had polled 7,104,779 votes to Bryan's 6,502,925. Even in defeat, Bryan had polled more votes than any victorious candidate before McKinley. As one awed Eastern society matron observed, he had swept the South and most of the West despite the combined opposition of "all the banks, all the trusts, all the syndicates, all the corporations, all the great papers." In defeat, moreover, he had provided an agrarian America, well beyond its zenith, with a troubador. His soaring voice would be that of the Democratic party for nearly two decades. Even his enemies could not help but marvel at his achievement. As Henry Cabot Lodge's wife mused when the election was over:

> The great fight is won . . . a fight conducted by trained and experienced and organized forces, with both hands full of money, with the power of the press—and of prestige—on one side; on the other, a disorganized mob, at first out of which burst into sight, hearing, and force—one man, but such a man! Alone, penniless, without backing, without money, with scarce a paper, without speakers, that man fought such a fight that even those in the East can call him a Crusader, an inspired fanatic—a prophet!

Part Three

THE PROGRESSIVE REPUBLIC

Chapter 8

The Imperial Experiment

The election of 1896 had been fought on domestic issues; the four years that followed were overwhelmingly occupied with foreign affairs. When McKinley and Bryan met again in the election of 1900, the major issue was no longer silver; it had become the question of imperialism.

When, in 1898, the Spanish-American War erupted, and with it the great outward movement of American hegemony, it came as a culmination rather than as a beginning. The extension of America's domain into the western Pacific and the islands of the Caribbean precipitated a great debate on the nature of American power. Was it to influence world politics by setting an example which would rouse in other races the desire for, and the determination to secure, self-government? Or was it to assume the responsibility of instructing peoples who were not yet equipped for self-government in its subtle art? In the course of the debate that followed, certain fundamental premises of American foreign policy in the twentieth century were laid down. The major interest of the United States branched out to include the Caribbean islands and Central America. A vigorous assertion of the interdependence of the Anglo-Saxon peoples reflected the growing confidence of Americans that they were destined to supersede Great Britain as the world's dominant power. The decision to annex the Philippines made the United States an oriental power, and in the subsequent Anglo-American efforts to stabilize Far Eastern affairs led to the formulation of the Open Door policy in China. This put the United States on record as being vigorously opposed to the domination of China—and the vast Chinese market—by any one power. Without quite realizing it, the United States had abandoned her isolation, and had projected her power thousands of miles beyond American shores.

AMERICA AND THE PACIFIC

The United States became a Pacific power in the 1840s. The restless energy that had sent Americans journeying westward now propelled them to establish American dominance in the Pacific. Gradually they came to assume that the Pacific Ocean was the American Mediterranean. From 1883 on, Congress steadily authorized the construction of steel warships, and made the United States a major naval power. It was argued by some that American principles condoned expansion only into territories contiguous to the United States; Senator Albert J. Beveridge of Indiana replied in 1898 that the American Navy would provide the connecting link. As American trade overseas approached nearly $2 billion in 1898, it was widely assumed that (in the words of one congressman) "like England, we will establish trading posts throughout the world, we will cover the oceans with our merchant marine, we will build a navy to the measure of our greatness. . . ." The foundations for this expansion of trade—especially coaling bases—were widely established between 1867 and 1897.

International Interests in Samoa. In 1867 the Navy occupied Midway Island, supposedly to obtain a coaling station; but efforts to dredge a harbor proved too costly. Under Grant, an abortive attempt was made to establish a protectorate over the Samoan island of Tutuila in order to secure exclusive rights in Pago Pago harbor. In 1878 a Samoan delegation petitioned at Washington for an American protectorate, but settled finally for a friendship treaty. Under this, the United States agreed to negotiate any difficulties which might arise between Samoa and outside powers in return for a coaling station at Pago Pago. When Germany decided in 1884 to extend her domination to Samoa, a crisis was precipitated which negotiations at Washington in 1887 failed to resolve. A fortuitous typhoon in March 1889 destroyed the American and German cruisers converging on Samoa to defend their respective claims. Three months later, on June 14, 1889, Britain, Germany, and the United States agreed in the Treaty of Berlin to establish a three-power condominium which left the façade of power to the Samoans while granting effective authority to the three signatories.

American Interest in Hawaii. As early as 1854, under President

Pierce, there was agitation to annex Hawaii. In 1867, Secretary of State Seward expressed the feeling that annexation with the consent of the islands' inhabitants would be preferable to close commercial ties. The feeling grew in governmental circles that economic union ought to have as its complement political union. Efforts to achieve a reciprocal trade agreement were renewed successfully in 1875, after Hawaiian sugar planters had threatened to switch their affections and trade to Great Britain. The results of the Hawaiian-American agreement proved more advantageous to the Hawaiians than to the United States Treasury, but the political advantages persuaded Washington to accept the loss. The treaty came up for renewal in 1884, but the United States Senate withheld approval until 1887, when an amendment was included granting the United States a coaling and naval base at Pearl Harbor.

Domestic Politics in Hawaii. By 1890 the islands' economic dependence on the United States was absolute. Its sugar crop had expanded tenfold under the stimulus of the trade agreement. The McKinley Tariff of 1890, however, granted a bounty to American sugar growers while putting the Hawaiian product on the same basis as foreign sugar. A growing political crisis within the islands now erupted. In 1887, the white families who dominated the Hawaiian economy and owned more than two-thirds of all Hawaiian real estate had succeeded in overthrowing the corrupt rule of King Kalakaua. A new constitution was established which made the king a figurehead and gave effective power to the legislature. The legislature, needless to say, was elected on a restricted franchise of the propertied classes. As the McKinley Tariff depressed the Hawaiian economy, the native Hawaiians made their discontent at the white usurpation of power increasingly obvious. When Queen Liliuokalani came to the throne in 1891 she seemed intent upon revoking the 1887 "reforms." Determined to regain their advantageous position in the American sugar market and to retain their political dominance, the white element decided to depose the queen and to ask for the annexation of Hawaii to the United States.

The Annexation of Hawaii. Hawaiian hopes for annexation were raised by encouragement from congressmen and members of Harrison's cabinet. On January 16, 1893, John L. Stevens, the pro-annexation American minister to Honolulu, landed armed sailors from an American warship—ostensibly to protect American property in the city. The annexationists now formed a committee of public safety and demanded the queen's abdication; Liliuokalani, faced not only with American hostility but with American guns, capitulated under protest. "The Hawaiian pear is now fully ripe," Stevens notified the State Department, "and this is the golden hour for the United States to pluck it." The Harrison administration indicated that it was fully prepared to incorporate the Hawaiian Islands as "an integral part of the territory of the United States." The annexation treaty reached the Senate just as Cleveland re-entered the White House for his second term. Uneasy at the circumstances surrounding the treaty, he withdrew it for further study, implying that he agreed with the doubts of Secretary of State Walter Gresham, who wondered whether "a great wrong done to a feeble but independent State by an abuse of the authority of the United States" should not "be undone by restoring the legitimate government?"

When the Blount investigation of the events surrounding Liliuokalani's deposal concluded that it was due to unwarranted American intervention, Cleveland dispatched Albert S. Willis as new Minister to Honolulu with instructions to restore the queen. But Sanford B. Dole, the Hawaiian president, refused to surrender his authority to anything short of American armed force. Cleveland had been checked. When the heavy imposts on Hawaiian sugar were lifted in 1894, the Hawaiian government pressed anew for annexation, its urgency sharpened by evidence that the Japanese were becoming increasingly interested in the islands. They unleashed a flood of propaganda describing the strategic implication of the islands for American aspirations in the Pacific, but were still unable to obtain ratification of an annexation treaty. In 1898, the annexationists in Congress turned to the device of a joint resolution, which required not a two-thirds vote but a simple majority. On July 7, 1898, when the nation was stirred by reports of Admiral Dewey's great victory at Manila Bay, President McKinley signed the joint resolution. Hawaii was a United States territory; sixty-one years later, she would achieve statehood.

AMERICA AND THE CARIBBEAN

The Expansionist View. The anti-expansion views of Cleveland extended to the Caribbean, where the hallowed premises of the Monroe Doctrine were understood to prevail; but unlike the expansionists, who read their own ambitions into the Doctrine, Cleveland insisted that it condoned no more than the maintenance of the status quo, with the strict nonintervention of European powers. "The mission of our nation is to build up and make a greater country out of what we have," Cleveland declared, "instead of annexing islands." Ironically, his stubborn anti-imperialism led him to take a stand in 1894 that almost precipitated war between the United States and Britain. He was willing to condone a unilateral assertion of American pre-eminence in the Caribbean that gained the almost universal approbation of American expansionists. "Today the United States is practically sovereign on this continent and its fiat is law upon the subjects to which it confines its interposition," Secretary of State Richard Olney had asserted. This overweening power was founded on "its infinite resources combined with its isolated position" which rendered the United States "practically invulnerable against any or all other powers."

Cleveland and Venezuela. The crisis that had led to this unique definition of American power in the Western Hemisphere grew out of a simmering territorial dispute between Great Britain and Venezuela over British Guiana's boundary with the latter nation. The discovery of gold in the interior of Guiana revived the dispute. Venezuela proposed arbitration, but the British insisted on discussing only the territories west of a line drawn in 1840 by Sir Robert Schomburgk. Relations between the two countries had been broken off in 1887, and, in response to Venezuelan pleas, the American State Department pressed the British government to accept arbitration. The appearance in 1894 of a pamphlet written by William L. Scruggs, a paid agent of the Venezuelan government, entitled *British Aggressions in Venezuela, or the Monroe Doctrine on Trial,* served to stir popular interest.

Early in 1895 a resolution calling for arbitration passed Congress. Under political and public pressure, Secretary of State Gresham began to prepare a diplomatic note, but his death in May put Olney in the State Department. The note which Olney prepared, and which was turned over to the British government, bristled with threats, and discussed the imaginary danger of the European powers dividing up South America as they had Africa; it concluded with the demand that the British reply to the call for arbitration in time for the President to submit the matter to Congress when it convened in December. The British Foreign Minister, Lord Salisbury, replied:

> The Government of the United States is not entitled to affirm as a universal proposition, with reference to a number of independent states for whose conduct it assumes no responsibility, that its interests are necessarily concerned in whatever may befall those states simply because they are situated in the Western Hemisphere.

Cleveland and his bellicose Secretary of State promptly went to work preparing a message to Congress which called for the establishment of a presidential commission to draw a boundary between Guiana and Venezuela. "When such report is made and accepted [by Venezuela],"

Cleveland concluded, "it will be the duty of the United States to resist by every means in its power, as a willful aggression upon its rights and interests, the appropriation by Great Britain of any lands . . . which . . . we have determined of right belongs to Venezuela." Despite the vigorous denunciation of Britain, Cleveland took care to note in his message that it would be "a grievous thing to contemplate the two great English-speaking peoples . . . as being otherwise than friendly."

The Threat of War. An upsurge of jingoistic patriotism found congressmen declaring that war would be a good thing; Civil War veterans volunteered their services; Theodore Roosevelt announced that the "country needs a war" and contemplated the conquest of Canada. Saner voices agreed with Joseph Pulitzer that a war between the United States and Great Britain would be "a colossal crime." The already serious economic crisis worsened as fear of war sent stock values plummeting by more than a half billion dollars. In Britain, the people, who hardly knew where Guiana *was,* and the vast majority of the ruling class, decided against war. The British government was increasingly preoccupied with its growing difficulties in South Africa, and had small desire to add an American war to them. The dispute was submitted to arbitration, and on October 3, 1899, a five-man commission settled the boundary—largely in Britain's favor. A more lasting result of the Venezuelan affair was the tacit agreement between the United States and Britain, despite the Senate's refusal to confirm a formal arbitration treaty, to settle future disputes through negotiation. "There is a patriotism of race as well as of country," Olney concluded, "and the Anglo-American is as little likely to be indifferent to the one as to the other." He expected that in the future the two countries "would be found standing together against any alien foe by whom either was menaced by destruction or irreparable calamity."

The Conflict within Cuba. Agitation for the annexation of Cuba had dwindled after the 1850s, but Americans retained their concern for the "Pearl of the Antilles." Few Americans doubted that Spanish authority was intolerable, and that Cuban efforts to overthrow it should be assisted, at least indirectly. During the Ten Years' War that afflicted the island between 1868 and 1878, many calls were issued for direct American action. Although the Spaniards mitigated one of the worst Cuban grievances when they abolished slavery in 1878, they did little else thereafter but collect heavy taxes which were chiefly used to reward Spanish officials and to service the war debt contracted during the ten-year upheaval. Trade stagnated, and Cuba, potentially so rich, lived on the edge of the barest poverty. American restrictions on imports sharpened economic want on the island. Finally, in February 1895, a republican government was established in Oriente province and a rebellion launched against Spain.

The United States provided sanctuary for Cuban refugees, who established a *junta* in New York and distributed propaganda and raised money to buy arms and supplies for the rebels. Soon, the brutal war raging in Cuba caught the attention of the yellow press. William Randolph Hearst and Joseph Pulitzer filled the columns of their newspapers with vivid and frequently exaggerated reports of Cuban atrocities. Millions of Americans now received a daily dose of irresponsible journalism concerning the Cuban plight.

Particularly offensive to Americans were the actions of the Spanish captain-general, Valeriano "Butcher" Weyler, and his 120,000 man army. To break the back of Cuban resistance, Weyler had decided on the "reconcentrado" policy, which meant that Cuban civilians were rounded up in the countryside and herded into urban camps where they were kept under armed guard. The resulting collapse of agriculture, assisted by the Cuban rebels' decision to lay waste to cane fields and sugar factories, led to wholesale famine and the death from starvation and disease of thousands of Cuban civilians.

American Involvement in Cuba. The rebellion proved costly to American investors who had put nearly $50,000,000 into Cuban sugar, tobacco, and mines. Sugar exports were reduced to a fifth of their normal flow, and exports on the whole declined by seventy-five per cent. It was hardly surprising that Americans with an economic stake in the island wanted their government to intervene and to settle the dispute by expelling the Spaniards. Self-interest was complemented by a genuine humanitarian impulse; "a pure spiritual Christianity," observed one senator, demanded that the United States "stand by the weak and defend the helpless, and advance the banner of mercy and justice over the world."

Cleveland did warn the Spaniards that if they continued their savagery the United States would be forced to intervene to halt "senseless slaughter"; but he insisted upon following a pacific course, and even threatened not to mobilize the Army if Congress did declare war. The business community, which was regaining its confidence after the prolonged depression, generally pooh-poohed war agitation, or regarded it as monstrously unthinkable. At the outset of his administration McKinley seemed no less set upon keeping the peace. Protest and indignation, plus indirect aid, seemed to represent the limits of American willingness to press the Cuban cause.

Businessmen were as determined to keep the peace under McKinley as they had been under Cleveland—a feeling shared by the influential Mark Hanna and accurately manifested by the President himself. Surrounded by businessmen, the gentle McKinley did not respond to the bellicose urgings of Theodore Roosevelt, Henry Cabot Lodge, Captain A. T. Mahan, Whitelaw Reid, and Albert Shaw, all of whom saw in Cuba a stage on which the true scope of American power could be revealed to the world. Whether the forces pressing for war could have

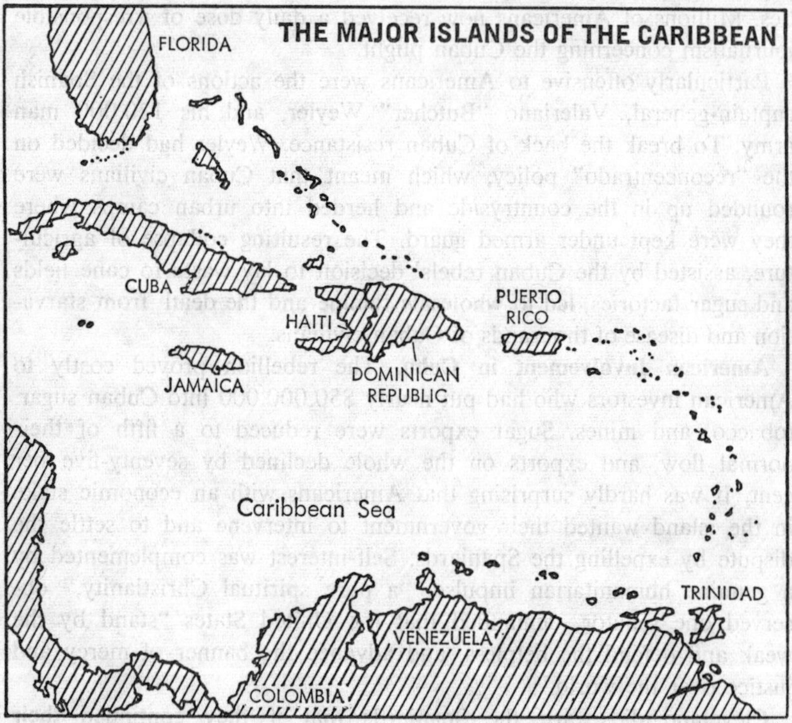

succeeded against the opposition of business and the President is questionable. But other events were to resolve the issue.

The Sinking of the Maine. On February 9, 1898, Hearst published a letter of Dupuy de Lôme, the Spanish minister, in which he described McKinley as "weak and a bidder for the admiration of the crowd." In the resulting storm, de Lôme resigned and the Spanish government apologized. Six days later the American battleship *Maine*, which had been dispatched to Havana in January to protect American citizens, mysteriously blew up at anchor with the loss of 250 men. The Spaniards, hastening to conciliate American opinion, agreed to allow an American court of inquiry to inspect the sunken craft. The court decided that a mine had caused the explosion, though there was no evidence that the Spaniards were responsible for its use; it was equally logical to assume that the Cuban rebels had blown up the battleship in order to bring about American intervention. Whoever was responsible, the drums of war beat louder as a result. Lodge raged that "this gigantic murder, the last spasm of a corrupt and dying society . . . cries aloud for justice."

Public doubt about Spanish atrocities was dispelled when Senator Redfield Proctor of Vermont reported to the Senate in March 1898 on his recent visit to Cuba. He graphically described the condition of the island and estimated that no less than 200,000 Cubans had died in reconcentrado camps. McKinley, still seeking to keep the peace, instructed the American minister at Madrid to press the Spaniards for an armistice until October 1, and a revocation of the reconcentrado order. The next day, March 28, McKinley let Madrid know that he felt Cuban independence would be the logical outcome of such an armistice. The Spanish government conceded both demands, but Congress, responding to popular outcry, still pressed the President for intervention in Cuba, threatening to pass a war resolution in the absence of definite presidential action on the matter. McKinley buckled, and asked, on April 11, for Congress to act "in the name of humanity" to stop the war in Cuba. Nine days later, the United States went to war with Spain.

THE SPANISH-AMERICAN WAR

Attitudes toward the War. America's excursion into belligerency was to last but three months. From the outset, despite general European antagonism toward the United States, few doubted that the Americans would emerge victorious. A demoralized Spain lacked the will to fight, and Great Britain made it obvious that she fully supported the American cause. "Unless all signs deceive," a British commentator observed, "the American Republic breaks from the old moorings, and sails out to be a 'world power.'" Rudyard Kipling wrote a poem welcoming the United States' decision to share the "white man's burden." At home, Senator Teller appended to the war resolution an amendment which pledged that "the United States . . . disclaims any disposition or intention to exercise sovereignty, jurisdiction, or control over [Cuba]." Thus the war began as a noble effort to secure Cuban independence; it would end, as the British suspected, in a scramble for conquest and empire.

The Invasion of Cuba. A fleet under Commodore William T. Sampson set about blockading the coast of Cuba. For a time, Americans were terrified by reports that a Spanish fleet under Admiral Cervera was on its way to bombard American coastal cities; but the fleet merely passed unchallenged through the blockade and anchored in the harbor of Santiago de Cuba. A large expeditionary force was now assembled at Tampa amid utter chaos, while the bulky General William R. Shafter struggled to establish order. Against a more skillful enemy, the confusion at Tampa might have ended disastrously, but in mid-June Shafter finally got his 18,000 man force afloat, and it was landed without incident at Daiquiri and Siboney. A steady advance, despite heavy losses, brought the Americans to San Juan Hill, overlooking Santiago. In a memorable charge, Theodore Roosevelt and his Rough Riders won the heights. The militant Theodore informed his friend Lodge that he was having "the time of my life." He described the affair at Santiago as "a bully fight," and decided that "the charge itself was great fun." When Roosevelt later wrote of the affair in *The Rough Riders,* Mr. Dooley, the mythical observer of public events created by Finley Peter Dunne, humorist and journalist, was moved to note that Roosevelt's memoir really should have been entitled *Alone in Cuba.*

The Invasion of Manila. The Spanish-American War was being fought, ostensibly, solely to free Cuba from tyrannical Spanish control. Imperialist appetites, however, added as "incidental" to the war the "liberation" of Spain's other colonies in the Western Hemisphere. In the Caribbean, Puerto Rico fell victim to American occupation with virtually no resistance whatsoever. In the Pacific, a little more effort was required. On May 1, Commodore George Dewey sailed into Manila harbor in the Philippines, sank the Spanish fleet, and dropped anchor. Americans, not quite certain where the Philippines were, nevertheless greeted the victory with exuberant hysteria. The Germans, who had hopes of gaining the archipelago, dispatched a fleet to the bay to buttress their claims, and managed to provoke Dewey into threatening war with Germany. When the British squadron in the bay proved conspicuously friendly to the Americans, suggesting that the Anglo-Saxon powers had their own understanding, the German fleet ceased its aggressive gestures. The fall of Manila on August 13, 1898, set the United States among the imperial powers.

The Spanish Surrender. On July 3, the six ships of Cervera's fleet emerged from the blockaded harbor. In the resulting battle Admiral Sampson destroyed the Spanish fleet at the cost of one American life; the next day, the American public was notified that "the fleet under Sampson's command offers the nation as a Fourth of July present the whole of Cervera's fleet." The destruction of the Spanish fleet was tantamount to Spain's striking her flag in the New World. Further fighting proved unnecessary when Spanish forces capitulated in Cuba on July 16. Nine days later an army under General Nelson A. Miles occupied Puerto Rico. The troops who had escaped bullets now fell victim to dysentery and the dreaded yellow fever. On August 12 a peace protocol was signed, and the "splendid little war" was at an end.

THE PROBLEM OF THE PHILIPPINES

America's Choice of Roles. Even as the war drew to its swift conclusion, Americans were debating the disposition of the Spanish Empire. They had extended their power into the Orient and the Caribbean; now they were obliged to decide whether they had come to liberate subject peoples or to replace the frayed power of Spain. For the out-and-out imperialist, the time had come (as a popular journal expressed it) for America to "welcome the golden dawn of the republic's full-grown manhood." For the anti-imperialist, whose most articulate spokesman was William Jennings Bryan, the issue was simply whether America would remain true to "the self-evident propositions that all men are created equal; that they are endowed by their Creator with inalienable rights; that governments are instituted among men to secure these rights; and that governments derive their just powers from the consent of the governed." Moderate imperialists insisted that the United States was morally obliged to "lead" less fortunate peoples to self-government. A great debate raged which converted the election of 1900 into a national referendum and ended with the creation of an American Empire.

Aguinaldo and the Native Revolt. At the heart of the debate was the future of the Philippines. These islands were located nearly 7,000 miles southwest of America's Pacific coast. Unlike territories previously occupied by the United States, the Philippines had a native population of several millions, ground down in virtual slavery by a system which permitted a few thousand Spaniards to treat the islands as a single huge plantation. When Dewey destroyed the Spanish fleet, the natives had already been in general rebellion for two years under their leader Emilio Aguinaldo, waging a guerrilla campaign similar to that of the rebels in Cuba. The savagery of the Spaniards' retaliation was summed up in the decree of a Spanish governor: "For the traitors no punishment seems . . . adequate and commensurate with the magnitude of the crime they committed against their king and country."

By February 1898, the American consul in Manila could report: "Conditions here and in Cuba are practically alike." When war began between Spain and the United States, Aguinaldo agreed to assist the Americans, having been assured that Philippine independence would follow. Though Spain tried desperately to retain her authority over the islands, the fall of Manila on August 13 settled the issue. The question now was whether an American or a Filipino government would assume control. It was a question fraught with danger, since American forces had effective control only over Manila and the Cavite naval base, while Filipino guerrillas dominated the hinterland. The ultimate outcome was a deadly war which cost the lives of at least 4,234 Americans and probably 220,000 Filipinos.

McKinley's Capitulation. The debate over imperialism would have ended early had McKinley not capitulated to the demands of the imperialists. From the outset of the war with Spain, he treated the conflict as a divine mission. "The faith of a Christian nation recognizes the hand of Almighty God in the ordeal through which we have passed," he notified the nation at war's end. "Divine favor seemed manifest everywhere. In fighting for humanity's sake we have been signally blessed." In early May the government decided to send an American expeditionary force of 15,000 to Manila. An upsurge of annexationist sentiment now pushed the administration along a path which left little doubt that the United States meant to absorb the Philippines. The occupation of Guam in June confirmed the imperialist expectations. Growing evidence that the Democrats, under the lead of Bryan, intended to oppose territorial expansion only strengthened the Republican insistence that Spain cede the whole of her empire to American control. McKinley's final surrender to these demands was preceded by much thought and a bout of hard prayer. Divine grace was at last vouchsafed him and, as he recalled the matter later, the answer came that "there was nothing left for us to do but to take them all, and to educate the Filipinos, and uplift and civilize and Christianize them, and by God's grace do the very best we could by them as our fellow-men for whom Christ also died." Under the Treaty of Paris, signed on December 10, 1898, Spain agreed to relinquish her authority over Cuba, ceded Puerto Rico and Guam to the United States, and surrendered the Philippines in return for the sum of $20,000,000.

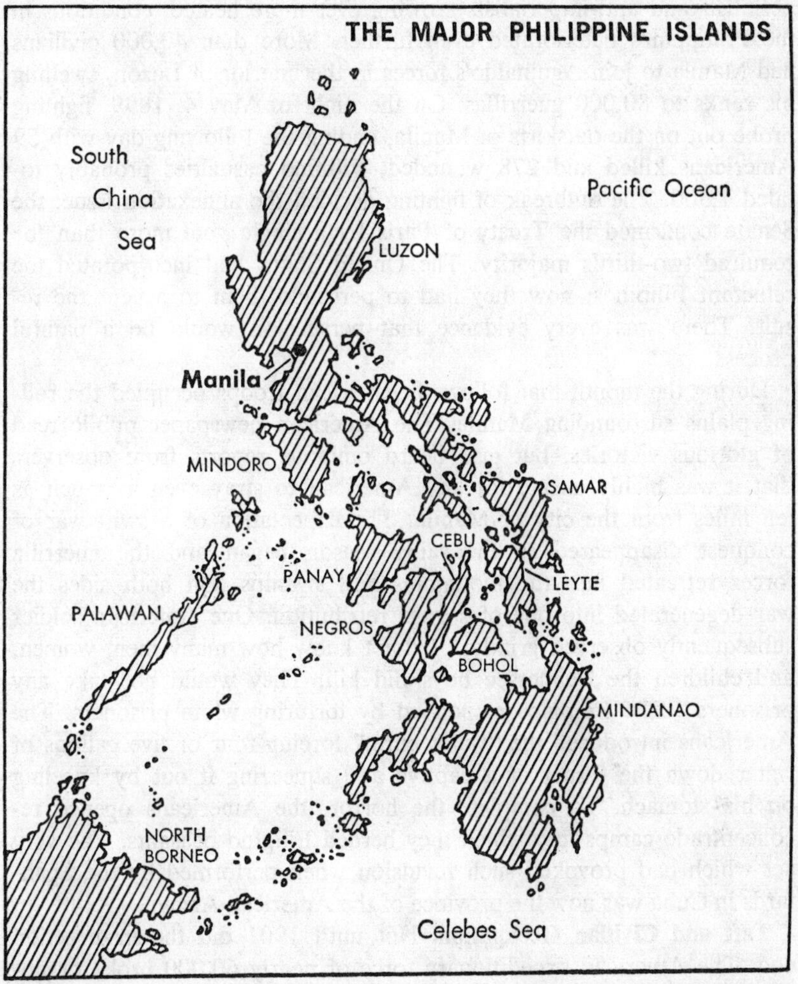

Military Occupation of the Philippines. Relations between the Filipinos under Aguinaldo and the American occupation forces swiftly deteriorated. As the American forces expanded to more than 22,000, little doubt remained that they would be used against the Filipino forces. As early as September 8, 1898, General Elwell S. Otis, the American commander, bluntly warned Aguinaldo that the Americans would use force to expel his men from the suburbs of Manila. There remained one last hope for averting conflict: the Senate might refuse to ratify the Treaty of Paris. As the Senate debated, with both imperialists and anti-imperialists growing ever more heated, conditions in the Philippines deteriorated even further. More than 40,000 civilians fled Manila to join Aguinaldo's forces in the interior of Luzon, swelling his ranks to 80,000 guerrillas. On the night of May 4, 1899, fighting broke out on the outskirts of Manila, ending the following day with 59 Americans killed and 278 wounded; Filipino casualties probably totaled 1,500. The outbreak of fighting decided the annexation issue: the Senate confirmed the Treaty of Paris by a single vote more than the required two-thirds majority. The United States had incorporated the reluctant Filipinos; now they had to persuade them to accept the result. There was every evidence that persuasion would be a painful process.

During the month that followed, American troops occupied the rolling plains surrounding Manila. The American newspaper public read of glorious victories, but also heard ominous reports from observers that it was highly unsafe for any American to stray even as much as ten miles from the city of Manila. The expectation of a swift war of conquest disappeared as the rainy season began and the guerrilla forces retreated into the mountains and swamps. On both sides the war degenerated into one of savage retribution. One American soldier subsequently observed grimly: "I don't know how many men, women, and children the Tennessee boys did kill. They would not take any prisoners." The Filipinos responded by torturing white prisoners. The Americans introduced the "water cure," forcing four or five gallons of water down the throat of a captive and squeezing it out by kneeling on his stomach. To complete the horror, the Americans opened reconcentrado camps into which they herded Filipino peasants. The very act which had provoked such revulsion when performed by the Spaniards in Cuba was now the province of the American Army.

Taft and Civilian Occupation. Not until 1901 did the insurrection end. The American expeditionary force of nearly 60,000 broke organized resistance by the end of 1899, but for two years more a murderous, secret, and silent war raged. Most Americans remained sublimely ignorant of these events. McKinley, who could not allow himself to remain ignorant of them, began to doubt the wisdom of his decision to take the islands. But he sent William Howard Taft to the islands in April 1900 to seek a settlement, recognizing no alternative but to accept the fact that "We've got them." Taft carried with him a program drawn up by Elihu Root which granted the Filipinos limited self-government, most of the Bill of Rights—with the exception of trial by jury and (revealingly) the right to bear arms—and a promise of land redistribution. Under Taft, civil authority replaced the military power except in the actual conduct of the war.

Implications of the Election of 1900. As the Americans strove to establish their authority, the guerrilla conflict reached bloodier heights. Some Americans, mostly Republicans, charged that Aguinaldo hoped to aid the cause of Bryan in his second campaign against McKinley. Since Bryan campaigned vigorously on an anti-imperialist platform, while the Republican nomination of Theodore Roosevelt for Vice-President seemed to re-emphasize their endorsement of imperial expansion, it seemed plausible to assume that a Bryan victory would mark America's repudiation of empire. But such reasoning overlooked two factors: first, prosperity had returned under McKinley and the Republicans had as one of their slogans "The Full Dinner Pail"; and second, most Americans knew little of what was happening in their distant possessions. When the votes were counted, McKinley had won a popular majority of nearly 900,000 and had increased his electoral vote to 292 as opposed to Bryan's 155. The new Vice-President made the future of the Philippines crystal clear when he noted that to grant them freedom under Aguinaldo "would be like granting self-government to an Apache reservation under some local chief." The death of McKinley from an assassin's bullet in September 1901 made Theodore Roosevelt President, and eliminated the last chance that the United States would relinquish its hold on the islands.

The End of Insurrection. Meanwhile, the American Army was carrying on a campaign of terror which involved the execution of a Filipino prisoner for every American killed, the burning of Filipino homes whenever telegraph lines were cut, the killing of domestic animals and the destruction of crops, and the summary execution of any native suspected of aiding the guerrillas. Such tactics finally broke the rebellion. The capture of Aguinaldo in March of 1901, and the subsequent capture of his chief lieutenant Malvar, in April 1902, marked the end. On July 4, 1902, President Roosevelt officially declared that the insurrection was at an end. Amnesty was offered to all Filipinos who would take an oath of allegiance to the United States, and civil government was established. Violence occasionally erupted thereafter, but America had achieved her primary goal: domination of the Philippines. The great American writer Mark Twain suggested a final touch:

> And as for a flag for the Philippine Province, it is easily managed. . . . We can just have our usual flag, with the white stripes painted black and the stars replaced by the skull and crossbones.

The American nation had traveled a long road since "Christian duty" had directed McKinley to take the Philippines.

THE POLICY OF EMPIRE

Hawaii, Puerto Rico, and Guam. The far-flung accessions of territory under McKinley made it necessary for the United States to set up colonial governments. In the case of Hawaii, the problem was swiftly solved with the passage of the Organic Act of 1900, which incorporated the territory and granted its residents self-government and the full rights of American citizenship. Under the Foraker Act, Puerto Rico was made an unincorporated territory with an elected legislature and an appointed governor and executive council. The Navy Department administered Guam directly. But in the cases of Cuba and the Philippines, policy followed an uncertain course.

Cuba. The Teller Amendment had committed the United States to the establishment of Cuban freedom. Though McKinley assumed "ties of singular intimacy" between the two countries, he meant to grant the island speedy independence. The army of occupation promptly went to work instituting administrative reform, establishing an effective judiciary, and organizing new educational, health, and public works programs. Under General Leonard Wood, major medical advances were made. Major William C. Gorgas instituted sanitation campaigns that nearly eradicated dysentery, typhoid, and malaria. A Cuban physician, Dr. Carlos J. Finley, had concluded that yellow fever was caused by the Stegomyia mosquito; when an Army medical commission established the correctness of this view, Gorgas swiftly eliminated the disease by extensive drainage programs and control programs. To complement these positive reforms, Secretary of War Elihu Root set to work making Cuba free. His ideas, which emphasized the need to establish intimate ties between the United States and an independent Cuba, were made into law in an amendment to the 1901 Army Appropriation Bill proposed by Senator Orville Platt of Connecticut. The Platt amendment gave the United States the power to intervene in Cuban affairs when the Cuban government proved unable to protect life, liberty, and property, and also secured American naval bases on the island. Despite a strong opposition, which charged that the Platt amendment made Cuba a protectorate, a Cuban constitutional convention decided, on June 12, 1901, to incorporate these two provisions into the Cuban constitution, a point that was further confirmed in the

Cuban-American treaty of May 22, 1903. By the end of 1902, most American forces had been withdrawn from the island.

The Philippines. The Philippines, wracked by revolt, presented a peculiar problem. As early as December 1899, Jacob G. Schurman headed a commission that recommended territorial status for the islands with civilian rather than military government. In March 1901, Congress, in a further amendment to the Army Appropriation Bill, assumed all military, civil, and judicial jurisdiction of the islands. It provided for the election of an assembly to serve as the lower house of the Filipino legislature—a commission appointed by the American government would serve as the upper chamber—the appointment of a civil governor with large executive powers, and the creation of a native civil service. In July 1902 the Philippine Organic Act confirmed these innovations, establishing a bicameral legislature, an appointed governor, and two Philippine commissioners resident in Washington. The act made the islands an unincorporated territory, and William Howard Taft took up residence in Manila as the first governor. In the ensuing forty-five years, the scope of Philippine independence was steadily broadened.

THE PROBLEM OF THE ORIENT

The Open Door. In August 1899 Secretary of State John Hay asked the State Department adviser on Far Eastern Affairs, William Rockhill, to submit his thoughts on American policy toward China. From this request emerged the "Open Door" policy whose primary purpose was to protect America's already large trade interests in China.

In the later nineteenth century, the disintegration of the authority of the Manchu dynasty threatened the division of the huge Chinese Empire into foreign spheres of influence, and precipitated a scramble for special concessions. The Germans extended their control of the Shantung peninsula; Russia ominously expanded into Manchuria and was challenged by the Japanese, who were already encamped in Korea and Formosa; the British, dominating southern China from Hong Kong, penetrated ever deeper into the Yangtze valley. The Americans feared that they would either be compelled to surrender their trade interests or to start carving out their own sphere of influence. Among commercial circles the strongest argument in favor of the occupation of the Philippines was its strategic relationship to the China mainland. The British, who were unwilling to face alone a possible coalition of Russian and German expansion, also pressed the United States to join with them in support of an Open Door policy. This would give all nations equal access to the Chinese market and would tacitly commit the participants to preserve an independent Chinese government.

Though at first reluctant to commit itself, the McKinley administration found growing domestic support for joint action by Britain and America to maintain "free and equal commercial relations for all time in the Orient." Rockhill himself was profoundly influenced by Alfred Hippisley, an Englishman employed by the Chinese Imperial Maritime Customs Service, whose primary concern was to maintain Chinese independence in the face of threatened partition. At his urging, Rockhill pressed for the United States to take the lead in promoting the Open Door. It was proposed that the United States ask all nations trading with China to declare themselves in favor of commercial equality, though respecting established spheres of influence. The right of China to collect all customs duties under the established treaty tariff would be maintained. Secretary Hay, who had originally favored cooperation with Great Britain, came to view the Open Door as an excellent opening for giving substance to the unofficial British-American understanding.

The International Agreement. On September 6, 1899, Hay forwarded a circular letter to Great Britain, Germany, and Russia setting forth the Rockhill-Hippisley proposals; in November they were sent to France, Italy, and Japan. By early January, all governments except the Russian had replied that they were ready to accept the principles of the Hay note. The Russians equivocated; their note from St. Petersburg declared that "the Imperial Government has no intention whatever of claiming any privilege for its own subjects to the exclusion of other foreigners," but seemed to insist on maintaining a Russian sphere of influence in China. Hay, acting with deft aplomb, merely announced on March 20, 1900, that all the replies were satisfactory, and that the United States considered the acceptance binding on the six powers. The Russians had been outmaneuvered.

The Boxer Rebellion. The United States had sought only to freeze the status quo; but some Chinese—nationalists inflamed by western incursions—wanted to expel all foreigners. When the Emperor attempted to institute a program of western reform, the Dowager Empress Tzu Hsi, allied with a secret society known to westerners as "Boxers," seized power and attempted to expel the "foreign devils." In the resulting upheaval, the western diplomatic colony in Peking was besieged, as were other foreigners resident in the city. During the summer of 1900 they maintained a tenuous existence, awaiting relief.

Hay recognized that the Boxer outrages might be used to justify a wholesale partition of China. To keep the Open Door alive, he set to work liquidating the outbreak while maintaining Chinese sovereignty. In a letter of July 3, 1900, while acknowledging the anarchic chaos in China and the importance of restoring order, he added a critical qualification: "but the policy of the government of the United States is to seek a solution which may bring about permanent safety and peace to China, preserve Chinese territorial and administrative entity, protect all rights guaranteed to friendly powers by treaty and international law, and safeguard for the world the principle of equal and impartial trade with all parts of the Chinese Empire."

The Boxer uprising collapsed on August 14 when a task force of Japanese, Russian, and American troops entered Peking. The Chinese government was forced to pay an indemnity of $333 million, of which the United States received nearly $25 million. Eventually the United States contributed three-quarters of its share to a Chinese government fund for educating selected Chinese students in the United States. The rebellion leaders were either executed or imprisoned, and foreign troops policed the Tientsin-to-Peking railroad. On October 29, 1900, Hay announced that the major powers had subscribed to the views set forth in his letter of July 3. Ironically, even as Hay pressed to preserve the territorial integrity of China he began tentative inquiries into the possibility of obtaining a naval base in Fukien province. The Japanese pointedly reminded him of his recent note; American was to be no exception to the Open Door policy.

Under McKinley, a man who seemed to epitomize the nineteenth century, the United States entered the twentieth century and became a world power. By annexing the Philippines and espousing the Open Door, the nation was now irrevocably involved in Far Eastern affairs and, though most countries gave nominal assent to the principles enunciated by Hay, it was the United States that had made the firmest commitment. In the end, it would risk war rather than surrender its pledge to China. A great break with the insular past had taken place, one recognized by Hay when he warned: "The United States of today can not go back to what the country was fifty or a hundred years ago. Whether we will or not, whether for better or for worse, we must go forward." Thus was the epitaph of the nineteenth century written.

Chapter 9

The Progressive Experiment

William McKinley was visiting the Pan-American Exposition at Buffalo, New York, on the afternoon of September 6, 1901, when he was shot by Leon Czolgosz, an anarchist. For a few days the President seemed to rally; but on September 14, murmuring the words of "Nearer My God to Thee," he died. Ohio Senator Mark Hanna, distraught at the death of his friend, is reputed to have moaned: "Now look, that damned cowboy is President of the United States." The forty-two-year-old Vice-President, Theodore Roosevelt, had been vacationing in the Adirondacks when he received word of McKinley's death. He dashed down the mountainside he had been climbing, reached a railroad station at dawn, and that afternoon, September 14, took his oath of office in Buffalo. The nation mourned the martyr President, and then turned to take a long, close look at his successor.

THE ERA OF THEODORE ROOSEVELT

Roosevelt the Man. Theodore Roosevelt was unlike any previous President. Born into a patrician New York family, educated at Groton and Harvard, well traveled, a historian of some repute, passionately interested in nature, well-versed in literature and art, he possessed (as the British minister noted) "the energy and enthusiasm of a twelve-year-old boy." His progress to the presidency had been unusually swift: he had been elected assemblyman from New York City; tried unsuccessfully for the mayoralty of New York City; served as United States civil service commissioner under Benjamin Harrison; thrived upon being police commissioner of New York City; made a considerable mark as assistant secretary of the Navy, a position in which he revealed a marked propensity to ignore the Secretary of the Navy, John D. Long; and, in 1898, the hero of San Juan Hill, was elected to the governorship of New York State.

It was only with reluctance that Roosevelt's nomination for the New York governorship had been approved by the Republican political boss Thomas C. Platt in the first place. And Roosevelt made it quickly apparent that Platt's fears were only too well founded; Roosevelt was not a man who could be bought, manipulated, or managed. In spite of Platt's opposition, Roosevelt was able to make inroads against the vested interests of big business, and even secured several notable victories from the Platt-controlled legislature. Anxious to rid himself of this thorn in his flesh, Platt resolved to eliminate Roosevelt from the realms of political power by having him nominated for the vice-presidency. It was a shrewd plan, and it succeeded—up to a point. When he received the nomination as his party's candidate for "the second most important" post in the nation, Roosevelt recognized that —for the time being, at least—his career as an effective power in politics was over. He even spoke regretfully of "taking the veil," and resigned himself to spending four years studying law. And then, quite suddenly, McKinley had been killed. The bullet that felled the President catapulted Roosevelt into a position of greater power than either he or Thomas Platt had dreamed of.

Under the impact of Roosevelt's dynamic personality, the staid, stuffy atmosphere of the White House seemed to disintegrate. In its place came an air of supercharged energy. Outspoken, less than mindful of the accuracy of his facts, Roosevelt questioned the responsibility of corporations and their managers, chaffed at the arrogance of the bankers, dismissed "mere wealth" as warranting no honor, and revealed an undisguised relish in the manipulation of power. A "conforming independent"—one who took issue with his party's leadership but never deserted the party standard—he had an opinion on every subject. He opposed birth control, detested pacifists, proposed lining up Populists and labor leaders and shooting them, and at every opportunity preached the virtue of the vigorous life. He possessed what Henry Adams described as "the singular primitive quality that belongs to ultimate matter—the quality medieval theology assigned to God—he was pure act."

Roosevelt and the Uses of the Presidency. Despite his many contraditions, Roosevelt, possessed a seething will to succeed and a sense of *noblesse oblige* that derived from his conviction that, as a member of America's gentry, he had an obligation to render public service. Always receptive to new ideas, convinced that the purpose of life was "work, fight, and breed," Roosevelt's political leadership created an environment within which reform agitation could flourish. In his fascination with change and innovation, the new President responded eagerly to the rising call by the urban middle-classes for social reform. And he brought to the effort a sense of moral urgency with which the American bourgeoisie agreed. The presidency became, in his hands, an instrument of power which permitted him to manipulate the scales of society; simultaneously it provided him with a pulpit from which to deliver sermons on the moral imperatives that govern human existence. He converted the presidency into an institution which not only enforced the law but which also provided direction and instruction to Congress. Unhesitatingly, he threw the power of the national executive behind reform, and used his extraordinary personal popularity to obtain a hearing for those who advocated change. But he took care that the agitation steered a middle course, repudiating the "stand pat" defense of the status quo by the Republican leadership as well as the radicals' call for drastic upheaval. Roosevelt accepted the need to tinker with the established condition in order to preserve it. Progressive agitation for reform appealed to him precisely because it sought to preserve and perfect the established system.

The Progressive as Intellectual. The progressive reformers possessed the vision of vigorous youth. Largely comprising those young adults who had come of age in the 1890s, and attracting as well the older members of both parties who saw a need for extensive reform of the basic political structure and a widespread adoption of new political and social philosophies, they spoke of returning government to the people, repudiated strict *laisser faire* doctrine as inadequate to modern needs, and argued for positive government intervention to correct social and economic abuses. For young Governor Robert La Follette of Wisconsin, in many ways typical of these young progressives, the dominant issue was the "terrific struggle" being waged between the American people and "the allied forces of organized wealth and political corruption." To meet this double challenge new and untested weapons had to be developed. The young progressive gave vigorous expression to the hopes and aspirations of the rapidly expanding urban middle class to which they belonged, a class increasingly resentful of the extensive consolidation of both economic and political power during the 1890s.

The progressive, conditioned to think in the context of an open society in which natural superiority would be recognized as a matter of course, treated concentrations of power as subversive of the natural order of things. Raised in a society in which "Social Darwinism" taught that economic success was an index of one's status in the evolutionary process, they rejected Spencer's dogma that society was a fixed condition. Instead, they returned to the core idea of Darwin's evolutionary theory that all things are in a state of flux, that (as Oliver Wendell Holmes, the great jurist, had noted) "the condition of life is change." If survival of a species was predicted upon its ability to adjust to an environment, the young reformer saw no reason why man should not be permitted free rein to manipulate his environment to best meet his needs. Indeed, the progressive reveled at the prospect of a world in which "free will" would prevail.

The Progressive as Moralist. As had been the case with most previous reform movements, the agitation of the progressives of the late nineteenth century was not only intellectual but also moral. Progressives—among them many ministers—recognized that Protestant Christianity, the religion of the majority of the country, was losing its effective power as a result of its long identification with *laisser faire* capitalism; the New Testament had ceased to be, for many, a source of divine religious revelation, but had become, instead, merely a guidebook of morals and ethics. Many viewed the decline of active participation in religion as evidence of the failure of Protestantism to adjust to modern needs. Ministers like Washington Gladden and Samuel Loomis believed that Christianity would have to be either the religion of the whole people or of none; unless Protestantism came to grips with the social and economic problems of the day, unless it was prepared to take a firm stand and an active role in the resolution of social and economic crises, Christianity was doomed.

Walter Rauschenbusch of Rochester Theological Seminary summed up what many considered to be the church's responsibility: "Our business is to make over an antiquated and immoral economic system; to get rid of laws, customs, maxims, and philosophies inherited from an evil and despotic past, to create just and brotherly relations between groups and classes of society."

The Progressive Demons. The first step in successful reform is the identification of those conditions and their sources which must be reformed. The progressive focused his attention on the abuses and dislocations that had grown up in the wake of the swift urbanization and industrialization of the late nineteenth century. The new tycoons provoked only their patronizing contempt. "Without restraints of culture, experience, the pride, or even the inherited caution of class or rank," charged Henry Demarest Lloyd, "these men think they are the wave instead of the float, and that they have created the business which has created them." Conspicuous wielding of industrial and financial power aroused the reformers' fear; but garish displays of wealth stirred their contempt. Each bit of evidence that indicated a growth in the power of economic organization, whether of labor or capital, excited their near-claustrophobic conviction that their futures were being circumscribed. As members of a supposedly beleaguered middle class they struggled to strike a balance between the draining pretensions of an opulent plutocracy and the rising aspirations of a depressed working class.

Confronted by a steady if normal rise in prices, amounting to thirty-five per cent between 1897 and 1913, people on fixed incomes struggled to resist the flaking away of their expectations. Their agitation increasingly took the form of consumer leagues designed to keep public check on prices, challenging them when they seemed out of line with costs. Legitimate profit within the context of defined quality was the rallying theme of organized consumers. No less disturbing for the urban middle class was the mounting evidence that local political power was passing with accelerating speed into the hands of the political bosses, usually Irish, who, it was contended, bankrupted democracy with their legions of immigrant voters. Throughout the 1890s a flood of articles warning against the Irish conquest of the cities filled middle-class journals. "Educated citizens of cities said, and I think they believed—they certainly acted upon the theory," Lincoln Steffens recalled, "that it was the ignorant foreign riff-raff of the big congested towns that made municipal politics so bad." Challenged in their assumed political prerogatives, uncertain of their future expectations, the progressives fought to maintain their status. Educated to believe they would be given automatic recognition as the natural leaders of society, they struck for reform, not to overturn established values, but to restore them to their pristine intention. The progressives were to reveal a tenacity in their fight that could only have been inspired by a defense of privilege.

THE CLIMATE OF SOCIAL ABUSES

The interdependence of modern society was a phenomenon that the progressive recognized, knew he must accommodate himself to, but, nonetheless, felt unease about. No matter how much modern man struggled to retain his autonomy he was increasingly compelled to depend upon the skilled technician. The supposedly self-contained society of an earlier America, in which one knew whom to trust and whom to distrust, seemed irrevocably lost. "Modern sins are impersonal," Edward A. Ross complained. "The hurt passes into the vague mass, the 'public,' and is there lost to view." Responsibility seemed illusive; one knew abuses existed, one felt the dislocations of the times, but the factual context which enabled one to understand the who and what of a dilemma, and the how of resolving it, seemed equally illusive. Out of this sense of frustration there grew within the middle class an insatiable appetite for information. For in knowledge, it was assumed, there existed the key to mastery of events. And as the appetite for information expanded, so did the brand of journalism that Theodore Roosevelt angrily branded as "muckraking."

The Muckrakers. The demand had created the response, and though he was not the creator of the product, no man played a more vital role in the shaping of muckraking than S. S. McClure, publisher of *McClure's Magazine*. He had developed an infallible technique for insuring a wide circulation: he made every middle-class housewife feel that without a subscription to *McClure's,* she had been delinquent in her duty as a woman. During its early days, the magazine had revealed little inclination to deal with major social problems. But late in 1901, McClure ordered his editor, Lincoln Steffens, to "Get out of the office, go to Washington, Newfoundland, California, and Europe. Meet people, find out what's on, and write yourself." From this decision there emerged a stunning series of articles on municipal government, articles that were to establish Steffens as a great American journalist of social protest.

While in St. Louis, Steffens met Joseph Folk, the new district attorney, who seemed to have an affinity for controversy, and whose insistence upon enforcing the law had revealed a relationship between business and politics which stirred antagonism rather than support from the city's newspapers and leading citizens. Steffens listened as Folk told how political leaders within the city had attempted first to dictate his conduct of the office, and how, when they failed, to intimidate him. Steffens made Folk's revelations the core of his exposé of municipal corruption. "It is good business men that are corrupting our bad politicians"; Folk insisted, "it is good business that causes bad government." In October 1902, *McClure's* carried the result of Steffens' investigation, "Tweed Days in St. Louis"; the following month, Ida Tarbell, whose girlhood experiences in the Pennsylvania oil regions had left their mark, began what soon was known as "the frightening" *History of the Standard Oil Company;* and the following January, Ray Stannard Baker exposed labor union abuses. McClure had almost unwittingly gone into the business of providing his middle-class readers with the details of the conditions which they instinctively felt: corruption permeated American life; it existed because of public indifference; it provided profits for public official and private entrepreneur.

The public response to the articles in *McClure's* brought on a deluge of exposés in the mass circulation magazines. David Graham Phillip wrote "Treason of the Senate" for *Cosmopolitan;* Samuel Hopkins unsettled national notions of health with his report in *Collier's* on patent medicine frauds; stock manipulation and fraud rivaled with reports of embalmed beef from the nation's packing houses for space in *Everybody's*. Ben Lindsey poured out his grievances against judicial malpractices in *The Beast,* and told how, upon learning that mere boys were being imprisoned along with adult males in the Colorado State Prison, he launched the agitation that resulted in the establishment at Denver of the nation's first juvenile courts. Upton Sinclair turned the nation's stomach as he detailed the horrors of packing-house practices in his novel *The Jungle*. Out of such exposures came the pressure that propelled the Pure Food and Drug Act through Congress. Burton Hendrick made the nation privy to the secrets of the insurance industry, precipitating the legislative investigation of New York insurance companies that brought Charles Evans Hughes to nationwide fame. Ray Stannard Baker reminded the nation of the plight of the Negro, and though he ended with a plea for Booker T. Washington's gradualism and the industrial education of the Negro, he precipitated a reaction that led to the formation of the National Association for the Advancement of Colored People under the leadership of men such as William E. B. Du Bois, and a militant call for according the Negro "absolute political and social equality."

The wealth of information contained in these exposures made the American middle class increasingly receptive to programs of comprehensive reform. Though the appetite for exposure waned after the first decade of the twentieth century, inexorable pressure for legislative action had built up. And unlike the reform agitators of the 1880s and 1890s, who had been mollified by bills that promised general corrective reforms, the progressives now demanded concrete action to meet specific abuses. Rugged individualists possessed by conscience, they set to work chaining the monsters who threatened their paradise. The muckraker had mapped the dimensions of the problems; the legislators would have to determine the solutions.

Trusts and Plutocracy. The progressive did not discover the trusts; he discovered that the Sherman Anti-Trust Act did not work. The publication in 1904 by John Moody of *The Truth about the Trusts* identified 1898, eight years after the passage of the Sherman Act, as the year in which "modern trust-forming" began. Out of 318 trusts examined, Moody noted that only 82, capitalized at $1,196,700,000, had been organized before 1898, while 234, with capitalization in excess of $6,000,000,000, had arisen afterward, dominating the steel, tobacco, copper, and an endless variety of other industries. The appearance of M. G. Cuniff's double page map of railroad consolidation in *World's Work* revealed that in 1902 nearly seventy-five per cent of all trackage was controlled by Morgan, Gould, Hill, Harriman, Rockefeller, and Vanderbilt. From the United States census bureau a stream of statistics revealed that in 1909 one per cent of American industrial corporations controlled forty-four per cent of all industrial production.

The staggering power of corporations, power of such dimensions that state governments proved inadequate to control, and that only federal power could be capable of dealing with—such power was fully revealed in the 1913 Pujo Committee Report on "The Concentration of Control of Money and Credit." Arsense Pujo, a Louisiana congressman, seemed to confirm fully the charge made by Henry D. Lloyd in 1894 that the masters of capital dominated the American economy. It was the overwhelming dimensions of the capital controlled by a few bankers that now unsettled the public imagination. The congressional findings were given wide circulation by Louis D. Brandeis in *Other People's Money,* which emphasized that "a few leaders of finance," most prominent of whom were J. P. Morgan; Kidder, Peabody of Boston; and Kuhn, Loeb & Co., had established "a vast and growing concentration of control of money and credit." Through this control, these fiscal masters dominated not only banking, but also insurance, transportation, mining, and industry. The progressive mind boggled as it read that Morgan & Company and its banking affiliates—the National City Bank and the Bankers and Guaranty Trust Companies—possessed "341 directorships in 112 corporations having aggregate resources or capitalization of $22,245,000,000," a sum that represented nearly fifteen per cent of the total national wealth in 1912. Such concentrations of wealth raised the obvious question: Could democracy survive in America? For many progressives the question took an even sharper form: How was America to be redeemed from the grasp of the new plutocracy that industrialization had created?

Big Labor. Finley Peter Dunne, creator of the fictional character Mr. Dooley, whose comments on the current scene commanded a wide audience at the turn of the century, noted that the middle class felt increasingly crushed between capital and labor. Though labor, in the context of the mid-twentieth century, could hardly be described as formidable in 1900, it revealed an increasing propensity to employ an organized effort to redress its grievances. The American Federation of Labor membership soared from fewer than 250,000 in 1896 to 1,676,000 in 1904. A militant effort to organize steel in 1900, accelerating agitation for closed shops, coupled with energetic strikes by miners in Pennsylvania and Colorado, made the public increasingly aware of a new tone in labor. *The Outlook* notified its readers in 1904 that during the thirty months following January 1902 no less than 180 union men were killed, 1,651 wounded, and 5,000 arrested during labor disturbances. Equally unsettling were evidences of labor's political action; despite the A.F.L.'s declared neutrality, Socialists won elections in Boston's suburbs, and labor candidates gained the mayorships of Hartford, Bridgeport, and Ansonia, Connecticut. The evidence of developing class warfare added a special note of urgency to progressive agitation.

Organized Business. In 1903, under the guidance of David M. Parry, the National Association of Manufacturers launched a counterattack, charging that a "socialistic" organized labor "knows but one law, the law of physical force—the law of the Huns and Vandals, the law of the savage." Muckraking journals contributed to the denunciation, implying that "unionism" and "violence" were synonymous. On October 29, 1903, the Citizens' Industrial Association, an organization of manufacturers, was formed in Chicago. Its statement of purposes revealed a distinct affinity for the progressive view of labor. It declared:

> The present industrial conditions have become so deplorable by reason of the indefensible methods and claims of organized labor that the time has come when the employing interests and good citizenship of the country must take immediate and effective measures to reaffirm and enforce those fundamental principles of American government guaranteeing free, competitive conditions. In its demand for the closed shop organized labor is seeking to overthrow individual liberty and property rights, the principal props of our government. Its methods for securing this revolutionary and socialistic change in our institutions are also those of physical warfare.

Appeals to class sentiment provoked only contempt from progressives, convinced as they were that the class orientation of both business and labor was "destroying American liberty." They subscribed wholeheartedly to Theodore Roosevelt's declaration that he "wished the labor people absolutely to understand that I set my face like flint against violence and lawlessness of any kind on their part, just as much as against arrogant greed by the rich, and that I would be as quick to move against one as the other." With increasing frequency the progressive appealed to the "higher interest" of the general public, a term which enabled them to universalize their own peculiar interests. For unconsciously, the middle class, both leveling and uplifting in its instincts, proposed to absorb into itself all other classes. It believed, as fully as the most dedicated Marxist, in the impending classless society, or, more accurately, the restoration of a society once governed by an equalitarian impulse.

The Americanism Campaign. Thomas Bailey Aldrich, the author and editor who may be considered the summation of middle-class intellect, stated: "Kipling described exactly the government of every city and town in the . . . United States when he described that of New York as being 'a despotism of the alien, by the alien, for the alien, tempered with occasional insurrections of decent folk!'" Aldrich expressed the increasing alarm that agitated the middle class as it viewed the Irish conquest of the city. For some, like William Allen White, there existed the certainty that the "clean Aryan blood" of the native American assured an "instinctive race revulsion to cross breeding" with the "inferior races" flooding urban alleyways. The continuation of unlimited immigration, *Harper's Weekly* acidly remarked in 1905, would "toll the passing of this great Anglo-Teuton people" and would signal the triumph of "the Latin and Hun." Already harassed by the thought of being crushed between the monoliths of business and labor, the middle class shivered at the prospect of a society in which the "pigsty mode of life" (as one contemporary described the customs of the southern and eastern European immigrant) would prevail. Nothing less than the purity of the American race was at stake—though few bothered to define exactly what was imagined to comprise the American race. Against such a vision, the plea of John Dewey for "a unity created by drawing out and composing into a harmonious whole the best, the most characteristic, which each contributing race and people has to offer" stirred only a handful of the most compassionate and enlightened.

For those Americans who felt that the new immigrant was totally beyond assimilation, the solution to the problem was restriction upon immigration. The possibilities of outright, complete termination of immigration, and termination disguised through the use of literacy tests or the quota system, commanded increasing attention.

For most progressives, however, the problem presented by the immigrant was neatly summed up by Charles Bonaparte, Roosevelt's Secretary of Navy and Attorney General, who, probably inspired by Sinclair's tale of the Lithuanian immigrant who fell into the sausage vat and thereupon found his way to the breakfast table, dismissed them as "sausages." Pliable, passive, often pathetically eager to share fully the promise of American life, the immigrant impressed numerous progressives as likely to respond to a program of Americanization and naturalization. The exotic habits and mores that the immigrant brought across the ocean would crumble upon exposure, through education, to the obvious superiority of American values and institutions. A campaign for the organization of night schools and citizenship classes set forth the promise that once the immigrant learned English, explored the glories of American history, and absorbed the lessons of citizenship, he would cease to be a problem and blend into the anonymity of American citizenship. The progressive naïvely dismissed the tenacity with which the immigrant, unconvinced of his inferiority, would cling to his distinctive customs. Moreover, the progressive failed to realize that the patronizing attitude Americans displayed toward these newcomers from Europe would compel them to retreat into a solemn restraint, dwelling (in the words of one historian) as "strangers in the land."

THE EFFECTS OF ROOSEVELT'S LEADERSHIP

The "Square Deal." Had Theodore Roosevelt achieved nothing else, he may be credited with setting the federal government firmly on the path toward effectively regulating the conditions of American life. Supremely conscious of the challenge of power, Roosevelt did not hesitate to use presidential authority in his attempt to stabilize American life. For him the presidency remained the one federal office dedicated to the interest of the whole people. In his own words, he would be "the progressive leader of the conservatives and the conservative leader of the progressives." Far from fearing the dimensions of American industrial power—its very size stirred his pride—he rejected pleas to dismantle it, preferring instead to concentrate on mastering it. Government was to him not the servant of a single interest or class, but the objective force that would arbitrate disputes and insure justice, or, as he put it, a "Square Deal," for all. Faced with a nation in internal conflict over unresolved problems, Roosevelt set out to be the patriot President; though profoundly political, he intended never to allow the collective interest to be submerged by the particular interest. As President he chose to personify the national power and conscience.

Trust Busting. Roosevelt assumed his presidential role with caution. Confronted by a Congress dominated by sturdy conservatives, and aware that he was President by grace of a bullet rather than a ballot, he steered an even course. Far from issuing a clarion call for reform, he proposed new legislation *sotto voce* to regulate corporate abuses, to implement the Interstate Commerce Act, to establish reciprocal tariffs, and to inaugurate a national program of conservation. Though sweetened with soothing words, his first congressional message contained the seeds of what was to become Roosevelt's call for a more effective federal power. The time had come for the creation of a national government commensurate with the challenge of a national economy.

There already existed, among both conservatives and liberals, agreement that more effective regulation of the economy was required. Roosevelt believed that the executive branch already possessed sufficient power to regulate if the President chose to use it. On February 19, 1902, Attorney General Philander C. Knox, at the direction of the President, announced that the federal government intended to start suit, under the Sherman Act, against the Northern Securities Company, a giant holding company for the Northern Pacific, the Great Northern, and the Chicago, Burlington, and Quincy Railroads. The company, backed by J. P. Morgan, John D. Rockefeller, James J. Hill, and Edward Henry Harriman, with a capital stock valued at $400,000,000 (one third of which was estimated to be water), had been formed in 1901 as a compromise settlement of the monumental struggle between Hill and Harriman to gain control of the Burlington system. If the company were allowed to exist, it would create a near monopoly of northwestern rail facilities; but if found illegal, its dissolution would not substantially disrupt the economy, since the company was still only in its formative stages. In the subsequent judicial proceedings, the Supreme Court found against the Northern Securities Company, concluding that Congress had in the Sherman Act "recognized the rule of free competition by declaring illegal every combination or conspiracy in restraint of . . . commerce."

In the Northern Securities case, Roosevelt had taken the measure of

Morgan, Rockefeller, and their ilk, and had earned the appellation "trust buster" among a delighted public. He had demonstrated the dimensions of executive power, while not affecting substantially the industrial-fiscal structure of the nation. The case also revealed Roosevelt's view of America's industrial growth: he accepted the inevitability of big industry, but also insisted that it be regulated, and, when necessary, controlled, by the federal government. Once Roosevelt won his massive re-election victory over Alton B. Parker in 1904, he decided that he had received a public mandate for renewed trust busting, and in 1906 and 1907 launched suits against the Standard Oil Company, the Du Pont monolith, the American Tobacco Company, and the Hartford, New Haven Railroad. In all, during his eight years in office, forty-four major antitrust battles were fought in the courts. Such prosecutions, Roosevelt believed, "gave a guaranty in this country that rich man and poor man alike were held equal before the law."

The Coal Strike of 1902. In a more spectacular intervention in the economy, made in 1902, Roosevelt played a major role in ending the crippling anthracite coal strike which had begun in May 1902 and which involved the 50,000 members of the United Mine Workers who worked the anthracite coal mines of northeastern Pennsylvania. Two years earlier, Mark Hanna, eager to eliminate all threats to the re-election of McKinley, had persuaded the mine operators to grant a ten per cent wage raise. Now the miners demanded union recognition, an eight-hour day, and wage raises that varied between ten and twenty per cent. Six railroads serving the anthracite region owned more than three-quarters of the mines, and under the unyielding leadership of George F. Baer of the Reading, and W. H. Truesdale of the Delaware, Lackawanna, and Western, they set out to break the union. Well aware that the urban centers of the East depended on anthracite for heating purposes, the railroad managers refused to negotiate, and closed the mines. The miners, led by John F. Mitchell and aided financially by bituminous coal miners, doggedly insisted that their demands be met, persisting in their stand into the autumn of 1902. As winter approached, the East faced the prospect of a fuel-less frigidity, and the urban centers became increasingly agitated as most journals of opinion expressed support for the coal miners. Baer defended his refusal to negotiate by blandly asserting: "The rights and interests of the laboring man will be protected and cared for by the Christian men to whom God has given control of the property rights of the country"; such self-righteousness provoked even conservatives into discussing the possibility of compulsory arbitration and government seizure of the mines.

Roosevelt's Intervention. An increasingly disturbed President, warned by Attorney General Knox, Senator Henry Cabot Lodge, and Secretary of State Elihu Root that he lacked the power to act in the matter, finally issued an invitation to the operators and union leaders to attend a conference at the White House on October 3. Mitchell proposed either direct negotiations or submission of the controversy to the binding decision of an arbitration commission appointed by Roosevelt. Baer flatly rejected negotiation and arbitration, demanding instead federal intervention, using federal troops if necessary, and the prosecution of the union under the Sherman Act. The Baer first proposal bore unexpected fruit when Roosevelt let it be known that he was prepared to send ten thousand troops into the coal fields—but with the purpose of removing the mine operators instead of compelling the mine union to desist from striking. News of the presidential intention shook Wall Street, and at a meeting on October 13 between Roosevelt and agents of Morgan, it was agreed to establish a seven-man commission to arbitrate the dispute, and the miners resumed work. The following March the miners received a ten per cent raise and an hour reduction in their work day, but failed to obtain union recognition. The coal operators accepted with pleasure a ten per cent rise in the price of coal.

Roosevelt and Labor. Roosevelt had come a long way from his early view of labor, which he had expressed in the 1890s by calling it one of "the ugly forces that seethe beneath the social crust." But he took prompt care to remove any suspicion that he would prove an automatic friend of labor. He repeated with frequent variations his belief that labor as well as capital had to accept government regulation. In his 1903 message to Congress he declared:

> Whenever either corporation, labor union, or individual disregards the law or acts in a spirit of arbitrary and tyrannous interference with the rights of others, whether corporations or individuals, then where the Federal Government has jurisdiction, it will see to it that the misconduct is stopped, paying not the slightest heed to the position or power of the corporation, the union or the individual. . . .

And he did not hesitate on several occasions to send troops to maintain labor peace, as in 1903, when he intervened at an Arizona mine upon the request of the territorial governor. But in 1904 he bluntly refused to send troops, when requested by the Western Federation of Miners, to restore order at Cripple Creek, Colorado, making it obvious that Roosevelt intended to establish government as a mediating force between labor and capital. But the comparative weakness of labor led him to question increasingly the use of the injunction against labor, and in

May 1906, he declared that he opposed allowing "any operation of the law turn into an engine of oppression against the wage worker." Determined to create a power equilibrium in the nation's economy, Roosevelt gave labor its first friend in the White House.

Railroad Regulation. At the beginning of the twentieth century the nation was almost totally dependent on railroads for transportation. They provided almost the only links between the great cities and the countryside. Much of the continuing public agitation for government regulation of the railroads mirrored resentment and unease at this dependence. The primary demand was for rate regulations and the strengthening of the Interstate Commerce Commission. But railroads also had their grievances against big business which they hoped to correct through remedial legislation. Particularly galling were rebates; railroads were being blackmailed into giving partial refunds on transportation charges in order to obtain the chance to move large quantities of goods. The hope of eliminating the rebate system explains why conservative congressmen supported the Elkins Act of 1903 which forbade rebates. And the trend toward concentration of railroad control alarmed both conservatives, preoccupied as they were with keeping compctition, and liberals, who feared the power such concentrations created.

Utilizing the power obtained through the Elkins Act, Roosevelt instituted numerous rebate suits, but the ease with which railroads had previously flaunted the law encouraged continued rebating. The weakness of the Interstate Commerce Commission, gutted by a succession of adverse Supreme Court decisions, permitted it to perform successfully only its statistic-gathering function. The obvious ineffectiveness of existing regulations resulted in renewed efforts by Robert M. La Follette in Wisconsin, Albert B. Cummins in Iowa, and John A. Johnson in Minnesota to institute rail reform in their states. Their success on the state level encouraged them to agitate for federal action. This effort was but one of many straws in the wind, with both Republican and Democratic journals editorializing for reform, while numerous businessmen and trade organs acknowledged that federal rate regulation was inevitable. The intensity of Western and Southern grievances toward rail practices expressed itself in the near-unanimous support (326–17) of the Esch-Townsend Bill by the House of Representatives. The stringency of rate regulation provided by the bill, however, provoked a massive railroad lobby that convinced the Senate it should reject the Esch-Townsend Bill.

The Hepburn Act. The Senate's action might have convinced a less determined politician to surrender all prospects of effective railroad regulation, but Roosevelt, frustrated in his efforts to obtain constructive legislation during the 1905 session, returned to an earlier concern, the need for tariff reform. He issued a brisk succession of threats to call a special session; suggested the need for tariff reduction; and renewed demands for rate regulations. The evidence indicates that Roosevelt had decided upon a war of nerves, a contest in which the threat of government intervention in interstate commerce disputes, a series of government legal actions against the rebate precedures of railroads and such formidable industrial giants as Standard Oil, and proposals for tariff adjustment combined to suggest to opponents of rate regulations that surrender was the better part of valor. In December 1905, the presidential message called for fair rates, the termination of special favors to corporations or individuals by railroads, and the provision of power which would permit the Interstate Commerce Commission to inspect railroad corporation books. Roosevelt described the abuses characteristic of railroad management as symptomatic of all corporations, the correction of which could be met only if the federal government were to intervene affirmatively in their affairs. When the railroads resorted to issuing propaganda favorable to their own interests, Roosevelt encouraged the publication of numerous muckraking articles that dealt with railroad malpractices and their cost to the public.

Roosevelt's consummate use of the presidency to shape public opinion began to bring results, as even the most formidable conservative wilted under the whiplash of public sentiment. The House of Representatives, ever ready to legislate on rates, passed (with only seven dissenting votes) the Hepburn Bill, which embraced most of Roosevelt's demands. But in the Senate the formidable talents of Nelson Aldrich of Rhode Island were put to work amending the bill into innocuousness. When Aldrich gave "Pitchfork Ben" Tillman of South Carolina, a ranking Democrat, sponsorship of the bill, he assumed that Roosevelt's distaste for Tillman would complicate the presidential task, but Roosevelt promptly parried by resuming friendly relations with Tillman. When Tillman proved unable to maneuver an acceptable bill through Congress, he turned to Senator Jonathan Dolliver, leader of the Progressive Republicans, and then to regular Republicans. Unable to gain his point, he turned, as William Howard Taft recalled, to "the conservative members of the Cabinet . . . to get him out of hot water." A compromise was hammered out which the Senate approved on March 18, 1906, by a vote of 71 to 3.

The newly approved Hepburn Act gave Roosevelt the railroad law he wanted. Though not as stringent as Robert La Follette of Wisconsin had wanted, it marked a substantial increase in federal regulation over private enterpise. It gave the Interstate Commerce Commision jurisdiction over all matters related to transportation; express and Pullman operations, pipelines, refrigeration and storage charges—all passed under the I.C.C. The Commission was further empowered to set aside railroad rates upon the complaint of a shipper and to set up temporary schedules until a decision was rendered by the courts. Railroad books were open to governmental scrutiny, and a uniform accounting procedure could be prescribed by the Commission. Railroads were also forbidden to carry goods processed or made by their own subsidiaries other than those consumed by their own operation.

Symbol for an Age. Roosevelt sensed and expressed, as no other man of his age had, that the free and easy business enterprise of the nineteenth century was no longer feasible in the twentieth. A single board of directors could make decisions which affected the remotest corner of the republic. Out of the competition of a *laisser faire* economy had emerged an oligopolistic economy in which a few great producers dominated whole segments of the economy. Often it seemed that the self-made man viewed his success as a license to ignore the social consequences of his acts, as a warrant to arbitrarily wield the economic power he possessed. To Roosevelt, born into a family possessing moderate wealth coupled with a mature sense of obligation, the *nouveau riche* seemed to regard "power as expressed only in its basest and most brutal form, that of mere money." His aesthetic sense was outraged at the contemptuous indifference with which too many business and political leaders met their responsibilities. A swelling chorus of complaints against the "galling serfdom to the monopolistic class" convinced Roosevelt by 1908 that he lived on the threshold of revolutionary upheaval. He saw reform was nothing less than the proverbial stitch in time. As the sentiment for change welled up in the nation, the President rode its crest, moving steadily leftward; and in the last two years of his administration, Roosevelt increased the tempo of his demands for reform.

Conservation. In no area did Roosevelt feel greater responsibility than the role of the federal government in preserving the natural resources of the country; and he brought to the subject of conservation the intensity of a devoted nature lover. At the time of Roosevelt's inauguration, some forty-five million acres of forest lands were being held by the federal government under a conservation program instituted by Benjamin Harrison and continued by Grover Cleveland. But the new President, with the yeoman assistance of Gifford Pinchot, provided conservation with a system. During the seven years of his presidency, an additional one hundred and fifty million acres were set aside, including not only forest lands but mineral lands, oil sites, and potential power stations. When in 1903 Congress granted a private individual the right to construct a power station at Muscle Shoals, Alabama, Roosevelt vetoed the measure. In the same year he threw his support behind Nevada's Senator Francis G. Newland's reclamation bill, which provided that a part of receipts from the sale of public lands be set aside for irrigation, reclamation, and dam projects. To administer the vast new program the Reclamation Service was established, and that bureau rigorously enforced restrictions on the use of the national domain, leading to extensive prosecutions and convictions of malefactors. When Congress attempted to limit the conservation program, Roosevelt beat the legislators to the punch by adding new territories to the public domain. Congress responded by denying support to the National Country Life Commission which sought to improve rural life, and the Inland Waterways Commission; but Roosevelt had established a conservation program under federal auspices that Congress might delay but could never arrest.

The Money Panic of 1907. On numerous occasions during his administration Roosevelt had received evidence that the nation's banking system was unsound. The conclusion of Nicholas Murray Butler, president of Columbia University, that "God was responsible" for the management of the nation's fiscal affairs, described the situation succinctly. In a rare revelation of humility, Roosevelt admitted that his knowledge of fiscal matters was nearly nonexistent. If any one man controlled the nation's banking system it was John P. Morgan; but his and other financiers' constant issuances of corporate securities had burdened the economy to a point where a deflation of stock values seemed inevitable. Most businessmen refused to acknowledge any responsibility whatsoever for the unstable condition, charging rather that Roosevelt's "policy of hostility against all corporations and their securities, particularly railroads" lay at the bottom of the impending crisis.

A severe break in prices on the New York Stock Exchange during March 1907 sent Morgan appealing unsuccessfully to Roosevelt for assurances that he would not apply the Hepburn Act too closely; on the other hand, Roosevelt would not use his influence to give a favorable slant to stock market conditions. The Treasury assumed the task of stabilizing public confidence by leaving federal moneys on deposit in New York banks. Nevertheless, stock prices steadily declined. In September, an expected industrial upswing failed to materialize; in October, New York banks proved unable to meet the need of interior banks for funds. There followed a wave of corporation and bank failures, but it was not until news leaked out that several New York trust companies had failed in an effort to corner the copper market that a major crisis exploded. As depositers hastened to remove their funds, the Knickerbocker Trust Company, the largest banking facility of its kind in the country, closed operations on October 23. Withdrawals reached panic proportions, and it seemed that the national banking system would collapse. Faced with a banking failure, Secretary of the Treasury George B. Cortelyou agreed to assist Morgan and other private bankers in supplying government and private funds to support hard-pressed banks. As the banking system tottered, the New York Stock Exchange reported sagging stock prices, and rumors of an impending crash circulated. The sudden weakening of one important brokerage firm led Morgan, after he had received assurances from Roosevelt that the government would not intervene, to purchase through the United States Steel Corporation the firm's heavy holdings in the Tennessee Iron and Coal Company. Thus the brokerage firm was saved, Wall Street was stabilized, and Morgan had gained control of a major producer of bituminous coal. When critics pointed out that as a result of the purchase the great steel combination had gained control of vast coal and iron resources, Roosevelt defended it as a necessary step in "the stoppage of the panic." Nonetheless, there remained the dangerous charge that Roosevelt, for all his reputation as a trust buster, had helped solidify a steel monopoly, a charge which when supported by Taft's administration in 1911 completed the break between Roosevelt and Taft.

THE PRESIDENCY OF WILLIAM HOWARD TAFT

The Closing Days of Roosevelt's Presidency. When Roosevelt had overwhelmingly won the election in 1904, he had announced: "Under no circumstances will I be a candidate for or accept another nomination." And with these words, he surrendered a powerful weapon with which to maintain his control in Congress as his second term drew to a close. The pent-up resentment of Congressional conservatives now poured out in criticism of the administration. Roosevelt responded with denunciations of "malefactors of great wealth." When his annual message was sent to Congress in 1908, it bubbled with radical proposals that included a call for income and inheritance taxes, more stringent regulation of railroad rates and securities, extension of eight-hour day and workmen's compensation laws, compulsory arbitration of major labor disputes, and, significantly, limitations of the use of labor injunctions. The latter foreshadowed the more extensive judicial reforms Roosevelt advanced on the 31st of January, 1908. His criticisms of the federal judiciary were provoked by the Supreme Court's disallowance of the Employer's Liability Act of 1906, which provided railway employees with a compensation law. Too frequently, the President charged, the Court behaved as if the Constitution were "a strait-jacket" designed to impede, rather than aid, necessary change. When the Supreme Court overturned Federal Judge Kenesaw Mountain Landis' $29,000,000 fine of the Standard Oil Company of Indiana for violations of the Sherman Anti-Trust Act, Roosevelt increased the tempo of his attacks. Equally emphatic was his denunciation of business irresponsibility, and his simultaneous call for "the moral regeneration of the business world." But Congress, its attention focused upon the impending change in the White House's occupancy, turned a deaf ear. As Roosevelt's term drew to a close, his power to influence Congress suffered a radical decline, a development which in turn provoked the President to renewed and intensified criticism. In his December 1908 State of the Union Message, his criticisms of the judiciary and business were more or less in keeping with past denunciations, but his censure of Congress was so strong as to provoke that august body to decline a subsequent measure of explanation from the President.

The Election of Taft. During the difficult closing days of his second term, Roosevelt admitted that he regretted being relieved of his official duties; nonetheless he worked with intense vigor to assure the nomination of William Howard Taft as his successor. Because he was convinced that unless he used the full power of appointment to assure the selection of Taft he himself would be renominated, Roosevelt's behavior would seem to have been without ulterior motive.

Taft, eager to please and congenial, impressed Roosevelt as a dedicated progressive who would continue the Square Deal. What Roosevelt failed to grasp immediately—though he would all too soon come to realize his mistaken impression—was that Taft was apt to respond to the strongest immediate pressure to which he was subjected, and that once Roosevelt himself was out of the picture Taft would gravitate steadily toward his own natural conservatism. The decision to make Taft the Republican nominee came without the genial Ohioan having made any real effort. He had performed well as Governor General of the Philippines, had served competently as Secretary of War, and had wanted to serve on the Supreme Court. Indeed, fewer presidential candidates seem to have been less interested in the presidency than Taft. But Roosevelt's determination swept the almost-reluctant nominee to a first ballot victory.

The Democrats chose Bryan for a third time on a pro-labor, progressive platform. In the campaign that ensued, it often seemed that Roosevelt, rather than Taft, was running; and when the votes were counted, Taft had won with less than half Roosevelt's majority of four years earlier. Of great significance were sizable Democratic gains in the key states of Indiana, Ohio, Minnesota, and North Dakota, where they won the governorships and additional Democratic seats in the House of Representatives. In every instance, however, progressive Republicans had done better than either conservative Republicans or Democrats. Taft would have had a difficult time following Roosevelt; his troubles were compounded by the presence of a Congress in which progressive sentiments were on the ascendancy. And the new President was at heart a conservative.

Taft the Man. Had Roosevelt deliberately set out to make a sharp contrast between himself and his successor, he could not have chosen better than Taft. Where Roosevelt possessed endless energy and probing intelligence, both of which thrived on controversy, Taft was phlegmatic, affable, physically fat, a man who viewed the presidency as a tedious chore. When faced with political controversy, he retreated, in the desperate hope that somehow the trouble would go away of its own accord. Throughout the Tafts' married life, Helen Herron Taft had been the one who provided the energy and ambition that propelled her husband to political success; but shortly after Taft assumed office the new First Lady fell grievously ill. Thus, at the time the President needed her guidance most, she was unavailable. Given these characteristics in the new President, characteristics which, in many respects, contradicted the national image of the ideal American, one can understand that the country did not warm immediately to Taft. So great was the contrast between public feeling for Roosevelt and public feeling for Taft, in fact, that when (after Taft had been duly installed in the White House) Roosevelt characteristically dashed off to Africa and went on a safari, more attention was paid in the popular press to Roosevelt's absence than to Taft's presence. The new President was not, to be sure, the first chief executive whose personality did not lend itself to inspiring a ready outburst of national affection; and it might have been assumed that with the passing of time Taft would have been able to form his own unique, personal, and valid image of the presidency. But, regrettably, Taft lacked the one ingredient that was essential to the formation of such an image: decisiveness.

The Insurgents and the Old Guard. When Nelson W. Aldrich, the conservative spokesman of the Senate, was informed that Roosevelt had left for Africa, he is reputed to have said, "Let every lion do his duty." The surging energy of the outgoing President, conservative Republicans sensed, was to be replaced by the blander, more accommodating qualities of the new President. For though Taft had promised in his inaugural address to uphold Roosevelt's reforms, he had indicated on numerous occasions that he had strong reservations about the efficacy of federal action to institute reforms. Nor had he any positive desire to use the presidency as a force in social disputes. If anything, he subscribed to the doctrine that in any dispute between management and labor, the latter interest must be wrong. As a Federal Circuit Judge, he had shown his anti-labor bias so frequently that he was known as "the injunction judge." At the heart of Taft's political philosophy was a profound suspicion of organized power, whether it be that of labor, corporations, or government, and the emphatic conviction that man was by nature an imperfect animal. His friendship with Roosevelt was an anomaly, for left to his own choice, Taft usually felt most at home with conservatives.

The result of Taft's inclinations was a swift estrangement from that element within the Republican party that the President dubbed "the Bryan wing." As is common among liberals, the members of this group possessed a formidable capacity for articulating their sentiments. Their aggressiveness disturbed the placid routine preferred by the chief executive. In fact, Taft completely ignored the progressive wing of the Grand Old Party when he formed his cabinet, emphasizing conservative appointments, particularly of men who possessed strong administrative qualities. But in one instance, at least, Taft seemed destined to follow a reform path, for he threw his support behind an effort to remove the "stand-pat" Speaker of the House, Joseph G. Cannon.

Revolt in the House of Representatives. Speaker Cannon epitomized the type of politician who provoked progressive condemnation. Widely known as "Uncle Joe," he ran the House with an iron hand, relying on the collaboration of a squad of conservative congressmen to squash any discontent. His cantankerous temper, his ever-present black cigar, and his widely known penchant for poker playing had made him a colorful figure. But his exploitation of former Speaker Thomas B. Reed's rules to suppress progressive measures and to penalize dissenters from his rule had brought the House to the verge of rebellion. Taft harbored a positive distaste for Cannon and seemed determined to clip his wings. Not only was he intent upon replacing him, but he also was determined to alter the rules upon which Cannon's edifice of power depended. (These rules permitted the Speaker to appoint all committees, a position that served as a powerful impediment to independent action.) Of equal significance was Cannon's role in the five-member Rules Committee, for it was this group which determined the conditions under which a piece of legislation would reach the floor—if at all. When Taft moved against Cannon, some thirty Republican congressmen, led by George W. Norris of Nebraska, Victor Murdock of Kansas, and Augustus P. Gardner of Massachusetts, announced that they would oppose Cannon's re-election. But when congressional conservatives, led by Nelson Aldrich and Henry C. Payne, Chairman of the House Ways and Means Committee, made it clear to Taft that Cannon's removal would prevent tariff reform, the President backed down. Upon his re-election to the speakership, Cannon systematically punished insurgent Republicans by depriving them of choice committee assignments; and the Republican Congressional Campaign Committee announced it intended to oppose their renominations in forthcoming primaries. Oddly, Taft, who privately continued to denounce Cannon, denied presidential patronage to the insurgents, although he indicated that he was so penalizing them because they failed to support his policies, whereas Cannon had given him loyal support.

The break between the insurgents and Taft came just as Norris led an insurgent-Democratic coalition to a successful challenge of Cannon during the first days of the March 1910 session. A new set of rules which enlarged the Rules Committee from five to fifteen, removed the Speaker from its membership, and left their election to the House rather than the Speaker, was passed. As evidence of progressive power grew, Taft steadily moved toward the right.

The Payne-Aldrich Tariff Act. On one subject Taft seemed settled: the reduction of tariff rates. During his efforts to gain the Republican nomination, he had called for a substantial lowering of the Dingley Tariff schedules. No sooner was Taft in the White House than he called a special session to deal with the question. Under the guidance of Payne, the House quickly passed a bill in which substantial revisions were made. But in the Senate Aldrich produced a bill that managed—in eight hundred amendments—to reverse the downward trend.

A group of progressive senators, led by the formidable La Follette of Wisconsin, Joseph L. Bristow of Kansas, Albert J. Beveridge of Indiana, and Albert Cummins and Jonathan Dolliver of Iowa, organized a systematic denunciation of Aldrich's proposed schedules. Accepting Taft at his word, they called upon him to aid their struggle; but despite his pledges and his halfhearted threats to veto the bill if it were passed, Taft wavered, and finally threw his support to the proposed legislation, assuming that he could compel changes in the Conference Committee as it attempted to iron out the differences between the two Houses' versions of the tariff. Although Taft failed to achieve the wholesale reform to which some observers thought he was committed, he did force downward modifications on hides, bootware, iron and coal, cotton, and oil. In addition, the bill established a tariff commission, and a tax on companies active in interstate commerce. Nevertheless, the over-all effect of the act was to maintain the high rates. The weight of Taft's action was to intensify the already sharp suspicions of progressive Republicans.

The Ballinger-Pinchot Controversy. Taft's alliance with conservative congressional leadership was publicly acknowledged in a transcontinental tour taken in the late summer and autumn of 1909. The widening rift between the President and the progressive Republicans needed only a galvanizing issue to become a permanent division. A dispute over conservation provided the circumstances—not only for a conservative-progressive division, but for a larger clash between Taft and Roosevelt.

Almost as soon as taking office, the new Secretary of the Interior, Richard A. Ballinger, took issue with the pro-conservationists whom he dismissed as "whoop 'er up boys." By the summer of 1909, Chief Forester Gifford Pinchot, a passionate exponent of conservation, viewed Ballinger's behavior with increasing suspicion, suspecting that Ballinger intended to surrender federal land reserves to private enterprise. The return of some million acres to the public domain by Taft, and a severe contraction of the Reclamation Service activities, brought the dispute between Pinchot and Ballinger to a boil. The Secretary of the Interior, however, acted with the certainty that he and the President were in accord on matters of conservation. But Pinchot would not be silenced, and when an investigator for the General Land Office brought him evidence that Ballinger was deeply involved in an effort to transfer Alaska coal lands from federal control to private hands prior to their sale to a Morgan-Guggenheim syndicate, the Chief Forester placed the evidence at the disposal of Taft. The President responded with a vigorous defense of his Interior chief, but also attempted to persuade Pinchot to desist from further action. Any doubt about the forester's intention disappeared when two articles appeared in *Collier's,* setting forth the charge that the administration was "whitewashing" Ballinger. The information, as Taft quickly realized, had come from Pinchot, who had written the President that Ballinger was "the most effective opponent the conservation policies have yet had." But the articles provoked a storm of demands for a congressional investigation, one that Pinchot pushed forward by admitting in a public letter to Senator Dolliver that he had indeed provided anti-Ballinger material to the press.

Upon this admission, Taft dismissed Pinchot. But irreparable damage had already been done to the President, who found large segments of the nation assuming that he and his associates wished to dismantle Roosevelt's conservation program. In the resulting congressional inquiry Ballinger was cleared; but under the clever and merciless interrogation of Louis D. Brandeis, the brilliant muckraking lawyer, Ballinger and Taft were both made to appear as though they had deliberately conspired to hide from the public the Interior chief's desire to gut conservation.

The Challenge to the Democrats. The blundering management of the affair by the administration, and the deep split it had caused in Republican ranks, led Brandeis to conclude: "If only there were a Democratic party, what havoc would be wrought!" The forthcoming mid-term elections were to provide the Democrats with their chance. For the first time in sixteen years they controlled the House of Representatives, and a coalition of Democrats and progressive Republicans proved increasingly dominant in the Senate. The Democrats also gained the upper hand in the key states of Massachusetts, New York, Ohio, and Indiana, and in New Jersey, where the recently resigned president of Princeton University, Woodrow Wilson, won the governorship. A political revolution impended.

THE RIFT BETWEEN TAFT AND ROOSEVELT

Roosevelt's Views on Taft. As Taft's blunders wore away his reputation, Roosevelt supporters recalled with longing the dynamic leadership of the old chief. When the former President returned to the United States from his grand tour of Africa and Europe, his name arose with increasing regularity as a possible replacement for Taft in 1912. Although Roosevelt took care to support Taft publicly, privately he expressed to a British friend his dismay at the political situation. He traced its deterioration to the President. "Taft," he wrote, "is a kindly well-meaning man, who was a fine judge and an excellent lieutenant in executive office, but he has no instinct of leadership and he takes his color so completely from his immediate surroundings that he is continually finding himself in situations where he really has broken his word, or betrayed some former associate. . . ." Although Roosevelt did not say so, there stirred deep within him the conviction that he himself was one of the betrayed. As early as April 1910 he complained to Henry Cabot Lodge: "I don't think that under the Taft-Aldrich-Cannon regime there has been a real appreciation of the needs of the country, and I am certain that there has been no real appreciation of the way the country feels." Thus, even as the official opposition surged forward in strength, the most formidable spokesman of the Republican party moved toward a split with the incumbent President.

Conflicting Views of the Presidency. At the heart of the impending rift between Roosevelt and Taft was a fundamental difference in their conceptions of the presidency. Roosevelt defined his view of the office as one in which "every executive officer, and above all every executive officer in high position was a steward of the people. . . ." In that role Roosevelt had done whatever he felt "the needs of the Nation demanded unless such action was forbidden by the Constitution or by the laws," and in the process had greatly broadened "the use of executive power." Lest anyone doubt his aim, he bluntly declared: "I did not care a rap for the mere form and show of power; I cared immensely for the use that could be made of the substance."

To such a conception of the office, Taft issued a vigorous dissent: "The true view of the executive functions," he argued in 1916, "is . . . that the President can exercise no power which cannot be fairly and reasonably traced to some specific grant of power or justly implied and included within such express grant as proper and necessary." He dismissed Roosevelt's stewardship theory as unsafe.

It was not Taft's bumbling but his reforms that brought the final split with Roosevelt. At heart, Taft lacked sympathy with the industrial tendencies of his day. "Monopoly" belonged in his lexicon of dirty words. Where Roosevelt had plumped in 1908 for a program of regulation to check the destructive tendencies of corporate power, implying that concentration was the order of the day, a position he was subsequently to state explicitly, Taft swung behind a campaign of judicial dissolution of corporate concentrations. As a first step, however, he accepted the need for strengthened railroad regulations, and in an unusually strong stand (at least for Taft), he threw the whole weight of executive power behind the legislative push to amend the Hepburn Act.

MAJOR ACTS OF TAFT'S ADMINISTRATION

The Mann-Elkins Act. Roosevelt had pressed for changes in the Hepburn Act, and Taft had energetically supported these proposals during the campaign of 1908. In January 1910, Attorney General George W. Wickersham submitted the new legislation to the House. The tangled debate that followed among regular and progressive Republicans and Democrats culminated in a deal between the "Regulars" and the Democrats; the latter agreed to support the proposed administration bill in return for the Regulars' support of the Arizona and New Mexico statehood bills.

The act that finally emerged established a Commerce Court with the power to hear appeals from rates set by the Interstate Commerce Commission, but it also vested in the I.C.C. the authority to regulate railroad and telegraph companies and to order rate changes. Most importantly, if a railroad objected to a rate, it had to prove its inequity. Oddly, both Taft and the progressives agreed that the end product had real merit; but in the struggle to achieve an acceptable bill their mutual suspicions had intensified. Once again, the easygoing Taft had revealed his remarkable facility for converting agreement into hostility.

Taft and the Income Tax. On February 25, 1913, the Sixteenth Amendment was formally incorporated into the Constitution. Although he had followed a devious course in its formulation, Taft himself had proposed its submission as an amendment. He did so to reconcile it with the 1895 Supreme Court decision declaring an earlier income tax unconstitutional; and he had labored hard to obtain its ratification. If one simply contemplates the revolutionary changes the income tax wrought, one would have to designate William Howard Taft an unwitting radical who in this single act propelled America further along the road to a social revolution than all other Presidents before or since. Ironically, in signing it, he signed the death warrant of the self-sufficient world he treasured.

Taft, Reform, and Trust Busting. As Roosevelt struggled to regain the presidency in 1912, he repeatedly denounced Taft as a reactionary. A fairer estimate would concede to Taft the designation moderate progressive. Although rarely thought of as friend to labor, the ponderous Ohioan consistently supported safety legislation covering mines and railroads; the eight-hour day in government employment; an Employers' Liability Act covering government contracts; and a federal Children's Bureau to supervise various matters, among them child labor.

Although generally considered a friend of business, no President pushed trust-busting activities with greater zeal. In his four years as President, Taft launched twice as many antitrust proceedings as Roosevelt had during his seven years. But there existed a fundamental divergence between the two men in their conception of such proceedings. For Roosevelt, antitrust proceedings were a means to an end: the establishment of effective business regulation. For Taft, they were an end in themselves: the perpetuation of American free enterprise and competition. Where Roosevelt saw concentration of control in the American economy as the inevitable wave of the future, Taft viewed it as an unnecessary evil, to be driven out of existence by court proceedings. This divergence of opinion was the major cause of the rift between the two men; and when the rift became an irrevocable split, it divided the Republicans into two warring camps.

The Rule of Reason. In November 1906, Roosevelt had opened legal proceedings against the Standard Oil Company, followed shortly by proceedings against the American Tobacco Company. The action against Standard Oil was particularly popular, since it epitomized for the public the evils of the trust; and in 1907, nearly 1,000 legal indictments were pending throughout the nation against Standard Oil. The lower federal courts had found against both companies, and on March 14, 1910, the Supreme Court opened hearings on a Standard Oil appeal. On May 15, 1911, Chief Justice Edward White finally found against Standard Oil, but limited the specific applicability of the decision by setting forth the "rule of reason," which decreed that the Sherman Anti-Trust Act applied only to "undue" or "unreasonable" restraints of trade. This decision meant that every new instance in which a corporation was charged with trust activity would require a Court ruling. On May 29, 1911, the same rule was applied in rejecting the American Tobacco Company's appeal from a lower court decision. Taft had originally opposed the Court's arrogation of power, but, once again revealing his automatic reverence for judicial findings, now claimed it strengthened the Sherman Act.

ROOSEVELT'S RETURN TO POLITICS

The U. S. Steel Prosecution. With the unfailing facility that had led Taft time and again to convert a reasonable political stance into unmitigated disaster, he initiated a suit against the United States Steel Corporation. A primary point in the government's case as it was finally revealed on October 26, 1911, proved to be the charge that the 1907 acquisition of the Tennessee Coal and Iron Company was a key step in the corporation's struggle to obtain a steel monopoly. Unfortunately for both Taft and the Republican party, Roosevelt had played a key role in United States Steel's absorption of the Tennessee corporation. Roosevelt, who had ten weeks earlier appeared before a Democratically controlled House committee to defend his role in the transaction, viewed the steel suit as a personal attack. All of his doubts about the Taft administration welled up into an absolute conviction that no matter what its progressive protestations, it represented "a kind of sincere rural toryism." As for Taft's efforts to dismantle big corporations, he dismissed it as equivalent to an effort at damming the Mississippi "to stop its flow outright." The real challenge of America's industrial tendencies, he concluded, was one of comprehensive regulation. "We should enter upon a course of supervision, control, and regulation of these great corporations—a regulation which we should not fear, if necessary, to bring to the point of control of monopoly prices. . . ." Roosevelt had re-entered the political wars and his target was none other than his self-chosen heir.

The Reasons for Roosevelt's Decision. Although Roosevelt had viewed the growing political warfare within the Republican party as likely to result in a Democratic victory in 1912, it was not until November of 1911 that he actually considered challenging Taft for the Republican nomination. Once he *had* contemplated the possibility, he began to shift his position, clearly indicating his newly formed conviction that only he could displace Taft and assure a Republican triumph. This conclusion was reached despite the fact that La Follette of Wisconsin had decided to challenge the incumbent. But Roosevelt did not believe in a La Follette victory, "simply because," as he explained it, "while people did not like Taft, they would in the majority of cases have gone for Taft against La Follette." It was also evident that Roosevelt, who found the "toryism" of Taft objectionable, would never accept the restoration of the agrarian America that was La Follette's dream. Both men, in his estimation, sought to repudiate the very aspect of American life which had brought the United States to the threshold of world dominance—America's bursting industrialism. To assure fulfillment of that destiny, Roosevelt, on February 24, 1912, announced his intention to campaign for the Republican nomination "through direct primaries."

The Primaries of 1912. Roosevelt's decision to enter the primaries was a calculated risk, for he realized that since Taft controlled the party machinery he was assured of Southern Republican support. Although the South provided little strength to the party, it controlled a third of the convention delegates, and supported candidates for the patronage they could offer. Taft, as the incumbent, pulled the patronage lever. Further, most state organizations which used the state convention system for instructing national convention delegates were under the control of conservative leaders. Roosevelt's supporters recognized that only by demonstrating at the primary polls their candidate's superior drawing power could they win. As expected, Taft drew heavy support in the South, and also in the convention states of New York, Michigan, Kentucky, and Indiana; and he and La Follette came home winners in the Massachusetts and North Dakota primaries. But following the April 9 primary victory in Illinois, Roosevelt swept on to a series of triumphs that culminated with his capture of Taft's home state of Ohio. When the Republicans gathered in Chicago early in June, Roosevelt had won more votes in the primaries than Taft and La Follette combined, and had carried traditionally Republican states. To the party leaders the former President issued the simple warning: "A clear majority of the delegates honestly elected to this convention were chosen by the people to nominate me." The issue was no less than a choice between honesty and popular will versus fraud and party hacks.

The Progressive Party. The gathering Republicans met amid scenes of angry controversy. No less than 254 delegates were contested. Of these, Roosevelt needed no more than 50 to win the nomination, and he expected easily to gain at least that number. But Taft controlled the convention committee which determined the result, and he received 235 delegates. Since all objective analyses give Roosevelt at least 50 delegates, the resulting nomination of Taft carried with it an aura of duplicity. Roosevelt made the point emphatic in a message to the Republican party: "Any man nominated by the Convention as now constituted would be merely the beneficiary of this successful fraud; it would be deeply discreditable to any man to accept the Convention's nomination under these circumstances; and any man thus accepting it would have no claim to the support of any Republican on party grounds, and would have forfeited the right to ask the support of any honest man of any party on moral grounds."

Rather than embrace an immoral slate, Roosevelt called upon his supporters to join together in a new party dedicated to progressive principles and ideals. Thus in early August the Progressive party—popularly known as the Bull Moose party—was formed. Out of its roaring enthusiasm came a surge of indictments and demands. "Democrats and Republicans alike," Roosevelt charged, "represent government of the needy many by professional politicians in the interests of the rich few." What was needed, the Progressive felt, was a combination of the short ballot, initiative, referendum and recall, a corrupt practices act, female suffrage, direct election of senators, recall of state judicial decisions, reform of the amendment procedures, and presidential primaries, in order to assure political democracy. In addition, stringent controls of industry and tariff reform, a more effective pure food law, child and women labor protection, minimum wage and maximum hour provisions, unemployment insurance, and old-age pensions were given a ringing support. When the convention adjourned on August 7, with the thunderous chords of the *Battle Hymn of the Republic* shaking the rafters, it had thrown aside the restraints of the past and revealed the aspirations of the future.

Fully a quarter of a century would be needed before its program would be substantially fulfilled, but although the Progressive party faded by 1916, it had made its indelible mark by delineating the future direction of reform. It had also cast the Republican party into a time of discontent that would last for eight years, and had assured the election of a Democrat named Woodrow Wilson. The floodtide of progressivism had been reached.

Chapter 10

Wilsonian Democracy

Democrats watched with increasing glee as the Republican party fell apart, sensing that the way to the White House was being paved for them by the rampaging Roosevelt. "Nothing new is happening in politics, except Mr. Roosevelt, who is always new, being bound by nothing in the heavens above or in the earth below," Woodrow Wilson noted. "He is now rampant and very diligently employed in splitting the party wide open—so that we may get in!" Sixteen years in the political wilderness seemed about to end for the Democrats and a wealth of presidential aspirants were prepared to make their bids when the Democratic faithful gathered at Baltimore in the final week of June 1912.

Until the disruption of the Republican party, it appeared that the progressive banner would be seized by the Democrats; but once Roosevelt had climbed aboard the progressive hobby horse, it no longer seemed important whom the Democrats chose, for their candidate was bound to win. William Jennings Bryan, however, was determined to assure the choice of a progressively inclined Democrat, and set to work frustrating conservative designs to organize the Baltimore convention. Only from Woodrow Wilson did he get clear-cut support. "The Baltimore convention is to be a convention of progressives," Wilson, then Governor of New Jersey declared, which would "express its convictions in its organization and in its choice of the men who are to speak for it." Although woefully short of the two-thirds support needed to assure his nomination, Wilson had carved out his niche as *the* progressive Democrat. For forty-six ballots the Democrats were deadlocked, as the various factions of delegates held fast for their respective candidates—Senator Oscar Underwood of Alabama, Speaker of the House Champ Clark of Missouri, and Woodrow Wilson. Finally, on July 2, Wilson won the nomination, and, most observers thought, the presidency.

THE ELECTION OF 1912

Wilson and Roosevelt Contrasted. Wilson himself strongly doubted his ability to win the presidency. He viewed Roosevelt from the outset as his real opponent. Gloomily he informed a friend, "I feel Roosevelt's strength is altogether incalculable. He appeals to their imagination; I do not. He is a real, vivid person, whom they have seen and shouted themselves hoarse over and voted for, millions strong; I am a vague, conjectural personality, more made up of opinions and academic prepossessions than of human traits and red corpuscles."

From the very beginning of the campaign it was evident that Roosevelt had lost none of his fire, and his personality alone assured him of national attention. In addition, most progressives had a far clearer idea of what Roosevelt represented than they did of what Wilson stood for. On the other hand, Wilson probably gained considerable progressive support precisely because Roosevelt's past too often impressed reformers as erratic and opportunistic.

But if Roosevelt's record lent itself to confirming the alienation of some progressives, Wilson's own position was either obscure or nonexistent. It was not until late August, after Wilson had met Louis D. Brandeis, that a well-defined program stating Wilson's position was formed. Only then could the voter begin to see clearly the ways in which Wilson differed from Roosevelt.

The New Nationalism. When Theodore Roosevelt returned from his African safari, he was eager to meet Herbert Croly, author of the ponderous but challenging book, *The Promise of American Life*. Roosevelt considered Croly's "the most profound and illuminating study of our national conditions which has appeared for many years." Croly's volume focused on the inadequacies and misguided objectives of the progressive effort to restore the *laisser faire* liberalism of the nineteenth century. "It cannot be restored even if we would," the waspish author asserted, "and the public interest has nothing to gain by its restoration." In a freewheeling criticism of progressive aspirations, Croly argued that the temper of the time called for greater collectivization, whether it be expressed in corporations, unions, or political machines. To assume that "the people" were victimized by these developments neglected the elementary fact that societies did not exist in isolation from the public, but were reasonably faithful reflections of the public temper. To combat natural selfishness of the human animal, Croly concluded, a movement was required by which men would learn that goodness would pay off. A collectivized society required a collective solution for its problems. Croly dubbed the solution he proposed "New Nationalism"; and he realized that acceptance of his solution was tantamount to repudiation of Jeffersonian individualism, now to be replaced by "a democracy devoted to the welfare of the whole people by means of a conscious labor of individual and social improvement; and that is precisely the sort of democracy which demands for its realization the aid of the Hamiltonian nationalistic organization and principle."

It was these ideas that Roosevelt excavated from Croly's dry tome and presented with his usual vigor. Beginning on August 31, 1910, at Osawatomie, Kansas, a locale heavy with memories of the avenging John Brown, Roosevelt launched the demand "that we work in a spirit of broad and far-reaching nationalism when we work for what concerns our people as a whole." The only agent sufficient to meet such needs was the national government, which alone could secure "the betterment which we seek." And then, in words which echoed Croly, Roosevelt declared:

> The American people are right in demanding that New Nationalism without which we cannot hope to deal with new problems. The New Nationalism puts the national need before sectional or personal advantage. It is impatient of the utter confusion that results from local legislatures attempting to treat national issues as local issues. It is still more impatient of the impotence which springs from over-division of governmental powers, the impotence which makes it possible for local selfishness or for legal cunning, hired by wealthy special interests, to bring national activities to a deadlock. This New Nationalism regards the executive power as the steward of the public welfare. It demands of the judiciary that it shall be interested primarily in human welfare rather than in property, just as it demands that the representative body shall represent all the people rather than any one class or section of the people.

A powerful federal government which regulated a rapidly centralizing economy and society had captured Roosevelt's imagination. It became the promised result should the Progressive party capture the presidency in 1912.

The New Freedom. The intellectual debt Roosevelt owed Croly was matched by that which Wilson owed Louis D. Brandeis. A wealthy former corporation lawyer, Brandeis had achieved a national reputation by his attacks upon the monopolistic practices of the New Haven Railroad and his conduct of the Ballinger-Pinchot hearings. He supplied Wilson with the specific proposals that put backbone into the Democratic candidate's belief that an inspired political leader provided the words which moved men to act. As early as 1909, Wilson had described a "man of the people" as:

> . . . a man who has felt that unspoken, that intense, that almost terrifying struggle of humanity, that struggle whose object is, not to get forms of government, not to realize particular formulas or make for any definite goal, but simply to live and be free. He had participated in that struggle; he has felt the blood stream against the tissue; he has known anxiety; he has felt that life contained for him nothing but effort, effort from the rising of the sun to the going down of it. He has, therefore, felt beat in him, if he had any heart, a universal sympathy for those who struggle, a universal understanding of the unutterable things that were in their hearts and the unbearable burdens that were upon their backs.

Unquestionably Wilson possessed outstanding rhetorical skill, but on close examination his speeches revealed a curious absence of substance. As one hostile contemporary noted: "His mind is like a light which destroys the outlines of what it plays upon; there is much illumination, but you see very little." Although committed to opposing the trusts, as more than one historian has noted, Wilson lacked an effective program with which to handle them. Only after his meeting with Brandeis did Wilson resolve to make the trust question "a second struggle for emancipation."

In a set of campaign speeches which came to be known collectively as the "New Freedom," Wilson diagnosed the national condition and prescribed a remedy. Aware that social and economic changes abounded on all sides, he hammered away at the idea that increasingly "the individual has been submerged." The agent of this submersion was the corporation; Wilson stated, "Your individuality is swallowed up in the individuality and purpose of a great organization"; and with the decline of the free individual came the exaltation of a few "to a power which as individuals they could never have wielded." The most striking evidence of this change was the shift in the everyday relationships of men, which, the Democrat noted, "are largely with great impersonal concerns, with organizations, not with other individuals."

Against this formidable shift of emphasis the antiquated laws were often wholly ineffective. Nothing short of a massive redrafting of the laws would provide the needed remedy. Under the prevailing system, claimed Wilson, the laws often pitted power against weakness, narrowed and stiffened the lines of endeavor, and squeezed out the small producer or compelled him to sell out and resign himself to being absorbed. The result was a stifling of ambition and the obliteration of free enterprise, a process which made it possible for a favored few to get preferential treatment and to extend their own exclusive network of control, ultimately allowing them to dominate every industry in the country. Against this process Wilson proposed a redirection of governmental energy. "What this country needs above everything else," he proclaimed, "is a body of laws which will look after the men who are on the make rather than the men who are already made." And nothing less than an energetic campaign to "bring the government back to the people" was required, a campaign which would "open up all the processes of politics and of public business . . . to public view." An informed public would work to restore through law a competitive economic system founded on traditional free enterprise.

Thus Wilson, like Theodore Roosevelt, saw the federal government as an agent capable of positively regulating the economy. But where Roosevelt viewed the federal task as a regulation of the new order through the extension of federal power, Wilson saw federal power as an agent for dismantling illegal corporate power and restoring unhampered competition. To achieve this end an informed people would have to dethrone the vested interests in politics, untrammel business by abolishing such evils as tariff favors, railroad discrimination, and credit denials, and all other forms of unjust handicaps against the little man, while humanizing industry "—not through the trusts,—but through the direct action of law guaranteeing protection against dangers and compensations for injuries, guaranteeing sanitary conditions, proper hours, the right to organize, and all other things which the conscience of the country demands as the workingman's right." Triumph for the New Freedom, Wilson promised, would open the gates of opportunity to all. In substance, he pledged redemption of the nation from the woes that had stirred the progressive to arms.

Wilson Elected. The Americans who trooped to the polls in 1912 to elect a President and Congress seemed to have espoused progressivism. Not only had Wilson and Roosevelt announced themselves progressive, but Taft, ostensibly the spokesman for conservatism, insisted on thinking of himself as a progressive. In addition, the Socialists, under the eloquent leadership of Eugene V. Debs, mounted a vigorous campaign. When the returns were counted, Wilson had won a landslide electoral victory, though he had garnered barely forty-two per cent of the total vote. His 6,293,019 votes had obtained 435 electoral votes; Roosevelt's 4,119,507 had gained only the 77 electoral votes of Michigan, Pennsylvania, South Dakota, Minnesota, and Washington, plus 11 of California's split electoral count, for a total of 88 votes. Taft's 3,484,956 votes had carried the 8 votes of Vermont and Utah, while the Socialists, with 901,873 votes, had no electoral votes at all—though, significantly, they had polled more heavily than ever before in their history. Of greater immediate significance was the Democrats' winning control of Congress, as a result of the Republican split, with 73 votes in the House and 6 in the Senate. The Democratic party, still a minority in the nation, had nonetheless won the chance to prove it was the party of progress, one which (in the definition of Wilson) had "a plan at its heart." It would not be Wilson alone who was to undergo testing; the party he led was now also on trial, and after sixteen years in the wilderness, it had now to justify its tenure and establish itself as the majority party.

THE BACKGROUND AND QUALIFICATIONS OF WOODROW WILSON

Wilson's View of Government. The complex, often elusive man who had entered the White House on March 4, 1913, seemed to many a distant, unapproachable figure. (William Allen White described him as "a frozen flame of righteousness.") His election and inauguration had stirred in him not pride but an impersonal detachment, a stance that he admitted robbed his life "of intensity, as it certainly does of pride and self-consciousness (and, maybe, of enjoyment). . . ."

The son of a Presbyterian minister, Wilson revealed a striking tendency to fuse his role as teacher with that of minister, spreading the true word, leading his flock into the light. His early career in the academic sphere, first at Bryn Mawr and at Wesleyan University, and then at Princeton, had strengthened his faith in "the inestimable force of chastened eloquence." As a public official he retained the conviction that his task was to teach the public that "liberty is not something that can be laid away in a document, a completed work," but is, instead, "an organic principle, a principle of life, renewing and being renewed." It was the citizenry's responsibility to recognize the constant mobility of democratic institutions.

Wilson had begun to form his convictions about government as a comparatively young man. As a graduate student, he had, in his striking thesis *Congressional Government,* leveled the charge that the dominance of the legislative branch during the final decades of the nineteenth century had resulted in bad federal government. Similarly, there were indications of his political temperament during his career as an educator. Early in his presidency of Princeton he earned national fame as he worked to make the university a model for democratic education; and his willingness to experiment ultimately resulted in the proposal of innovations and reforms so far-reaching as to drive the dean of the graduate school, Andrew Fleming West, into open opposition. The ensuing clash occupied public attention; and when Wilson was finally forced to accept defeat, he resigned Princeton's presidency, on October 20, 1910. But by this time, his political career was already well launched, as in mid-September of 1910 he had been given the Democratic gubernatorial nomination in New Jersey.

From Governor to President. Wilson did not conceal his reasons for accepting the nomination; he saw it as "the mere preliminary of a plan to nominate me in 1912 for the presidency." Although the candidate of "Boss" James Smith and of "Boss" Robert W. Davis, he flatly declared his independence the moment his nomination was secured. Although he had originally been thought of as the conservative candidate, he emphatically espoused progressive reforms, warning his boss sponsors that they, like the "young lady of Niger who went for a ride on a tiger," stood a good chance of being gobbled alive. His repeated pledge that he stood for the regeneration of the Democratic party, combined with the public detestation for Taft, swept Wilson into office with a generous margin of 50,000 votes.

The vigorous program of reform that followed resulted in the establishment of the direct primary, a corrupt practices act, a law regulating public utilities, and a workmen's compensation law. These major acts, along with a host of lesser reforms were rammed through the state legislature in six weeks of March and April, 1911. The whole nation viewed with admiration the remarkable record of reform established under the guidance of an "unsophisticated school-master" (as Wilson called himself).

Wilson revealed himself an effective mobilizer of public opinion and a vigorous party leader. Though the election of 1911 resulted in the defeat of the Democrats, with the Republicans gaining solid control of both Houses, and in spite of the deadlock between Wilson and the legislature, a solid progressive platform had been built from which the energetic governor now pressed for the presidential nomination. With his election to the presidency, Wilson again revealed qualities that had proved mighty weapons both at Princeton and Trenton; a vigorous, forward-looking, well-thought-out set of proposals was handed to Congress. Within little more than five months of Wilson's inauguration, the New York *Times* editorialized: "this Congress has a President on its back, driving it pitilessly. . . . Never were Congressmen driven so, not even in the days of the 'big stick.'" The New Freedom was to mature in a surge of legislation.

WILSON'S FIRST TERM

As governor, Wilson had inherited a legacy of long agitation for reform in New Jersey; it had set the stage for his subsequent success in 1911. The same condition prevailed in 1913 when he entered the White House. Although there existed no consensus on specific reforms to be pressed, there was near-unanimous agreement on the need for reform. It was Wilson's good fortune to sense and share the national mood for change and to be ready to guide it toward specific fulfillment. Throughout his first four years as President, he would move ahead—but always with reverence for the past. The value of the American inheritance was not to be repudiated; but the promise of a better future also needed fulfillment. "Men's hearts wait upon us; men's lives hang in the balance; men's hopes call upon us to say what we will do," Wilson had declared in his inaugural address. To meet these aspirations, he had pledged to try his uncompromising best. Such a pledge the new President would never take lightly.

The Federal Reserve Act. The fiscal crisis of 1907 convinced both progressives and conservatives that substantial reforms were needed to keep the nation's financial structure on an even keel. A stopgap measure, the Aldrich-Vreeland Act (1908), had provided for the issuance of emergency banking notes on critical occasions and, more importantly, for the setting up of a National Monetary Commission (made up of members of Congress) to investigate banking conditions and to make recommendations for the reconstruction of the American banking system. In 1912, under the guidance of Nelson Aldrich, the Commission issued a comprehensive critique of the existing system, and called for a National Reserve Association which would have all the earmarks of a central bank. The proposed bank would have a capitalization of no less than $100,000,000; some fifteen branches controlled by member banks and distributed sectionally; and the power to issue currency, backed by gold and commercial paper, which would be its own—rather than the government's—liability. It would also provide reserve and discount facilities, in addition to holding the deposits of the federal government. Thirty of its thirty-nine directors would be chosen by the branches and businessmen of the proposed fifteen districts into which the banking nation would be divided. The plan had the undoubted support of most bankers, but among numerous old line Democrats it triggered the unhappy memory of the unlamented Second Bank of the United States. The subsequent issuance in 1913 of a report by the Pujo Committee, announcing the existence of a money trust, lent weight to charges that the proposed National Reserve Association was merely a new engine of privilege. The new administration found itself obliged to follow a delicate path between the demands of the bankers and those of their critics. Notable among the latter was Brandeis, who had popularized the Pujo findings in a series of muckraking articles subsequently published as *Other People's Money*. Finally, however, it was agreed that fiscal reform transcended other issues.

Even before Wilson's inauguration, Congressman Carter Glass of Virginia, chairman of a House Banking Committee subcommittee, had opened hearings on fiscal reform proposals. Glass opposed a central bank, supporting instead a loose system of reserve banks under private control. As emphatic in his views was William Jennings Bryan, the newly designated Secretary of State, who plumped for a reserve system under federal control. Wilson, who had given little if any prior thought to the problem, entered into consultation with Glass and his chief adviser, H. Parker Willis, and gave his tentative approval, but he insisted on a supervisory board which would keep a check on the system. When news of the proposal leaked out, it threatened to cause a major split in the party. Secretary of the Treasury William Gibbs McAdoo proposed instead that the reserve system be made an adjunct to the Treasury. To further complicate the administration's position, Senator Robert L. Owen of Oklahoma, chairman of the Banking Committee, raised his powerful voice in opposition to Glass's proposal. An uneasy Wilson, faced with the threat of an irreparable party split, turned to Brandeis for guidance, and obtained the advice that government control of the banking system and government responsibility for the issuance of currency was imperative. Wilson deferred to this stand

and with the assent of Glass and Bryan, on June 23, 1913, notified Congress that "the control of the system of banking and issue, which our new laws are to set up, must be public, not private, must be vested in the Government itself, so that the banks may be the instruments, not the masters, of business and of individual enterprise and initiative."

Further complications arose once the bill had been introduced into Congress, as a shifting coalition of Southern and Midwestern congressmen attacked the Glass bill for its failure to forbid restrictive banking practices and interlocking control of banks. Further protests were directed against the absence of provision for short-term agricultural credits, the use of commercial paper as security for currency issuances, the decision to reaffirm the gold standard, and the role of private bankers in administering regional banks. With the assistance of Bryan the attacking congressmen managed to gain the inclusion of a provision for short-term agricultural credit, and on September 18 a contented House gave the bill a thumping approval, 285 to 85. Despite a torrent of criticism from the banking world and the temporary bottling up of the House bill in the Senate Banking Committee, the bill was finally released, and on December 19 the Senate gave it a 54 to 34 backing. Four days later, after both Houses agreed to the changes reached in conference, Wilson signed the act into law.

The new administration had taken a giant step forward in the struggle to reform the economic administration of the country. The act as finally approved provided for the establishment of between eight to twelve Federal Reserve Banks, which were to serve as central banks in their districts, and for the creation of a Federal Reserve Board to supervise and formulate policies of the Reserve Banks. All national banks and certain state banks and trust companies were to be members of a system in which the Reserve Banks issued Federal Reserve notes and bank notes, discounted and fixed discount rates on members' paper, held deposits for member banks, and provided clearing facilities for members' checks. The final result was to provide a neat fusion of private enterprise and public regulation.

The Underwood Tariff. The long tradition of Democratic hostility to protective tariffs insured a renewed effort to reduce the high rates of the Payne-Aldrich tariff. In fact, only the veto by Taft of three Democratic tariff acts had prevented their reduction. Representative Oscar Underwood of Alabama, chairman of the Ways and Means Committee, faced with a friendly President, set to work to reintroduce a comprehensive reformulation of tariff schedules. Despite an original effort to provide protection for raw wool and sugar, wool was placed on the free list and sugar was given temporary protection for an additional three years. Of greater significance, over-all rates were reduced from an average of forty per cent to between twenty-four and twenty-five per cent, and in all instances where American industry was competitively secure, protection was abolished or made nominal. To meet an expected decrease of $100,000,000 in customs receipts, an income tax, which provided for a low graduated surtax and generous exemptions, was passed. Early in May the House approved the new tariff with a resounding vote of 281 to 139. The Senate was brought into line by Wilson's vigorous attacks upon lobbyists who sought "to overcome the interests of the public for their private profit." On October 2, 1913, a self-confident President signed the measure into law, satisfied by the knowledge that he had secured his dominance within the Democratic party.

The Clayton Anti-Trust Act. During the fight over the Federal Reserve System, Wilson had promised to handle interlocking corporate directorates in a proposed reform of antitrust legislation. In addition, he had built his 1912 campaign around promises to restore free competition through effective regulation. Once the tariff and the currency reforms were safely tucked away, he set to work redeeming his campaign pledges. Addressing a joint session of Congress on January 20, 1914—the personal appearance of a President before Congress was a startling innovation that Wilson had resorted to first when he called a special session of Congress in early April of 1913—he appealed for the passage of antitrust laws in a spirit of "quiet moderation, without revolution of any untoward kind." The bill presented to Congress, which bore the name of Alabama's Henry D. Clayton, chairman of the House Judiciary Committee, enumerated and forbade unfair trade practices such as price-cutting for the purpose of destroying competition; extended criminal liability to owners and directors of enterprises guilty of violating antitrust legislation; restrained one corporation from holding stock in another corporation if it reduced competition; made interlocking directorates illegal; and made injured private parties the beneficiaries of any damages collected in antitrust judgments. As the legislation was drawn up, provisions were made for the creation of an Interstate Commerce Commission to provide the Justice Department with the means to enforce the new legislation. Upon the advice of Brandeis, the I.C.C. was authorized to regulate the issuance of new railway securities.

One serious defect remained, one that labor and its friends insisted should be remedied by eliminating labor unions from liability under the antitrust laws. Since the 1912 Democratic platform had specifically pledged such exemption to farm and labor organizations, Samuel Gompers, president of the American Federation of Labor, saw its inclusion as nothing less than the condition of a continued support by labor of the administration. In a final compromise, the act granted to labor the right to jury trials in cases of criminal contempt; limited the use of injunctions; and excluded farm and labor organizations from designation as "illegal combinations" so long as they lawfully struggled to achieve their rights. Subsequently, in the Senate, Albert B. Cummins of Iowa obtained the inclusion of the assertion "that the labor of a human being is not a commodity or article of commerce." On this lofty note, labor's fight ended. But although Gompers designated the act's labor provisions as nothing less than labor's Magna Carta, within a decade it became apparent that labor's gains had been small, and that the great struggle for its equality was still unfought. The Clayton Act's passage, on October 14, 1914, ended the effort to reform the trusts. What finally emerged was superficially vigorous, but as Wilson privately complained, it was "so weak that you cannot tell it from water." A harsher criticism came from Senator James A. Reed of Missouri, who denounced the act as "a sort of legislative apology to the trusts, . . . accompanied by assurances that no discourtesy is intended." But the administration's real hope for trust reform was embodied in an act passed a month previously.

The Federal Trade Commission. Proposals for antitrust legislation seemed inevitably destined to bog down in the problem of how to dismantle trusts without crippling American industry. There existed the further problem that each new piece of trust legislation created endless wrangling in the courts which only served to convince the businessman that he was unjustly used, and to make the complainants resentful at the absence of a just settlement. Wilson also sensed that a general pattern of restraining legislation neglected a fundamental fact about the economy: it was ever changing, with new practices developing constantly, making it almost impossible to define with precision "legal" and "illegal" practices. If free enterprise has a compelling justification, it is that it encourages human ingenuity to seek new ways to resolve economic needs; but by its very nature, it places a premium on being able to avoid uncomfortable consequences or obstructions to one's enterprise. It was hardly surprising to learn that American businessmen had revealed a startling capacity to reverse the intent of even the most punitive laws, making them yield to business's own needs.

Thus it was that a considerable sentiment had developed for a new approach, one which would settle for a general statement of illegal trade practices, and which would establish a federal trade commission empowered to bar impediments to competition through an intimate supervision of the daily activities of the business world.

Without quite realizing it, Wilson, influenced by Brandeis, was espousing a measure that commanded considerable support among such vigorous exponents of the New Nationalism as Herbert Croly. In addition, such influential agents of business sentiment as the United States Chamber of Commerce had swung behind the proposal for the establishment of a trade commission which would advise businessmen about the legality of their proposed actions. For so long as restraints on trade practices existed, there remained the danger that steps taken at considerable expense in time and money would be disallowed. As a number of businessmen had observed, the tenacity with which they struggled to reverse the meaning of a law was inspired by fear at the loss they would sustain if the law were upheld. In a sense, the proposed commission would save both businessmen and government considerable expense, time, and energy. At first Wilson wavered; whether from political reasons or simple uncertainty is unknown. But on June 10, 1914, he swung behind the proposal, and three months later, on September 26, 1914, the bill establishing the new commission was signed into law. The passage of the Clayton Act seemed almost anticlimactic.

The Decline of the New Freedom. The feeling was now growing that the New Freedom had petered out. Ominous signs for the future appeared, as the 1914 elections reduced the Democratic House majority from 73 to 25, while Republicans had made large gains in the key states of New York, Pennsylvania, Illinois, Ohio, New Jersey, and Wisconsin. A real question existed as to whether Wilson could win re-election in 1916. It caused the President to search for a new direction, one which would lead him and the Democratic party to renewed power, built not upon the divisions in the Republican party, but on the designation of the Democratic party by a majority of the American electorate as its choice.

THE SEARCH FOR SOCIAL JUSTICE

"Modern politics," Henry Adams noted in his *Education,* "is a struggle not of men but of forces. The men become every year more and more creatures of force massed about central power houses." For

Wilson, flushed with a succession of legislative triumphs, the Democratic decline at the 1914 polls seemed a personal repudiation. "It costs to be used by the American people as a means of guiding their affairs!" he gloomily complained. "It exhausts a chap utterly to keep up with them." The vast reforms he had instituted in the administration of the economy were commended on all sides; but the fickle democracy did not dwell on favors received, but contemplated rewards yet unattained. The instinctive nineteenth century liberalism that imbued Wilson's original program had led him to declare in his inaugural, "Our work is a work of restoration," but the coming of World War I in 1914 threw into sharp focus the apparent bankruptcy of nineteenth-century ideals. "Is it not a possibility," wrote one contributer to the *New Republic,* "that what is taking place marks quite as complete a bankruptcy of ideas, systems, society, as did the French Revolution?"

Such sentiments struck a responsive chord in the younger generation that Randolph Bourne had described as "a little deficient in gaiety of heart, unduly confident in the strength of its insight, and amazingly disrespectful of its elders. In compensation it is fearless, honest, and terribly serious." And, unlike Wilson, the new generation was inspired by the conviction that the role of the federal government was to act positively to solve a whole host of social problems.

The Rising Call for Reform. Active in doubting the efficacy of the New Freedom's effort to restore *laisser faire* were a host of reform organizations such as the National Child Labor Committee, the National Association for the Advancement of Colored People, the National Consumers' League, women suffrage leagues, and the Anti-Saloon League, all of which saw legislation as the key to solving their grievances. Many of these reform groups had followed Theodore Roosevelt to Armageddon in 1912; but once the election result was in, Roosevelt retreated from the progressive standard, arguing as he did so that the absence of "loaves and fishes" made it impossible to hold together the Progressive party. In addition, the Rough-rider's distaste for Wilson, whom he described as "the worst President by all odds since Buchanan with the possible exception of Andrew Johnson," laid the foundations for the former President's reconciliation with the Republican party in 1916. Numerous progressives were increasingly at loose ends politically. To Wilson they appeared as a potential source of renewed strength; but to reap such votes, something more than a program of administrative reform of the economy was needed. Nothing less than a commitment to social justice was required. Wilson's administration had shown little, if any, inclination to press for such reforms; but by late 1914, the pressure began to grow for a shift in this direction.

Wilson and Social Justice. "The Government should concern itself with the matters that are of most importance to the average man and average woman," Theodore Roosevelt had declared, adding "it should be its special province to aid in making the conditions of life easier for these ordinary men and women, who compose the great bulk of our people." But for Wilson such a conception of the role of government came with difficulty. If there exists a single explanation of his political philosophy, it is that he was a Southerner, whose first recollection was "of standing at my father's gateway in Augusta, Georgia, when I was four years old, and hearing someone pass and say that Mr. Lincoln was elected and there was to be war." He had passed his boyhood, adolescence, and youth in a South first engulfed by war, and then afflicted with the agony of reconstruction. As the grown man admitted, "A boy never gets over his boyhood, and never can change those subtle influences . . . that were bred in him as a child." His reluctance, therefore, to extend the power of the federal government reflected his belief in the essential worth of state rights, in the merit of a government which strove to keep to a minimum its interferences in the everyday life of the individual, and in a political system founded on the antique maxim that that government governs best which governs least. In a real sense, Wilson never fully reconciled himself to the progressive demand for positive government.

Negro Rights. By the end of the first decade of the twentieth century, the American Negro had been made the target of a vast system of discriminatory legislation throughout the South. The conservative leadership of Booker T. Washington, who had enjoined his fellow Negro to learn, work, and win the respect of the white man, had struck militant Negroes and white sympathizers as grossly out of pace with the realities. Under the leadership of William E. B. Du Bois, a militant call was issued for a campaign to assure Negroes "absolute political and social equality," and from this call there emerged in 1910 the National Association for the Advancement of Colored People. Wilson openly appealed for Negro support during the 1912 campaign with the promise to stand "for everything by which [he] could assist in advancing the interest" of the Negro; but shortly after he entered the White House, Wilson declined to establish a National Race

Commission under presidential auspices. He justified his stand by referring to the opposition of certain Senators. The sentiment within the administration carried a profoundly anti-Negro bias, one that avoided the flagrant race baiting of some of the more vehement racists, but which, nonetheless, had a deeply Southern cast. With the consent of the President a program of tacit segregation was introduced into federal employment. Booker T. Washington, after spending several days in Washington, grimly summed up the new atmosphere in the capital: "I have never seen the colored people so discouraged and bitter as they are at the present time."

The La Follette's Seamen's Bill. Wilson had shown a marked unwillingness to press aggressively for an extension of labor's rights during the debate over the provisions of the Clayton Act. Although he was not unaware of the needs of labor, he made it abundantly clear, in a speech made when dedicating the Federal Labor Building, that he was not "at liberty to think of any one class of our fellow citizens to the exclusion of any other class," an attitude which labor sympathizers felt was hardly conducive to redressing the inequities under which labor operated. Nonetheless, Wilson's administration was to witness labor reforms of considerable dimensions.

One of these was the La Follette's Seamen's Bill, the brainchild of Andrew Furuseth, president of the International Seamen's Union, who had devoted his life to improving the life of the sailor. This bill contained provisions for strict safety requirements and for improved seamen working hours and working conditions, and relieved seamen of the threat of imprisonment if they broke their labor contracts. Wilson, when made aware that some of the provisions abrogated treaty pledges, was persuaded at first to veto the bill, but reversed his stand when subjected to the impassioned pleas of Furuseth. If anything, Wilson's stand emphasized the absence of a strong presidential plan for meeting labor's needs; but his willingness to respond if a suitably powerful appeal was made to his sense of justice was a hopeful sign.

Child Labor Reform. No private organization was more active or more successful in alleviating labor conditions than the National Child Labor Committee. It had successfully maneuvered through state legislatures the establishment of minimum ages at which children could be gainfully employed. By 1914, forty-seven states had instituted such restrictions, with fourteen as the usual age. When A. Mitchell Palmer was persuaded, in January 1914, to introduce into Congress a bill which prohibited the transit of the products of child labor in interstate commerce, Wilson, despite the overwhelming support given the bill in the House of Representatives, refused to lend his support to the proposal, taking the stand that it was unconstitutional. There the issue languished until 1916 when Wilson, probably seeking to assure continued Democratic dominance, threw his support behind a campaign to convince the electorate that the Democratic party alone stood for progressive aspirations. Wilson now placed the full prestige of his office in a successful fight to obtain congressional approval of the Keating-Owen Child Labor Bill which severely restricted the use of such labor. A similar evidence of change was Wilson's wholehearted espousal of the Kern-McGillicuddy Bill, which set up a federal employee workmen's compensation measure that its authors hoped would be a model for similar measures to cover other workers. Presidential opposition to the Hollis-Buckley Bill providing for federally supported rural credits abruptly ended in 1916, when it gained his cordial support. For many social reformers the climactic event which revealed the "new Wilson" was his decision, in January 1916, to nominate Louis D. Brandeis as an associate justice of the Supreme Court. In the taxing fight to get the appointment approved, Wilson never wavered, and on June 1, 1916, Brandeis was confirmed. One last great measure remained to be enacted to secure Wilson's claim to the banner of social justice.

The Adamson Act. A major labor dispute was coming to a head during the late spring of 1916. A series of demands by the four railroad brotherhoods for an eight-hour day with no reduction in pay, and for time and a half payments for overtime, were rejected by rail managers, although they agreed to submit to arbitration. When mediation failed, and the railroad brotherhoods signified their readiness to strike, Wilson decided to intervene to compel his own settlement. He called for acceptance of the eight-hour day, but relinquishment of the time and a half proposal. The brotherhoods accepted Wilson's terms, but management, despite Wilson's passionate pleas, refused to heed. At the Capitol, Wilson and the Senate's Democrats composed a solution which established the eight-hour day and provided for compulsory arbitration of future rail disputes by a federal commission. Although the railroads appealed to the courts, the Supreme Court subsequently upheld the Adamson Act in Wilson *v.* New. Against a storm of Republican abuse, Wilson, now in hot haste for a second term, issued a clarion call for social justice, a call that identified the Democratic party as the agent of humanity.

THE ELECTION OF 1916

When the Republicans gathered in Chicago in 1916 to nominate Charles Evans Hughes, they did so with the knowledge that the cement of the Progressive party, Theodore Roosevelt, had decided to support the Republican nominee. Although the last poor remnants of the Progressive party still offered Roosevelt their nomination, the erstwhile Bull Moose of 1912 declined. No one could estimate the implications, for no one could calculate how Roosevelt's 1912 vote would now split. The dramatic emergence of Wilson as a champion of social justice brought with it a veritable flood of reformers into the Democratic camp. His forceful support of labor added the American Federation of Labor, the railway brotherhoods, and other labor organizations to his unabashed backing. Equally impressive was the swing of organized farm support to the President. Independent support for Wilson was also growing.

Against this evidence of an upsurge of Democratic strength, Hughes could point to the near-unanimous support of the business community, and to increasing strength among those Americans who wanted the United States to take a more forceful stand in the world crisis precipitated by World War I. But the Republican candidate labored under a major handicap: the still-raw wounds of the 1912 fight. In his effort to straddle the gap between Progressive and Old Line Republicans, he managed to alienate as many votes as he gained. Nevertheless, he had a major asset: a united Republican party possessed a solid majority which could well afford considerable losses and still win.

This situation in the Republican party, however, applied to normal circumstances, and in 1916 the overshadowing issue for the nation was the raging world conflict, World War I. Out of the memory of the civil holocaust and the aftermath that had blighted his own youth, Wilson threw his full energies behind an effort to keep the nation at peace. Although no one can determine with exactitude the effect of this effort, it is unquestionably true that the Democratic slogan, "He Kept Us Out of War" appealed to deeply felt aspirations of the American people, particularly to the millions of newly enfranchised women who had gained from their states, mainly in the Great Plains and the West, the right to vote. (Full national female suffrage did not come into being until the 19th Amendment to the Constitution was adopted on August 26, 1920.) In almost every state where women voted Wilson either carried the day or ran an extremely close race. In the end, a tiny margin of a few thousand votes in California converted the supposed victory of Hughes on election night to a Wilson triumph the morning after. When the final tally was in, Wilson had 9,129,606 popular and 277 electoral votes as opposed to Hughes' 8,538,221 popular and 254 electoral votes. But Wilson had picked up almost three million votes over 1912, proving the efficacy of his stand in support of social justice and peace. The re-elected Wilson faced a growing international crisis and minuscule Democratic majorities in Congress with the consoling knowledge "that it can no longer be said that I represent a minority of the nation."

Chapter 11

America Abroad

By the last decades of the nineteenth century it had become apparent to most observers that America was destined to assume a predominant role among the major powers of the world. The great naval historian, Admiral A. T. Mahan, asserted: "Whether they will or no, Americans must now begin to look outward"; and Senator Albert J. Beveridge declared that God "has marked the American people as His chosen nation to finally lead in the regeneration of the world."

The sense of power which increasingly permeated American conceptions of the nation's destiny soon led to the universal conclusion that the question was no longer whether America would enter the arena of world politics, but when she would do so, and how.

During the administration of Theodore Roosevelt an answer to the question was proposed. The administration of Woodrow Wilson provided a different answer to the same question. Each had its own importance and validity, and American foreign policy has alternated between the two positions ever since.

FOREIGN POLICY IN LATIN AMERICA

The nineteenth century ended with the United States firmly committed to the preservation of the Monroe Doctrine; determined to extend her influence within and dominance of the Pacific Ocean; and inclined to espouse an unofficial Anglo-American alliance. Although the exact extent of each commitment was uncertain, America's stand on the Monroe Doctrine had been so emphatically stated that few nations doubted the United States' intention to retain against all challenges its exclusive dominance within the Western Hemisphere. The American people agreed upon America's right to pre-eminence in its own hemisphere; less unanimity of opinion existed over how best to secure this interest. Similarly, in regard to America's larger role in the world, few questioned that such a place was in order, but there was disagreement over whether it would most effectively be brought about by the physical power of the nation, or by the moral example of the American experiment. The gulf between Roosevelt's and Wilson's concepts of foreign relations is indicated by the former's emphasis upon might and the latter's appeal to morality.

Presidential Authority in Foreign Affairs. The Constitution is ambiguous on where ultimate responsibility for foreign relations is vested; it divides power in this area among the President, the Senate, and Congress. Yet as John Jay noted in Federalist Paper No. 64, "although the President must, in forming treaties, act by the advice and consent of the Senate, yet he will be able to manage the business . . . in such a manner as prudence may suggest." Under normal circumstances, as Jay suggested, the President is the dominant force in the formulation of foreign policy; but he invites trouble if he assumes that he is the only power. The President does possess a formidable complement to his foreign affairs power, that of Commander-in-Chief of the nation's armed forces. So long as Congress provides the wherewithal to support those forces, the President can use them to implement foreign policy (short of war) without the immediate consent of Congress. In fact, as more than one historian of presidential power has noted, he can even commit the armed forces to action, leaving no choice to Congress but to provide the means after the event. (An example of this is Theodore Roosevelt's decision to send the American fleet on a trip around the world, although funds were lacking, knowing that Congress could hardly abandon the fleet, once it had been launched on its errand.) The actual meaning of these implicit powers of the President was to receive its most dramatic definition at the hands of Theodore Roosevelt. It would not be too much to argue that the energetic New Yorker provided a definition of executive power in foreign affairs, the complete implications of which have still not been fully explored.

The Big Stick. During his early days in Republican politics, Roosevelt had enjoyed citing a West African proverb to explain his attitude toward the New York party bosses: "Speak softly and carry a big stick; you will go far." To act from a position of strength remained for Roosevelt a cardinal principle, one which he carried to extraordinary lengths in his relations with Latin America. In 1904, he set forth the principle of "the big stick" policy, subsequently known as Roosevelt's corollary, with a blend of soft words and menacing threat:

> It is not true that the United States feels any land hunger or entertains any projects as regards the other nations of the Western Hemisphere save such as are for their welfare. All that this country desires is to see the neighboring countries stable, orderly, and prosperous. Any country whose people conduct themselves well can count upon our hearty friendship. If a nation shows that it knows how to act with reasonable efficiency and decency in social and political matters, if it keeps order and pays its obligations, it need fear no interference from the United States. Chronic wrongdoing, or an impotence which results in a general loosening of the ties of civilized society, may in America, as elsewhere, ultimately require intervention by some civilized nation, and in the Western Hemisphere the adherence of the United States to the Monroe Doctrine may force the United States, however reluctantly, in flagrant cases of such wrongdoing or impotence, to the exercise of an international police power.

With equal emphasis Roosevelt warned Europe to avoid intervention in affairs of the Western Hemisphere, asserting in effect, that what was good for the goose was very ill-advised policy for the gander, a point which he made sharply to Secretary of State Elihu Root when he wrote: "If we intend to say 'Hands off' to the powers of Europe, sooner or later we must keep order ourselves." Whatever Roosevelt might have intended, he gave the distinct impression that the United States claimed a suzerainty over Latin America, and later events were to demonstrate that the claim "justified" American intervention.

The Panama Canal. The most spectacular example of American intervention in Latin American affairs was Roosevelt's decision "to take Panama." The weight of political opinion in the United States subscribed to Admiral Mahan's opinion that the physical proximity of a territory provided a "ground for national self-assertion." Since the signing of the Clayton-Bulwer Treaty in 1850, the United States had made it clear that any proposal to construct a canal across the isthmus of Panama without American participation would be viewed as an unfriendly act. Rutherford B. Hayes had reminded the world that our primary interest was founded on the fact that "our merely commercial interest in it is greater than that of all other countries." This view was echoed by Secretary of State James G. Blaine, who described an isthmus canal as "forming substantially a part of our coast-line." When

Ferdinand de Lesseps, the builder of the Suez Canal, launched a French company in 1879 to construct a canal across Panama, he had to devote a considerable part of his formidable energy to quieting American fear of the enterprise. Ultimately, de Lesseps's project floundered, overwhelmed by engineering difficulties and yellow fever.

In the aftermath of the Spanish-American War, however, American interest in an isthmus canal revived. Early in 1900 a proposal to build a canal across Nicaragua was introduced into Congress. Although such a proposal went against the Clayton-Bulwer Treaty, Great Britain, eager to cement its friendly ties with the United States, negotiated the Hay-Pauncefote Treaty (February 5, 1900) which permitted the United States to build, own, and neutralize a canal across the isthmus on condition that it not be fortified. When a storm of protest against this restriction arose in the United States, the proposed treaty failed to gain Senate ratification. But Britain indicated it was prepared to concede this point, and on November 18, 1901, a second Hay-Pauncefote Treaty was negotiated; this version not only conceded the United States' dominant interest in an isthmian canal, but also conceded American pre-eminence in the Caribbean.

Considerable lobbying for the Panama route was conducted by the New Panama Canal Company, which had replaced de Lesseps's enterprise. Faced with evidence that both Congress and Roosevelt favored a Nicaragua route, the French directors of the Company agreed to sell their interest for $40,000,000. Fearful that they would lose even this sum, Philippe Bunau-Varilla, a large stockholder in the New Panama Company, set to work influencing the Senate. His efforts were successful; at least, a House bill authorizing a Nicaraguan canal was amended by the upper Chamber to provide for a possible Panama route. But, as finally approved on June 28, 1902, the bill stipulated that unless Colombia was persuaded to provide a right of way "within a reasonable time and upon reasonable terms," the Nicaraguan route would take preference.

Colombia, through its Washington ambassador, Tomas Herran, negotiated a treaty which gave the United States control in perpetuity over a zone six miles wide in the isthmus of Panama which belonged to Colombia at that time, in exchange for a cash payment of $10,000,000, and an annual rental of $250,000. The Bogota government refused to accept the Hay-Herran Treaty, proposing instead a payment of $20,000,000 by the United States, and an additional $10,000,000 from the $40,000,000 to be paid the New Panama Canal Company. The Colombians also expressed strenuous reservations about the failure to define explicitly Colombia's continuing sovereignty over the canal zone. Roosevelt responded to these Colombian maneuvers with the blustering charge that Bogota was attempting to "blackmail" the United States. Rather than submit, the President considered either starting the Nicaragua canal or acting to secure the Panama route by direct intervention; but when a revolution broke out in Panama on November 3, 1903, the work of a New York *junta* financed by Bunau-Varilla and his American agent William Nelson Cromwell, an American warship, the U.S.S. *Nashville,* blocked the landing of Colombian troops to suppress the uprising. The newly independent Panama promptly designated Bunau-Varilla to negotiate a treaty which provided for a zone ten miles wide to be granted the United States in perpetuity for a down payment of $10,000,000 and an annual rent of $250,000—the same terms originally offered to Colombia for a smaller zone.

Despite the blunt charge by Senator John T. Morgan of Alabama that Roosevelt had actually started a war against Colombia, on February 23, 1904, the Senate overwhelmingly approved the Hay-Bunau-Varilla Treaty. Precisely who was responsible for the sequence of events that had detached Panama from Colombia remained uncertain until 1911, when the former President boasted:

> I am interested in the Panama Canal because I started it. If I had followed traditional, conservative methods I would have submitted a dignified State paper of probably 200 pages to Congress and the debate on it would have been going on yet; but I took the Canal Zone and let Congress debate; and while the debate goes on the Canal also does.

Most contemporary estimates of Roosevelt's action concede that it hastened the construction of the canal by a few months.

Wilson and Panama. Colombia viewed with dismay the sequence of events that had detached its Panama province. Insistent upon obtaining compensation, it proposed that its grievances be submitted to arbitration, but neither Roosevelt nor Taft was prepared to concede that a Republican administration might have erred. It was left to the less restrained Wilson, therefore, to support the passage in 1914 of a treaty which provided Colombia with an apology, and with an indemnity of $25,000,000. Roosevelt promptly appealed to Henry Cabot Lodge, the powerful Massachusetts senator, who arranged to have the proposed treaty shelved. Seven years later the treaty—this time without an apology but still providing for the $25,000,000 payment—was passed. As critics of the agreement noted, the discovery of oil in Colombia had convinced influential oil interests that an apology was due, even if only in cash. Furthermore, Roosevelt had died by this time. Roosevelt's opinion on the matter, however, had not died, and his words remained to do great damage to the country: "The payment," he had written, "can only be justified on the ground that this nation has played the part of a thief, or of a receiver of stolen goods."

Venezuela and the Dominican Republic. The increased stature of the United States in world politics after the Spanish-American War led to involvement in a serious crisis in the chaotic affairs of Venezuela. Italy, Germany, and Great Britain, irate over the failure of Venezuela's dictator Cipriano Castro to pay debts held in those countries, blockaded five Venezuelan ports and bombarded the forts guarding Puerto Cabello. The United States, aware that none of the participating powers planned territorial seizures, accepted the blockade and bombardment, but readily agreed through Roosevelt to arbitrate the dispute. When during the arbitration, however, a German warship bombarded Fort Carlos, America became incensed; and Roosevelt's suspicions of German intentions deepened even further when Berlin accepted arbitration by the World Court at The Hague only with obvious reluctance.

No sooner had the Venezuelan crisis moved toward settlement than a revolution broke out in the nearly bankrupt republic of Santo Domingo. France, Italy, and Germany threatened intervention in the country's affairs unless it met its debt obligations. President Morales of the country requested that the United States assume a protectorate over his republic. The threat of German intervention, Britain's positive encouragement of American assumption of supervisory responsibility for Caribbean affairs, and strong popular support at home for intervention finally persuaded Roosevelt to issue his famous corollary to the Monroe Doctrine. One month later, the Santo Domingan government agreed to accept an American as supervisor of its finances and collector of its tariffs. In the face of senatorial opposition, Roosevelt resorted to an executive agreement to gain his point. Simultaneously, American bankers expressed considerable interest in the plan for American banks to assume responsibility for consolidating and administering the debts of the Caribbean countries. The promise of stabilizing the region's fiscal obligations, thereby closing off any justification for further European intervention, had been further sweetened by the prospect of profits for American entrepreneurs.

FOREIGN POLICY IN THE FAR EAST

Roosevelt and Eastern Affairs. Although the Open Door policy had nominally committed the United States to support of the territorial integrity of China, primary American concern was for the security of American commercial interests in the Celestial Empire. The Chinese-American Trade Treaty of 1903 granted the United States equal trade privileges in Manchuria, and in so doing threw American support behind Japanese efforts to restrain the attempts of Russia to dominate the region. The administration was equally interested in persuading American banking combines, such as J. P. Morgan and Company and Kuhn, Loeb and Company, to play an active role in the construction of Chinese Railroads. In spite of its altruistic veneer, however, the Open Door policy increasingly took a form in which the overriding concern was, as Brooks Adams expressed it, "To make Asia pay." To this intention President Roosevelt gave his unqualified support, declaring in his First Annual Report (December 3, 1901), "we . . . claim parity of treatment, . . . throughout the [Chinese] Empire for our trade and our citizens with those of all other powers."

The Russo-Japanese War. Russia's stubborn refusal to withdraw from Manchuria, coupled with its persistent effort to close the region to any but its own exploitation, threw the Roosevelt administration into a quandary; it wanted to uphold American rights, but doubted the willingness of the public to support military intervention. Instead, Congress gave its wholehearted support to the Anglo-Japanese Alliance of 1902, and indirectly encouraged, by friendly approval, Japan's increasingly aggressive opposition to Russia's Manchurian policy. When Japan inaugurated war in February 1904 by suddenly attacking and sinking the Russian fleet at anchor in Port Arthur, Manchuria, United States policy explicitly supported Japan. As the developing war brought Japan sweeping successes both on land and sea, America began to have second thoughts. The Russian peril was receding, it was true; but now there were uneasy reflections on the "yellow peril." A complete triumph of Japan, Roosevelt noted, would end in "a real shifting of equilibrium as far as the white races are concerned." To protect the established situation, Roosevelt decided to use his good offices to encourage a negotiated peace.

The Treaty of Portsmouth. By late spring of 1905, the Czar's government had been overwhelmed by defeat on the field, and, further threatened by the possibility of revolution at home, it was receptive to the presidential proposals. Tokyo was also eager to resolve the dispute, for the financial drain of war now threatened fiscal collapse. That Roosevelt's interest was not motivated solely by concern for restoring peace is indicated by the advance assurance he extracted from Japan that she would adhere to the retention of the Open Door policy in Manchuria, restoring that province to China. In the negotiations held during the late spring of 1905 at Portsmouth, New Hampshire, Japan obtained the southern half of Sakhalin Island from Russia, and was given control of Port Arthur and the Russian railroads in Manchuria; in addition, St. Petersburg recognized Japan's dominant interest in Korea, and Japan recognized China's sovereignty in Manchuria. Subsequently, to eliminate the chance that Japan might turn her expansionist urge toward the Philippines, the Taft-Katsura Memorandum of July 1905, again recognized Japan's control of Korea, but stated that Tokyo had no aggressive designs on the Philippines. A brief interlude of good feelings permeated Japanese-American relations.

The Gentlemen's Agreement. Diplomacy has no place for permanent friendships—only for parallel interests. Roosevelt and the United States gained international acclaim for the tactful handling of the Portsmouth negotiations, but international memories are short. Within a brief time, the United States and Japan were involved in an acrimonious dispute which cast American racial practices into vivid relief. The unpleasant truth was that Orientals, no matter what their condition or status, were often the victims of discriminatory legislation, particularly on the West Coast. Typical were the laundry regulations, a series of restrictions limiting the operation of hand laundries, passed by San Francisco in the 1880s, which, although nominally impartial (as the Supreme Court noted), were enforced with an unequal hand against Orientals. Restrictions on Chinese immigration and abusive treatment of Chinese visitors in the United States led to a Chinese boycott of American goods, a boycott which was so effective that it almost persuaded Roosevelt to order military intervention at Canton. A factor which tended to mitigate Chinese resentment was its government's obvious inability to protest forcefully against such mistreatment, and the real desire of the administration to prevent unnecessary harassments of Chinese students and visitors in the United States.

Less amenable to settlement was the dispute between Japan and the United States over the treatment of Japanese nationals. The swift growth of a Japanese population in America during the last decade of the nineteenth century led to increasing fears of a "Japanese menace."

Efforts to cut back on Japanese immigration were only partially successful, and an Oriental Exclusion League began active agitation in California for effective restrictive laws. On October 11, 1906, San Francisco segregated all Oriental children in the public school system. Japan viewed this action, and subsequent West Coast anti-Oriental riots, as deliberate insult and provocation. Roosevelt, fearful that California's discriminatory actions might precipitate a war, assured the Tokyo government that Washington was deeply disturbed "with the outrageous agitation against the Japanese." But despite Roosevelt's angry denunciations the Californians refused to retreat from their stand. Finally, aware that browbeating was getting no results, Roosevelt changed tactics, and with quiet persuasion obtained the retraction of the offensive school practices in San Francisco. At the same time, in a series of diplomatic notes, both governments agreed to halt the further immigration of Japanese coolies to the continental United States. These documents were known collectively as the Gentlemen's Agreement of 1907–1908, and the term has subsequently come to designate any unwritten agreement to discriminate against a minority.

The Root-Takahira Agreement. Once the dispute was settled, Roosevelt hastened to impress upon the Japanese that any warlike intentions they might harbor had better be dispensed with. In a striking gesture designed to remind them that American naval power was the second greatest of the world, he ordered the American fleet to make a trip around the world. It was greeted with surprising warmth wherever it touched down, and in Japan the enthusiasm was so complete that thousands of Japanese children learned to sing the American national anthem in English. The absence of Japanese hostility has led historians to conclude that Roosevelt deliberately manufactured a crisis atmosphere to persuade Congress to appropriate funds for two more battle wagons. Whatever the reason, relations between the United States and Japan took a new turn on November 30, 1908, when the terms of the Root-Takahira Agreement were revealed. In this treaty, Japan and the United States pledged to maintain "the *status quo* in the Pacific area." The nations agreed to respect each other's territorial possessions, and to uphold the Open Door policy in China, with the express purpose of supporting "by pacific means" China's independence and integrity. With the Root-Takahira Agreement, the great powers of the Pacific Ocean seemed determined to pursue a policy of peaceful negotiations of future disputes. The pugnacious Roosevelt had departed on a note of sweet reason.

DOLLAR DIPLOMACY

Taft's Approach to Foreign Affairs. In his message to Congress on December 3, 1912, William Howard Taft described the diplomacy of his administration as governed by the "modern ideas of commercial intercourse." Warming to the subject, Taft described his policy as one which substituted dollars for bullets. He added significantly, "It is one that appeals alike to idealistic humanitarian sentiments, to the dictates of sound policy and strategy, and to legitimate commercial aims." The President might also have mentioned that unlike his energetic predecessor, he had been content to allow his Secretary of State, Philander C. Knox, to manage the foreign affairs of the nation.

As he viewed the future of America's international relations, outgoing President Roosevelt had concluded that the country's major antagonist would most likely be Japan, and that the countries of the Caribbean area would remain comparatively tranquil, presenting few problems to American diplomats. Subsequent events proved him wrong. With the exception of a few bumbling attempts by Knox to advance American commercial interests in China, there was little active involvement by the United States in the Orient during Taft's administration. Instead, both Taft and Knox increasingly viewed the Caribbean as the region in which diplomatic strategy was of paramount importance. America's dominance of the Panama Canal seemed to justify the taking of an active role in Latin American matters; and whether one designated that role as "cooperation" or "interference," the results were the same. And the possibility that Latin American feelings might be ruffled seems never to have entered Philander Knox's mind.

Intervention in Nicaragua. What followed from this attitude was a firm encouragement of American investors to participate in the management of Honduran and Haitian financial affairs. Even more drastic, America took an active part in the revamping of Nicaraguan finances and tariff collection—with the assistance of American naval strength. When repeated violence shook Nicaragua, Marines were landed to protect American interests. During such episodes of intervention, Knox repeatedly tried to reassure Americans with his firm pledges that the United States did not intend to annex any territory. It is hardly surprising, however, that repeated intervention by Marines struck critics of Knox's policy as the equivalent of asserting a protectorate over Nicaragua; that banana republic may have been nominally free, but for practical purposes it had become an American colony.

Negotiation with Canada. The policy of direct intervention in the Caribbean had been initiated by Roosevelt; with equal emphasis, he had set forth a policy of amicable negotiation with Canada. This latter policy had been formulated when the two nations had become embroiled in a dispute over the location of the Alaskan-Canadian boundary, finally settled in favor of the United States. Settlement by negotiation was again employed in 1911 to resolve disputes over seal hunting and over the use of the Newfoundland fisheries. In the first instance, the excessive hunting of the pelagic seals had threatened these animals with extinction. After complicated negotiations, Great Britain, Japan, the United States, and Russia signed the North Pacific Sealing Convention which forbade the killing of seals at sea. In the second instance, a dispute between New England and Newfoundland fishermen over use of fisheries adjacent to that island was submitted in 1909 for settlement by the Hague World Court. Its decision of September 7, 1910, which guaranteed the rights of New Englanders and confirmed the local jurisdiction of Newfoundland, was subsequently confirmed in the Anglo-American Convention of July 20, 1912.

Canadian Reciprocity. The Payne-Aldrich Tariff, passed in 1909, had not only displeased Progressives, it had also offended the Canadians, who found their agricultural produce denied access to the lucrative American market. When Canadians threatened to retaliate against American manufactured goods, Taft, influenced in some measure by Aldrich, decided to meet domestic criticisms of the high prevailing tariffs by negotiating a reciprocal trade agreement with Canada. In January 1911, Knox negotiated an understanding that placed most agricultural goods, iron, steel plate, and paper pulp on the free list, while substantially reducing tariffs on canned meats and vegetables, flour, and numerous manufactured items. Business and commercial interests welcomed the agreement, but agricultural factions viewed it as a deliberate betrayal of their interests. The House promptly approved the measure, but the Senate, fully aware of the opposition, dawdled, and finally adjourned. Taft recalled Congress in April 1911 to consider the question, and finally, in July 1911, the measure was approved. Ironically, the American opponents of reciprocity now received an unexpected boost from Canadian manufacturers, who feared American competition, and a stirring appeal to Canadian nationalism that charged "Reciprocity Means Annexation!" When the Conservative party won the Canadian general elections of 1911, the Ottawa parliament rejected the proposed treaty. The only evident result of the dispute was an emphatic assertion by Canadians that they meant to keep Canada free.

The Mexican Revolution. Taft had actively interfered in the Caribbean; he had fostered a policy of conciliation toward Canada. Now, confronted with the problem of the Mexican Revolution, he devised a third policy: ambiguous containment. After almost four decades of absolute dictatorship, Porfirio Díaz was overthrown in 1911, leaving a record of harsh political repression, of systematic discrimination in favor of the aristocratic rich, and of extensive exploitation of Mexican resources by foreign capital. The sentiments of the forces that had fostered the revolution became apparent in May 1911, when Francisco Madero organized a government which announced its hostility to foreigners and their property. Although few observers realized it, Mexico was on the verge of one of the truly great revolutions of modern times, one that would drastically alter Mexican institutions, raising the Indian peon majority to control of the country for the first time. The Mexican revolutionists were bent upon making the Mexicans masters of their own house.

Despite misgivings, Taft seemed ready to accept the Mexican right to self-determination. Although he placed a force of 20,000 troops on the border, he emphasized that their role was defensive rather than aggressive. When elements of the navy revealed a willingness to provoke a fight, he worked to restrain them. Even when bullets whizzed across the frontier in border towns, he urged Americans to avoid retaliation. But Taft's efforts to keep the peace were not shared by those whose interests were threatened by the revolution; their prime concern was the major American investments—valued at two billion dollars—that had been made in Mexico. To secure these investments against loss, many Americans revealed a willingness to resort to extraordinary and mean action. A stronger President might have been able to control the situation (although it is doubtful), but Taft revealed his inability to persist firmly against strong pressure. He finally resolved his dilemma by averting his gaze from the obvious fact that some Americans were intervening extensively below the Rio Grande. Francisco I. Madero, the man who had replaced Díaz, was a gentle visionary who sought to place Mexico on the democratic path. Although some of his radical supporters, men like Emiliano Zapata, felt that he did not press swiftly enough for agrarian and other reforms, recent scholarship indicates that he was committed to a drastic but carefully planned program of reform at every level of Mexican life. His plans were thwarted on February 18, 1913, when a military *coup d'état* led by General Victoriano Huerta overthrew him, and shortly thereafter Madero's bullet-ridden body was found in the outskirts of the capital. Huerta, who had been brought to Mexico City by Madero to suppress a revolt of Felix Díaz, nephew of the overthrown dictator, now proclaimed himself head of the government and requested recognition from Washington. He received the energetic support of the American ambassador Henry Lane Wilson. America's role in the serious events in Mexico was severely compromised by Ambassador Wilson's strong—and well-known—detestation of Madero. The available evidence clearly suggests that the ambassador had urged Madero to resign and even threatened him; and when Madero persisted in his refusal to step down from office, that Wilson had actively encouraged Huerta to depose the Mexican President. The State Department chose to withhold recognition from Huerta, however, hoping thus to politely blackmail Huerta into making concessions in unsettled disputes between the two countries. Such was the situation that Taft bequeathed Woodrow Wilson; it was to prove a major headache for the new President.

ATTEMPTS AT IDEALISM IN FOREIGN POLICY

Wilson's Approach to Foreign Affairs. "Mutual respect," President Wilson declared, was "the indispensable foundation of friendship between States." With this ideal he committed the United States to a new policy toward Latin America. As spokesman of the Democratic party, he firmly supported Bryan's opposition to expansion overseas, no matter how such expansion might be disguised. On October 27, 1913, in an address given at Mobile, Alabama, Wilson defined in detail the spirit which would guide future American policy in Latin America. After defining the economic tutelage to which most of our southern neighbors were subjected, he called for American assistance in aiding the Latin American struggle for economic emancipation. "We must prove ourselves their friends and champions," he declared, "upon terms of equality and honor." He went on to point out that "equality" demanded that the United States comprehend the interest of Latin America "whether it squares with our own interest or not." For a brief moment, it seemed that an era of good feelings was opening in hemispheric relations. In fact, Wilson contemplated a Pan-American treaty of nonaggression and cooperation. Wilson thus anticipated the goals of Franklin D. Roosevelt's Good Neighbor Policy and John F. Kennedy's Alliance for Progress. Unfortunately, however, words are not policy;

and Wilson's deeds were shortly to contradict the lofty sentiments of his speeches.

Wilson and Mexico. Shortly after Wilson took office, considerable publicity was directed against Henry Lane Wilson's complicity in the Huerta coup against Madero. A profoundly disturbed President set to work obtaining information about the Mexican situation. The reports he received from his personal representative, William Bayard Hale, convinced him that Mexico was struggling to escape centuries of exploitation. He refused to recognize the Huerta government and threw the weight of the American government into a campaign to force its collapse. Although the State Department and Bryan emphasized that their chief's policy was one of "disinterested friendship" which intended to give "the most scrupulous regard to the sovereignty and independence of Mexico," many Mexicans, even those who opposed Huerta, viewed Wilson's attitude as a presumptuous interference in the domestic policy of their country. Huerta, whom President Wilson characterized as "a diverting brute," shrewdly exploited his nation's resentment of Yankee interference to gain the upper hand over his opponents. Unable to dispose of Huerta directly, Wilson, in the early autumn of 1913, decided to encourage negotiations between Huerta's provisional government and its Constitutionalist opposition. Again his proposal went aglimmering, as Venustiano Carranza, the Constitutionalist chief, declared his intention to gain the upper hand through conquest. Thus the best American intentions seemed to worsen rather than improve the Mexican crisis.

American Intervention in Mexico. Wilson's belief in a righteous world intruded itself upon his solution of the Mexican upheaval. In the May 23, 1914 edition of the *Saturday Evening Post,* he wrote: "My ideal is an orderly and righteous government in Mexico." Although he qualified this with the demand that any settlement reached be made in behalf of the whole Mexican population rather than the favored few, it became increasingly apparent that the continuing upheaval threatened the interests of the United States. To rid himself of Huerta, Wilson considered the use of naval power to overthrow the provisional government at Mexico City. On February 3, 1914, he committed the administration to support of the Carranza faction, but Huerta stubbornly clung to power. In April, the administration seized upon the temporary detention of some American sailors at Tampico as an excuse for intervention; on April 21, naval forces seized Vera Cruz after a hard fight with Mexican cadets and civilians. The action struck most Americans as peculiar, following so closely upon Wilson's many peaceful pledges. Nor was the national confusion lessened when the Carranza forces threatened to join in repulsing American aggression. But when, late in April, the fortuitous offer was made by Brazilian, Argentine, and Chilean representatives to Washington to mediate the dispute, the immediate danger of a larger war was removed.

The Overthrow of Huerta. The slow campaign to overthrow Huerta ended at last with his downfall on July 15, 1914. A little over a month later, Carranza's forces entered the Mexican capital. But the long struggle was far from ended, for no sooner had Carranza and the Constitutionalists triumphed than their leading general, Pancho Villa, launched a counterrevolution. In a tragic display of misjudgment, Wilson and Bryan decided to support Villa's bid for power. Again events escaped Washington's control, as Carranza organized a military campaign that inflicted a series of overwhelming defeats on Villa. The threat of intervention by Wilson only brought the counterthreat that all Mexicans would unite in opposition to such intervention. Wilson could truly conclude that he was damned if he did and damned if he didn't. Further complicating Wilson's delicate task were the hostility of Theodore Roosevelt to efforts to keep the peace, and Roman Catholic agitation against Carranza's government because of its anticlerical attitudes. Nonetheless, on October 19, Wilson, following the lead of his new Secretary of State, Robert Lansing, gave *de facto* recognition to Carranza's government.

The Pershing Expedition. The American decision to recognize Carranza brought a violent response from Villa, who not only executed those Americans he captured in Mexico, but also attacked Columbus, New Mexico, where nineteen residents were killed. An agreement was drawn up which allowed both American and Mexican authorities to pursue bandits across the border, and shortly afterward a punitive expedition led by Brigadier General John Pershing set out after Villa, crossing the border on March 15, 1916. Within less than a month, almost 7,000 American troops had penetrated some three hundred miles into Mexico. Carranza viewed the development as considerably more than a pursuit of bandits; it appeared to him no less than an invasion, and on April 12 a bloody clash that resulted in the killing of forty Mexicans and two Americans at Parral, Mexico, brought the two nations to the brink of war. Once again a resort to negotiations seemed to be moving both nations toward peaceful settlement, when Villa's attack upon Glen Springs, Texas, inflamed American sentiment. The movement of new American troops into Mexico determined Carranza to force a showdown, and the United States mobilized forces to meet the challenge. In spite of a nasty skirmish at Carrizal, Mexico, in late June 1916, however, the desire of both Wilson and Carranza to keep the peace moved both countries away from actual war. The establishment of a Joint High Commission, composed of three Americans and three Mexicans, permitted a sensible analysis of issues under dispute between the two governments, and in January 1917, Pershing and his forces were withdrawn from Mexico. Shortly thereafter the Mexicans elected a new assembly to draw up a new constitution; and on March 13, the United States accorded *de jure* recognition to Carranza's government. The Mexican nation settled down to working out the massive reforms that would make their revolution a unique experiment in the development of social and economic justice. Wilson, despite his moralizing and seeming failure to maintain a balance between his words and his deeds, had kept the peace and prevented American power from being used to undo the Mexican experiment in democracy.

The Panama Tolls Dispute. Wilson's effort to steer an even course in foreign affairs received a further testing in his efforts to settle amicably a dispute over Panama Canal tolls. The dispute had its origin in Congress's decision to exempt American coast shipping from tolls. The British government promptly protested that this violated the Hay-Pauncefote Treaty of 1901, which pledged: "The canal shall be free and open to the vessels of commerce and war of all nations . . . , on terms of entire equality, so that there shall be no discrimination . . . in respect of the conditions or charges of traffic." Wilson, who had supported the exemption during the 1912 campaign, had second thoughts after his election, and concluded: "The exemption constitutes a very mistaken policy." He skillfully exploited the Mexican difficulties in persuading the Congress to revoke the exemption. Both Houses recognized that the British had a strong case, and, although some congressional Anglophobes allowed their antipathy free rein during the debate, they saw no reason why London's friendship should be alienated; in late spring of 1914, the two Houses, by comfortable margins, repealed the American Tolls exemption.

Caribbean Policy. At no point was Wilson's policy as stated in the Address at Mobile less supported by action than in the Caribbean region. Although Secretary of State Bryan had called for American government assistance in freeing the small republics of the Caribbean from banker control, Wilson rejected the proposal as too radical. The presence of almost 2,700 Marines in Managua, Nicaragua, assured continuation of a conservative government, friendly to United States interests.

The situation in Santo Domingo was not helped by the blundering appointment which put a political hack, James M. Sullivan, into a strategic diplomatic position there. For a time Sullivan used his power as minister to keep an unpopular President in office despite widespread protest, and finally a revolution was touched off. When various elements within the country proved unable to cope with the situation, Wilson finally sent in Marines on May 15, 1916, to occupy the country and restore order. A similar effort to restore peace in Haiti resulted in American occupation of the country, and the bloody fighting that followed resulted in the death of no less than 2,000 Haitians. When the last resistance was crushed, a disguised protectorate was imposed upon the distracted country. It often seemed that Wilson had learned far too well Roosevelt's injunction: "Speak softly, but carry a big stick."

WORLD WAR I AND NEUTRALITY

The outbreak of World War I found America wholly unsuspecting and unprepared. "I had a feeling that the end of things had come," mourned Secretary of Agriculture David Houston. "I stopped in my tracks, dazed and horror-stricken." For Woodrow Wilson, the world tragedy followed close upon a personal tragedy, the death of his wife, Ellen Axson Wilson. On August 19, 1914, he pleaded with the nation to be "neutral in fact as well as in name." Time and again he would appeal to the Americans to consider their good fortune and their great opportunity. "Look abroad upon the troubled world. Only America at peace!" he pointed out. "Among all the great powers of the world, only America saving her power. Only America using her great character and her great strength in the interests of peace and prosperity." To his Secretary of Navy, Josephus Daniels, he added, "Every reform we have won will be lost if we go into this war." But any acute observer realized that the polyglot population of the United States could not escape some measure of emotional and psychological involvement in the cause of one or more of the belligerents. Sadly Wilson complained to Walter Hines Page, his Ambassador to England, "More and more, from day to day, the elements (I mean the several racial elements) of our population seem to grow restless and catch more and more the fever of the contest." Even Page, as Wilson noted, ran the risk of allowing his "intense feeling . . . for the English case" to jeopardize the objective view and the primary concern for American interests which were his responsibility. Wilson shared with Page an earnest desire to keep the peace, yet both also admitted an unquenchable sympathy for the western allies. It was the latter sentiment that proved, ultimately, to be the decisive influence in the conflict over retention of genuine neutrality.

The Economic Cost of Neutrality. The war's immediate impact on the American economy brought tumbling stock prices, as European investors liquidated their American holdings. Only the closing of the Stock Exchange, and prompt government issuance of "emergency currency" as authorized by the Aldrich-Vreeland Act, kept the economy from buckling; not only was the investment market demoralized, but the commodity market, which traditionally depended upon the European market to absorb substantial portions of American staple crop production was also threatened. Faced with a heavy drain upon the American gold supply, the administration braked the efforts of European governments to float American loans. For a time it seemed that Bryan's belief that "money is the worst of all contrabands" would prevail, and that the United States would follow a rigid neutrality. But the consequence of a policy based on the promise that American loans to any nation at war would be inconsistent with true neutrality soon proved too costly. A major part of the American economy depended on overseas markets; to close credit to the British and French would, therefore, be tantamount to compelling Americans to accept belt-tightening as the cost of neutrality; and Jefferson's efforts to do as much during the Napoleonic Wars had already demonstrated that such a demand was not likely to generate much enthusiasm.

Although the administration modified its restrictions on commercial loans to belligerents as early as October 1914, it was not until the spring of 1915, as the western allies began to flood the American market with orders for American commodities, that American banking firms freely extended loans to European governments. When it became apparent that the deficit in the British balance of trade with the United States would exceed $2,500,000,000 for 1915 alone, pressure accelerated for a massive loan to subsidize British purchases. Faced with domestic economic demoralization, unrest, and suffering, the administration agreed, during the summer of 1915, to allow a syndicate of American bankers, headed by the Morgan firm, to float a $500,000,000 loan to underwrite French and British purchases. The loan did not prove particularly popular with American investors—the heaviest purchasers were firms such as Du Pont, Westinghouse, and Bethlehem Steel, which had large allied war contracts—but the United States now moved steadily toward becoming an arsenal for the western allies. American prosperity and the cause of the western allies had become one; as William Jennings Bryan observed, "Where your treasure is, there your heart is also."

Preparedness. At the outbreak of war in Europe, Americans simply could not comprehend the possibility of direct involvement. A century of isolation from European conflicts, and the security which the oceans provided, had left Americans unable to believe that their fundamental interests or safety could be threatened by European problems. At first, only a handful of Americans seriously agitated for preparation against the contingency of direct involvement. Most active was Theodore Roosevelt, who viewed the expansion of American armed might as an assurance that America's honor would not be trailed "in the dust." Preoccupied with the implications—both immediate and far-reaching—of a German triumph, the former President viewed preparedness for war as the best precaution against actual engagement in war with Germany should that power win the conflict in Europe. Wilson's agonizing indecision, as he struggled to keep peace with both Mexico and the European powers, caused Roosevelt to denounce the White House "scholar" as "cowardly," "supine," and "yellow." Faced with the evidence of mixed emotions among America's vast immigrant population, Roosevelt threw himself into a campaign against hyphenated loyalties, sounding a call for an Americanism that would make the sole loyalty of the nation respond to "one flag, one language, and one people."

Against such belligerence Wilson maintained a firm stand, insisting that traditional American antipathy to militarism should not be abandoned. As Germany resorted to submarine warfare, however, and as the propaganda campaigns of the Navy League and Army League—which contended that in strength was the surest guarantee of peace—made their impact, the administration shifted its ground. In the summer of 1915, Wilson directed the War and Navy Departments to prepare plans that would put the nation in a posture of effective response to aggression. In mid-October, plans to launch a $500,000,000 naval construction program over a five-year period received presidential approval, and a similar program of Army expansion, involving not only increases in the regular forces but the establishment of a special 400,000 man reserve, was approved. Against the severe criticisms of the pacifistic League to Limit Armament, Wilson argued: "We have it in mind to be prepared, not for war, but only for defense; and with the thought constantly in our minds that the principles we hold most dear can be achieved by the slow processes of history only in the kindly and wholesome atmosphere of peace, and not by the use of hostile force." He also maintained that a neutral but powerful United

States would be able to force a just peace when the exhausted belligerents turned from conflict to negotiated settlement. As the preparedness program developed, what the administration emphasized was its necessity. Slowly, despite considerable skepticism, Congress agreed to double the size of the Regular Army (from little more than 105,000 to almost 220,000) and to expand the National Guard to almost 460,000, and an even larger expansion of naval forces was approved. Construction of government plants to insure essential war supplies, and the creation of the United States Shipping Board to provide federal aid in the construction of merchant ships and to regulate already existing shipping, were also approved. But every measure taken to increase American might carried with it the pledge that the new strength would buttress the peace rather than provoke war. It was to prove a doubtful premise.

The British Blockade. Almost from the outbreak of the war, it was apparent that American rights to free navigation of the seas would be infringed upon. The British, whose land forces were minuscule when war began, of necessity insisted upon exploiting its sea dominance. The blockade that resulted soon provoked controversy, for the British arbitrarily redefined contraband to include not only obvious instruments of war but ultimately all materials, on the grounds that in modern warfare anything which permitted intricate modern economies to function was contraband. The Order in Council of August 20, 1914, which expanded the meaning of contraband, precipitated an avalanche of American protests; but the British, who received assurances from the American ambassador, Walter Hines Page, that these protests could be safely ignored, persisted in extending their blockade. The right of visit and search was redefined to compel merchant ships to tie up in allied ports. These long enforced stays were frequently so costly that ship owners proved less willing to use their vessels in trade that either directly or indirectly might aid the central powers. To implement their blockade of German ports, the British also mined the North Sea, obliging neutrals sailing the area to rely on the British Navy for guidance. This necessity substantially simplified the British blockade problem. The success of the British effort was graphically demonstrated as trade with the central powers was reduced from $169,289,775 in 1914, to a bare $1,159,653 in 1916, even as allied trade zoomed from $824,860,775 to $3,214,480,547 in the same period. The latter fact best explains why the State Department, despite strong protests, tolerated British interference. The profits drawn from allied trade were so vast that they more than absorbed losses sustained from the end of German trade.

Submarine Warfare. As the British blockade tightened and American supplies assumed a growing role in allied war calculations, the Germans decided upon a course of action that ultimately proved the primary factor in America's decision to go to war. On February 4, 1915, Berlin announced that it would establish a war zone around the British Isles, and attack all enemy ships found in the area. When this declaration of U-boat warfare raised the possibility that, contrary to traditional practice, merchant and passenger ships would be sunk without warning, the Germans, echoing the British, argued that necessity dictated their action. Of particular importance to the United States was Germany's warning that they could not guarantee that neutral shipping sailing in the area would be free from attack. Six days after the German declaration, the State Department warned Germany that it would be held to "strict accountability" for all American lives and ships lost. Once U-boat warfare opened in earnest, on February 18, 1915, it was only a matter of time before American citizens would lose their lives. On March 28, an American was lost when the British passenger line *Falaba* was sunk; and on May 1, the American tanker *Gulflight* escaped sinking when torpedoed, but three lives were lost.

The Sinking of the Lusitania. "Both sides," Wilson privately complained in early March of 1915, "are seeing red on the other side of the sea, and neutral rights are left, for the time being, out of their reckoning altogether. They listen to necessity (and to necessity as they interpret it), not to reason, and there is therefore no way of calculating or preparing for anything." Wilson was still struggling to strike a balanced attitude, but because of his private conviction that "England is fighting our fight," a single bit of evidence of Germany's intent to resort to a ruthless course would be enough to transform his inherent bias in favor of the allies into action. "The first German U-boat campaign," as Winston Churchill, then First Lord of the Admiralty, noted, "gave us our greatest assistance. It altered the whole position of our controversies with America." The German Ambassador to Washington, Count Johann Heinrich von Bernstorff, fearful lest sinking of a passenger liner would result in the loss of many American lives, published an advertisement on May 1, 1915, in New York papers, warning Americans that they sailed on British ships at their own risk. On May 7, the notice assumed fatal significance when the great Cunard liner *Lusitania* was sunk without warning. A shocked America read that 1,198 persons had been killed, of whom 270 were women, 94 children, and 124 American citizens. The response proved explosive, as moral shock and a demand for retribution combined to deal Germany a major propaganda defeat. "The torpedo that sank the *Lusitania,*" a leading American publication editorialized, "also sank Germany in the opinion of mankind."

Wilson, although shocked by the event, refused to use it to break the peace. Instead, he decided to force Germany to guarantee that her unrestricted submarine warfare would be ended. The harshness of his tone precipitated a major crisis in the cabinet; Bryan, unable to follow a policy which he feared would precipitate war, resigned. To meet Washington's demands, the German government issued on June 6 an order that its submarines no longer attack large passenger liners. When the British liner *Arabic* was sunk on August 19, 1915, with the loss of two American lives, the crisis renewed, but Germany pledged a stringent effort to prevent a recurrence of such incidents. Wilson had demonstrated, even to the satisfaction of Roosevelt, that patience paid.

The Sussex Pledge. In spite of German pledges, submarines continued occasionally to attack allied passenger vessels. When the French liner *Sussex* was torpedoed—though not sunk—on March 24, 1916, Robert Lansing delivered a note on April 18 threatening the severance of diplomatic relations unless U-boat warfare was stopped. Sixteen days later the Germans pledged to refrain from sinking unresisting merchant ships without warning. For the moment, relations with Germany improved, even as relations with Britain suffered a severe strain. Americans protested London's search of American mails, as well as the issuance of a blacklist that forbade British trade with eighty-five American firms and persons suspected of aiding the central powers.

AMERICA ENTERS THE WAR

Final Bid for Negotiated Peace. Through the summer and autumn of 1916, Americans were preoccupied with the upcoming national election, which brought well over 3,000,000 new voters to the polls. In the campaign, it was emphasized by the Democrats that Wilson had kept us out of war, and Americans were urged to "Put America First"; and this issue of neutrality gave Wilson a narrow victory. He promptly set about sounding out the belligerents concerning the terms on which they would consider peace. On January 22, 1917, Wilson reported to the Senate that although his appeal had obtained little in the way of tangible results, it was apparent that both sides had revealed an interest in the prospect of peace. Wilson believed that the time had come for the United States to prepare actively to bring about the peace—and also that the peace so secured must be one "without victory." Even more important to Wilson was the need to create a "League for Peace" which would provide an agency in which future differences could be negotiated rather than fought over.

Increased German-American Tensions. All hopes for a negotiated peace disappeared on January 31, 1917, when Germany announced the beginning of unrestricted submarine warfare. Berlin had decided that even if such action resulted in war with the United States, the chance to deliver a knockout blow to Britain was worth the risk. The only question that seemingly remained was the circumstances that would lead to the final American-German confrontation. The conviction that Germany was bent on war received further confirmation on March 1, 1917, when a note from the German Foreign Minister Arthur Zimmermann, proposing a German-Mexican alliance in case of war with the United States, was revealed. Its promise that in case of a German victory Mexico would obtain Arizona, New Mexico, and Texas added to the rising American dismay at Germany.

The Declaration of War. By early March, Wilson had authorized the arming of American merchant ships and directed that they shoot on sight any submarines in the war zone. The sinking of the American *Algonquin* on March 12, 1917 was followed by the sinking of three more American vessels. A heartsick Wilson, convinced at last that war was inescapable, appeared before Congress on April 2, 1917, to request a declaration of war. With six senators and fifty representatives in opposition, war was declared. Wilson, pale as a ghost, is reputed to have responded to the vigorous cheers of Congress with the cry, "Think what it was they were applauding. My message today was a message of death for our young men. How strange it seems to applaud that." With that somber thought in mind, he set out to convert the savage bloodletting of the western front into a crusade to make the world safe for democracy. War was to be justified by its moral result.

Mobilization. Germany had taken a calculated risk when she resumed U-boat warfare. She assumed that victory could be won quickly, before the United States could further affect the balance of power—and Germany had good reason to believe that the impending collapse of Russia would release enough additional German troops to permit a breakthrough on the western front. Moreover, a war-weary France witnessed troop mutinies as the *poilus*—the French foot soldiers—viewed with increasing anger the reckless gambling of their lives; and unrestricted warfare by U-boats was bringing Britain to the brink of starvation. As events demonstrated, German hopes were ephemeral. The American mobilization proved both swift and efficient, and the allied powers knew that they had only to hold on until the Yanks arrived. A trickle of American troops appeared as early as the summer of 1917, and by the spring of 1918 no less than 300,000 troops had landed. Then a flood of over 1,700,000 Americans poured into France, providing, as one British general noted, an army of "men of splendid but risky ease of mind." The sagging morale of the allies soared as fresh American troops stiffened their lines. At the Second Battle of the Marne, fought in mid-July, the German drive broke against lines manned by Americans. American forces under General Pershing drove the Germans out of the Argonne Forest, at the cost of 120,000 casualties, during September and early October. The simultaneous breeching of the German lines by the British and French further to the west brought the German Empire to its knees on November 11, 1918.

The Home Front. As American manpower swung the balance on the western front, the American economy floundered. Most of the equipment used by Pershing's troops was supplied by the British and French. American shipyards failed to supply any quantity of ships until after the war was over, although the American Navy played a vital role in the destruction of the submarine menace. When the railroads floundered, Wilson turned to Bernard Baruch, who vigorously directed the War Industries Board to an efficient management of the war effort. Supervisory federal boards proliferated, as the Fuel Administration, the War Trade Board, the Railroad Administration, the Emergency Fleet Corporation, and the National War Labor Board each assumed responsibility for a segment of the economy. By war's end, the government was operating the nation's railroads, telephone and telegraph companies, and warehouses. Under the leadership of Herbert Hoover, vast quantities of foodstuffs were shipped to the allies. And millions of women poured into the factories to replace their drafted men. America had obtained by war's end a brief insight into the extraordinary capacities of the American economy when subjected to government management. It was a lesson that would be recalled in the depression-ridden economy of 1933.

The Fourteen Points. From the moment the United States entered the war, Wilson emphasized that his country had "no selfish ends to serve." Above all other considerations, the American sacrifice and that of the other belligerents would be justified only if it resulted in a just and lasting peace. Yet Wilson sensed that it was unlikely that the terrible sacrifices exacted from the European combatants would permit the necessary detachment to achieve such a peace. Only America, distant from Europe's hatreds, and still unshattered by the fierce bloodletting of the previous three years, possessed the detachment to assure a peace of reconciliation. Wilson understood that his nation's century-long isolation left a legacy of suspicion that a vindictive peace would quickly ignite. If America were to take its place in the world community, she had to be convinced that the World War had purified old and corrupt Europe.

As Wilson struggled to convince his countrymen that Europe had learned its lessons, the new Bolshevik government, which had achieved power through the Russian Revolution in 1917, in Petrograd, Russia, revealed the allied agreements and treaties that seemed to promise a peace of reward. The President decided to seize upon the allied powers' discomfiture to set forth his own idea of a peace; on January 8, 1918, he delivered to Congress his Fourteen Points, which pledged the Americans to a program for world peace that included open covenants of peace, absolute freedom of navigation, an equality of trade conditions, reduction of national armaments, and impartial adjustment of all colonial claims. Eight other points called for the evacuation of Russian territory, restoration and reparation for Belgium, the return of Alsace-Lorraine to France, rectification of Italy's borders, the establishment of a free Poland with access to the sea, and the extension of self-determination to the peoples of Austria-Hungary, the Balkans, and the Turkish portions of the Ottoman Empire. Culminating this series of demands was the call for "a general association of nations . . . under specific covenants for the purpose of affording mutual guarantees of political independence and territorial integrity to great and small states alike." It was a program that Wilson believed workable. When told that Lloyd George of Great Britain and Georges Clemenceau of France had dismissed the League of Nations, Wilson replied, "I know that Europe is still governed by the same reactionary forces which controlled this country until a few years ago. But I am satisfied that if necessary I can reach the peoples of Europe over the heads of their rulers."

The importance of the Fourteen Points was universally recognized on October 6, 1918, when Germany requested an armistice based upon Wilson's plan. It seemed that the statesman in the White House had fathomed the heart of a war-weary continent. In a world grown cynical, the shimmering words of Wilson sparked a hope. On November 11, 1918, as the guns finally fell silent, Wilson sent a message to

Congress. In it he declared, "To conquer with arms is to make only a temporary conquest; to conquer the world by earning its esteem is to make permanent conquest." Such a peace as Wilson dreamed of, however, was not to be drawn at Versailles.

Part Four

THE NEW REPUBLIC

Chapter 12

Aftermath of World War I

The armistice was scheduled to take effect at 11 A.M., November 11, 1918. As the hour of peace approached, the American sector of the western front was suddenly rocked by artillery bombardment. The hour of cease-fire came and went, but the competition for firing the "last" shot of the war continued.

Americans soon joined the other combatants, however, in the awful evaluation of the magnitude of loss caused by the war. The total number of dead and wounded exceeded 29,500,000—almost fifty-eight per cent of all forces involved. Even excluding consideration of the numbers of wounded, the losses were staggering: German deaths totaled 1,774,000; Russian, 1,700,000; French, 1,358,000; Austrian-Hungarian, 1,200,000; British, 908,000; Italian, 650,000. In comparison, the death of 126,000 Americans seemed almost insignificant.

As the ravaged continent of Europe turned to the overwhelming tasks of reconstructing physical ruins and obliterating psychic scars, Wilson perceived his own tragic obligation; it was his responsibility to convince the world that words could cut as deeply as swords, and that good might finally emerge from the great holocaust. Europe, scarred and skeptical, would doubt him; America, eager to get on with business, would desert him.

CASUALTIES OF WORLD WAR ONE

Country	Dead	Wounded	Total
AUSTRIA-HUNGARY	1,200,000	3,620,000	4,820,000
BELGIUM	13,716	44,686	58,402
BRITISH COMMONWEALTH	908,371	2,090,212	2,998,583
BULGARIA	87,000	152,390	239,390
FRANCE	1,357,800	4,266,000	5,623,800
GERMANY	1,773,700	4,216,058	5,989,758
GREECE	5,000	21,000	26,000
ITALY	650,000	947,000	1,597,000
JAPAN	300	907	1,207
MONTENEGRO	3,000	10,000	13,000
PORTUGAL	7,222	13,751	20,973
RUMANIA	335,706	120,000	455,706
RUSSIA	1,700,000	4,950,000	6,650,000
SERBIA	45,000	133,148	178,148
TURKEY	325,000	400,000	725,000
UNITED STATES	126,000	234,000	360,000

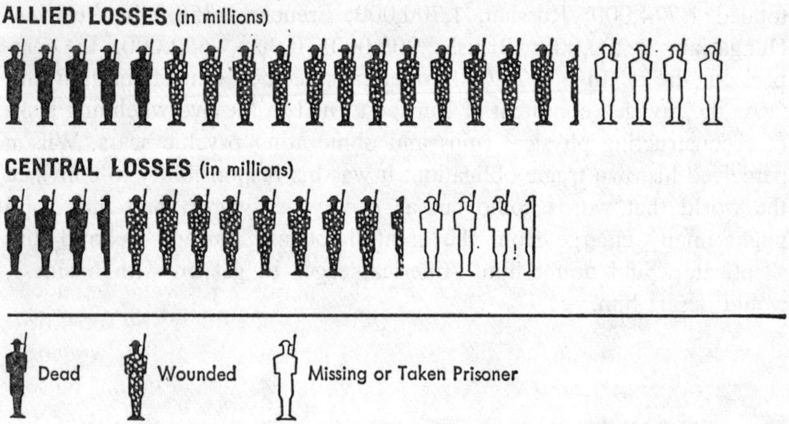

THE TREATY OF VERSAILLES AND THE LEAGUE OF NATIONS

Conflicting Attitudes toward Peace. Even as war ended, the American public had repudiated Wilson politically. Despite a presidential appeal for approval of his leadership through the return of a Democratic Congress, the Republicans gained small majorities in both Houses (47 in the House and 2 in the Senate). But in the flush of military victory, Wilson seemed to have regained political ascendency. As President, he would be the personification of the country at the peace negotiations, and, at least at the outset, his voice would be that of the nation. As William Howard Taft reminded the Republican Congress, a congressional rejection of the final treaty would not be tolerated "for any but the gravest reasons." Yet within the Republican party there existed strong reservations about Wilson's appeals for a generous peace. The influential independent Republican journal, the Washington *Post,* had insisted that "'Unconditional surrender' are the words that should be inscribed on every bullet and bomb that goes to Germany." A dictated peace, as opposed to a negotiated settlement, commanded considerable support in Republican circles. No less threatening was the personal hostility toward Wilson of the new chairman of the Senate Foreign Relations Committee, Henry Cabot Lodge. The idea of "a peace without victory" left him cold. "It seems to me incredible that people who have made such awful sacrifices," he wrote to the British historian Trevelyan, "should be content to forego the prospect of victory." With the revelation in January 1918 of the secret treaties by which the western allies meant to impose a victor's peace, many supporters of Wilson's generous terms felt as Oswald Garrison Villard, publisher of the *Nation,* felt: "At the Peace Conference the whole fight [would center] on how far Mr. Wilson could set aside the underhand bargains contained in those documents." Both friend and foe, therefore, were nervously watching Wilson's conduct as the negotiations opened.

The Treaty Delegation. Wilson's announcement on November 18, 1918, that he meant to head the American delegation at Versailles took the nation by surprise. Since the other major belligerents intended to have their delegations led by their top political leaders, Wilson's decision was understandable. But as the Republicans immediately recognized, it would give the President a formidable advantage in any subsequent discussion of the treaty ratification. Their unease gave way to dismay when, on November 29, the American peace commission's personnel was announced. Beside Wilson it consisted of Secretary of State Lansing, Colonel Edward House (the President's closest confidant), General Tasker Bliss, and a career diplomat, Henry White. Only White had any affiliation with the Republican party—and it was not very strong at that. The simple truth was that Wilson's relationships with more prominent Republicans were so strained that he felt he could take none of them along. A further irritant for the touchy Senate was the presidential failure to include one of their number in the delegation, or even to consult with them about his plans. Since any treaty would ultimately require a two-thirds Senate approval, it was a fatal defect.

The Treaty Negotiations. Whatever doubts Wilson may have had melted as an ecstatic Europe rendered him a greeting that led one French journal to announce, "Never has a king, never has an emperor received such a welcome." When the Conference finally opened on January 12, 1919, Wilson seemed to have the weight of world opinion on his side; he was more convinced than ever that he commanded an "irresistible . . . moral force." What he failed to understand was that there could exist a considerable divergence on what constituted a "just" peace. The re-election of Lloyd George to the British Prime-Ministership on the slogan "Be tough on Germany" was an ominous sign. Georges Clemenceau, the irascible French Premier, privately reassured the Chamber of Deputies that he would press for the dismemberment of Germany. And the French press opened an officially inspired newspaper campaign designed to discredit Wilson's high ideals, a campaign that was terminated only when Wilson threatened to call for the removal of the negotiations to the neutral climate of Geneva. And back in America a subtle campaign was begun to undermine national faith in Wilson's most cherished hope, the establishment of the League of Nations.

Although the United States was pledged to full publicity for all negotiations, and despite Wilson's struggle to gain that point, the other participants kept the dissemination of information on the treaty to a minimum. This refusal to cooperate foreshadowed Wilson's fate through all subsequent negotiations. Time and again he was forced to concede points to the vindictive Clemenceau and the suave Lloyd George, until John Maynard Keynes, the influential economist, dismissed him as a "blind and deaf Don Quixote." Even when he managed to swing Italian support behind the League idea, the price involved was a departure from the principle of self-determination. By granting the Italians the Brenner Pass as their frontier, he had placed 200,000 reluctant Tyrolean Austrian-Germans under Italian control. Nevertheless, despite all the retreats, the President stubbornly hewed to a single line; the critical decision was whether the League of Nations would be made part of the treaty. This point was won on January 25, 1919, when it was so decided, and Wilson, chairman of the League commission, set to work drawing up the Covenant of the League. Twenty days later, a jubilant Wilson read to the Versailles assemblage the final Covenant, a document that he decribed as "a vehicle of life," in which he saw the permanent means of rectifying any shortcomings of the Peace Treaty and a method for resolving future national conflicts of interest. As such, Wilson declared, "It is a definite guarantee of peace. It is a definite guarantee against the things which have just come near to bringing the whole structure of civilization into ruin." So far as he was concerned, the treaty negotiations were fulfilled. Eager to assure its ratification by Congress, he returned home to present and explain the finished Covenant to the Senate leadership. But the Republican leadership obtained 39 signatures on a round robin declaration:

> Resolved: That it is the sense of the Senate that while it is their sincere desire that the nations of the world should unite to promote peace and general disarmament, the constitution of the league of nations *in the form now proposed* to the peace conference should not be accepted by the United States.

The gauntlet was down. Henry Cabot Lodge, who had assumed major leadership of the Republican opposition to Wilson after the death, on January 6, 1919, of Theodore Roosevelt, set the tone of the impending controversy over the Covenant when he observed jocularly, "As an English production it does not rank high. It might get by at Princeton but certainly not at Harvard."

The Treaty of Versailles. In gaining his position on the League, Wilson had seemingly surrendered the substance of the Fourteen Points. What he had held to had been further compromised by Secretary Lansing and Colonel House during his absence. When the weary President re-entered the negotiations on March 14, 1919, he attempted to restore the originally temperate spirit of the negotiations. Although the justice of France's demands for reparations was conceded, the now ill President firmly rejected all French efforts to incorporate the Rhineland into France. Presidential stubbornness and moral conviction led an enraged Clemenceau to contend that "talking to Wilson is something like talking to Jesus Christ!" A compromise which permitted the French to occupy the Rhineland and which gave them economic control of the Saar Basin was at last settled upon. Both Britain and the United States agreed to support France against any future "unprovoked" German attacks. Similarly, Japan was granted the right to exploit economically the former German possessions on China's Shantung peninsula. Italy was momentarily frustrated in her demands for Fiume, an Adriatic port that provided Yugoslavia with her only developed outlet to the sea; and the principle of national self-determination was neatly ignored when the Austrian-Germans were forbidden to unify with Germany. In addition, Germany was obliged to admit her guilt for the war, and—what was most foreboding—denied any participation in the formulation of the treaty. The final result was Hobson's choice; a disarmed Germany accepted it under protest, but the sum effect was to render Wilson's appeal for "a peace without victory" meaningless, a point that his enemies at home intended to emphasize.

The Great Debate. In all probability, given the hatreds and fears that four years of war had engendered in Europe, the final treaty was as good as could have been expected. To protests that the treaty was bad, Colonel House observed "that empires cannot be shattered and new states raised upon their ruins without disturbance." Despite the protests of Irish-Americans, who resented Wilson's failure to support Ireland's right to self-determination at the negotiations; of Italian-Americans, who believed Italy's right to Fiume had been ignored; and of German-Americans, who felt the substance of the treaty contradicted the golden words of Wilson, the vast weight of American opinion supported the League. In the Senate, however, eighteen senators, led by William E. Borah of Idaho, proclaimed their irreconcilable opposition to the League. "Your treaty means injustice. It means slavery. It means war," Borah rumbled in the Senate. Lodge gathered around him a group of senators who insisted on reservations, particularly that which left it to Congress to fulfill Article X of the Covenant, the article which pledged League members to uphold the independence and territorial integrity of any member threatened with external attack. Despite Wilson's care to have included in the final Covenant Republican demands for the exclusion of domestic issues from League scrutiny, and reassurances that the Monroe Doctrine was in no way superseded, it soon became apparent that nothing short of rejection of the League would satisfy Lodge. Fearful that the Senate might approve it, the Massachusetts senator opened hearings on the treaty, determined to keep it bottled up in committee. After two months of unproductive hearings, Wilson realized that only a great public outcry could force the senators to unbend and bring the issue to a vote. Therefore he decided to take the question to the people.

The Appeal to the People. On September 3, 1919, Wilson set out on a journey of more than 8,000 miles over a twenty-two day period, during which he delivered thirty-seven hour-long speeches. He defended the League Covenant as "in spirit and essence . . . an American document." Confronting the world and the nation was a single alternative: "armed isolation or peaceful partnership." Throughout the West he was greeted by crowds that defied the imagination, and Wilson responded with eloquent appeals that America lead the way into an Eden regained. In Wilson's wake came a band of irreconcilable senators, led by Borah and Hiram Johnson of California. They intended to meet his appeal with a counterappeal. On September 25, at Pueblo, Colorado, Wilson pleaded that the nation keep faith with its war dead. It was a moving climax to a desperate effort, for the strained health of Wilson finally began to crack. Rather than risk his health further, his second wife, Edith Bolling Wilson, finally convinced him to return to Washington. There, on October 2, 1919, he suffered a stroke which left him almost completely incapacitated. At a critical juncture in the struggle for ratification, Wilson had been removed from the fight.

The Rejection of the League of Nations. Wilson's stroke had completely paralyzed the left side of his body. For the remainder of his life he would be a partial invalid; but even as he was able to resume his daily activities, he remained inflexibly opposed to any compromise, particularly those that would compel him to resume negotiations with other members of the League. Against the rock of Wilson's stubbornness, the League foundered. On November 19, 1919, the treaty, with Lodge's reservations, was rejected by a vote of 55 to 39, and an unamended treaty was turned aside by a vote of 53 to 38. Wilson had proved that if he could not have his treaty, there would be no treaty at all. Although all but sixteen senators were prepared on November 19 to accept the treaty in some form, Wilson had refused to compromise. Since politics is the art of compromise, he had, by his action, thrown aside political accommodation. All that was left was Wilson's grim prophecy: "Arrangements of the present peace cannot stand a generation unless they are guaranteed by the united forces of the civilized world." Twenty years later, events would bear out the prophecy.

THE DECLINE OF AMERICAN CIVIL LIBERTIES

The Charges of the Super-Patriots. The night before Wilson went to Congress to request a declaration of war, he had somberly warned an editor friend:

> Once lead this people into war, . . . and they'll forget there ever was such a thing as tolerance. To fight you must be brutal and ruthless, and the spirit of ruthless brutality will enter into the very fiber of our national life, infecting Congress, the courts, the policeman on the beat, the man in the street.

The primary value of a society at war, Wilson predicted, would be "conformity . . . and every man who refused to conform would have to pay the penalty." Presidential expectations were soon realized. The Governor of Iowa responded to public clamor for the exclusive use of the English language with a proclamation that made English the only medium of instruction, the only language to be used in public conversations, on telephones, or in public addresses; the proclamation further demanded that "those who cannot speak or understand English conduct their religious worship in their homes." Elsewhere, attacks were made on Americans of foreign extraction, as dozens of self-styled patriotic organizations sought out suspected traitors. German culture became the principal target, as throughout the country German language, music, literature, and art were forbidden. The final absurdity came with the demand that the old German vegetable dish, sauerkraut, be known in the future as "liberty cabbage."

The decline of outrages against civil liberties that many observers believed would follow the war failed to materialize; in fact, the situation was the reverse. A definite upsurge of intolerance developed toward radical political thinking. The long battle over the League of Nations had exacerbated native suspicions of foreigners. In addition, the Bolshevik seizure of power in Russia had sent a chill of fear through the western world. Public journals warned against the growing conspiracy fostered by "the Lenin-Trotsky murderers" to undermine established institutions. "The American citizen, native or naturalized, who willfully spreads the spirit of destruction and violence is a traitor," warned one newspaper. "He deserves death." A prominent evangelist announced that his method of ridding the country of Socialists and I.W.W.s would be to stand them up before a firing squad. In Indiana, a jury acquitted a murderer because his motive was to punish the victim for the latter's outspoken criticism of the United States. "The man who scatters the firebrands of anarchy in his speech," wrote one newspaperman, "and then, when called to account, takes refuge in the right of free speech, is no better than the murderer who disguises himself in his victim's clothing in order to escape." National sentiment was succinctly summarized in one editor's statement: "The enemy is not without the gate, but within."

The Palmer Raids. Wilson's illness left a massive gap in the leadership of the Democratic party. One man who seemed ready to fill the breach was Attorney General A. Mitchell Palmer. A Quaker, he had refused appointment in 1913 as Secretary of War, as pacifism was a basic tenet of his faith. He had played a major role in the reform of child labor laws and in the enactment of female suffrage. Now there were other pressing social problems to which he could turn his energies.

After the war the nation was plagued by strikes in the coal and steel industries. Even more unsettling was the Boston police strike, during which the capital of Massachusetts fell victim to numerous riots and wholesale depredations on property. A singularly unnerving experience for Palmer occurred in June 1919 when a bomb exploded in front of his home. The discovery of many other bombs, addressed to such prominent Americans as John D. Rockefeller, Oliver Wendell Holmes, and Secretary of Labor William B. Wilson, intensified fears that the nation was in the grip of a vast radical conspiracy. In August 1919, Palmer authorized the establishment of an Anti-Radical Division (ultimately to become the F.B.I.) under Justice Department auspices to be directed by J. Edgar Hoover. On November 7, the new division swung into action with the first of the "Palmer raids." Throughout the East, some 250 members of the radical Union of Russian Workers were arrested and manhandled, although only 39 were subsequently deemed deportable. Four days before Christmas, 1919, the old troop transport *Buford* sailed from New York with 249 aliens, of whom the most famous was the anarchist Emma Goldman; its destination was that part of Russia under Bolshevik control. The New York *Times* dismissed the action with a blunt editorial that concluded, "Well, Americans know the revolutionary agents now. They are determined that these soldiers of disorder shall be driven out."

With such support, Palmer and J. Edgar Hoover now turned their attention to Communists, Socialists, and members of the I.W.W. (International Workers of the World). The latter group had opposed American entrance into the war and compliance with the draft laws;

some one hundred of their number had been convicted for violating the espionage and selective service acts, fined $2,300,000, and given prison sentences ranging from one to twenty years. In late January, well over four thousand suspected Communists were arrested across the country; hundreds of those arrested proved to be innocent citizens who happened to be visiting the buildings where the raids were conducted, or, in some instances, who had just been passing by. For a time after this nationwide raid, numerous citizens found themselves unable to obtain legal counsel, bail, or even the opportunity to inform their families of their imprisonment. In a supposed effort to rid the nation of a subversive element, the Justice Department had indulged in a wholesale violation of civil liberties rarely paralleled in the nation's history. In New York State the legislature expelled its five Socialist members, although they represented a legal political party. The leader of the Socialist party, Eugene V. Debs, languished in federal prison as an ailing Wilson stubbornly refused to pardon him for his wartime opposition to the draft laws.

The Panic Subsides. In mid-winter of 1920, a few voices began to be raised against this trend. Such eminently conservative spokesmen as Warren G. Harding and the Chicago *Tribune* questioned the implications of attacks upon Socialists. When the Senate passed a peacetime sedition bill, on Palmer's insistence, in January 1920, the American Newspaper Publishers Association bitterly opposed the proposal. Twelve prominent judges charged that the Justice Department, by its violation of civil liberties, was stirring up more radical sentiment than any agitator ever had. And a number of the members of the Republican National Committee went on record as opposing further repressive measures. With evidence that the public had had its fill of repression, the Labor Department, under the guidance of its Assistant Secretary Louis F. Post, a fierce defender of civil liberties, insisted upon the extension of full legal protection to all suspected radicals. Post and Secretary of Labor William B. Wilson swiftly removed charges from more than half of the approximately five thousand suspected radicals. (In the end, only one-tenth of those originally charged were deported.) With the disappearance of the substance of Palmer's supposed vast internal conspiracy against the nation went his presidential hopes. Even the explosion on Wall Street on September 16, 1920, of a bomb which killed thirty-three persons and injured hundreds more, failed to re-ignite national fears. On December 25, 1921, Warren G. Harding, seeking to undo the damage wrought, pardoned

Eugene V. Debs and invited him to the White House. So ended a painful chapter in American history.

Sacco and Vanzetti. Though federal interference with civil liberties had come to an end, there were still to be continued attacks upon aliens, non-whites, admitted radicals, and non-Protestants by the xenophobic nativists. No single incident of American disregard for civil liberties shocked world opinion and claimed international attention to a greater degree than the Sacco-Vanzetti case.

Nicola Sacco and Bartolomeo Vanzetti, Italian-Americans and avowed radicals, were arrested in May 1920 for the robbery and murder of two payroll guards at South Braintree, Massachusetts. The evidence on which the men had been arrested, and the testimony which was given at the trial, could, at best, be described as slight; many observers, less generous, called it nonexistent. From the very beginning of the trial, in July 1921, it became apparent that ostensible charges notwithstanding, Sacco and Vanzetti were actually being tried for their political views, their ethnic backgrounds, and their anarchist sentiments. In a case riddled with violations of elementary judicial safeguards, both men were convicted by Judge Webster Thayer and condemned to die. As public furor mounted and controversy over the case raged, a number of legal appeals were made, and execution was thus postponed for six years; ultimately, however, both men were electrocuted on August 23, 1927. Though Sacco and Vanzetti died, they were not forgotten. For many they had become martyrs in the cause of justice.

To this day, many historians have examined and re-examined the records of the Sacco-Vanzetti case; and though there is still disagreement over whether or not the men were actually guilty of the crime of which they were accused, the consensus of opinion is that the entire judicial procedure, from beginning to end, had been converted into a mockery by prejudice, bias, corruption, and illegality. The repercussions of the Sacco-Vanzetti case were to continue sounding for many years.

The Ku Klux Klan. Outbreaks of nativist agitation are a recurring phenomenon in American history. Throughout the nineteenth century and into the early twentieth century, Americans joined anti-foreign organizations and called for restrictions on the inflow of aliens. In early autumn of 1915, the Ku Klux Klan of reconstruction days was revived by William J. Simmons of Georgia. It retained the anti-Negro bias of the old Klan, but added to its litany of hate anti-Catholic and anti-Jewish attacks. It was not until 1920, however, that the Klan, skillfully managed by two publicity agents, expanded into a national movement that knew no sectional boundaries. It preyed upon the fears of native Americans who were appalled at the decline of rural mores, and at the inadequate adjustments made by a changing society under the impact of a rapidly expanding industrial-urban complex. "One by one all our traditional moral standards went by the boards," complained the Klan's Imperial Wizard and Emperor, "or were so disregarded that they ceased to be binding." American cities were depicted as the breeding places for "many racial hybrids and some ethnic horrors that will be beyond the powers of future anthropologists to unravel." A not uncommon complaint of Klan newspapers charged "that the Jews dominate the economic life of the nation, while the Catholics are determined to dominate the political and religious life." It is hardly surprising that Hiram Wesley Evans, one of the Klan's leaders, should have concluded: "the Nordic-American today is a stranger in large parts of the land his father gave him." By the beginning of 1924, between three and four million Americans had enlisted in the Klan's ranks, not only in the South, but also in Indiana, Ohio, Colorado, Pennsylvania, and upstate New York. The Klan's leaders cynically exploited the movement for personal gain, and as rumors of their behavior circulated, finally erupting into public scandal, the organization's membership steadily declined. Moreover, in areas where immigrants, Catholics, and Jews were numerous, anti-Klan action was taken, often resorting to the same sort of violence that the Klan had so long fostered. Although declining as an organization, Klan sentiments persisted in many minds, quietly lying dormant. They would be heard again—even louder than before—in 1928, when a Roman Catholic, Alfred E. Smith, made his bid for the presidency.

THE RETURN OF FULL-SCALE CORRUPTION

"Normalcy" and Warren G. Harding. That Warren G. Harding should succeed Woodrow Wilson surely suggests that self-interest tends to triumph over idealism. Harding was an ordinary man, possessed of simply decency, naïve trust, and sublime ignorance. The reform agitation of the previous twenty years seemed to have run its course, and the American people were now ready to settle into "normality." When the Republican bigwigs chose the handsome senator from Ohio in preference to the belligerent General Leonard Wood, the competent Illinois Governor Frank O. Lowden, and the progressive Hiram Johnson, they were settling for the candidate who stirred the least resentment. What they were also choosing, unwittingly, was a genial incompetent who, after his election, would confess: "My God, but this is a hell of a place for a man like me to be!" In the Senate, his pathetic desires to be liked and to help others were useful attributes; in the presidency, they were disastrous. Far too many of his friends proved ready to use him, to exploit his geniality, to compromise his decency, to destroy what shreds of integrity a lifetime of petty politics had left him. William Allen White, the crusading Kansas journalist, recalled Harding complaining, "I have no trouble with my enemies. I can take care of my enemies all right. But my damned friends, my God-damn friends, White, they're the ones that keep me walking the floor nights!" The most striking fact about Harding's less than thirty months in the White House was its singular corruption.

Slightly more than sixty-one per cent of the American voting population cast their ballots in 1920 for the ticket of Harding and Calvin Coolidge, and against that of James M. Cox and Franklin D. Roosevelt. Although Wilson had dreamed of viewing the election as a final referendum for the League, it more accurately represented simply a vote for change. The national mood comprised resentment against the progressive effort to remake American society and resentment against the inadequacy of the effort. For eight years, Americans had listened to the soaring words of Wilson, had heard the call to gird up their loins for another battle to redeem the world and the nation from the failings of humanity. They had had enough. For a decade some struggled to defend or restore the vanishing rural virtues, while others sought new solutions for the problems of a radically changing America. As Walter Lippmann noted, "The evil which the old fashioned preachers ascribe to the Pope, to Babylon, to atheists, and to the devil, is simply the new urban civilization, with its irresistible scientific and economic and mass power. The Pope, the devil, jazz, the bootleggers, are a mythology which expresses symbolically the impact of a vast and dreaded social change." The election of Harding was a final appeal to the virtues of small town America; when, after his death, the full scope of the corruption in his administration became known, it was obvious that the old order was bankrupt.

The Cabinet Appointments of Harding. Harding made several excellent cabinet appointments, but not as many as he should have. Charles Evans Hughes proved a distinguished Secretary of State; Henry Wallace brought considerable knowledge to the Agriculture Department; and Herbert Hoover introduced efficient management into the Commerce Department. But the former senator from Ohio had the distinction of appointing the only cabinet officer ever sent to prison for malfeasance in office: Secretary of the Interior Albert B. Fall. Moreover, Navy Secretary Edwin Denby was guilty of monumental incompetence, and Attorney General Harry M. Daugherty truly belonged in prison. The other executive appointments also revealed Harding's great lack of judgment. Actually, the primary requirement for a presidential appointment seems to have been that the appointee be an old friend from Ohio.

The Forbes and Daugherty Scandals. One of Harding's least inspired appointments made Charles R. Forbes, a chance acquaintance, head of the Veterans Bureau. After Harding's death, it was discovered that Forbes had perpetuated a $200,000,000 swindle by selling veterans hospital supplies to commercial outlets at a fraction of their true cost, and by permitting fraudulent charges to be added to the bills for purchases of hospital sites, and to construction contracts.

Even more appalling is the fact that Attorney General Daugherty conducted a flourishing business through his friend, Jesse Smith, selling pardons and paroles for federal prisoners; immunity from government prosecution; appointments to federal office; and liquor withdrawal licenses. The flood of money was so great that it awed even the perpetrators themselves, Daugherty and Smith. Harding's knowledge of these undertakings is uncertain, although the suicide—it may have been murder—of Jesse Smith, in late May of 1923, exposed enough of the illegal and immoral operation to leave the President visibly shaken.

Teapot Dome. Death mercifully claimed Harding on August 2, 1923, before the worst of the scandals came to light, that involving the naval oil reserves at Teapot Dome, Wyoming, and Elk Hills, California. These reserves had been transferred to private control on noncompetitive bidding by Secretary of the Interior Fall, after Harding had moved control of them from the Navy Department to the Interior Department. Fall's transfer of the reserves, which had raised suspicions, created a furor when it was discovered that Fall had obtained a $100,000 interest-free loan, $233,000 in Liberty Bonds, and a herd of blooded cattle in the transaction. Fall was indicted, prosecuted, and sentenced to a year in prison and a fine of $100,000. The Secretary of the Navy, who was guilty of stupidity in permitting the original transfer, was forced to resign. The scandal also revealed something of the moral tone prevalent in far too many American circles. When the scandals were revealed, loudest criticism was directed against Montana's Democratic Senators Thomas Walsh and Burton K. Wheeler for their investigating zeal. Typical of the response was the New York *Times* description of them as "assassins of character." It was hardly an atmosphere conducive to responsible or respectable government.

THE ROARING TWENTIES

Prohibition. On January 16, 1920, the Eighteenth Amendment to the Constitution went into effect. For the next fourteen years, until December 5, 1933, Americans were forbidden "to manufacture, sell, or transport any intoxicating liquor." A struggle to establish temperance as a way of life had been finally brought to fruition by the combined efforts of the Woman's Christian Temperance Union and the Anti-Saloon League. "Prohibition" seemed to its supporters a giant step forward in the fight to lift the moral tone of American life; but experience proved it to be unenforceable, making violation of the law a national sport. Moreover, prohibition stimulated crime, as the underworld fought to gain the right to supply illegal liquor to a thirsty public. Former President Taft had warned against the experiment, with the skeptical assertion, "I am opposed to the presence of laws on the statute book that cannot be enforced and as such demoralize the enforcement of all laws." The prohibitionists took advantage of the war to agitate for restriction of liquor production, arguing that the grain so saved could be used to make bread to feed the hungry millions of ravaged Europe. With the nation at war, it was easy to argue that beer was a German drink, the consumption of which was tantamount to treason. In an almost absent-minded way, first Congress and then forty-six state legislatures—Rhode Island and Connecticut alone did not act—approved prohibition. To put power behind the amendment, Congress passed the Volstead Act, which limited production of alcoholic beverages to medical needs; specified penalties ranging from fines of $1,000 to $10,000 and imprisonment of from six months to five years; and made the Commissioner of Internal Revenue responsible for enforcement. A Prohibition Commissioner was appointed to head a force of 1,520 men whose job it was to keep production within authorized limits, to prevent smuggling of liquor into the country, and to restrain consumption. Agents' salaries ranged between $1,200 and $2,000; but though the number of agents grew to 2,836 in 1930, and compensation increased to between $2,300 and $2,800, the task proved unmanageable. As one Harvard professor noted:

> Few people really want [prohibition]. But nobody cares to say so. Politicians wait in vain for the sign that is not given. Judges on the

> bench hand out reluctant sentences, wondering what they will do when the stock of wine in their own cellars is exhausted. Lawyers, doctors, professors and merchants sit by tamely awaiting the extinction of their private comfort. The working man watches the vanishing of his glass of beer and wishes that he was a man of influence with power to protest. The man of influence wishes that he were a plain working man and might utter protests without fear of injury of his interests.

With public opinion against it, prohibition was honored more in the breach than in the observance. Illicit stills poured out a flood of illegal liquor; bootleggers smuggled vast quantities of foreign production into the country; Chicago witnessed bloody battles, as gangsters fought for control of the clandestine industry. Newspapers followed the careers of such colorful figures as Al Capone, Dion O'Bannion, and Johnny Torrio as they resorted to murder and systematic corruption of the police and municipal officials, and defied all authority with impunity. As one reporter noted, "The Holy Experiment bred unholy results." The Governor of New Jersey summed up the national sentiment with his promise that he would make his state wetter than the Atlantic Ocean. The very passage of the Eighteenth Amendment contained within itself the seeds of its own repeal; for the dedicated souls who had agitated for its passage had forgotten one small detail: they were a minority, attempting by legislation to enforce their own personal scheme of goodness upon the majority. The majority responded with a wholesale campaign of civil disobedience that effectively negated the power and intent of the law.

The Puritan in Babylon. A mourning nation rallied around the new President on the death of Harding in the summer of 1923. Calvin Coolidge had gained fame when, as Governor of Massachusetts, he had broken the Boston police strike in September 1919 with the pointed comment that there existed "no right to strike against the public safety by anybody, anywhere, any time." A dour, pinched-faced Vermonter, Coolidge was as close with words as Ebenezer Scrooge was with his pennies. Coolidge took his oath of office by lamplight in his father's remote Vermont farmhouse—a symbolic gesture, perhaps; for the new President set promptly to work cleaning up the Harding scandals, and infusing into the capital a wholesome air of bucolic morality. The White House, which had been the camping ground for Harding's unsavory friends, resumed its traditional role as the residence of a family whose daily lives were models of decorum. Otherwise, the new President took care to avoid innovation. He operated on the simple principle, "Never go out to meet trouble. If you will just sit still, nine cases out of ten someone will intercept it before it reaches you." So guided, Coolidge gave the nation almost six years of deafening silence.

The Wealth of the Nation. Politically, the American people of Coolidge's time lived in an aura of naïve and blissful placidity. Economically, socially, and intellectually, however, the twenties was a time of surging energy. A vast redistribution of population took place as urban centers boomed at the expense of rural areas. The census returns of 1920 revealed that, for the first time, over half the population dwelt in urban centers of more than 2,500 inhabitants each. The process accelerated until by 1930, 44.6 per cent of the entire population dwelt in ninety-six metropolitan areas with more than 100,000 inhabitants each. Equally dramatic was the fact that for every 46 farmers, 54 workers labored in manufacturing industries that created wealth three times as valuable as that created on the farm. Physical distances no longer presented the problems of isolation they had once, as the automobile industry found an eager market for its product. Between 1919 and 1929, auto registrations increased from 6,771,000 to 23,121,000. Highways cut across the countryside, putting an end to the golden age of railroads, and giving city dwellers such mobility that suburbs sprang up all across the countryside. States and municipalities whose funds for road building were matched dollar for dollar by federal funds, as provided by the Federal Highways Act of 1916, had expended almost half a billion dollars on highway construction in 1921. Henry Ford achieved world fame by his dynamic role in the production of the cheap automobile. The construction industry surged ahead, from over twelve billion dollars in sales in 1919 to substantially more than seventeen billion dollars in 1928. The skylines of many cities were marked by towering skyscrapers. Sales of radios, which totaled a bare sixty million dollars in 1922, had increased almost fiftyfold by 1929, and Americans were now able to hear news almost as it happened. The movie industry also soared, with weekly admissions reaching over 100,000,000,000 in 1930. Charlie Chaplin, Theda Bara, Rudolph Valentino, Amos 'n Andy, and Rudy Vallee became national idols and household names, as both the radio and movies broadened the daily experience of millions of citizens. The productivity of American industry was paralleled by a significant increase in wages; between 1922 and 1927, the purchasing power of the dollar increased by some thirteen per cent. Mass prosperity revealed itself in such other statistics as the increase of telephones from a bare ten million in 1915 to well over twenty million in 1930; in the expanded use of such new products as aluminum, pyrex cooking ware, and synthetic fibers such as rayon and celanese; and in the doubling of the consumption of canned goods. As 1929 approached, Americans were better fed, better clothed, and better housed than ever before in their history. And they could believe that life would get even better and better, until America would be a material paradise for all. But beneath the glittering prosperity, there existed questioning doubts, ill-formed fears of the meaning of the rushing change that altered the urban and rural landscape, and dismay as, in the words of T. S. Eliot, more Americans achieved "awareness of the decay of the individual consciousness and its fixed relations to the world."

The Lost Generation. For Americans born as the nineteenth century faded into the twentieth, there was no simple, codified system of values that could be readily accepted. Instructed in the virtues of a rural arcadia, shaped by the freewheeling individualism of a maturing capitalism, they had to accommodate their vision of a good life to the crowded turbulence of the city, to the lonely anonymity of the urban complex. Moreover, Europe, which many Americans had traditionally looked to as the source and center of cultural, intellectual, and artistic growth, was now decimated as the result of World War I, no longer politically or economically stable, and rendered incapable of giving new meaning and direction to those Americans who looked to her in their search for stability. The parent had become as bewildered as the child. The difficulty of establishing meaningful values in such an unstable society created the group known collectively as "the Lost Generation." A silent revolution had taken place in the dingy alleyways of Pittsburgh, in the slums behind the Chicago stockyards, in the tangled industrial complexes of northern New Jersey, Birmingham, Alabama, Detroit, Michigan, and a thousand other factory towns. The hordes of immigrants from central, southern, and eastern Europe that had inundated America between 1880 and 1920 were no longer content to remain circumscribed by their ghetto walls. The established order repressed them, so they questioned it; the accepted mores baffled them, so they failed to give them homage; and as the blood and flesh of the city, they sat at the throttle of the coming America. As the K.K.K. and the Prohibitionists struggled, each group in its own peculiar way, to salvage a vanishing America, American poets and writers were composing a long lament, a final requiem for a dying past. The tender words of the Lost Generation, as critic A. K. Whipple noted, "which look as if they were ushering in a new epoch are in truth ushering out an old one."

"I feel persuaded that here are destined to be discovered certain as yet undefined spiritual quantities," the poet Hart Crane wrote in an optimistic tone, "perhaps a new hierarchy of faith not to be developed so completely elsewhere." But Crane's abiding faith in the American experience was to be betrayed; in 1932, he took his own life. Crane's disillusionment was echoed by other artists of the time. T. S. Eliot saw the twenties as comprising "Shape without form, . . . gesture without motion." Against the soaring expectations of the publicist, Eliot juxtaposed a world ending not with a bang but a whimper. Ernest Hemingway and John Dos Passos captured the isolation of the people, and the pervasive loneliness of a crowded modern life; but they struggled also to find some hope in the enduring tenacity with which the ordinary man clung to life. Others launched ripping attacks into the homage rendered to common man. "I enjoy democracy immensely," H. L. Mencken declared. "It is incomparably idiotic, and hence incomparably amusing." Sinclair Lewis painted with harsh exactitude the bleak emptiness of Main Street and the vapid wasteland of middle-class American life; yet after writing twenty-three novels that exposed many an American foible and rubbed many an American nerve raw, Lewis could still declare, "I love America, I love it, but I don't like it."

The words of American writers had musical accompaniment: jazz. This peculiarly American musical idiom added the final note to general despair. Jazz had had its beginnings as funeral music, played to lift the spirits of mourners returning from New Orleans Negro funerals. Given the temper of the times, it had a curiously appropriate tone.

Of all the spokesmen of the twenties, however, none captured the fundamental tragedy and innocence more completely than F. Scott Fitzgerald. For him, the golden decade had coincided with the full vigor of his manhood. In an America wracked by the necessity of accepting change, Fitzgerald clung to his youth as old women cling to their heirlooms; in retrospect, he seems both symbol and victim of the times. In his words we can find an acute appraisal of what life and the world were like for the Lost Generation:

> Now once more the belt is tight and we summon the proper expression of horror as we look back at our wasted youth. Sometimes, though, there is a ghostly rumble among the drums, an asthmatic whisper in the trombones that swings me back into the early twenties when we drank wood alcohol and every day in every way grew better and better, and there was a first abortive shortening of the skirts, and girls all looked alike in sweater dresses, and people you didn't want to know said "Yes, we have no bananas," and it seemed only a question

of a few years before the older people would step aside and let the world be run by those who saw things as they were—and it all seems rosy and romantic to us who were young then, because we will never feel quite so intensely about our surroundings any more.

DOMESTIC AND FOREIGN AFFAIRS

The Election of 1924. The confrontation of urban and rural ideas took place most clearly during the Democratic national convention of 1924, which met at New York's Madison Square Garden. The "dry" wing of the party, under the leadership of William Jennings Bryan, clashed head on with the "wet" wing, headed by New York's gravel-voiced Alfred E. Smith. For nine broiling days, the convention was deadlocked; the casting of ninety-five ballots had not brought victory to either of the favored candidates, Alfred E. Smith and William G. McAdoo. The two leading candidates therefore agreed to withdraw; eight ballots later, on the one hundred and third ballot, the Democrats came forth with the incongruous ticket of John W. Davis, a Wall Street lawyer, and Charles Bryan, brother of silver-tongued William Jennings Bryan. (The Republicans settled for the wordless Coolidge and the bombastic Charles Dawes.)

Disgusted with the major tickets, a coalition of disgruntled Midwestern farm progressives, socialist reformers, intellectual professional men, and railroad union leaders met at Cleveland to organize a revitalized Progressive party. Their ticket, Senators Robert La Follette and Burton K. Wheeler, pledged to end the control "of government and industry by private monopoly." They proudly sported the slogan of New York's energetic Congressman Fiorello La Guardia, who threw his support to the party with the declaration, "I would rather be right than regular." The new party called for government ownership of railroads, establishment of congressional review of Supreme Court decisions, support of collective bargaining, government control and development of all water power resources, and direct election of the President. Despite divided support from labor, small resources, a minimum of organization, and steady rise in farm prices, the Progressives polled 4,826,471 votes. The Democrats fell below their 1916 and 1920 totals with 8,385,586 votes and the Republicans piled up 15,275,003 votes, at the same time gaining a sixteen vote majority in the Senate and a sixty vote margin in the House. The Democrats were at low ebb, and the Progressives had shown that they could command a massive vote of protest.

The Farm Problem. The twenties proved to be golden years for many, but for the American farmer they marked a quickening approach to the final death of the age-old agrarian dream. In contrast to the prosperity of the city, agricultural income declined from sixteen per cent of the national income in 1919, to a bare nine per cent in 1929. Prices broke sharply immediately after the end of World War I, and the loss of world markets condemned ever-larger numbers of farmers to marginal incomes which were insufficient to supply rural dwellers with the new products flooding the markets. A vast revolution impended; hundreds of thousands of family farmers abandoned the land to take refuge in the city, and great corporations began farming vast acreages with machines and gangs of itinerant workers. In 1921, the Farm Bureau Federation, one of the nation's most powerful farm groups, sponsored the organization of a congressional "farm bloc" to unite rural congressmen behind farm relief measures. Beginning with the Packers and Stockyards Act of 1921, which established public regulation of meat packer rates; the Grains Futures Act of 1921, which permitted regulation of grain rates by the Secretary of Agriculture; the Capper-Volstead Act of 1922, which freed farm organizations from antitrust laws; and the Agricultural Credits Act of 1923, which provided credit facilities that would extend loans to farmers, came a series of measures which drastically curtailed the traditional free enterprise of American farmers.

The McNary-Haugen Plan. The demand for equalization of farm income with that of manufacturing income culminated in a proposal for the establishment of parity prices that would guarantee the farmer prices equivalent to those he had earned during the golden years between 1909 and 1914. This plan, the brainchild of George N. Peek, a farm implements manufacturer, who argued, "You can't sell a plow to a busted customer," was embodied in the proposal of Senator Charles L. McNary of Oregon and Representative Gilbert N. Haugen of Iowa that eight basic commodities—wheat, flour, corn, cotton, wool, cattle, sheep, and swine—plus derivatives from the latter three, be covered by parity prices. But since the proposal called only for the support of domestic prices, cotton producers, whose main market was abroad, viewed the parity plan with indifference. In 1927, after provisions were included to cover cotton and tobacco growers, the McNary-Haugen Act was passed, placing not only cotton and tobacco but also wheat, rice, corn, and hogs under the equivalent of parity prices, and committing the government to regulating production. Coolidge, however, vetoed the bill, on the ground that it was an unnatural intervention of government in the regulation of economic processes. Faced with the obvious fact that agriculture was in deep trouble, the administration settled for a do-nothing policy.

When the Republicans met at Kansas City in 1928 to nominate a presidential candidate, they chose Herbert Hoover, who was known as an enemy of parity; and although the party platform pledged the creation of a federal farm board to promote a farm-marketing system of farmer owned and controlled stabilization corporations which could prevent and control surpluses through orderly distribution, it flatly opposed, "putting the government into [the] business" of agriculture. The seven decades of identification by Northern agricultural interests with the Republican party was beginning to wear thin.

The National Origins Act. On May 26, 1924, the greatest folk migration in history came to an end. On that day, Calvin Coolidge signed the National Origins Act, restricting immigration into the United States. It marked the end of a century-long experiment with the melting-pot idea, as well as the firm establishment of the quota principle that had been instituted during Harding's administration by the Emergency Quota Act of May 19, 1921, which limited the annual migration to three per cent of "the number of foreign-born persons of such nationality resident in the United States" as determined by the 1910 census. The 1924 act reduced the national quotas to two per cent, and provided a formula which would guarantee that the bulk of future immigration would come from northwestern Europe. For millions of Americans who came from central, southern, and eastern Europe, the act came as a premeditated insult; and in the nation's bursting cities, the act added one more log to the fire of discontent with the ruling Republican party.

War Debts and Reparations. America's rejection of the League of Nations did not mark a return to total isolationism. It was, however, an indication that national self-interest would prevail. The Americans were quick to express their suspicions of foreign intentions, assuming that the world had cast the United States in the role of international patsy. Typical was the view that the Europeans were reneging on repayment of $10.3 billion in debts contracted for war and rehabilitation purposes. When more reasonable observers pointed out that the Europeans lacked the means to pay, that the five per cent interest charges added to the already unwieldy burden, and that countries like France were burdened with enormous reconstruction costs, Calvin Coolidge expressed dominant sentiment with the abrupt retort, "They hired the money, didn't they?"

The establishment of the World War Debt Funding Commission on February 9, 1922, served notice on the world that the United States expected payment in full within twenty-five years at an interest rate of 4.25 per cent. Eventually, these terms had to be modified to cover a sixty-two year period at 3.3 per cent, when Britain negotiated a settlement. But other European countries proved even less amenable, with France settling for a 1.6 per cent interest rate, and Italy for a bare 0.4 per cent.

Since Europeans viewed repayment as conditional upon their obtaining German reparations, the firm American position on the debts served to revive European war-induced antagonisms. In 1924, the Dawes Plan outlined a method for liquidating war debts, by which surplus German funds would go into the servicing of the American debts rather than into reparations to other countries. These payments were further modified in 1929 by the Young Plan, which reduced German reparations to about the same level as the debt payments. In a curious way, the United States had managed to become the sole legatee of German reparations, even while claiming that she had refused to accept any punitive compensation. The final ironic touch came through German borrowing of funds in the United States market to develop the German economy. These loans, which amounted to at least $2.6 billion, were equivalent to payments on the outstanding war debts. Thus, America was supplying through investments the money that would pay the war debts owed to America.

The Washington Conference. On November 11, 1921, a conference convened at Washington, at the request of Secretary of State Charles Evans Hughes, to bring about international naval disarmament. The "big five" naval powers—the United States, Great Britain, Japan, Italy, and France—were joined by four lesser powers, China, Belgium, Portugal, and the Netherlands. The major purpose of the conference was to settle smoldering differences between Japan and the other Pacific powers. To the surprise of the other attending nations, Hughes gave the world an insight into America's espousal of open diplomacy, for he publicly announced the American plan for a wholesale reduction of the world navies. After careful negotiations, a formula was set forth which provided for construction of five ships apiece for the United States and Britain for every three possessed by Japan, and for every 1.75 built by Italy and by France. Japan obtained a major concession when both Britain and the United States pledged to refrain from strengthening their bases in the western Pacific region.

For all practical purposes, Japan had been given hostages (Guam, the Philippines, and Hong Kong) that could be seized at will should war erupt between Japan and the Anglo-Saxon powers. Furthermore, the limits on tonnage of capital ships and the agreement to restrict capital ship construction during the life of the treaty—it was due to expire in 1936—precluded a successful American effort to match Japanese sea power in the western Pacific. Perhaps of greatest significance was the renewed pledge to uphold the Open Door policy in China. Whether the American public realized it or not, such a pledge carried with it the ultimate obligation to intervene in China's defense should any power threaten to infringe upon it. Less than a decade after the signing of the Washington Treaty, Japan would enter into a campaign to subjugate China, and the United States would begin moving steadily toward a position of unyielding opposition that would culminate in World War II.

The Kellogg Peace Pact. On April 6, 1927, French Foreign Minister Aristide Briand announced that France wished to join the United States in outlawing war. A vigorous campaign led by Nicholas Murray Butler, president of Columbia University, Professor James T. Shotwell, also of Columbia, and Senator William Borah culminated in late December of 1927, when Secretary of State Frank P. Kellogg called for a multi-power declaration. On August 27, 1928, after extended negotiations in which amendments permitting defensive war were attached, the United States and fourteen other nations signed the Pact of Paris, renouncing war "as an instrument of national policy." On January 15, 1929, the Senate, by a thumping 85–1, ratified the "Peace Pact." Though sophisticated opinion agreed with Senator Carter Glass of Virginia, who viewed the pact as "worthless, but perfectly harmless," sixty-four nations ultimately subscribed to the pact. Though it lacked the substance to make it meaningful, the declaration seemed to reveal a universal longing for continued peace.

The Election of 1928. When the Democratic party met at Houston, Texas, on June 26, 1928, there was no doubt that the candidate would be New York's Governor Alfred E. Smith. A self-made man who had risen from the tenements of the Lower East Side of New York City, his nasal voice and ever-present brown derby seemed to symbolize the coming to power of the urban masses. Though Smith's long identification with Tammany Hall was certain to alienate numerous Democrats, and his Roman Catholicism and "wet" sentiments would provoke vigorous opposition to his candidacy, the Democrats realized that to pass over him would lose millions of urban, Catholic, and immigrant voters. In an effort to placate "dry" fundamentalist Protestants from the South, Senator Joseph Robinson of Arkansas was made the vice-presidential candidate. The Democratic platform also attempted to appeal to those interests offended by the unrestrained favoritism shown to business by the Republican party.

The Republicans, who had chosen Hoover and Curtis at Omaha, would probably have won no matter whom the Democrats nominated; the flood tide of prosperity assured that. But the most memorable aspect of the campaign was the tidal wave of anti-Catholic diatribes that flooded the nation, warning of the dangers of putting a Roman Catholic into the White House. Virginia's Republican National Committeewomen, for example, called upon the nation's women to "save the United States from being Romanized and rum-ridden." The K.K.K. circulated vast quantities of literature warning that the election of Smith would place the nation at the mercy of the Pope. The vicious dimensions of these attacks upon a religious minority stunned American Catholics, and moved the great Protestant theologian, Reinhold Niebuhr, to mourn that "the relations between Catholics and Protestants in this country are a scandal and an offense against Christian charity." Equally revealing was the patronizing contempt with which Smith's humble origins were treated. One Southerner, seeking to explain the extensive opposition to Smith within his section, wrote:

> I think we would naturally prefer a man of high culture and character, such as Woodrow Wilson, for president, to a product of the slums of New York with only a Tammany training, and whose highest ambition is to see the time come when he can put his foot on the brass rail and blow the foam off again.

Although Hoover disassociated himself from these attacks, numerous Republicans exploited them, reducing the campaign to Smith's efforts to establish his ability to fill the presidential post irrespective of his religion and his stand on prohibition, and of Hoover's solemn invocations of "rugged individualism." The result was an overwhelming victory for Hoover, who carried all but eight states—including five from the Solid South—and had a majority of almost six and a half million votes. Congress also remained Republican—by 267 to 163 in the House, and 56 to 39 in the Senate. But the overwhelming defeat of Smith masked a development of major importance: he had attracted almost six million new voters into Democratic ranks; had carried the great cities for his party, reversing a previous Republican dominance; and had firmly attracted millions of future Catholic voters and new immigrants to the Democratic party. In defeat, Smith had laid the foundations of Democratic dominance; in victory, Hoover stood on the threshold of an economic catastrophe that would terminate the golden twenties and open the lean thirties.

THE WALL STREET CRASH

The economic catastrophe that engulfed Hoover in 1929 was not his fault. Democrats have every reason to be grateful that their man was not in the White House; otherwise *they* would have had to assume responsibility for the depression against which the Republicans would struggle for two decades.

The Prelude to Disaster. The depression which had affected the nation between 1919 and 1921 had steadily receded, until by 1925, except for agriculture, coal mining, and the textile industry, the economy was booming. In the mid-twenties, however, a speculative movement started in the stock market; stocks valued at $27 billion on January 1, 1925, were inflated to valuation higher than $87 billion on October 1, 1929. It was not until the spring of 1928, however, that the speculative fever completely replaced reasoned restraint. In a single week, stocks such as Wright Aeronautical advanced 34¾ points, while Radio Corporation of America roared ahead by a full 21½ points in a single day. It was obvious that quoted stock prices had no relation to earning power. Through 1928, and into 1929, the market forged ahead, declined precipitously, and then forged ahead again. Its erratic behavior, when charted, resembles a blueprint for a roller-coaster. But for the investor, assured by such learned pundits as Yale's Professor Irving Fisher and Bernard Baruch who claimed that stock prices had reached what appeared to be a permanently high plateau, the dizzying ride held forth the lure of a golden pile. Working on borrowed margin, investors sent stock prices skyrocketing by their frantic bidding. The time had come to put on the brakes; but Hoover, who realized that the market was heading for a fall, proved reluctant to use federal power to restrain the speculation. He settled for the extraordinary notion that ultimate responsibility for regulation of the Wall Street market rested with the Governor of New York. By late spring of 1929, factory production turned downward. For a little while longer, men clung to the illusion that the value of stocks could be divorced from the value they originally expressed. A terrible awakening awaited them in October 1929.

Black Tuesday. Although the summer of 1929 revealed a small but steady decline in production indices, the stock market kept its balance. An erratic pattern of rise and fall in stock prices continued through

September and into early October, but on October 18 sharp declines were registered in the traditionally strong blue chip stocks such as United States Steel, General Electric, and Westinghouse. Decline proved contagious, and through the following week formidable giants such as American Telephone and Telegraph joined the slide; over-all industrial averages registered declines of as much as 31 points in a single day. But it was Thursday, October 24, 1929, that the terrible word "panic" crept into the market vocabulary. In a single day, some 12,894,650 shares poured through the market, shattering dreams of wealth, and sweeping prices down at a pace that exceeded the ticker tape's ability to record the disaster. Only the direct intervention of Richard Whitney, acting president of the Stock Exchange and a Morgan floor partner, who represented the New York banking community's decision to make large purchases of stock to stabilize the market, finally arrested and partially reversed the downward movement. For a few days longer, collapse was forestalled; but on Tuesday, October 29, the end came. Industrial averages fell 43 points, 16,410,030 shares were traded, and such industrial giants as Westinghouse awoke to the fact that their stock had declined by 160 points in less than two months. The cold, chill realization that the economy was profoundly sick slowly crept through the nation. The spectacular breaks in the stock market were superseded by a slow wasting away of value. The time of the locust had arrived, and with it the end of untold expectations. The Great Depression had begun.

Chapter 13

The Era of the New Deal

During the decade of the 1930s, America passed through a domestic upheaval the dimensions of which have not yet been fully measured: depression, want, growing international crises (half the world was victim to rampant tyranny), and the collapse of accepted values. But the same years saw experimentation to resolve social problems, dynamic legislation, constructive and imaginative leadership, and indomitable hope. The past was seen to be bankrupt, and there were no well-defined programs ready-made to meet the economic crisis of the thirties. Americans therefore had to create their solution out of whole cloth; and the course they chose was a pragmatic approach that attempted to meet the crisis piecemeal, without a comprehensive, binding, underlying scheme. Throughout the depression, Americans held fast to their conviction that their political system was basically healthy and that only a program of change *within* the established system was needed. Faced with the very collapse of capitalism, Americans turned not to revolutionary or alien ideologies but to the established political system for solutions. At just the time Germany had turned to Hitler and Nazism, the United States, true to democracy, chose Franklin D. Roosevelt. The era of the New Deal remains, therefore, a testament to the durability of American institutions and American faith in those institutions.

THE GREAT DEPRESSION

The Plight of the Workingman. Between October 1929 and March 1933 the United States slid into an abyss of despair. Although the business community voiced optimism for the future, and although Hoover greeted 1930 with the announcement that "business could look forward to the coming year with greater assurance," industrial production stagnated and unemployment grew. By the spring of 1930 almost 4,000,000 workers were without jobs; a year later, the number approached 8,000,000; in 1932, some 12,000,000 crowded the army of the unemployed; and by March 4, 1933, somewhere between 13,577,000 and 16,000,000 of the work force—almost one out of every three workers—were in search of jobs. For those who kept their positions wages were drastically cut, first through a reduction in hours, and then in hourly earnings. The average work week in 1929 was 48 hours; two years later it had been cut to 38. Wages, too, fell—from an average weekly salary of $28.50 in 1929, to $22.64 in 1931, and to $18.46 in 1932. Over-all income receipts declined by almost sixty per cent during the 1929–32 period. The employed and unemployed were separated only by comparative degrees of poverty.

The Plight of the Farmer. For most farmers, who had been fighting a losing battle through the twenties to keep income abreast of costs, the great depression dealt a final crushing blow. A grim joke of the era had a farmer saying, in reply to a question, "Naw, we don't grow corn—we grow poorer." In 1931 and 1932, nearly twenty-five per cent of all farms in the great Corn Belt were foreclosed. The acuteness of farm poverty moved one Iowa lawyer to protest:

> I have represented bankrupt farmers and holders of claims for rent, notes, and mortgages against . . . farmers in dozens of bankruptcy hearings and court actions, and the most discouraging, disheartening experiences of my legal life have occurred when men of middle age, with families, go out of the bankruptcy court with furniture, a team of horses and a wagon, and a little stock as all that is left from twenty-five years of work, to try once more—not to build up an estate—for that is usually impossible—but to provide clothing and food and shelter for the wife and children. And the powers that be seem to demand that these not only accept this situation but shall like it.

Amidst the abundance of America, there existed the irony of want. While city dwellers grubbed through refuse for food, wheat was left uncut in Montana fields because it did not pay to cut it; apples rotted in Oregon fields; cotton remained unpicked; Western roads teemed with dispossessed farmers and their families. In the South, the share-cropper tenant was cast adrift, as landlords found themselves unable to advance further credit. Thousands of Negro tenants (as one Alabama congressman reported in 1932) were "now in the middle of a winter, practically without food and without clothes, and without anything else. . . ." And to protests that the farm situation simply could *not* be as black as it was painted, a congressman replied: "Any thought that there has been no starvation, that no man has starved, and no man will starve, is the rankest nonsense."

The Failure of "Relief." If the spectre of hunger haunted the countryside, it cut its ugly scar across the city. The depression brought Americans face to face with the inadequacy of traditional charity methods. Among the great industrial nations, only the United States lacked all rudiments of a social security system. Normally, the poor were expected to look to private charity or local government for sustenance; but the sheer dimension of the present need crushed the traditional system, whose resources were hopelessly inadequate drops in the proverbial bucket. Herbert Hoover, wedded to custom, stubbornly refused to accept federal responsibility for the extension of relief; finally, in the summer of 1932, he reluctantly signed the Emergency Relief Act, which authorized the Reconstruction Finance Corporation to loan the states up to $300,000,000 for welfare aid. But even this measure did little to alleviate the problem, for only a tenth of the designated sum was loaned by the end of the year.

It is doubtful whether even the whole sum would have done more than scratch the problem. In the city of Philadelphia alone, 298,000 persons were out of work in May of 1932, with some 55,000 families each subsisting on a weekly relief grant of $4.23. In Birmingham, only 8,000 of the 108,000 workers earned their normal income, and thousands eked out an existence on grants of $2.50 to $4.00 a week. New York City reported that its Health Department found "that 20.5 per cent of the school children examined were suffering from malnutrition in 1932." In Chicago, where teachers were frequently unpaid, it was revealed that an average of 11,000 children were being fed from funds raised by teacher contributions.

Unemployment affected both the well-educated and the uneducated. Tens of thousands of college graduates found no need for their training. As a social worker observed, suffering drew no distinction; "all creeds, all groups, all races; everybody is suffering together."

The Rise of Protest. The initial response of the man in the street to the depression was bewilderment. But as the bread lines lengthened, and as government action failed to alleviate the public's need, ominous signs appeared which seemed to threaten social upheaval. An Oklahoma newspaperman testified before a congressional hearing on unemployment that he heard a cattleman declare, "We have got to have a revolution here like they had in Russia. . . ." The staid and proper *Harper's* magazine wondered what the army of unemployed would do if matters worsened, and nervously questioned: "Will they not demand retribution?" During 1931 and 1932 more and more newspapers reported "hunger riots," during which grocery stores were sacked. Sharpest action came from farmers in the Upper Middle West. There, such farm organizations as the Farmer's Holiday Association, under the fiery leadership of Milo Reno, warned, "If you continue to confiscate our property and demand that we feed your stomachs and clothe your bodies we will refuse to function." The traditionally individualistic farmer talked increasingly of a production "strike," and reports of violence began to be made as groups of farmers ranged through the countryside, dumping milk and destroying produce.

The appearance of some 30,000 veterans in Washington, during the spring of 1932, to support the proposal of Representative Wright Patman of Texas that the veterans' bonus authorized in 1924 for payment in 1945 be paid immediately brought the human evidence of the depression right to the steps of the Capitol. There, thousands of men, some with their families, encamped in shacks on the Anacostia flats. But, as *The New Yorker* observed, the "bonus army . . . was something more than a lobby: it was the expression of men's desire to huddle together when their courage was gone." Although the House approved the Patman Bill on June 15, 1932, by a vote of 209–176, the Senate, on June 17, voted it down by an overwhelming margin of 62–18, even as some 12,000 bonus veterans kept vigil outside the Capitol. When the veterans remained in their encampment, the District of Columbia police decided on July 28, 1932, to dispossess the Anacostia squatters. Some resistance was met, and President Hoover ordered troops, under Douglas MacArthur, to drive the bonus army out of Washington. The encampments were burned to the ground, two veterans and an eleven-week-old baby were killed, and well over a thousand veterans, bystanders, and police were injured. The bonus army had been dispersed, but as one sensitive reporter, who had watched the burning of Anacostia, noted:

My mood was one of despair. It was an experience that stands apart from all others in my life. So all the misery and suffering had finally come to this—soldiers marching with their guns against American citizens. I had nothing but bitter feelings toward Herbert Hoover that night.

THE ADMINISTRATION OF HERBERT HOOVER

Herbert Hoover. Few men had entered the White House with a sounder reputation than Herbert Hoover. During World War I he had managed with unusual skill the American Relief Administration's efforts to alleviate suffering in the aftermath of war. To many observers, Hoover was one of the truly great figures to emerge from the war. His ability was again demonstrated in his excellent administration of the Commerce Department under Harding and Coolidge. Moreover, his long and highly successful career as a mining engineer had led him around the world, exposing him to the complex realities of the international situation. But Hoover was victim to a tragic limitation: he was a self-made man who had risen from near-poverty to wealth and fame, and like many others of that breed, he held the firm conviction that capitalism was inherently capable of riding out every storm without important government intervention. Few men of high national responsibility have believed so intensely in the innate value of a *laisser faire* individualism. "While I can make no claim for having introduced the term 'rugged individualism,'" he declared in 1934, "I should be proud to have invented it." Faced with the great depression, he accepted it as a necessary shaking out of an economic system suffering from overproduction, overpricing, overspeculation, and an absence of confidence overseas.

The Hoover Policies. At the outset of the depression, the administration worked to reassure the public that "the fundamental business of the country, that is, the production and distribution of commodities, is on a sound and prosperous basis." Privately, however, Hoover conceded that "the depression must last for some time." But the gradual changes that would come to pass as the depression worked its wonders of economic readjustment would culminate, Americans were told, in a period of prosperity greater than ever before. At no point did Hoover understand that a mature system of production had woefully outstripped the American ability to consume the goods produced.

Timid efforts to combat the depression were finally launched, and these implicitly committed the federal government to taking a measure of responsibility for the mitigation of the depression. But, by their very paucity, they only accentuated the seeming unwillingness of Washington to face up to the dimensions of the collapse. The Agricultural Marketing Act of 1929, with the Federal Farm Board as its agent, designated federal funds for the purchase of farm produce when prices sank below a certain level. It was viewed as an occasional, rather than a permanent, necessity; but the tide of farm surpluses soon revealed the inadequacy of the act. By 1932 the Hoover administration was experimenting with creation of artificial scarcity, as agents of the Federal Cotton Corporation tried to persuade cotton farmers to plow up a third of the prospective crop. Faced with increasing evidence that local and state facilities for the relief from want were breaking beneath their burden, Hoover established, in October 1930, an Emergency Committee on Unemployment Relief—while at the same time cautioning against shifting responsibility for economic and social questions from the local community to Washington. Against the efforts of such Democratic senators as William G. McAdoo of California to launch a massive federal relief program, Hoover responded with the flat pronouncement that he was "opposed to any direct or indirect government dole." Only outright starvation, Hoover noted, would persuade him to think otherwise. In the fall of 1931, a new Organization on Employment Relief, under the direction of Walter S. Gifford, president of the American Telephone and Telegraph Company, was organized to stimulate private charity. A community warned of an imminent hurricane decided to prepare for a spring rain.

International Fiscal Collapse. The collapse, in May 1931, of the Kreditanstalt, Austria's largest bank, sent a spiraling economic crisis sweeping first through central Europe and then through the whole world. On September 21, 1931, the British government went off the gold standard. Soon, large blocks of American stock were dumped on the market by European investors, and large amounts of gold were drained from the country as foreign accounts in American banks were withdrawn. Desperately, on June 21, 1931, Hoover declared a moratorium on payment of intergovernmental debts and reparations. But the damage to the nation's banking system could no longer be met with stopgap efforts; in October 1931 alone, some 522 banks failed. Under presidential pressure, insurance companies were persuaded to halt foreclosures on delinquent mortgages and bankers agreed to form a $500 million pool to aid threatened banks; but again, all that was achieved was delay, rather than cure. Bank failures decreased briefly, and then began to mount again. Now, at long last, Hoover called on Congress to establish the Reconstruction Finance Corporation. In January 1932, Congress complied.

The Reconstruction Finance Corporation. The new act granted the Reconstruction Finance Corporation $500 million of capital, and allowed it to borrow up to $1,500 billion through the sale of tax-free bonds. Under the guidance of Eugene Meyer, governor of the Federal Reserve Board, and former Vice-President Charles G. Dawes, it opened offices in thirty cities. Within a year, some $1,500 billion in loans had been poured into the nation's banks, insurance companies, and other fiscal institutions, as well as into railroads. A further aid to business was provided by the Glass-Steagall Act of February 27, 1932, which reduced reserve requirements under the Federal Reserve System, and which lowered the rediscount rates. But Hoover stubbornly refused to provide either individual relief or public-works projects, and in July 1932, he vetoed the Garner-Wagner Relief Bill. Such refusals, combined with the R.F.C.'s habit of lending primarily to large banks and corporations, convinced growing numbers of the electorate that Hoover and the Republican party were dedicated to government of the few, by the few, for the few.

The Smoot-Hawley Tariff. As the depression dragged on, Hoover increasingly traced its origins to foreign sources. Such thinking permitted him to believe that the "American System" of *laisser faire* individualism was still fundamentally healthy. Insisting on a republic founded on "free-choice," "maximum efficiency," "equality of opportunity," and (above all) "liberty," Hoover, nonetheless, saw fit to sign into law, on June 17, 1930, the Smoot-Hawley Tariff. He defended his action as beneficial to American business, but failed to understand that the tariff repudiated all the values he struggled to maintain. Substantially, the measure placed a protective wall of sixty per cent tariffs around all American industry. Although it precluded the possibility that foreigners could successfully compete in the American markets, it also eliminated the possibility that foreigners could consume United States goods. In fact, the act stirred an orgy of international self-sufficiency, as approximately fifty other nations clamped down restrictions on imports. The American market, already overloaded with goods, now found its gluts assuming monstrous dimensions.

The Election of 1932. The Republicans approached the presidential election of 1932 surrounded by mounting evidence that they had lost the nation's confidence. In the mid-term elections of 1930, the

Democrats had picked up enough seats in the Senate to gain an even division with the Republicans; some 40 seats in the House of Representatives, which, along with subsequent Republican deaths, permitted the Democrats to organize the House; and 17 governors, as against the Republican 12. No Democratic victory was more spectacular than Franklin D. Roosevelt's re-election to the governorship of New York by 725,000 votes. The rejection of Republicans in the 1931 elections was even more emphatic.

It is hardly surprising, therefore, that when the Republicans gathered in Chicago on June 14, 1932, reporters described the convention as "mournful as a wake." Dutifully, the delegates renominated Hoover and Curtis, reaffirmed Hoover's policies, and then went forth to be slaughtered. The Democrats, meeting in the same city some ten days later, gathered with the soaring certainty that they had come to nominate a winner. Under the skillful guidance of James A. Farley and the gnomelike Louis Howe, Franklin D. Roosevelt was nominated on the fourth ballot. To the boisterous strains of "Happy Days Are Here Again," the Democrats opened a slashing attack on the Republican depression, and—unexpectedly—pledged repeal of prohibition. Their candidate gave the nation a preview of his willingness to experiment by flying to Chicago to accept his nomination. There, before a roaring convention, he set the note for the future when he declared: "I pledge you—I pledge myself to a new deal for the American people." Seventeen thousand miles, and at least a thousand speeches later, Roosevelt swept to a massive victory of 22,809,638 votes to Hoover's 15,758,901, carrying forty-two states (with 472 electoral votes) to the incumbent's six states (and 59 electoral votes). The Congress was to be overwhelmingly Democratic, with 59 Democrats, 36 Republicans, and 1 Farm-Laborite in the Senate, and 313 Democrats, 117 Republicans, and 5 Farm-Laborites in the House. Nothing was more revealing of the fundamental conservatism of the American voter than the poor showing of left-wing parties: Norman Thomas running as a Socialist gained 885,458 votes, while William Z. Foster, the Communist, had a bare 103,152. Of greatest significance for the future, Roosevelt had consolidated the urban vote that Smith had dented in 1928, sweeping every major city except Philadelphia, Buffalo, Newark, and Hartford. An urban coalition of labor, Catholics, Jews, new immigrants, and Negroes had fused with the traditionally Democratic South to establish a new political majority that would dominate the future of American politics.

THE FIRST ADMINISTRATION OF FRANKLIN D. ROOSEVELT

F.D.R. the Man. The President who entered the White House on March 4, 1933, was to the manner born. A member of an affluent, influential family, Roosevelt hardly seemed the man most likely to become identified with the greatest social revolution America has ever witnessed. Educated at Groton and Harvard, assured from birth against want, he had been elected to the New York State Senate in 1910, served in Wilson's cabinet as Undersecretary of the Navy, and was chosen to run as the Democratic vice-presidential candidate in 1920. In August of 1921 he contracted infantile paralysis, an illness which left him permanently crippled. Although he struggled to overcome his disability, he finally accepted its permanence, and set to work building a new political career. As Governor of New York State between 1929–33, he proved competent rather than outstanding, conscientious rather than inspired. Walter Lippmann cuttingly described him as "a highly impressionable person, without a firm grasp of public affairs, and without very strong convictions," and added, "He is a pleasant man, who, without any important qualifications for the office, would very much like to be President." In the most striking speech Roosevelt had made during his campaign for the presidency, the Commonwealth Club Speech at San Francisco, he had pointedly supported government interference in the economy; but he had also said, significantly, "The government should assume the function of economic regulation only as a last resort, to be tried only when private initiative, inspired by high responsibility, with such assistance and balance as government can give, has finally failed."

And lest anyone misapprehend his intentions, he added: "As yet there has been no final failure, because there has been no attempt; and I decline to assume that this nation is unable to meet the situation." Thus Roosevelt made it clear that, no less than Hoover, he believed in the American System, but that he meant to experiment until the crippled American experiment was made whole again.

The New Deal. Roosevelt's Inaugural Address of March 4, 1933, was a clarion call for hope and faith in the future. Bluntly the new President declared his conviction that "the only thing we have to fear is fear itself—nameless, unreasoning, unjustified terror which paralyzes needed efforts to convert retreat into advance." The jaunty optimism and the confident tone which permeated the presidential call to action convinced the nation that a man had finally been found to lead it out of the wilderness of economic despair.

The new deal which Roosevelt had promised the American people was not long in coming; "newness" marked Roosevelt's approach to every matter and situation. The liberal aura of his cabinet lent weight to the expectation of change. The long fight of the new Secretary of State, Cordell Hull, for lower tariffs promised needed reforms in that persistent problem. The presence of Henry Morgenthau, Jr. (who replaced William H. Woodin upon the latter's illness) in the Treasury secretaryship gave that office a diligent, thoughtful leadership during twelve crucial years of complex fiscal activities. Roosevelt's appointment to the cabinet of two progressive Republicans, Henry A. Wallace in the Agriculture Department and Harold L. Ickes in the Interior Department, suggested that liberals of either party would find a welcome in the new administration. To emphasize the new President's willingness to break with the past and to experiment with novelty was the appointment of Frances Perkins as Secretary of Labor, making her the first woman cabinet member in history. Dispensing patronage was the consummately shrewd politician James A. Farley in the Postmaster Generalship. Rounding out the cabinet were Homer S. Cummings (who succeeded Senator Thomas J. Walsh of Montana who had suddenly died) as Attorney General; Claude A. Swanson, the long-time senator from Virginia, as Secretary of the Navy; Daniel C. Roper, a South Carolinian who had served under Wilson, as Secretary of Commerce; and George H. Dern, the former liberal Governor of Utah, as Secretary of War. It was a cabinet with a liberal bent, and one which gave due recognition to the traditional sources of Democratic strength.

The Brain Trust. Many observers viewed Roosevelt's election as an instance of an ordinary man, fortunate enough to be in the right place, winning the White House for want of a better alternative. It is undoubtedly true that Roosevelt had revealed little originality in his thinking prior to his election, and that, despite charges to the contrary, he was committed to the saving of "the system of private profit and free enterprise after it had been dragged to the brink of ruin." More than once he reminded the public of his fundamentally conservative intention, insisting (with variations) that "The New Deal is an old deal—as old as the earliest aspirations of humanity for liberty and justice and the good life." As Frances Perkins later recalled, to suggestions that the depression be allowed to run its course without federal intervention, Roosevelt, horror-stricken, protested: "People aren't cattle, you know!" Thus the new President regarded the problem of preserving the old values as a matter that had to be governed by simple humanity. Faced with a novel situation, he revealed a willingness to experiment, to look for new solutions, and to take advice from intellectuals.

Even before Roosevelt was elected, there developed around him a "brain trust" of social critics, academicians, social workers, and reformers. At the center of this group was Raymond Moley, a former Columbia University professor, who revealed an unusual knack for supplying Roosevelt with striking ideas to be implemented through a program of economic reforms; Samuel Roseman, who had realized that Roosevelt possessed a good temper but that he needed expert advice on many of the social abuses and economic dislocations of the times, and who therefore proposed the formation of a group of scholars as advisers; and the President's long-time friend and adviser, Louis M. Howe. Through Moley, a number of young Columbia faculty members were directed to assist in supplying Roosevelt with ideas. Among them were Adolph Berle, a fiscal expert; Rexford Tugwell, an adviser on agriculture; and Lindsay Rogers, a tariff consultant. During the twelve years of Roosevelt's presidency, a steady stream of such advisers would find their way into Roosevelt's camp. And, perhaps most important of all, there was Anna Eleanor Roosevelt, the First Lady, who brought an acute social conscience and an unwearying energy into the White House. No worthwhile cause failed to obtain her friendly attention and interest, no social problem was beyond her ken. For Eleanor Roosevelt, the role of First Lady was an object lesson in good citizenship.

The Closing of the Banks. Despite Roosevelt's initial optimistic tone, the administration was well aware that the nation stood on the brink of chaos. Secretary of the Treasury William H. Woodin, whose ill health would soon require his replacement by Henry Morgenthau, Jr., realized that only the drastic action of closing the banks would prevent the collapse of the nation's banking system. From Homer Cummings he obtained the information that such action was constitutional. Although considerable pressure existed for the nationalization of the banking system, Roosevelt had resolved on attempting to effect banking recovery through cooperation with the nation's bankers. As a preliminary to drastic reforms, he called Congress into emergency session for March 9, and simultaneously ordered the closing of the nation's banks and suspension of gold payments. He then sent examiners into the closed banks to determine which banks were basically sound and which needed to be liquidated. When Congress convened on March 9, it passed with dazzling rapidity an Emergency Banking Bill which validated the presidential action already taken, extended executive control over gold transactions, established a system of conservators under the Comptroller of the Currency to supervise the assets of closed banks, and permitted solvent banks to resume business. During the following week, 4,507 national and 567 state banks reopened, and the nation's banking seemed once again viable. In a single day, Roosevelt had demonstrated the possibilities of a forceful executive leadership. On March 12, he made use of radio to deliver the first of many fireside chats during which he explained his plans for recovery to the nation. For the first time in history, the presidential voice became a household sound. The nation was ready for three months of experimentation.

Congress' First Hundred Days. Once Congress had launched its program, it developed a seemingly insatiable appetite for reform. To provide some national cheer until the necessary three-fourths of the states approved the Twenty-First Amendment repealing prohibition, Congress approved the manufacture of 3.2 beer and returned responsibility for regulation of liquor laws to the states. On March 20, the Economy Act, providing for cuts in federal salaries and veterans' pensions, and for reorganization of federal agencies, insured a saving of $250,000,000 in federal expenditures. Momentarily, at least, Roosevelt seemed destined to keep federal finances on a bone-bare basis. But on March 31, the organization of the Civilian Conservation Corps, designed to provide work for eventually 500,000 youths in various conservation projects for subsistence and monthly wages of $30 apiece, set in motion a spending program that would soon make economy seem an improbable illusion. To fiscal traditionalists, the decision on April 19 to abandon the gold standard came as an unnerving surprise. This was supplemented, on June 5, with the abrogation of the gold clause in public and private contracts. On May 12, the government committed itself to further expenditures by the passage of a Federal Emergency Relief Act, which placed at the disposal of the states $500 million to relieve want; the Agricultural Adjustment Act, which established a system of federal farm subsidies and regulation of farm prices to insure farmers a fair return on their effort; and the Emergency Farm Mortgage Act, which permitted the Farm Credit Administration to assist farmers in staving off foreclosures. Senator Elmer Thomas of Oklahoma had added an amendment to the Agricultural Adjustment Act, giving Roosevelt the power to inflate the currency as he saw fit; the President had accepted this provision to avoid the likelihood that Congress might pass a compulsory inflation

UNEMPLOYMENT STATISTICS FOR THE GREAT DEPRESSION

Showing percentage of work force unemployed

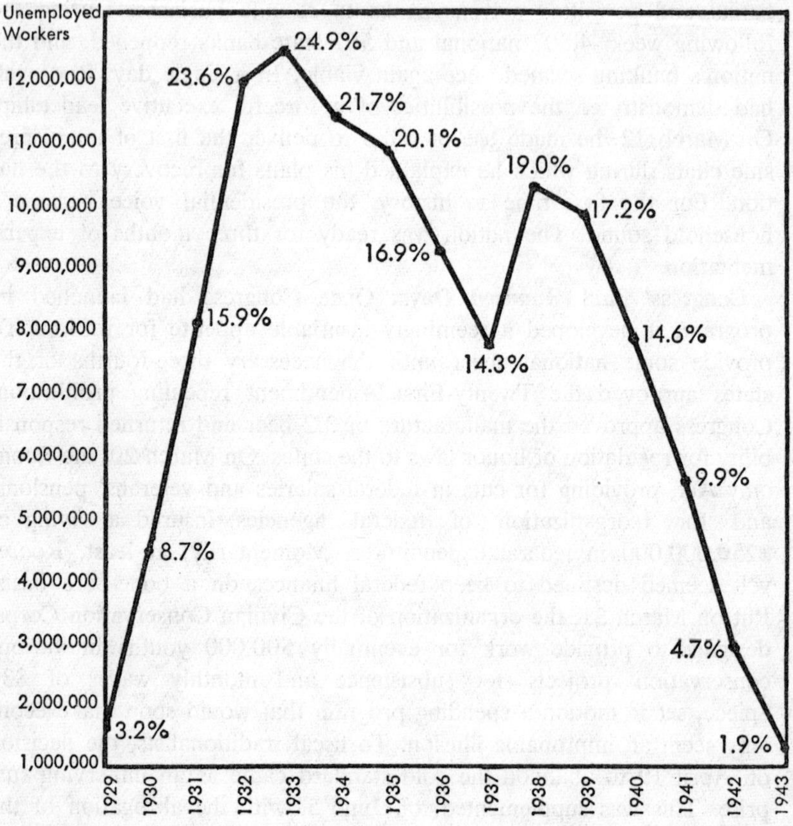

act. Six days after this series of acts was passed, the Tennessee Valley Authority Act, which committed the federal government to a systematic development of the Tennessee Valley, was passed. Its passage signaled for Senator George Norris of Nebraska, its long-time sponsor, "the dawning of that day when every rippling stream . . . shall be harnessed and made to work for . . . man." On May 27, the Truth-in-Securities Act, which required brokers and underwriters to provide investors with full information on the supporting value of stocks and bonds, was passed, and the Securities and Exchange Act of June 6, 1934, went even further, establishing a commission to police stock and bond sales. The Glass-Steagall Banking Act of June 16, 1933, organized the Federal Deposit Insurance Corporation to insure deposits up to $5,000 against loss. It also separated commercial from investment banking, thereby sharply restricting the likelihood that bankers would speculate with their depositors' funds. Three days earlier, the Home Owners' Loan Act had been passed, providing funds with which to refinance home mortgages, and on the same day that witnessed the passage of the Glass-Steagall Act came the Farm Credit Act, which reorganized federal agricultural credit activities, and the Railroad Coordination Act, which authorized a Federal Coordinator of Transportation to supervise railroad practices were passed.

The National Industrial Recovery Act. The finishing stroke of the one hundred days of legislation was the National Industrial Recovery Act, the purpose of which was to restore industrial production and revitalize employment. Its intention, as its administrator Hugh Johnson noted, was the achievement of "concerted action in industry and agriculture under government supervision looking to a balanced economy as opposed to the murderous doctrine of savage and wolfish individualism. . . ." The act provided a comprehensive system of codes to regulate production, prices, costs, distribution, and labor charges. To insure the workability of the codes, regulating prices and production antitrust laws were suspended. Section 7a set forth basic labor reforms which established maximum hours and minimum wages, the right to collective bargaining, and the prohibition of child labor. At the heart of the proposed reforms was an effort to establish a system of industrial planning which would free the economy from the vagaries of unrestrained competition. With the passage of the N.I.R.A. (to be carried out by the National Recovery Administration) the first one hundred days were finished. But for Roosevelt, the critical test had just begun.

The London Economic Conference. As the New Deal struggled to restore the nation's economy, other nations throughout the world wrestled with similar problems. Although depression had reached world-wide proportions, it was everywhere approached as if it were only a national difficulty. Country after country inaugurated programs of recovery which were characterized by a strident economic nationalism. Both the National Industrial Recovery Act and the Agricultural Adjustment Act provided for increases in the going tariff rates should foreign competition threaten to invade the American market. In addition, Roosevelt devalued the dollar's gold content. It was hoped that such action would reduce the gold value of our imports while increasing the dollar value of our exports. At the heart of this expectation was the widespread belief among Roosevelt's advisers in the "commodity dollar," which held that the value of money was determined by its purchasing power rather than its gold content. Concurrent with the program of domestic recovery, the President was pledged to participate in the London Economic Conference in June 1933. Its supporters, among them Cordell Hull, hoped to achieve international cooperation in the reduction of tariffs and the stabilization of monetary rates. All hopes for the Conference's success ceased, however, on July 3, when Roosevelt bluntly informed the assemblage that the United States had no intention of returning to the gold standard, planned to reduce further the gold content of the dollar, and intended to look to its own economic recovery without concerning itself with the international consequences. For the time being, Roosevelt had turned his back upon the Wilsonian legacy of international cooperation.

The Fight for Recovery. The second part of the N.I.R.A. had authorized a vast program of public works. Under the title of the Public Works Administration, Secretary of Interior Harold Ickes was authorized to borrow $3.3 billion with which to launch road and other construction projects. Roosevelt stated that the program's purpose was "to create employment as fast as we can," but he added the strategic proviso that "we should not pour money into unproved projects." Ickes took the injunction so literally that his careful scrutiny of each project effectively checked a speedy utilization of the authorized expenditures. As criticism of the dawdling behavior of the P.W.A. grew, the energetic social worker and chief of the Federal Emergency Relief Administration, Harry Hopkins, managed to divert some of the P.W.A.'s funds into the establishment of the Civil Works Administration. Briefly, the C.W.A. provided a vivid example of what could be done to put large numbers of unemployed to work. Through the winter of 1934, some four million unemployed labored at "make-work" projects which frequently struck critics as both wasteful and useless. In the spring of 1934, the C.W.A. was terminated, and unemployment immediately pressed peak depression figures.

No less emphatic was the growing evidence of the N.R.A.'s failure. From consumer organizations, labor leaders, and small businessmen came a surge of charges that the N.R.A. favored big business. Similar criticisms were leveled in Congress, and a common joke was that N.R.A. stood for the "National Run-Around." No less severe criticism came from businessmen who charged that the codes favored labor. The sharp turndown in the economy, after the short summer boom of 1933 (during which industrial production reached 101 per cent of the 1923–25 level and prices on the wholesale level rose from 60.2 in

March to 71.2 in October on the national price index), lent weight to the charge that the program had failed. When Clarence Darrow and the Review Board appointed by Roosevelt to investigate charges against the N.R.A. found that the codes resulted in price-fixing, further weakened the bargaining position of labor, and accentuated the trend toward concentrating monopolistic power in the hands of a few large producers (although the administration refused to print these findings), it was apparent that the experiment was nearing its end. The administration's hope that employer-employee strife could be kept minimal through a program of patriotic cooperation went aglimmering.

In September 1934, Roosevelt conceded in a fireside chat that the entire program needed overhauling. As legislative plans were made to eliminate the monopolistic and price-fixing aspects of the codes, the Supreme Court, on May 27, 1935, settled the N.R.A.'s fate by declaring, in Schecter Poultry Corporation *v.* United States, that it was unconstitutional in its entirety. So ended the first great experiment in recovery.

Disillusionment with Roosevelt. As the first stage of the New Deal ended, a surge of protest from both the right and the left threatened Roosevelt's experiment. Conservative businessmen, frightened by evidence that the administration contemplated stringent antibusiness measures, organized (under the leadership of Alfred E. Smith) the Liberty League. "In the view of those who comprise the membership of the League," declared the conservative Democrat Jouett Shouse, "the superficially drawn distinction between 'human rights' and 'property rights' is a catch-phrase and nothing more." Conservative charges that the administration contemplated a fascist dictatorship were now replaced by conservative charges that Roosevelt and his advisers conspired the establishment of "absolute communism." A vast radio audience listened to the weekly charges of the "radio priest," Father Charles E. Coughlin, that "the money-lenders" dominated the administration. His calls for an inflation of the currency stirred uneasiness in an administration bent upon maintaining traditional capitalist values. Peculiarly frightening was the evidence of the demagogic appeal of Senator Huey "Kingfish" Long of Louisiana's "share the wealth" plan among the many poor farmers of both North and South. The discontent of the aged was vividly illustrated in the large support given Dr. Francis Townsend's program of increased old-age pensions.

The Election of 1934. The impending off-year elections of 1934 raised questions as to whether Roosevelt's emphasis upon a nonpartisan approach to the nation's problems would pay off at the polls. Emphasizing that the administration was committed to the well-being of all, rather than to the interest of the few, to a government "run less for political purposes and more for the general good than it has been in some time," Roosevelt jauntily dismissed the surge of protest, and predicted that "the voters as a whole are pretty well satisfied that we are going some place and . . . still want action." The November results more than justified his confidence: the Democrats picked up 10 Senate seats, and increased their House seats from 313 to 322. No less dramatic was the upheaval in the state houses, where the Republicans managed to retain only 7 of 48 governorships. No one could doubt that the electorate had called for more reform rather than less, or that Roosevelt had demonstrated a powerful appeal as he reversed the usual off-year losses of the party-in-power.

The Wagner Labor Relations Act. No aspect of the New Deal was more important than the legislative recognition obtained by organized labor. In this area of legislative reform, however, Roosevelt followed rather than led. Section 7a of the original N.R.A. had been included largely as a result of the efforts of John L. Lewis, chief of the United Mine Workers, and of William Green, head of the American Federation of Labor. Secretary of Labor Perkins perceptively noted of her chief:

> There were many things about trade unions that Roosevelt never fully understood. I doubt that he understood what solidarity really means in the trade-union movement. He tended to think of trade unions as voluntary associations of citizens to promote their own interests in the field of wages, hours and working conditions. He did not altogether grasp that sense of their being a solid bloc of people united to one another by unbreakable bonds which gave them power and status to deal with their employer's terms.

At no time did Roosevelt militantly enforce Section 7a. Senator Robert F. Wagner of New York assumed the relinquished function, and as head of the National Labor Board concluded that the collective-bargaining clause of Section 7a lacked enforcement power. Despite efforts to strengthen the Board in February 1934, Wagner concluded that only a new act which specifically forbade employers to use unfair labor practices would prevent a dangerous deterioration of labor relations. Anxiously he warned:

> The struggle for a voice in industry through the process of collective bargaining is the heart of the struggle for the preservation of political as well as economic democracy in America. Let men become the

> servile pawns of their masters in the factories of the land and there will be destroyed the bone and sinew of resistance to political dictatorship.

He added emphatically that "Fascism begins in industry, not in government . . . the seeds of communism are sown in industry, not in government." Unless laboring men were given a chance to "know the dignity of freedom and self-expression in their daily lives," the drastic reforms being agitated on the right and left might sweep the American Experiment into the limbo of lost causes. But Roosevelt was not yet ready to support Wagner; in fact, in June of 1934 he abolished the National Labor Board, and established a new Labor Relations Board without Wagner. But the Supreme Court disallowed Section 7a along with the rest of the N.R.A., in May 1935, and Wagner, who had been conducting hearings on a new bill since March 1935, swiftly moved into action. By the end of May, the Senate had approved the Wagner bill by a thumping 63 to 12, and in mid-June the House passed it by a voice vote. After minor alterations in a joint House-Senate conference, the bill was signed into law on July 5 by the President. The act established a bipartisan National Labor Relations Board, with the power to compel employers to bargain in good faith, to prohibit employer interference in labor activities, and to conduct employee elections of their bargaining representatives. In addition, employers were forbidden to penalize employees who actively advocated organization. Congress had given labor the green light to open its greatest sustained effort at organization, but as Frances Perkins noted: "It ought to be on the record that the President did not take part in developing the National Labor Relations Act, and, in fact, was hardly consulted about it. . . . All the credit for it belongs to Wagner." Thus one of the greatest pieces of New Deal legislation came into existence in spite of, rather than because of, Roosevelt.

The Works Progress Administration. The 73rd Congress convened with the knowledge that the voter wanted more dramatic action. It sensed that the crosscurrents of dissent were derived from the inadequacies of the early New Deal. It also knew that the social and economic dislocations of the depression were hardly dented. The Congress was ready to send the federal government into a fuller participation in the nation's economy; it was prepared to use federal credit to buy the country out of the depression. On April 8, 1935, it authorized the expenditure of $4.8 billion to provide work for the unemployed. The funds to be used were obtained through deficit financing, by borrowing and increasing the national debt. Implicit in this provision were the ideas of the British economist John Maynard Keynes, who argued that government could spend its way out of a depression by pouring purchasing power into the hands of the consumers. Although Roosevelt viewed this arrangement as only a temporary expedient, he accepted it as necessary for the establishment of a vast public welfare program which would maneuver the nation out of the economic doldrums. To administer the program, the President authorized the establishment of the Works Progress Administration under the direction of Harry L. Hopkins. Hopkins viewed the new program as a dynamic alternative to the Emergency Relief Program which, he feared, would condemn the unemployed to a permanent dole, "unwillingly unproductive, and held in a straitjacket of idleness." Under the W.P.A. some $11 billion would be expended between 1935 and 1941 on 250,000 projects, ranging from the construction of public buildings and facilities to subsidy of the arts. Children were provided with hot lunches at school; the National Youth Administration made available funds to help young people continue their secondary and college educations; the Rural Electrification Administration assisted farmer cooperatives to build with W.P.A. labor power lines to bring electricity to regions that private power companies did not believe self-sustaining; and the Resettlement Administration tried (unsuccessfully) to shift marginal farmers to more productive land and slum dwellers to newly developed suburbs. The W.P.A. provided employment for as many as 3.5 million workers, at wages of from $15 to $90 a month. Although charges were made that the whole project was a boondoggle, a political machine, and a well of corruption, little evidence was obtained to support such extremist views. Further, the W.P.A. brought about a revitalization of the economy until 1937, when Roosevelt, assuming that the economy had finally revived, permitted the wholesale dismissal of most W.P.A. workers. Immediately, the economy sagged into renewed depression. And as an irate senator who had opposed the original bill observed, the federal government had assumed "an obligation never heretofore recognized, namely, the duty of providing a job for those in need."

The Social Security Act. "We advocate," the 1932 Democratic platform promised, "unemployment and old-age insurance under State laws." It was a tacit acknowledgment that the time was fast approaching when the United States should emulate the other great industrial nations which had introduced extensive social security coverage, often as much as a full generation or more earlier. During the 1920s eight states had established optional pensions laws, and in the early 1930s more than half of the states instituted mandatory legislation based on need. Under the guidance of Wagner, proposals for a federally aided program of unemployment insurance were introduced into Congress in February 1934 and the plan of Senator Clarence Dill of Washington and Representative William P. Connery, Jr., of Massachusetts to grant states a third of all funds paid out as old-age pensions received favorable attention. But Roosevelt was persuaded that piecemeal development of social security legislation would prove wasteful, and probably inadequate to meet the nation's needs. Therefore, in late June 1934, he appointed a cabinet Committee on Economic Security, with Frances Perkins as its director, to investigate the matter. He made it apparent that he favored a program that would cover everyone from the "cradle to the grave." On January 17, 1935, the President submitted a bill, based on the Committee's findings, which provided three types of coverage: (1) federal grants-in-aid to assist states in maintaining relief programs for the unemployed and for state welfare aid to the sick, dependent mothers and children, and the physically handicapped; (2) a one per cent payroll tax to help states establish unemployment insurance programs; and (3) a federal social security tax, to be paid equally by employers and employees, which would insure employees against old age, providing pensions of varying amounts to workers at age sixty-five (since reduced to sixty-two), widows, and dependent children of deceased workers, plus a small death benefit to cover funeral expenses. A basic program which provided essential security against such fundamental problems as old age, unemployment, and disability was thus established and, despite criticisms which complained of its inadequacies or denounced it as a threat to self-reliance, the program would be expanded and adjusted as experience dictated.

Other Reforms. By mid-summer of 1935, the New Deal had launched itself on a program of massive reform. Experiment was the order of the day. The organization of the Federal Housing Administration, in August 1934, stimulated home construction by providing federal insurance of home repair notes and home mortgages. Three years later, in the Housing Act of 1937, the federal government sponsored slum-clearance and low-rent housing. Profoundly important was the passage, on August 30, 1935, of extensive tax reforms which emphasized the principle of tax graduation, placing the heaviest burden of taxation on the wealthy. The Wealth-Tax Act of 1935, when attacked as intentionally hostile to the wealthy, obtained from Roosevelt the response that its purpose was not "to destroy wealth, but to create broader range of opportunity, to restrain the growth of unwholesome and sterile accumulations and to lay the burdens of Government where they can best be carried." Four days earlier, after a bitter legislative fight, the Public Utility Holding Company Act was passed, ordering the dissolution within five years of all utility holding companies that could not prove their usefulness to consumers. Of lesser import were the Air Mail Act and the Motor Carrier Act, which extended the Interstate Commerce Commission's regulatory power to these agents of transportation. The Banking Act of 1935 completed government control of banking policy by reorganizing the Federal Reserve Board into a presidentially appointed Board of Governors with effective power over every phase of the Federal Reserve System's operations. The Gold Clause Act, the Federal Power Act, and the Tennessee Valley Authority Amending Act were all designed to strengthen existing legislation. Rarely, if ever, in American history has a single session of Congress been so productive of reforms. Without anyone quite realizing it, the federal government had been endowed with massive powers that made it paramount in any field it chose to pre-empt. Neither friend nor foe was prepared to deny the accuracy of Roosevelt's judgment of the meaning of the new legislation when he declared that it established that "Government by the necessity of things must be the leader, must be the judge of the conflicting interests of all groups in the community, including bankers." In 1936, at the polls, the voters would give a hearty assent to the presidential belief that "the Government is the outward expression of the common life of all citizens."

THE SECOND ADMINISTRATION OF FRANKLIN D. ROOSEVELT

The Election of 1936. The Roosevelt who fought the campaign for re-election in 1936 had progressed a long way from the candidate of sweet moderation who had campaigned in 1932. He now thundered denunciations of "economic royalists," and before a roaring audience in Madison Square Garden, he savagely castigated his opposition, denouncing it with cold scorn:

> We had to struggle with the old enemies of peace—business and financial monopoly, speculation, reckless banking, class antagonism, sectionalism, war profiteering. They had begun to consider the Government of the United States as a mere appendage to their own affairs. And we know now that Government by organized money is just as dangerous as Government by organized mob.
>
> Never before in all our history have these forces been so united against one candidate as they stand today. They are unanimous in their hate for me—and I welcome their hatred.

Since June 27, 1936, when before 100,000 packed into Philadelphia's Franklin Field, Roosevelt accepted renomination, he had fought a caustic campaign against the Republican candidate, Kansas' liberal governor Alfred M. Landon, and the right-wing Union party ticket of the maverick North Dakota congressman William Lemke and Boston railroad attorney Thomas C. O'Brian. By October, the surging crowds that massed wherever Roosevelt went made it obvious that the incumbent was well on his way to a sizable victory. James A. Farley insisted it would be landslide unmatched since 1820; and as the Postmaster foretold, Roosevelt carried every state but Maine and Vermont, for a total of 523 out of a total 531 electoral votes, and 27,476,673 to 16,679,583 popular votes. The Democrats controlled the House by 328 to 107, the Senate by 77 to 19. Roosevelt had surged to the crest of his popularity; the nation had given him a massive endorsement.

The Supreme Court and the New Deal. No single development in the year before his re-election had so thoroughly irritated Roosevelt as the increasingly obstructionist stand of the Supreme Court. There the four conservative justices, Pierce Butler, James C. McReynolds, George Sutherland, and Willis Van Devanter, had more and more often gained the support of Owen Roberts to achieve a majority of the Court. The liberal minority of Louis D. Brandeis, Benjamin N. Cardozo, and Harlan F. Stone had, in the early stages of the New Deal, held the support of Owen Roberts and the Chief Justice Charles Evans Hughes on a New York statute regulating milk prices, and on a Minnesota moratorium on mortgages. The decision to abrogate the gold clause in federal and private contracts was barely upheld in the Gold Clause cases, but the Court's finding that this refusal to honor the gold clause in Treasury Bonds was a breach of contract under the Constitution forced Congress to pass the Gold Clause Act of August 28, 1935, denying consent to anyone who attempted to sue the federal government. As early as January of 1935, in the "hot oil" cases, the Court had found unfavorably against a section of the N.I.R.A. on the ground that it unconstitutionally delegated legislative power to the executive. On May 6, 1935, the Railroad Retirement Act was disallowed, raising serious doubt as to the Court's future findings on the Wagner Labor Relations Act and the Social Security Act. But it was the three decisions of May 27, 1935 that seemed to set the administration and the Supreme Court on a collision course. The Court disallowed the Frazier-Lemke Farm Mortgage Act of 1934, on the grounds that the five-year stay in mortgage foreclosures constituted denial of the use of private property without due process; it denied that the President had the power to remove an unfriendly commissioner—in this instance, a Hoover appointee, William E. Humphrey—from the Federal Trade Commission; and—most important—it declared the N.R.A. unconstitutional. On January 6, 1936, the Agricultural Adjustment Act went under, as did the Guffey-Snyder Coal Conservation Act on May 18, 1936. Lest the states assume they could attempt to regulate labor conditions, on June 1, 1936, in a 5 to 4 decision, the Court disallowed a New York State law regulating minimum wages for women. Future Justice Robert Jackson set the tone of the administration's response when he protested:

> In striking at New Deal laws, the Court allowed its language to run riot. . . . In overthrowing the A.A.A. the Court cast doubt upon all federal aid to agriculture; in laying low the N.R.A., the Court struck at all national effort to maintain fair labor standards; and in outlawing the New York Minimum Wage Law . . . the Court deliberately attempted to outlaw any form of state legislation to protect minimum wage standards. The Court not merely challenged the policies of the New Deal but erected judicial barriers to the reasonable exercise of legislative powers, both state and national, to meet the needs of a twentieth-century community.

Once re-elected, Roosevelt set about removing the judicial roadblock.

The Court-Packing Fight. The 1936 returns seemed to demand further reforms; at least, that was the interpretation that Roosevelt put upon his re-election. In his Second Inaugural Address, he described the abiding national challenge as the task of raising above "mere subsistence . . . one-third of a nation ill-housed, ill-clad, ill-nourished." Perhaps the presidential feeling that new schemes of social justice were required explains his decision, on February 5, 1937, to present to Congress his Judiciary Reorganization Bill without prior consultation with key congressional leaders. Or perhaps it was his feeling that, in the wake of his electoral victory, anything went. Whatever his reasoning, Roosevelt badly miscalculated. Consulting only Attorney General Homer Cummings, he asked for the power to appoint up to six additional Supreme Court justices and forty-four additional federal circuit and district judges when incumbent justices or judges failed to retire at the age of 70. He supported his stand with the claim that the advanced age of too many judges was resulting in serious and unnecessary delays in judicial processes. In strong words, Roosevelt argued:

> Modern complexities call also for a constant infusion of new blood into the courts, just as it is needed in executive functions of the Government and in private business. A lowered mental or physical vigor leads men to avoid an examination of complicated and changed conditions. Little by little, new facts become blurred through old glasses fitted, as it were, for the needs of another generation; older men assuming that the scene is the same as it was in the past, cease to explore or inquire into the present or the future.

Such arguments offended many of the New Deal's stanchest supporters, especially since the greatest liberal on the Court, Justice Brandeis, was over eighty. When Hughes leaked the information that the Supreme Court had an up-to-date docket, it made the presidential indictment seem foolish if not disingenuous. Nor did the fact that both Hughes and Roberts intended to vote with the three liberals to uphold the constitutionality of major New Deal measures help Roosevelt. On March 29, 1937, the Court upheld the Washington State Minimum Wage Act and the second Frazier-Lemke Farm Mortgage Act. Two weeks later, it upheld the Wagner Labor Relations Act. On May 24, the Social Security Act passed judicial review. For all practical purposes, the Reorganization Bill was dead. The decision of Justice Van Devanter to retire on May 18 simply accentuated the futility of Roosevelt's stubborn persistence in support of the act. Finally, in mid-July, the President threw in the sponge and allowed Congress to redraft his proposals in the form of the Judicial Procedure Reform Act, which became law on August 24. But the struggle had been costly: the Democrats had been deeply divided, and Roosevelt had sacrificed the momentum of his 1936 victory. Congress would now view reform proposals with increasing skepticism.

Problems in Organized Labor. When the American Federation of Labor opened its 1935 convention at Atlantic City, a bitter dispute arose over the organization of industrial unions. A group of union leaders, headed by David Dubinsky of the Ladies Garment Workers Union, Charles Howard of the Typographical Union, and the stentorian John L. Lewis of the United Mine Workers Union, submitted a report which concluded, "In the great mass production industries, and those in which the workers are composite, specialized and engaged upon classes of work which do not qualify them for craft unions membership, industrial organization is the only solution." When it became apparent that a majority of the A.F.L.'s leadership would not support the demand, Lewis and other labor leaders who backed industrial organization set to work, on November 10, 1933, to establish a Committee for Industrial Organization to "encourage and promote organization of workers in mass production and unorganized industries of the nation. . . ." When the A.F.L. refused to allow the Committee to continue its organizational efforts and expelled the participating unions, the C.I.O. assumed the role of a competing national labor organization. The new organization's leadership chose to view the Wagner Act as a presidential command to the unorganized to organize—an assumption made more emphatic by the massive Democratic victory, which the C.I.O.'s leaders viewed as partially traceable to its own efforts. There erupted in the latter months of 1936 and the early months of 1937 a series of sit-down strikes which soon paralyzed the automobile industry. As first General Motors Corporation and then the United States Steel Corporation capitulated to unionization, the drive for unions spread into the aluminum, cement, chemicals, meat packing, transportation, electrical, and other industries. As the C.I.O. convened in October 1937, it had almost 4,000,000 members. When efforts were made, however, to organize the Little Steel companies in the late spring of 1937, Republic Steel's anti-union Tom Girdler opposed them so strenuously that a strike broke out. On May 30, police in South Chicago opened fire on dispersing pickets, killing ten strikers and wounding many others. When Roosevelt refused to intervene in support of the strikers, Lewis angrily denounced the President as an ingrate. The administration's relations with one of its major sources of support had entered a dangerous phase. But, for the moment, the rapid organization of labor was arrested as the economy slumped.

The Recession of 1937. Between 1935 and August of 1937 the economy steadily progressed, until, in the words of Marriner Eccles, chairman of the Board of Governors of the Federal Reserve, the administration became fearful of a "rapid and speculative building up of business inventories." To brake what it thought might prove a boom followed by a crash, the administration cut back on government expenditures. Several slashes in W.P.A. rolls in 1936 and 1937 reduced the total number of workers to about 1.5 million. Contractions in P.W.A. projects cut back in construction. And deflationary policies inaugurated by the Federal Reserve System severely reduced credit. In the cabinet, Secretary of the Treasury Morgenthau revived agitation for a balanced budget, adding pressure to demands for contraction in federal expenditures. Roosevelt, who had never been possessed of a sophisticated knowledge of economics—some critics thought his knowledge was nonexistent—responded to growing evidence that the economy was faltering by convening, on November 15, 1937, a special session of Congress. After calling upon business to revive production, he added the threat that if private effort failed, the federal government would begin priming the pump again. A steady decline in production, prices, employment, and wages through the spring of 1938 finally persuaded the administration to call upon Congress to commence heavy federal expenditures again. Slowly, almost painfully, the administration, Congress, and the nation were coming to realize that the federal government would have to play a major role in stimulating future economic prosperity and growth.

The Twilight of the New Deal. Faced with the oncoming 1938 congressional elections, the Democratic leadership in Congress pressed for the passage of legislation that would please the voters. As Roosevelt vacillated on the course to follow in curing the recession, Congress, with presidential approval, passed a Housing Act designed to stimulate slum-clearance projects. On February 16, 1938, the second Agricultural Adjustment Act was passed, establishing the "ever-normal-granary" in which farmers could obtain loans of up to seventy-five per cent of parity by agreeing to place in government storage bins that produce which could be sold in times of shortage. A food stamp plan was set up under the Surplus Marketing Administration; this allowed indigent families to purchase food surpluses at reduced costs. Congress also established the Federal Crop Insurance Corporation, which insured farmers against natural disasters. On June 24, 1938, the Food, Drug, and Cosmetic Act substantially strengthened the Pure Food Act of 1906, by compelling manufacturers to list their products' ingredients and restrain their advertising. The following day, the Fair Labor Standards Act set in motion the establishment of a 40¢ minimal hourly wage and the forty-hour week. It also severely limited the use of child labor. In addition, the appropriation of some $3 billion and the loosening of credit began to stimulate the economy. But the passage on May 27, 1938, by a coalition of Republicans and conservative Democrats, of a tax bill that favored big corporations and wealthy individuals convinced the President that the time had come to force a liberalization of Congress, and his resentment over his failure to gain congressional assent to reorganization of the executive department gave extra sharpness to his decision to purge conservatives from the Democratic party.

The Purge of 1938. In a fireside chat on June 24, 1938, Roosevelt announced to the nation his intention to intervene in primary elections to defeat conservative Southern opponents of his program, with such party warhorses as Senator Walter George of Georgia, "Cotton Ed" Smith of South Carolina, and Millard Tydings of Maryland designated as his major targets. As the election returns were counted, it became apparent that the campaign had backfired. Except for Congressman John O'Conner of New York, every candidate singled out by Roosevelt for defeat emerged victorious. All that Roosevelt had achieved was a revelation of the limits of his own power. He had helped solidify the conservative opposition, one which was accentuated by the 1938 election of 7 new Republican senators and 80 Republican representatives. Only two years after the greatest presidential triumph in history, an effective congressional block to further reform had been erected; for a time, as Judge Samuel Rosenman recalls, Roosevelt contemplated trying to create "a combination of the liberal forces then existing in each party." But a darkening international scene increasingly held his attention. The man who had been elected as isolationist in 1932 prepared to lead his people into acceptance of a responsible international role. The generation he had guided through depression, he would now guide through war.

Chapter 14

World War II

When the guns fell silent on November 11, 1918, most men of good will tried to believe that a chastened world would now devote all its energies to preserving peace. For them, the Armistice marked the end of savage bloodletting for all time. Some perceptive observers, however, like Woodrow Wilson and John Maynard Keynes, recognized that the peace gained was only an interlude in a growing struggle that would end finally only in a world changed beyond imagination—if, that is, it did not end in the destruction of the world altogether. Soaring expectations soon plummeted as the realities of peace reminded men that for most of them there still remained what Henry David Thoreau had described as "lives of quiet desperation." For those who had drained the cup of defeat, there remained only bitter reflection and a savage urge for revenge. For one German corporal in particular, news of Germany's defeat was unbearable. "Everything went black before my eyes again," Adolf Hitler recalled, "and I staggered and stumbled my way back to the dormitory, flung myself upon my cot and buried my burning head in the blanket and pillow." Out of such despair the unmaking of the peace was born. Twenty-one years later, the guns that had been stilled in 1918 would soar again, and another war—more monstrous than the first—would stalk across the land.

FOREIGN POLICY IN THE 1930s

Stimson Doctrine. As the Hoover administration struggled to find its way out of domestic depression, the first threat of new international crisis was raised. On the night of September 18, 1931, an explosion on the South Manchuria Railroad was used as a pretext by the Japanese to seize the vast northeastern Chinese province of Manchuria. With almost clocklike precision Japanese armies overcame Chinese resistance, and by the early days of 1932 they controlled the whole province. When the League of Nations invited the United States to join it in efforts to restore the peace in the Orient, the administration (despite strong protests from the isolationist press) agreed to fulfill its responsibilities under the Kellogg-Briand Pact. Secretary of State Henry L. Stimson, while careful to maintain traditional American independence of League action, on January 7, 1932, set forth in identical notes to China and Japan the proposition that the United States did "not intend to recognize any situation, treaty, or agreement which may be brought about by means contrary to the covenants and obligations of the Pact of Paris of August 27, 1928, to which treaty both China and Japan, as well as the United States, are parties." The threat of invoking nonrecognition was the core of the Stimson Doctrine, and although neither Britain nor France adopted so firm a stand, Stimson held to his position. When the Japanese attacked Shanghai on January 28, 1932, the administration considered economic sanctions, but finally settled for joint pressure on Japan with the other Pacific powers. On May 31, 1932, Japanese troops withdrew from the great city. A brief but significant departure from usual American neutrality had occurred; Stimson had revealed that the United States viewed the Open Door as a vital policy, one to be maintained with something more than indifference. In August 1932, Stimson reminded the world that the Kellogg-Briand Pact made war "an illegal thing." Significantly, he concluded: "Hereafter when two nations engage in armed conflict, either one or both of them must be wrongdoers—violators of the general treaty. We no longer draw a circle about them and treat them with the punctilios of the duelist's code. Instead we denounce them as lawbreakers." No one doubted that by "lawbreaker" Stimson was referring to Japan. The first strain on American-Japanese relations had been made.

New Deal Isolationism. When Franklin D. Roosevelt entered the White House, he was publicly identified with opposition to American entry into the League of Nations. Although Secretary of State Stimson attempted to persuade President-elect Roosevelt to take a hard stand toward Japan, and though the new administration sympathized with China's plight, the New Dealers viewed domestic problems—which were, indeed, pressing—as superseding any possible foreign adventures. Except for efforts to revitalize friendly relations with Latin America, the new foreign policy re-emphasized American neutrality. Roosevelt turned aside efforts at international cooperation in meeting the world economic crisis, and did little to deter a welling call in Congress for positive neutrality. The Congressional sentiment was summed up by California's Senator Hiram Johnson, who declared it was ". . . the policy of the United States of America to keep out of European controversies, European wars, and European difficulties." Convinced that the nation had been dragged into World War I in part because of European bond sales in the United States to finance their war purchases, Johnson obtained passage of an act on April 13, 1934, which forbade future sales of such bonds in the United States by any power which had defaulted in its repayment of the war debt. When war threatened between Ethiopia and Italy in the summer of 1935, Senator Key Pittman of Nevada introduced a neutrality bill into Congress which established a six-month embargo on the export of arms or ammunition to the ports of any belligerent states; created a National Munitions Control Board under the Secretary of State to license the sale and shipment of munitions, and to restrict the use of American shipping for the transportation of munitions; and made traveling on the ships of belligerents an act of personal risk.

The act became law on August 31, 1935, but its mandatory embargo section lapsed within six months. When Congress reassembled in January 1936 it promptly set to work extending the embargo, a decision made more urgent when the threatened war between Italy and Ethiopia finally erupted on October 3, 1935. Roosevelt called for legislation which would not permit belligerents to prosecute war with American arms, ammunition, or implements of war. In subsequent debate over what manner of new bill should be passed, it was finally agreed to extend the arms embargo until May 1, 1937.

Even as the act was being signed into law, thoughtful critics, including one Minnesota congressman, charged that the embargo was discriminatory toward peaceful nations, since it made no effort to discriminate between aggressors and victims of aggression. As the congressman warned:

> While for a time we may escape involvement in foreign wars, the ultimate outcome will be that a few powerful, militaristic nations, unchecked by anything, will gradually create a situation of world-wide conquest, and the time will come when we alone will be left in the way of their complete world dominance. As surely as we take this attitude of smug indifference now, we ourselves will then become the object of attack and invasion.

In a world rapidly being engulfed by totalitarian aggression, such warnings were the first symptoms of a growing American awareness that neutrality might elevate the national morality but might also endanger the national existence, particularly if it were to make no distinction between dictator and democracy, tyranny and representative government.

The Good Neighbor Policy. No aspect of early New Deal foreign policy attracted a more favorable response than that toward Latin America. Labeled by Roosevelt the "Good Neighbor Policy," it commanded the wholehearted assent of the old Wilsonian who was to be Roosevelt's Secretary of State, Cordell Hull, who had renounced (at the Montevideo Pan-American Conference of December 1933) the right of one nation to intervene in the affairs of another country. In his First Inaugural Address, Roosevelt had declared that the United States stood "ready to carry on in the spirit of that application of the Golden Rule by which we mean the true good-will of the true good neighbor." To implement these intentions, the State Department announced, on May 29, 1934, that the United States was abrogating the Platt Amendment which gave the United States the right to intervene to keep the peace or independence of Cuba intact. And by January 1935, American Marines who had been stationed in Nicaragua and Haiti to keep order were withdrawn. Five years later, the Dominican Republic was permitted—after thirty-five years—to resume its own tariff collections. When, in March 1938, Mexico City nationalized all foreign oil holdings in Mexico, despite vigorous protests from American investors, the Washington government, rather than intervening, settled for notes demanding adequate compensation. Modifications of American treaty arrangements with Panama were also agreed to in March 1936. A new note—cooperation rather than coercion—had been introduced into the nation's ties with its Latin neighbors. But as one Latin American newspaper sharply commented, the new policy of nonintervention threatened to preserve "a league of 'mestizo' dictators" in the Caribbean region, "with the United States destined to guarantee the slavery of Latin American peoples." What with Fulgencio Batista in

Cuba, Rafael Trujillo in the Dominican Republic, and Anastasio Somoza in Nicaragua, the charge was dangerously close to the truth.

The Spanish Civil War. The successful Italian aggression on Ethiopia in 1935 inaugurated a European crisis that culminated four years later in World War II. The revolt of the Spanish army on July 17, 1936, spread rapidly from Morocco to the Spanish mainland, where it settled into a savage thirty-two-month-long civil war. Although the western democracies declared their neutrality, the Fascist dictatorships of Germany and Italy poured assistance into the rebel war effort under the leadership of General Francisco Franco, while the Communist dictatorship of Russia granted massive aid to the loyalist government in Madrid. Soon American public opinion was deeply divided, with leading American Catholics—particularly strong in their support was the Catholic hierarchy—openly supporting Franco, and numerous American liberals and radicals backing the republican government in Madrid. Some efforts to reduce the adverse effects of the embargo on the Spanish republican war potential were checked (as Harold Ickes subsequently recalled) because Roosevelt feared it "would mean the loss of every Catholic vote." But pressure to take more positive steps to align the United States against the growing Fascist menace grew. From Spain, Ambassador Claude Bowers warned "that with every surrender beginning long ago with China, followed by Abyssinia, Ethiopia and then Spain, . . . the prospects of a European war grow darker." Such a prospect moved the administration to re-evaluate its neutral posture.

The Quarantine Speech. On July 7, 1937, a clash between Japanese and Chinese troops near Peking, China, led to an undeclared war that soon spread to Shanghai and the Yangtze River Valley. Suddenly the administration, whose sympathies were with the Kuomintang government of China's Chiang Kai-shek at Nanking, found itself confronted with the dilemma of invoking the neutrality legislation with the knowledge that it would adversely affect the Chinese. Rather than risk such a result, the administration took advantage of the fact that no formal declaration of war had been made and chose not to invoke an immediate arms embargo. But when three American citizens were killed in the bombing of Shanghai, and when, on August 20, 1937, a stray shell struck the American cruiser *Augusta,* killing a sailor and wounding seventeen others, the State Department urged American citizens in China to come home, and the Navy Department reinforced the Marine garrison in Shanghai's International Settlement. Roosevelt took a further step to limit possible American involvement on September 14,

1937, when he announced that government-owned ships would be forbidden to transport war equipment to either the Chinese or Japanese, and that privately owned American vessels transported such goods "at their own risk." Faced with the prospect of a worsening world crisis, the President, on October 5, denounced "the present reign of terror and international lawlessness," and suggested that, faced with "an epidemic of world lawlessness," the time had come to impose a quarantine on aggressors. "There must be," he affirmed, "positive efforts for peace." When pressed to elaborate on the meaning of "quarantine," however, Roosevelt proved circumspect, for despite a favorable press and public response, he seems not to have developed a policy with which to implement his dramatic proposal. An administration originally committed to isolation, yet now partially aware of the threatening international situation, had only begun to grope its way toward a fuller participation in meeting that challenge. America shared the disease of the other western democracies: while the monstrous political doctrine known as Nazism was preparing the world for a descent into hell, she slept.

THE COMING OF WORLD WAR II

For a brief time in December of 1937, war between the United States and Japan seemed possible. A deliberate bombing by Japanese planes of the gunboat U.S.S. *Panay* as it lay at anchor in the Yangtze angered the country, but an apology and indemnity from Tokyo restored the uneasy peace. Actually, the arena for determining the future of war or peace had shifted to Berlin, where Adolf Hitler, having consolidated his power in Germany, launched his campaign to unite all Germans under his rule.

The Rise of Hitler. Hitler had annexed Austria in March 1938 without difficulty. During the summer that followed he agitated for the incorporation of the Sudeten Germans of Czechoslovakia into the Third Reich. By September, Europe seemed on the brink of war, but a conference of Neville Chamberlain, Prime Minister of Great Britain; Eduard Daladier, Premier of France; Benito Mussolini, Dictator of Italy; and Adolf Hitler at Munich during the final weeks of September 1938 resulted in the dismemberment of Czechoslovakia. Possessing Hitler's pledge that the remnant of the Czech state would be respected, Chamberlain returned to London and assured the British that he had brought "peace in our time." Roosevelt, whose role in the crisis was peripheral, privately felt relief at the result.

Two months later, Hitler seized upon the murder of the third secretary of his Paris legation by a young Jewish refugee, Herschel Grynszpan, to justify a sickening attack upon German Jews and their property, at which America's conscience was stirred—but not enough to increase the immigration quotas for Jewish refugees. The illusion that Hitler's expansionist appetite could be placated received a death blow on March 15, 1939, when German troops seized the guaranteed remnant of Czechoslovakia, and some nine million Czechs were incorporated into a supposedly German Reich. In the same month, Franco finally triumphed in Spain, Hitler absorbed the Lithuanian port of Memel, and Italy occupied Albania. In mid-April, the Berlin government indicated that it thought the time had come to resolve the Danzig and Polish Corridor questions.

The Declaration of War. Through the spring and summer the pressure grew, as intricate maneuverings between the great European powers culminated with the announcement, on August 24, of a Russian-German Pact. Hitler, having thus freed Germany of the threat of a two-front war, charged on September 1 that the German minority was being mistreated by the Warsaw government, and used this as an excuse to invade Poland. Two days later, Britain and France honored their pledges to the Polish nation and declared war on Germany. The second world war in a generation had begun. To an uneasy nation, Roosevelt warned: "You must master at the outset a simple but unalterable fact in modern foreign relations. When peace has been broken anywhere, peace of all countries everywhere is in danger."

Repeal of the Neutrality Act. The Gallup poll taken shortly after the war began left little doubt where American sympathies rested; no fewer than eighty-four per cent wanted an Allied victory. Yet the Neutrality Law of 1937 forbade the rendering of any assistance to belligerents, no matter what the circumstances of their involvement in war. On September 5, two neutrality proclamations were issued, placing an embargo on the export of arms and forbidding American citizens from giving illegal aid to any belligerent. Restrictions on the travel of Americans aboard belligerent ships plying the North Atlantic were also announced.

The President, however, set to work to repeal the Neutrality Law; he wanted to resume the traditional cash-and-carry policy toward belligerents. In a larger sense, he had determined that the United States could not ignore its moral obligations to western civilization, or neglect the fact that the fate of this nation was inextricably bound up with that of the other western democracies. "Destiny first made us, with our sister nations on this hemisphere, joint heirs of European culture," he declared. "Fate now seems to compel us to assume the task of helping to maintain in the western world a citadel wherein that civilization may be kept alive." On November 4, 1939, after a lengthy congressional debate, Roosevelt signed a revision of the neutrality legislation which lifted the arms embargo, but put such purchases on a cash-and-carry plan and denied American ships access to belligerent ports. The simultaneous proclamation that the Baltic Sea and the Atlantic Ocean from southern Norway to Spain was a combat zone simplified Hitler's submarine warfare against Britain, for it eliminated the immediate risk of conflict with the most powerful neutral: the United States. Despite the latter disadvantage, however, Prime Minister Chamberlain hailed the repeal as a major victory which ". . . reopens for the Allies the doors of the greatest storehouse of supplies in the world."

THE WAR'S EARLY YEARS

The "Phony" War. Within three weeks of Hitler's invasion of Poland, that country lay prostrate, its territory divided between Russia and Germany. Except for Finland's plucky fight against Russian invasion, between November 1939 and March 1940, the war—or more accurately, the absence of war—in the west was contemptuously dismissed by numerous observers as a "phony" war. Even as the administration worked to alleviate the stringency of the Neutrality Law, it joined with the other foreign ministers of the Western Hemisphere, on October 3, 1939, to issue the Declaration of Panama, which forbade naval warfare in a zone 300 to 1,000 miles wide below the Canadian border. The ineffectiveness of the declaration, however, could not conceal the fact that the unilateral support of the Monroe Doctrine had been replaced by multilateral action. The deceptive calm of the European war ended abruptly on April 9, 1940, as Germany swarmed into Denmark and Norway. Within hours the Danes were overrun and, although they fought doggedly, the Norwegians capitulated after little more than six weeks. The German war machine now stood revealed as the mightiest armed force the world had ever seen. In mid-spring of 1940, it would bring the European order crashing into ruins.

The Fall of the Low Countries. On May 10, the full might of German force surged into the Low Countries. In hardly the time it took to traverse the country, Luxembourg fell; Dutch efforts to block German advances with floods failed, and on the fifth day of the invasion they surrendered. (Their decision did not, however, spare the great port of Rotterdam, which was turned into a shambles by a slashing air attack after it was declared an open city.) On May 28, King Leopold III of Belgium, his armies backed against the English Channel, ordered his people to lay down their arms. From Belgium the road to France lay open.

The Fall of France. German air power ravished French towns while their armored forces swept along the poplar-lined French highways, cutting to pieces the vaunted French army, terrifying millions of French civilians into panicked flight southward, and cornering the British Expeditionary Forces at Dunkirk. Only by a prodigious evacuation effort was the British force saved, but the end for France had come. On June 10, the government fled Paris, and on the same day, Italy entered the war against the British and French, provoking from Roosevelt the grim observation that "the hand that held the dagger has stuck it into the back of his neighbor." Twelve days later, at Compiègne forest, in the very railway car where the Germans had surrendered less than twenty-two years earlier—an expression of Hitler's sense of the ironic—France capitulated. Suddenly, only Britain stood between Hitler and total domination of Europe. A stunned America witnessed the French collapse. Few Americans were prepared to challenge Harold L. Ickes's somber fear that "We are a long way from being able to defend ourselves successfully if we should be attacked by Germany and Italy, especially if these two countries should possess the British and French fleets." The reality of Nazi blitzkrieg—lightning warfare—now compelled the administration to move swiftly for a massive program of preparation against the prospect of a beleaguered America.

Military Mobilization. Traditionally, in time of peace the United States maintained only a minimal military establishment. It was possible for the average American citizen to pass his entire life without ever seeing a military uniform. As early as October 11, 1938, however, military expenditures had increased by $300 million, and shortly afterward the government extended a $25 million loan to the Chiang Kai-shek government. These were the first intimations of what was to prove the greatest mobilization in history. Beginning on May 16, 1940, when Roosevelt called for the creation of a mechanized army and the building of 50,000 planes, Congress appropriated during the remainder of the year some $18 billion to expand the Army to over a million two hundred thousand men, and to build a two-ocean navy second to none. The mobilization effort obtained a bipartisan cast when, on June 19, 1940, Roosevelt announced the appointment of Henry L. Stimson as Secretary of War and Frank Knox, publisher of the Chicago *Daily News,* as Secretary of the Navy. These long-time Republicans had taken a militant stand in favor of all aid to Britain short of war. Their position was made clear when, on July 2, before the Senate Committee on Military Affairs, Stimson declared, "I do not believe that we shall be safe from invasion if we sit down and wait for the enemy to attack our shores." This new militancy reflected itself in Congress's approval of the first peacetime draft, signed into law on September 16, which made all males between the ages of twenty-one and thirty-five liable to a year of military service. Previously, on August 27, the President had been authorized to call into service the National Guard and the Organized Reserves. Under the expert guidance of Major General Lewis B. Hershey, more than a million men were inducted into the service. The foundations of a vast military establishment had been laid.

The Election of 1940. As mobilization proceeded, the nation prepared for a presidential election. The Republicans—outraged at the appointment of Stimson and Knox, which they viewed as a typically Machiavellian maneuver by Roosevelt—met in angry session in Philadelphia. Rejecting both Thomas E. Dewey of New York and Robert A. Taft of Ohio, on June 27 the convention chose Wendell L. Willkie, a hoarse-voiced public utilities executive who had recently switched his political affiliation from the Democratic party. Oregon's Senator Charles L. McNary was given the vice-presidential nomination. When in mid-July the Democrats gathered at Chicago, the main question was whether Roosevelt would accept a third term. The available evidence indicates that by late May, as the international situation worsened, Roosevelt had decided upon a third try. Under the expert guidance of Chicago's Edward "Boss" Kelly, the convention was swept into renominating him in spite of his declared intention of not running. As Roosevelt's mate, the controversial Secretary of Agriculture, Henry A. Wallace, was chosen.

The vigor of Willkie's campaign could not disguise the fact that he lacked a single issue with which to corner Roosevelt. When he presented himself as the candidate pledged to keep the peace, Roosevelt immediately trumped him with the promise that no American boy would be "sent into any foreign wars." The President's slashing indictment of the Republican party as the party of "Martin, Barton, and Fish" (three ultraconservative Republican congressmen) accentuated the choice as one between a liberal, humanitarian Roosevelt and a reactionary Republican party. On November 5, 1940, Roosevelt swept to victory with 27,244,160 votes, as opposed to 22,305,198 for Willkie.

The electoral count was a lop-sided 449 to 82. Another tradition—a maximum of two terms for one man—had crumbled.

The Destroyer Base Deal. As the United States hastened to expand its military forces, Great Britain underwent a smashing air bombardment. From Ambassador Joseph Kennedy in London came the grim prediction that England was gone. Winston S. Churchill, who had replaced Chamberlain as Prime Minister on May 10, rallied the British people. With eloquent confidence, he pledged:

> I have, myself, full confidence that if all do their duty, if nothing is neglected, and if the best arrangements are made, as they are being made, we shall prove ourselves once again able to defend our island home, to ride out the storm of war, and to outlive the menace of tyranny, if necessary for years, if necessary alone. At any rate, that is what we are going to try to do.

The British managed to keep intact the bulk of their manpower in the French debacle; but most of their arms had been abandoned in the Dunkirk evacuation. Roosevelt made a calculated gamble to help the British until their factories could replace the lost arms. Utilizing an old 1917 law, the administration arranged for the transfer to England of about 150 war planes, 600,000 Lee-Enfield rifles, 800 artillery pieces, plus machine guns, mortars, and tons of ammunition. Roosevelt had practically turned over the entire armed equipment of the nation to the British, but his purpose was to buy time by helping the British continue their resistance. On September 3, 1940, in reply to urgent pleas from Churchill for help in replacing the depleted British destroyer fleet, the administration agreed to turn over to the British fifty overage destroyers in return for bases on Newfoundland, Bermuda, the Bahamas, Jamaica, Antigua, St. Lucia, Trinidad, and British Guiana. The previous day London had made the solemn pledge that no matter what happened to the home islands, the British fleet would never be surrendered or sunk. To a generally approving country, the President described the arrangement as "the most important action in the reinforcement of our national defense that has been taken since the Louisiana Purchase."

The Lend-Lease Act. The United States had moved a long way from neutrality, but all previous assistance faded when compared to the Lend-Lease proposals introduced into Congress in January 1941. After several weeks of bitter debate, during which Senator Taft of Ohio snorted that "Lending war equipment is a good deal like lending chewing gum. You don't want it back.", Congress approved the bill by large majorities, and on March 11, 1941, Roosevelt signed the measure. Specifically justified as a defense measure, the act authorized the President "to sell, transfer title to, exchange, lease, lend, or otherwise dispose of . . . any defense article for the government of any country whose defense the President deems vital to the defense of the United States." Within a year, no less than thirty-five countries besides the British Commonwealth were drawing vast quantities of supplies from the American arsenal.

The act was a wholesale underwriting of the enemies of Hitler, whether democratic or not. In June 1941, the Germans, after swiftly overrunning Greece and Yugoslavia in April and May, poured into Russia on a thousand-mile front extending from the Baltic Sea to the Black Sea. All doubts as to American response to this new development ended the following day, when Acting Secretary of State Sumner Welles told the press, "In the opinion of this government, . . . any defense against Hitlerism, any rallying of the forces opposing Hitlerism, from whatever source these forces may spring, will hasten the eventual downfall of the present German leaders, and will therefore redound to the benefit of our own defense and security." Churchill was even more specific: "If Hitler invaded Hell I would make at least a favourable reference to the Devil in the House of Commons."

The Undeclared War. For all practical purposes, by the spring of 1941 the United States had become an undeclared enemy of Germany and Italy. The seizure of sixty-five ships of the Axis (the term used to designate the Berlin-Rome Alliance) and the imprisonment of a thousand Axis seamen brought protests from Berlin and Rome, which protests the United States ignored. Early in April, American forces occupied Greenland as a defensive measure, and on July 7, 1941, American troops began to replace British soldiers occupying Iceland. The sinking of the American merchantman *Robin Moor* in the South Atlantic, on May 21, 1941, brought swift retaliation from Washington, where orders went out to freeze all Axis assets. Subsequently orders were also issued to close German and Italian consulates. Further economic retaliation came when in mid-July some eighteen hundred Latin American firms known to have Axis connections were blacklisted. Instructions went out on July 11 to American warcraft to convoy ships as far as Iceland, a move which substantially reduced the demands on the severely taxed British escorts. When a German submarine fired two torpedos at the United States destroyer *Greer,* and several American merchant ships were sunk, Roosevelt, on September 11, 1941, ordered American warships to shoot Axis warcraft on sight in areas of the Atlantic under American supervision. On October 9, Congress received a request for repeal of the limiting provisions of the Neutrality Act of 1939 which forbade arming of American merchant ships and which denied American ships the right to sail to belligerent ports. The torpedoing and damaging, on October 17, 1941, of the destroyer *Kearny,* with the death of eleven seamen, and the sinking of the destroyer *Reuben James,* on October 30, 1941, with the loss of seventy-six officers and seamen, resulted in the requested modification of the act on November 13, 1941. The intimacy between the British and American governments was further accentuated in early August 1941, when Roosevelt and Churchill met on British and American warships off Newfoundland to issue an eight point Atlantic Charter, which pledged both governments to work for a peace that would give assurance "that all men in all lands may live out their lives in freedom from fear and want." For all practical purposes, in everything but an official declaration, the United States was at war, by the end of November 1941, with Germany.

The Crisis in the Pacific. Hitler's military triumph in western Europe stripped the far-flung Dutch, French, and British possessions in Southeast Asia of their accustomed protection. Fearful that Japan might seize the weakness of the western allies as an opportunity to assert her dominance in the region, the United States moved her Pacific fleet forward from San Diego to Pearl Harbor, a move that Secretary of State Hull subsequently admitted served as a "double-barreled shotgun" in future talks with the Tokyo government. As conditions in Europe worsened, Japan pressured Petain's collaborationist government in Vichy, France, to allow a Japanese military mission free access to French Indochina; the Dutch authorities in the East Indies were similarly pushed by Tokyo to guarantee delivery to Japan of essential raw materials; and England faced demands to remove her garrison from Shanghai, to seal the Hong Kong-China border, and to close the Burma Road, the Chiang Kai-shek government's main link with needed war goods. After some uncertainty, Washington resolved upon a policy of firm opposition to Japanese expansionism. When evidence developed that the military authorities in Japan eyed the riches of the East Indies, Cordell Hull responded with a covert hint that force against the Dutch might be answered with force by the Americans, although privately Admiral Harold R. Stark, Chief of Naval Operations, admitted to Admiral James O. Richardson, Commander-in-Chief of the American Pacific fleet, that he did not know what the United States would do if the East Indies were attacked. In late July 1940, Roosevelt inaugurated a series of economic moves against Tokyo by banning the export of oil and scrap metals without a license and, even more tellingly, restricted sales of aviation gasoline to the Western Hemisphere. The Japanese responded on September 27, 1940, with a treaty that pledged Germany, Italy, and Japan to go to war with any power, other than Russia, that might attack one of them. The implication was clear: from the Axis powers' perspective, the United States represented a growing threat to their aspirations. Continued American aid to the Chinese government further accentuated the American-Japanese rift. On July 23, 1941, the Japanese obliged the French to cede them bases in southern Indochina, and the United States promptly froze Japanese assets in the United States, an action which Tokyo reciprocated. The replacement of the Konoye cabinet on October 16 by one headed by General Hideki Tojo, an expansionist militarist, indicated that Tokyo had determined on a showdown. These expectations were sharply delineated on November 10, 1941, when Churchill publicly avowed that Britain would declare war on Japan "within the hour" if the United States went to war with Japan.

THE UNITED STATES AT WAR

Pearl Harbor. In the last weeks of November and the first week of December 1941 a professional Japanese diplomat, Saburo Kurusu, and the Japanese ambassador, Kichisaburo Nomura, explored with Cordell Hull the chances of keeping the peace. The American position emphasized maintenance of the status quo in the Pacific except when peacefully altered. The Japanese responded that American aid to China was a primary disruptive force in the Pacific. On November 20, 1941, the Japanese offered to withdraw its troops from southern Indochina in return for supplies from the United States and the East Indies, and for a cessation of further American aid to China. The United States countered with an offer on November 26 to stabilize relations with Japan if Tokyo would withdraw its forces from both Indochina and China. Hull made it clear that the American counterproposal "was offered for the consideration of the Japanese Government as one practical example of a program to be worked out." The Tojo government chose, however, to treat the proposals as tantamount to an ultimatum, and as a consequence, they determined that war had become inevitable. In Washington, where authorities were fully aware that Japan had decided on war—a year earlier the United States had broken the Japanese secret code—the raft of messages that poured in led them to conclude that the attack would come in the Far East. No one in authority seems to have expected a direct attack upon the great Hawaiian naval base at Pearl Harbor. Thus, though the Japanese fleet had set sail from Japan on November 25 for its fatal rendezvous, the American military contemplated the problem of defending the Far East. On December 6, Roosevelt made a personal plea to the Emperor of Japan to help keep the peace by withdrawing Japan's troops from Indochina. On December 7, at 7:50 A.M. Hawaiian time, as Kurusu and Nomura prepared to give Hull a formal declaration of war, Japanese planes attacked the Pacific fleet at anchor. Within an hour, most of the Pacific battle wagons were destroyed or severely damaged; more than two thousand sailors, marines, and soldiers had been killed; and the bitter debate on whether the United States should intervene or remain aloof from the raging war ended abruptly. Few Americans disagreed with Roosevelt's description of December 7 as "a date which will live in infamy." By a vote of 82 to 0 in the Senate, and by 388 to 1 in the House, war was declared on Japan. On December 11, Germany and Italy declared war on the United States, and Congress replied in kind. The war which had begun some twenty-seven months earlier in the Polish Corridor had finally become global.

Full American Mobilization. When faced with the prospect of American intervention in European affairs, Hitler had dismissed it with the observation:

> There are new weapons which are effective in such cases. America is permanently on the brink of revolution. It will be a simple matter for me to produce unrest and revolt in the United States, so that these gentry will have their hands full of their own affairs. . . . Our strategy is to destroy the enemy from within, to conquer him through himself.

Rarely has an expectation been wider of the mark. Within hours of the outbreak of war, plans for the girding of America's power were well launched. Under the auspices of a nine-man War Production Board headed by Donald Nelson, a torrent of war material poured out of the nation's factories. Within a year of America's entry into the war some 49,000 planes were manufactured; by 1944 the figure exceeded 96,000; and by war's end, total aircraft production pushed 300,000. No less staggering was the 55 million tons of shipping constructed. Deprived of much of its natural rubber, an industrial apparatus capable of producing 762,000 tons of synthetic rubber had been built by 1944. Equally impressive was the sheer quantity of war goods being produced; in 1942 alone American production equaled that of the Axis, and by 1944 it was twice as much. To operate this vast industrial complex, millions of women poured into war production, as some 15,050,000 men between the ages of seventeen and thirty-eight entered the armed forces. Well over 200,000 young women served in various auxiliary forces.

To stabilize prices and assure a fair distribution of limited supplies, the Office of Price Administration under Leon Henderson instituted price controls and rationing of food, gasoline, clothing, and shoes. Federal expenditures exceeded $321 billion between 1941 and 1945, but these costs were met through heavy taxation and a vast sale of government bonds to private citizens, corporations, banks, and other public institutions. As the dimensions of the war effort grew, a nation which had floundered through a decade of depression finally achieved full employment. Full mobilization had revealed the intrinsic health of the American economy; it set a standard that Americans would insist upon when peace was restored.

The Early War in the Pacific. As the Japanese air armada devastated Pearl Harbor, vast numbers of Japanese troops landed in the Philippines, Guam, Hong Kong, and the Malay Peninsula. Within less than six months, Japanese forces had overrun Burma, the Dutch East Indies, Singapore, the western Aleutians, Wake Island, New Guinea, and the Solomon Islands, as well as Guam, the Philippines, Hong Kong, and Malaya. By spring of 1942, the Japanese were hammering at the gates of India, Australia, and Hawaii. After a desperate struggle, first under the command of General Douglas MacArthur and then under Major General Jonathan Wainwright, some 15,000 American troops and 40,000 Philippine scouts held off 200,000 Japanese troops—first on Bataan Peninsula, and then on the island fortress of Corregidor, until May 6, 1942, when the Japanese triumphed. The survivors of this ordeal were then forced to make the infamous "Bataan Death March," during which thousands of sick and starving captives perished.

Even as this tragedy was beginning, Admiral Chester Nimitz, convinced that the battleship had seen its day, skillfully employed aircraft carriers in the Battle of the Coral Sea on May 7 and 8, 1942, to turn back a Japanese attack on Port Moresby, New Guinea. From June 3 to 7, a massive Japanese assault on Midway Island, preparatory to an attack upon Hawaii, was also smashed by air power. A bitter campaign that raged between August 1942 and January 1943 on Guadalcanal, a major island in the southern Solomons, finally culminated in an American victory. The destruction of a Japanese fleet and convoy during the Battle of Bismarck Sea of March 2 and 3, 1943, confirmed that the tide had finally and fully turned. Through all the bitter fighting ahead, the Japanese would be in retreat.

The North African Campaign. As the United States desperately fought to hold the Japanese at bay in the Pacific, the Russians struggled to arrest the German onslaught upon their country. By the end of the summer of 1942, the Nazis had surged to Stalingrad on the Volga River, well over a thousand miles inside Russia. Simultaneously, the German Afrika Korps under Marshal Erwin Rommel drove to within seventy miles of Alexandria, Egypt, and seemed within inches of cutting the Suez Canal.

In late October, however, the course of war began to reverse when the heavily reinforced British Eighth Army, under Lieutenant General Bernard L. Montgomery, smashed Rommel's army at El Alamein. The following month, the Russians trapped several hundred thousand Germans at Stalingrad, laying the groundwork for a massive Nazi defeat when that army surrendered on January 31, 1943. On November 8, 1942, Lieutenant General Dwight D. Eisenhower led an American-British army of 290,000 ashore in Morocco and Algeria. After a brief struggle, French forces on the scene capitulated. The survivors of the Afrika Korps, having abandoned Libya, retreated into Tunisia, where a bitter battle was fought until early May 1943. Then some 300,000 Axis troops surrendered, inflicting upon the Axis powers another defeat as catastrophic as Stalingrad. Hitler had used the African invasion to complete the occupation of France, but all signs pointed to an impending catastrophe for Hitler's Germany.

The Italian Campaign. On June 11, 1943, Allied forces seized the Italian island fortress of Pantelleria, and one month later, on July 10, an American-British expeditionary force swarmed ashore on Sicily. In little more than five weeks, the island was firmly in the hands of the Allies, and on July 25, Benito Mussolini, the Italian dictator, was forced to resign. The new Italian government under Marshal Pietro Badoglio sued for, and received, an armistice on September 3, 1943, the same day that the British Eighth Army began landing in Italy opposite Sicily. Shortly afterward, General Mark Clark led the American Fifth Army ashore near Naples, and on October 7, the great southern Italian port fell to the Allies. The Germans moved swiftly to counter these developments, first liberating Mussolini from captivity and establishing him as a puppet in Milan, and then securing a powerful defensive line based on Cassino and its famous old monastery, some seventy-five miles below Rome. Through the winter of 1944, despite an Allied landing at Anzio beach a few miles below Rome, the Germans clung tenaciously to their lines. Only in May were the Allies finally able to break through to Rome, a city that greeted its liberators on June 4, 1944, with undisguised rapture. Again the Germans revealed a defensive ability that arrested the Allied push for the remainder of the year in the vicinity of Florence and Bologna. Only with the collapse of Germany itself in April of 1945 would the German defense finally disintegrate. The Italian campaign had been a heartbreaking struggle, but it had reduced the Allies' enemies by one, and added to the German burdens.

D-Day: June 6, 1944. In the early days of the war, the German Luftwaffe—air force—had practically dominated the skies; but in 1940 and 1941 it met its match in England's Royal Air Force. Unable to smash British resistance in daytime attacks or to continue to bear up under the heavy losses sustained, the Luftwaffe switched to night bombings of British cities. Through the autumn of 1940 and during 1941, London, Bristol, Birmingham, Liverpool, and Coventry reeled under savage bombings. In 1942, however, the German cities' turn came, and for the remainder of the war they were converted into massive ruins. In the North Atlantic, by 1943, the German submarine menace was brought under control, and a flood of American manpower and equipment poured into Britain, until journalists predicted that the island would sink under the weight of the supplies. As 1944 dawned, it was apparent that the time was fast approaching for the liberation of western Europe.

On June 6, 1944, a vast American, British, and Canadian force, totaling almost three million men, under the command of General Eisenhower, began landing on the Normandy beaches of northern France. For six weeks a sanguinary battle raged below the beaches, but on July 25, American forces broke out of Saint-Lô, and the German front disintegrated. During the next two months, Allied troops swept across France, as the American Seventh Army debarked in southern France, and a Free French force under General Charles de Gaulle liberated a delirious Paris, on August 25. In late September, after liberating most of Belgium and Luxembourg, American and British airborne troops freed southern Netherlands. The United States First Army, under Lieutenant General Omar N. Bradley occupied the German city of Aachen in October, while Lieutenant General George S. Patton's swiftly moving Third Army, in November, seized the great fortress city of Metz, reached the Rhine at Strasbourg, and entered Germany's Saar Basin.

THE END OF THE WAR

The Collapse of Germany. On July 20, 1944, an effort to assassinate Hitler in his East Prussian headquarters failed. With savage swiftness, Hitler crushed the thin ranks of opposition to himself; no longer able rationally to consider his predicament, the psychotic German dictator determined that if he were to perish, Germany would perish with him. Confronted on the east with a horde of Russians who stood on the Vistula at Warsaw, and in the Balkans by the surrender of Rumania and Bulgaria, Hitler determined on one more effort in the west. On December 16, 1944, Field Marshal Karl G. von Rundstedt launched a massive attack with some 250,000 troops on the thinly manned American line in the Ardennes mountains of Luxembourg and Belgium. For ten days the German forces advanced, reaching the Meuse River some sixty miles beyond their departure point. But the stubborn resistance of the 101st Airborne Division under Brigadier General Anthony C. McAuliffe at Bastogne, Belgium; the swift movement of Patton's Third Army from the south; and the redirection of the American First Army and Field Marshal Montgomery's forces in the north first halted, and then drove back, the German onslaught. The "Battle of the Bulge," as the struggle was called, ended in late January, with some 8,000 Americans killed and almost 70,000 wounded or captured; German losses totaled 220,000 in dead and captured. The end was in sight, for during January and February the Russian army had surged to the Oder River, barely thirty miles from Berlin, while Allied forces pushed across the Rhineland to the Rhine River. On March 7, 1945, by a stroke of luck, American troops captured intact the Remagen Bridge across the Rhine, and in a swift action established a bridgehead on the east bank of the Rhine. From the east and west two great armies now overran the German heartland, with Russian and American troops meeting on the Elbe River in late April. Hitler, on April 30, deep in a bunker, surrounded by the burning ruins of Berlin, committed suicide. Two days later, Axis forces in northern Italy and Austria capitulated, and on May 7, 1945, at Rheims, France, General Alfred Jodl surrendered all German forces to Eisenhower. The war in Europe was over; but the Japanese still tenaciously resisted.

The Final Phases of the Pacific War. In mid-1943 the war in the Pacific settled into a strategy of "island-hopping" devised by General MacArthur and Admiral Chester Nimitz. Rather than attempt to subdue every Japanese base, the American forces concentrated on destroying major enemy bases, leaving the lesser bases to be starved into submission. Between June 30, 1943, and April 1944, MacArthur's forces cleared the Solomon Islands and New Guinea in the South Pacific. No less spectacular were combined Army-Navy operations in the Central Pacific. Between November 1943 and August 1944, Tarawa in the Gilbert Islands, Kwajalein and Eniwetok in the Marshall Islands, and Saipan and Guam in the Mariana Islands were taken. From air bases in the latter two islands, American superfortress bombers set forth to reduce Japanese cities. On October 20, 1944, MacArthur waded ashore with his army on Leyte Island in the Philippines; four days later, on October 24 and 25, in the Battle of Leyte Gulf, the Japanese navy was permanently maimed by the loss of four aircraft carriers, two battleships, nine cruisers, and numerous lesser craft. By mid-February, Manila, after a devastating battle, was retaken. The time was fast approaching for a direct invasion of the Japanese home islands. On February 19, 1945, a Marine force invaded Iwo Jima, an island a mere 750 miles from Tokyo, and on April 1, Okinawa, the main island of the Ryukyu group, was invaded. For eighty-three days, the Japanese fought desperately, employing *kamikaze* planes, piloted by suicide aviators, which crashed deliberately into American ships. When the battle finally ended on June 22, after the suicide of the two commanding Japanese generals, American losses in the Pacific numbered 49,151 men, of whom 12,520 were killed or missing. No less than 36 American ships had been sunk and 369 were damaged. But Japanese losses exceeded 110,000 men and 7,830 planes. The last great battle of the war had been fought; a new and fearsome weapon was about to be introduced into warfare.

Hiroshima and Nagasaki. Shortly after the invasion of France, the Germans began to bombard Britain with rockets. Had this weapon been introduced into the war earlier, it might well have compelled the British to surrender. It provided a somber foreshadowing of a new dimension to future warfare. In the United States, the secret "Manhattan Project" under General Leslie R. Groves, employing the talents of such gifted scientists as J. Robert Oppenheimer, Enrico Fermi, and Nils Bohr, and unstintingly backed by President Roosevelt, explored the possibilities of harnessing atomic energy. In 1943, at Los Alamos, New Mexico, construction of the first atomic bomb began, and on July 16, 1945, at Alamogordo, New Mexico, during the early days of Truman's administration, the bomb was successfully exploded. At about 8:11 A.M., on August 6, 1945, an American superfortress, *Enola Gay,* began its run over the Japanese military base at Hiroshima. Shortly afterward, a terrible explosion shattered the city, killing 78,150, injuring 37,425, and leaving missing 13,500 of Hiroshima's 343,969 citizens. Three days later the port of Nagasaki was similarly visited, and some 38,500 of its 252,630 citizens were left dead. To an astonished world, President Harry Truman described the new weapon as "an atomic bomb. It is a harnessing of the basic power of the universe. The force from which the sun draws its power has been loosed against

ESTIMATED CASUALTIES OF ATOMIC BOMBINGS

	HIROSHIMA	NAGASAKI
Total population	343,969	252,630
Dead	78,150	38,500
Injured	37,425	40,000
Missing	13,500	7,000
Mortality rate per square mile destroyed	15,000	20,000

those who brought war to the Far East." Faced with annihilation or surrender, Japan's Emperor Hirohito called upon his people, on August 15, 1945, to cease resistance and to display restraint and fortitude in enduring the pangs of defeat. On September 3, 1945, six years from the day that Britain and France had gone to war with Germany, the Japanese formally surrendered on the battleship *Missouri* in Tokyo Bay.

World War II was over. The fate of mankind remained in the balance. The time for peacemaking had come; it was a task that would occupy the men who had made the war, and that would continue to occupy those who followed.

Chapter 15

The Trials of Power

The United States, at the end of the war, found herself on a lonely eminence of power, prestige, and wealth. Unlike the other great nations with whom she had shared the victory, America alone had emerged from the war with no grievous physical damage: cities, factories, farms, and institutions were whole and intact, freeing this nation from the heavy economic burden of rebuilding from ruins. Compared with the problems confronting most of the other combatants, the matter of demobilizing American manpower and returning industry to peacetime pursuits was a minor one. The United States was further isolated from the common postwar experience of the rest of the world by her exclusive possession of the atomic bomb.

In spite of the fact that the wealth and power enjoyed by the United States in 1945 exceeded that of any previous nation at any previous time in history, they were to bring her neither contentment nor security. America's very prominence and eminence *created* problems for her rather than solved them; and during the years that followed the war—now almost two decades—these problems were to increase and multiply, making solution ever more complex and remote.

It was inevitable that the postwar balance of relative power, initially so greatly in the United States's favor, should shift, reducing the gap between her and the other major nations of the world. It was also inevitable that the secrets of atomic and nuclear arms should be discovered independently by other nations. As western Europe, eastern Europe, and the Orient have recuperated from their positions of 1945,

America has had to learn how to live with other powers who are almost her equal—and on a planet which technology has made ever smaller. It has not been an easy task, and it is one that the United States even now has not yet fully mastered.

THE MAPPING OF PEACE

The Grand Alliance. The rise of Hitler had forced into existence a coalition of powers whose major immediate objective was to destroy the Nazi government and military machine. But beyond the immediate objective loomed a great question: What was to be the nature of the relationship among the great Allied powers in the time of future peace? Between Roosevelt and Churchill there existed an easy rapport; Churchill foresaw that it would result in an ever-expanding interdependence between Britain and the United States. A far more complex relationship existed between the western Allies and Joseph Stalin, dictator of the Soviet Union. A harsh tyrant who had not hesitated to liquidate or imprison tens of thousands of opponents—both real and imagined—in the 1930s, Stalin had struggled desperately to buy peace from Hitler. (If the opinion of Stalin's successor, Nikita Khrushchev, is correct, Stalin almost lost the war altogether by failing to provide the necessary means with which to meet the first German onslaught.) The available evidence indicates, however, that once the Red Army became locked in battle with Hitler's legions, Stalin fought to obtain from his western partners maximum aid, pressing always for more supplies and for a second front. Operating on the principle that "time is our ally," Stalin never lost sight of the fact that the interests both of the Union of Soviet Socialist Republics and of international Communism demanded that peace be prepared for. To Moscow, the alliance against Hitler was a momentary interlude which softened, rather than suspended, the larger ideological struggle between capitalism and communism. Even as Stalin fought his war against Hitler, he prepared the groundwork of a renewed ideological warfare with the west once Allied victory had been attained.

The Casablanca Conference. Any chance that the western Allies might negotiate a settlement with Hitler was ended in January 1943, when Roosevelt and Churchill met at Casablanca, Morocco. There, on January 24, Roosevelt issued his now-famous statement:

> Peace can come to the world only by the total elimination of German and Japanese war power. . . . The elimination of German, Japanese, and Italian war power means the unconditional surrender by Ger-

> many, Italy, and Japan. That means a reasonable assurance of future world peace. It does not mean the destruction of the population of Germany, Italy, or Japan, but it does mean the destruction of the philosophies in those countries which are based on conquest and the subjugation of other peoples.

A rigid application of the "unconditional surrender" terms was not made in the case of Italy, however, for the prospect of depriving Hitler of Italian aid led, in September 1943, to the granting of an armistice to the Badoglio government and the subsequent acceptance of Italy as a co-belligerent in the struggle against Hitler. Japan also obtained modification of the terms, being permitted to retain her Emperor, although this latter concession was deemed an advantage to the victorious Americans. Germany, alone, was compelled to accept total surrender.

The Cairo and Teheran Conferences. In late October of 1943, Churchill and Roosevelt met with Chiang Kai-shek at Cairo, Egypt. The major result of this conference was the declaration that Japan would be stripped of all territory other than the four home islands. China was promised restoration of Manchuria, Formosa, and the Pescadores; Korea was promised its freedom; and although not specifically stated, the restoration principle seemed to imply the return to Russia of the southern half of Sakhalin Island.

This latter provision was confirmed in late November when, at Teheran, Roosevelt and Churchill met with Stalin for the first time. Here, plans for concerted strategy against Hitler were settled upon, with Roosevelt and Churchill informing Stalin of the massive cross-channel invasion they had agreed to during their earlier August conference at Quebec, Canada. Considerable discussion developed around such peripheral questions as the ultimate fate of Iran, Turkey, and Finland, and the creation of an international organization to help keep the peace after the war. One astute American observer, after considering Stalin's proposals for Europe after the war, concluded grimly: "The result would be that the Soviet Union would be the only important military and political force on the continent of Europe. The rest of Europe would be reduced to military and political impotence." But for the moment, the three Allied leaders declared: "We express our determination that our nations shall work together in war and in the peace that will follow."

The Election of 1944. As the war progressed, Americans at home prepared for the next presidential election. At Chicago, in June of 1944, the Republicans nominated Governor Thomas E. Dewey of

New York, with Governor John Bricker of Ohio as his running mate. A month later, in the same city, the Democrats chose Franklin D. Roosevelt for a fourth term, but replaced Henry A. Wallace with Senator Harry Truman of Missouri. The scrappy Missourian had made a substantial reputation for himself as chairman of a Senate committee investigating war contract frauds. In spite of rumors about Roosevelt's declining health, on November 7, 1944, 45,531,000 Americans re-elected him by a majority of more than three million votes, and an electoral count of 432 to 99. No one could know that, in effect, two Presidents had been elected. On April 12, 1945, at Warm Springs, Georgia, Roosevelt succumbed to a cerebral hemorrhage. A stunned nation sympathized with Truman's remark, upon his accession to the presidency, that he felt as if "the moon, the stars, and all the planets" had fallen on him. The new President would have, as a legacy, the results of Roosevelt's last and most momentous war conference, held at Yalta in Russia's Crimea.

The Yalta Conference. Between February 4 and 11, 1945, Churchill, Roosevelt, and Stalin met together for the last time. The impending victory was uppermost in everyone's mind, and the strategy for military victory was now to be superseded by a strategy for political triumph. Many significant decisions, of far-reaching consequence, were reached at Yalta. The American delegation, still faced with what promised to be a bloody struggle against Japan, was eager to obtain firm pledges from Russia for full participation in the war against Tokyo. (Many critics of the agreement, gifted with hindsight of the atomic bomb, have questioned why any Russian aid in this project was required. They forget that the explosive force of the bomb was not expected to exceed a thousand tons of TNT, little more than the destructive power of a single flight of bombers.) An agreement was reached confirming the proposals which had been made at Dumbarton Oaks, near Washington, D.C., in September 1944, by delegates of China, Great Britain, the Soviet Union, and the United States, to establish an international association that would function as a world court. The complex question of Poland was partially resolved with the acceptance of the Curzon line—an ethnic boundary between Poland and Russia originally proposed in 1919, which had been used in 1939 by Germany and Russia to partition Poland—as the Polish eastern boundary; as compensation, Poland was to receive German lands in the north and west, and the Soviet authorities pledged free elections for the Poles. The demands of the Royal Yugoslavian government-in-exile were also seemingly met with the pledge that the government of guerrilla leader Marshal Tito would be expanded to include "members of the former Yugoslav Parliament who had not collaborated with the enemy." Elsewhere in the Balkans, Russia's interest was recognized (at least tacitly) in Rumania, Bulgaria, and Hungary, while that of Britain was assumed to prevail in Greece. The real rivalries that existed among the Allies in eastern Europe were momentarily disguised by the joint declaration which avowed the Big Three's "mutual agreement to concert during the temporary period of instability in liberated Europe the policies of their three governments in assisting the peoples liberated from the domination of Nazi Germany and the peoples of the former Axis satellite states of Europe to solve by democratic means their pressing political and economic problems." Any doubt as to the real situation should have been put at rest by Russian Foreign Minister V. M. Molotov's blunt earlier statement that "It was not necessary for the Soviet Union to conclude an armistice with Hungary since the Red Army was practically the master of that country. It could do what it wished." In a real sense, therefore, the future division of Europe was determined by whose armies—those of the west or those of the Soviet Union—liberated the country.

Yalta's Secret Terms. In addition to those matters already mentioned, the Yalta Conference produced a number of decisions and agreements which were kept secret at the time. In exchange for a firm promise that the Soviet Union would enter the war against Japan once the war with Germany was over—a pledge which the Soviets honored on August 8, 1945—the western Allies made some damaging concessions. The independence of Outer Mongolia was acknowledged; Russia's pre-eminent interest both in the Manchurian port of Dairen and in the two Manchurian railroads which connected it with eastern Siberia was acknowledged; Russia was further granted a lease of the naval base at Port Arthur. It was charged subsequently, and with considerable accuracy, that the United States had cavalierly compromised basic Chinese interests; but it ought to be noted that if eastern European developments are an accurate guide, Russian intervention would probably have assured their ultimately gaining most of what they had been conceded at Yalta. In all probability, therefore, the United States lost an ethical advantage rather than anything of tangible substance. Of critical subsequent significance, the right of and necessity for Soviet troops to occupy part of Korea was acknowledged. Finally, faced with the request that two or three of the constituent Soviet republics be admitted to the proposed organization that would ultimately become the United Nations, the western Allies agreed that the Ukraine and Byelorussia should be admitted. (Roosevelt hoped that the larger the Russian stake in the world court, the more apt they would be to support it firmly.)

The wisdom of the secret Yalta accords is highly suspect; most certainly, the carrying out of these agreements has led to many major international problems. But before they be subjected to wholesale condemnation, it should be recalled that the men who made them thought they were saving Allied lives, a noble—if diplomatically limiting—consideration.

THE AFTERMATH OF WAR

The Cost of World War II. When peace finally came in late summer of 1945, the world took time to count its losses. Fifty million men, women, and children had perished on the battlefield, in the ruined towns and cities, in detention and concentration camps, and in numberless forgotten waystops. Such great capitals as Warsaw and Manila had been virtually annihilated. Berlin, Tokyo, Budapest, London, Munich, and countless other cities were either shattered ruins or harbored raw wounds. The industrial plants, public utilities, agriculture, transportation, and communications of Europe and large parts of Asia were decimated. The specter of famine and disease threatened half the human race. And perhaps more importantly, six years of war and occupation had shattered the confidence of whole societies in the workability of their past institutions.

Changes in the Social Order. In the aftermath of Hitler's war, humanity's struggle to free itself from the disabilities of the past would result in major social revolution. This would be particularly true of those people who were subjected to colonial rule; if Japan had done nothing else, it had revealed that non-whites were not innately destined to be subjected. Moreover the scope of Japanese conquests had irrevocably weakened the fabric of colonial power, while the long struggle against Hitler had drained the wealth of western Europe. The great colonial powers would have all they could do to restore their own economies without enduring the sapping costs of colonial wars.

Even more shattering to the world's concepts of stable society had been Hitler's assaults on the westerner's moral and ethical code. In such concentration camps as Buchenwald, Dachau, Auschwitz, and Belsen, six million Jews and millions of other victims had perished. Had Hitler triumphed, whole peoples, such as the Poles and the Russians, were destined for either extermination or enslavement. The destruction of almost the whole of European Jewry had proven the literal possibility of genocide; but this savage act had been effected only with the wholesale collaboration of Europeans. The traditional anti-Semitism of the Christian world had borne an evil fruit, one which, the non-white colonial world quickly pointed out, revealed the moral bankruptcy of the white man. One overwhelming fact had emerged from two world wars; the white man's technological superiority was not supplemented by a superior humanity.

Retribution. The monstrous crimes of Nazism and of Japanese militarism confronted the world with a major legal problem, since no provision existed to cover them. Faced with this difficulty, the Allies resolved on the use of *ex post facto* law. At Nuremberg, Germany, beginning in November 1945, trials were held that ultimately resulted in the conviction of nineteen leading Nazis, twelve of whom (most importantly Hermann Goering) were condemned to death; at similar trials in Tokyo, seven members of the Japanese war governments (Hideki Tojo being the most famous) were similarly condemned. Such trials for "war crimes" would continue to be held for many years. One of the most famous of the later trials was that of Adolph Eichmann in Israel in 1962. Future war leaders now knew that the price of defeat in war was a hangman's noose.

The United Nations. Punishment of war criminals seemed to many like closing the barn door after the horse has run away. No amount of retribution could undo the horrors of six years of war. At San Francisco, on April 25, 1945, two hundred delegates from forty-six countries gathered to form the international organization that had long been proposed to keep the peace. Two months later, on April 26, the Charter of the United Nations as drafted by the delegation was submitted for ratification to fifty member nations. (By June of 1963, the UN membership would number one hundred and eleven nations.) The Charter as approved provides for an eleven-nation Security Council, five members of which—United States, Soviet Union, Great Britain, France, and China—are permanent members, vested with the power to veto any discussion of, or action against, aggression; and six members of which are elected. Every member has a vote in the General Assembly, the body which possesses the power to debate relevant issues and to make recommendations to the Security Council. A Secretary-General heads the administrative apparatus which is called the Secretariat. The three men who have served as Secretary-General—Trygve Lie, Dag Hammarskjold, and U Thant—have made the post increasingly vital in conducting negotiations to ward off war. A number of associate offices were also created by the delegation: the Trusteeship

Council, to administer former Japanese and some other colonies; a fifteen-man International Court of Justice, located in The Hague, the Netherlands, to adjudicate international disputes; the United Nations Educational, Scientific, and Cultural Organization (UNESCO), given the task of creating international contacts to broaden international understanding; and the eighteen-man Economic and Social Council, which supervises the International Labor Organization, International Monetary Fund, and the World Health Organization among others.

The Potsdam Conference. No problem was more pressing at war's end than the future of Germany. To resolve this difficulty, Churchill, Stalin, and Truman met at Potsdam, Germany, between July 17 and August 2, 1945. On July 28, Clement Attlee replaced Churchill, whose Conservative party had been beaten at the British polls. Two declarations were issued: the first, a surrender ultimatum to Japan on July 26, 1945, which threatened her with destruction if she did not capitulate, but also promised her a chance at economic recovery and self-government; and the second, on August 2, 1945, which was tantamount to the partition of Germany. The eastern section of Germany beyond the Oder and Neisse rivers (except for the northern half of East Prussia) was placed under Polish administration. The supposedly temporary nature of this occupation has since become permanent, involving the expulsion of some nine million Germans and their replacement by several million Poles. The remainder of Germany was divided into four administrative zones: the eastern third under Russia, and the remaining two-thirds under Britain, France, and the United States. Berlin was similarly divided in spite of the significant geographic fact that the city was located some one hundred and ten miles inside the Russian zone. Subsequently Austria was also divided, but the partition ended on May 15, 1955, when the Austrians pledged themselves to neutrality. In Germany, however, when the Soviet Union refused to treat the various zones as part of an economic unit, the three western powers in 1946 fused their zones for economic purposes, and on May 23, 1949, the Federal Republic of Germany was proclaimed; it was finally accorded full sovereignty on May 5, 1955.

The Berlin Blockade. On October 7, 1949, Russia responded to the creation of the Federal Republic of Germany by establishing a puppet government, the German Democratic Republic, in the Russian zone. But as Nikita Khrushchev observed, West Berlin remained a bone caught in the Russian throat. As early as April 1, 1948, the Russians had tried to force western withdrawal from Berlin by denying overland access to the city. Until September 30, 1949, when the blockade was finally lifted, an American and British airlift flew almost two and a half million tons of food and fuel to the city. From then on the city provided a vivid contrast between the extent of recovery in western and eastern Europe, and also served as an escape hatch for millions of East Germans, whose flight created economic chaos for Communist authorities in East Germany. Finally, in mid-August of 1961, the German Communists erected a wall dividing East and West Berlin, and simultaneously closed communications and transportation into the city. For all practical purposes, the partition of Germany had been completed, although almost two decades after the war no German peace treaty had yet been drawn.

American Recovery Plans. The war had hardly ended when President Truman terminated Lend-Lease, a decision which he subsequently admitted was a mistake since it deprived Europe and Asia of much needed economic assistance at a critical moment. By 1946, the crucial financial predicament of Great Britain was met by extending a $3,750 billion loan to England, but this help proved to be only a stopgap measure; in the late winter of 1947 the British government notified Truman that it would have to end aid to Turkey and Greece by March 31, 1947. The President, who always displayed a remarkable firmness in foreign policy, called on Congress in early March to provide some $400 million with which to assist the two countries in defending themselves. The Truman Doctrine, as it was called, marked the moment when the United States underwrote the containment of further Communist expansion.

A larger, more creative proposal for European recovery was made by Secretary of State George C. Marshall, on June 5, 1947. The Marshall Plan offered American financial and technical assistance to any government which provided a viable plan for recovery. On March 31, 1948, Congress agreed to the passage of the European Recovery Act, based on the Marshall Plan, opposition having been effectively spiked by Republican Senator Arthur H. Vandenberg of Michigan, who had defended the plan as an economic answer to Russia's expansionist designs. Few observers doubted the wisdom of his conclusion that "There is no guarantee that his European Recovery Plan will 'work' . . . but we cannot afford not to take that chance." Under the administration of Paul G. Hoffman the United States poured $12 billion into European recovery between 1948 and 1951, an investment which put Europe on the highroad to prosperity.

The North Atlantic Treaty Organization. A further supplement to European recovery was made on April 4, 1949, when the United

States, France, Great Britain, Italy, the Low Countries, Portugal, Norway, Denmark, Iceland, and Canada signed the North Atlantic Treaty, which pledged that an attack on any one signatory would be considered an attack on all. Greece and Turkey joined the alliance in 1951, and the Federal Republic of Germany joined in 1955. An integration of military arms on land, sea, and air was provided for, and a Supreme Headquarters, Allied Powers, Europe, under General Dwight D. Eisenhower, was established in December 1950. The existence of a collective power capable of threatening any aggressor with massive retaliation had been established; but, as Senator Robert A. Taft noted, such a treaty placed in jeopardy a peace founded "upon the establishment of law and justice among nations, with international action by joint force against an aggressor." He noted further that it started an armament race which, if the general history of such competitions was a guide, "led to war, not to peace." The awesome possibilities of such a conflict were underscored by Russia's successful development prior to 1949 of an atom bomb, and the harnessing between 1950 to 1953 by both the United States and Russia of thermonuclear energy in bombs. On March 1, 1954, the United States tested a twenty-megaton bomb, an explosive power almost ten times as great as all the explosive power used during World War II. By 1962, a single American army division had the fire power of all the armed forces that existed on the day Japan surrendered. Against such armed power, one could not help but wonder if the prospect of war was not in fact the prospect of the human race's suicide.

THE ADMINISTRATION OF HARRY S. TRUMAN

Harry S. Truman's mother had brought him up to "hew to the good line"; he obeyed. Straightforward, uncomplicated, stubborn when necessary, he had made the journey from haberdasher to President without losing the virtues and strengths of small-town America. His honesty was incorruptible, and his Midwestern twang sounded "homey"; Eastern sophisticates might dismiss him as simple, but his openness concealed a shrewd, incisive mind that enabled him to change from a seeming presidential failure in 1946 to at least a near-great President in 1953.

Domestic Problems. The task of returning the nation to a peacetime economy was bound to be difficult. Almost ten million veterans returned to civilian pursuits, and the economy had to be substantially revamped to accommodate them. Americans, weary of the deprivations of a decade and a half of depression and war, longed for the good life. Shortages in sugar, clothing, meat, and housing were particularly vexing. Through 1946, a campaign against price controls eroded away all restraints, with a consequent rise of thirty-two per cent in the price levels during the year. Labor agitated against wage controls as the lid blew off prices, and strikes shook the automobile, steel, coal, and electrical industries. Only Truman's threat that he would seize the railroads ended a strike in May. The Republicans smoothly exploited public dissatisfaction with the slogan "Had Enough?", and gained control of Congress in the off-year elections of 1946. The conservative Republican leadership set to work restraining labor.

The Taft-Hartley Labor Law. Congressional sentiment in 1947 favored a rewriting of the Wagner Act of 1935; it was felt that the law leaned too far toward favoring labor at the expense of management. Under the shrewd guidance of Ohio's Senator Taft—"Mr. Republican" to his party—a Labor-Management Relations Bill was enacted into law over Truman's veto on June 23, 1947. The Taft-Hartley Labor Law forbade the existence of the "closed shop" (which made union membership a pre-condition for a job) as well as of the "union shop" (which made union membership obligatory once a job was obtained). The latter restriction was removed by a 1951 amendment to the original act. Restraints were placed on jurisdictional strikes (which were disputes between two unions), "featherbedding" (which obliged an employer to hire more men than he actually needed), and "check-offs" (which forced employers to withhold union dues from their employees' wages). Employers also gained the right to oppose unions, the right to sue unions which violated their contracts, and the right to request the National Labor Relations Board to hold elections among their employees to determine who represented them. Unions were required to submit to a 60-day "cooling-off" period before striking, to make annual financial reports to the Secretary of Labor, and to refrain from making political contributions. Finally, all labor leaders had to submit affidavits that they were not Communists, and the President could enjoin strikes that endangered the national welfare. A new tone of reciprocal responsibility had been established in labor-management relations.

The Election of 1948. A confident Republican party nominated Thomas E. Dewey and Earl Warren, Governor of California, as their standard bearers for 1948. A divided, squabbling Democratic party grudgingly nominated Truman and Senator Alben Barkley of Kentucky. A state rights wing of the party, angered at Truman's efforts to extend Negro civil rights, defected to nominate South Carolina's Governor J. Strom Thurmond and Mississippi's Governor Fielding L. Wright on a "Dixiecrat" ticket; while a left-wing element of the Democratic party defected to form the Progressive party, nominating Henry A. Wallace and Senator Glen Taylor of Idaho, with a platform that called for increased social reform, reconciliation with Russia, and an end to all racial discrimination. With such divisions within what had been the New Deal coalition, the Republican candidates concluded that to insure an overwhelming victory they had nothing to do but avoid alienating prospective voters. Truman chose to campaign actively, making a whistle-stop tour across the country, giving the "do-nothing Eightieth Congress hell." Reporters traveling with Truman were impressed by the size and response of the crowds he attracted, but the pollsters announced that Dewey had a solid lead. To everyone's surprise but his own, Truman polled 24,105,000 popular and 303 electoral votes to Dewey's 21,970,000 popular and 189 electoral votes. The Dixiecrat and Progressive candidates polled a little over 1,100,000 votes each. The scrappy man from Missouri had staged the greatest political upset in the nation's history, and his party had swept to a solid control of Congress.

The Fair Deal. Re-election seems to have given Truman new confidence, and when Congress convened in January 1949, he called upon it to enact a program of reform he dubbed the "Fair Deal." It was a call that went largely unheeded, although minimum wages were raised in 1950 from forty to seventy-five cents, social security benefits were extended, and some $2,700 billion was appropriated for slum-clearance projects. But the national attention was focusing on Communist subversion, as evidence accumulated that some highly placed Americans had used their posts to advance Communist interests and, probably more important, as Americans felt increasing frustration at an international situation that seemed destined to remain forever at crisis pitch.

The Korean War. On Sunday, June 25, 1950, the American people awoke to learn that during the previous night Communist forces from North Korea had invaded South Korea. Suddenly they were reminded that at Yalta the Allies had pledged independence to Korea; that at Potsdam the country had been temporarily divided, for military purposes, at the 38th parallel; and that the division had become, by 1947, seemingly permanent, with a Communist government firmly entrenched in the North and a conservative—some thought reactionary—government under the authoritarian Dr. Syngman Rhee dominant in the South. The withdrawal of the Soviet army from the North in December 1948 and of American forces from the South in June 1949 appeared to leave the future of Korea in the hands of rival Korean factions. Truman and his Secretary of State Dean Acheson left the extent of the American commitment to South Korea unnecessarily vague, particularly since the January 26, 1950 American-South Korean defense pact had been preceded by an Acheson speech which seemed to place Korea beyond the American defense perimeter. Once news of the invasion reached Truman, however, he determined on firm action, for drawing upon the remembrance of the failure to challenge the Axis powers' early career of aggression, he concluded "that if South Korea was allowed to go unchallenged it would mean a third world war." Rather than act unilaterally, the issue was presented to the UN Security Council which then voted 9 to 0 to order North Korea to withdraw its forces. Fortunately, from the American viewpoint, Russia's veto power was not used since she had chosen to boycott the Council so long as the Nationalist Chinese and not the Communist Chinese held China's seat on the Council. During the next five days, with Security Council approval, the United States committed men and material under the command of General Douglas MacArthur to the aid of the South Koreans. Subsequently Great Britain, Canada, Australia, New Zealand, Turkey, Thailand, and the Philippines sent manpower into the battle. What ensued was a bloody campaign that drove United Nations forces (as the armed assistance to South Korea was designated) into a narrow perimeter around the South Korean port of Pusan. In mid-September a brilliant combined land and sea offensive expelled the North Koreans from all South Korea. Then, with authorization from the General Assembly, General MacArthur launched an invasion of North Korea which, by the end of November, brought some United Nations forces to the banks of the Yalu River which separated North Korea from Manchuria. MacArthur, preparing to launch a final offensive on November 24, assured reporters, "The war very definitely is coming to an end shortly." Instead, a massive intervention of Communist Chinese troops hurled the United Nations forces back into South Korea, and demands swelled in the United States for a direct attack on China. Truman wrote grimly: "I have worked for peace for five years and six months and it looks like World War III is near."

Truman and MacArthur. Article II, Section 2 of the Constitution firmly places ultimate military authority in the hands of the President. As the Korean War worsened, President Truman concluded that General Douglas MacArthur was deliberately working to undercut the administration's military policy. On October 15, 1950, at a Wake Island conference, MacArthur had assured Truman the Chinese Communists would not intervene—and that if they did, they would be slaughtered. The events following the November 26 offensive proved the general completely wrong; MacArthur responded by calling for attacks upon the "privileged sanctuary" of the Chinese in Manchuria. The administration, which had resolved upon a war of limited objectives (the restoration and maintenance of South Korea's independence), viewed MacArthur's stance as an implicit challenge to civilian control of the military. When Washington declined to use troops from Formosa, Joseph W. Martin, House Republican minority leader, solicited MacArthur's views on the subject and made them public on April 5. The key paragraph read:

> It seems strangely difficult for some to realize that here in Asia is where the Communist conspirators have elected to make their play for global conquest, and that we have joined the issue thus raised on the battlefield; that here we fight Europe's war with arms while the diplomats there still fight it with words; that if we lose the war to Communism in Asia the fall of Europe is inevitable; win it, and Europe most probably would avoid war and yet preserve freedom.

For Truman this paragraph "was the real 'clincher.'" Abruptly, on April 11, 1951, he removed MacArthur from his command. An extraordinary military career had come to an end, and the administration had settled for a war of limited objectives, one which would drag on to the increasing dismay of the American public until 1953.

The Red Scare. Out of national frustration with a war that seemed without victory or end, Senator Joseph R. McCarthy of Wisconsin would weave a tapestry of charges, innuendo, and outright lies which left the impression that the federal government was ridden with Communists and riddled with treason. The conjunction of the Communist Chinese takeover of China between 1947 and 1949, the emergence of Russia as an atomic power, and the revelation that numerous Americans had served the Communist cause lent substance to the charges. (What was not revealed and publicized, but which was very much to the point, was the fact that most Americans who had espoused the Communist cause, either in practice or in sympathy, had done so during the 1930s, a time when American political and social practices were particularly questionable and unsatisfying to thoughtful citizens, causing the Lost Generation—or large segments of that group—to see in the idealistic Communist experiment in Russia a hope of a better way of life. By the 1940s, however, when the ideals of the Communist experiment in the U.S.S.R. had been overshadowed by brutal purges; when the Soviet Union appalled western Communists by signing a non-aggression pact with Fascist Germany; and when the political, economic, and social climate in the United States had so much improved, most American Communists and so-called fellow travelers had become thoroughly disillusioned with Communism and deserted the cause.) Even more important, the unnatural conditions which at the end of World War II had left the United States the supremely powerful nation had been steadily altering; as recovery from World War II continued and other nations regained their traditional power, America's power was relatively declining. Faced with the realization that the United States would have to settle down to long, aggravating, often exhausting negotiations to gain its points, some Americans preferred to seek easy solutions and explanations for the nation's problems. These consisted usually of appeals for preventive war, best defined as a large war fought now to prevent a larger war fought later, and charges that wholesale domestic subversion accounted for all Communist advances; in essence, the followers of McCarthy were unable to concede that anything short of American betrayal could reduce America's supremacy of power. Particularly spectacular support for this position was obtained in 1948 when Alger Hiss, a former State Department official, was revealed by Whittaker Chambers, a self-confessed Communist agent, to have passed information to a Soviet espionage ring. The trial and subsequent executions of Julius and Ethel Rosenberg in 1951 for passing atomic secrets to Russian agents was looked upon as further proof of the threat. Such were the circumstances that accounted for the extraordinary career of Joseph R. McCarthy.

The McCarthy Hearings. Even those who attribute high-minded motives to McCarthy recognize that he was an opportunist. He did not create anticommunism, but took advantage of it. Many Republicans, frustrated by their defeat in 1948 and unwilling to accept the obvious permanence of the New Deal reforms, were prepared to tar their political enemies with damning labels. Thus, in February 1950, McCarthy charged that there were no less than 205 Communists in the State Department; within twenty-four hours, he had reduced the number to 57. The headlines that greeted his charges showed McCarthy that he had discovered a major power lever, one which he would manipulate for four years. The defeat in 1950 of Senator Millard Tydings, the long-time conservative Senator from Maryland, after McCarthy intervened with deliberately fabricated evidence of Tydings' supposed ties with Communists, added a frightening dimension to his power. With the elections of 1952 approaching, the Republican leadership, particularly Robert A. Taft of Ohio, studiously refrained from disciplining him. The Communist label when tagged to Democrats was believed to be vote-producing for the Republicans. Once the Republicans had successfully elected Dwight D. Eisenhower in 1952, however, McCarthy turned upon his own party's administration. In a series of freewheeling investigations, he charged that the United States Information Service's shelves contained subversive books; that the Protestant clergy was infiltrated with Communists; and that the United States Army "coddled Communists." The latter charge carried an implicit challenge to President Eisenhower which he attempted to sidestep by refusing, as he said, to "get in the gutter with that guy." As efforts to placate McCarthy proved unavailing, the Army launched a series of countercharges, indicting McCarthy and his aides for seeking special favors on pain of wrecking the Army if they were not forthcoming. Finally, on April 22, 1954, a Senate Subcommittee, under the direction of South Dakota's Karl E. Mundt, opened a televised investigation of the Army charges, and for thirty-six days the nation watched as Joseph Welch, the gentle but passionate Army counsel, revealed the moral and ethical shoddiness of McCarthy. When the hearings were ended, the Wisconsin senator had irretrievably damaged his reputation, and on December 2, 1954, upon recommendation of a Select Committee of the Senate chaired by Senator Arthur V. Watkins of Utah, the Senate voted 67 to 22 to censure McCarthy for tending to bring the Senate into disrepute.

THE ADMINISTRATIONS OF DWIGHT D. EISENHOWER

The Election of 1952. Twenty years of Democratic control of the executive office ended in 1952. The Twenty-second Amendment to the Constitution, ratified on March 1, 1951, had limited the presidency to two terms of office but had exempted Harry S. Truman from its provisions. The incumbent, who had firmly stated "There is no indispensable man in a democracy," eliminated himself from further consideration on March 30, 1952. When the Democratic National Convention convened on July 21, 1952, it discovered the eloquence of Illinois' Governor Adlai E. Stevenson, and it nominated him. Millions of Americans were inspired by his appeals to the nation to accept the fact that "Sacrifice, patience, understanding and implacable purpose may be our lot for years to come. . . ." The Republicans, meeting in Chicago in early July, chose General Dwight D. Eisenhower over Robert A. Taft. As his running mate, they nominated Richard M. Nixon, the controversial

Senator from California. Eisenhower's campaign emphasized the need to place the national interest above the particular interest. The campaign was a mélange of Stevenson's eloquence, Eisenhower's homilies, calls to clean up the "Truman mess," and charges that Nixon had accepted a "slush fund" from a group of California millionaires. On Election Day, in an outpouring of voters never previously exceeded, Eisenhower swept to victory with almost 34 million popular votes to slightly more than 27 million votes for Stevenson; the electoral count was 442 to 89. But it was a personal, rather than a party, victory for Eisenhower; the Republicans held a bare eight-vote edge in the House, and were able to organize the Senate only because the Vice-President's vote broke a 48–48 tie. In the 1954 off-year elections, the Democrats would further reveal their intrinsic strength by regaining control of both Houses of Congress.

Eisenhower's Domestic Policies. The moderate conservatism of the new President was made sharply evident in his domestic policies. To a South Dakota audience he announced that he had "instituted what amounts almost to a revolution in the federal government as we have known it in our time, trying to make it smaller rather than bigger and finding things it can stop doing instead of seeking new things for it to do." In fact, despite unsuccessful efforts to shift some of the TVA's activities to private enterprise, Eisenhower emulated the Truman program of modest domestic reforms. In 1954, social security coverage was extended to some ten million individuals and benefits were raised. The following year saw the minimum wage lifted to $1.00 an hour, and Eisenhower personally supported a bill making the Salk antipolio vaccine available to all children. Of enormous future significance for the economy, the President, on June 26, 1956, signed the Federal-Aid Highway Act and Highway Revenue Act which created a thirteen-year, $27 billion program of federal aid for state highway construction. At the behest of Secretary of Agriculture Ezra Taft Benson, the Soil Bank Act of 1956, which paid farmers to withdraw land from crop production, was passed; as usual, the result was to maintain a high level of payments to farmers without materially reducing the staggering farm surpluses. Nonetheless, Benson, who was committed to returning agriculture to an unsupported free enterprise system, doggedly but unsuccessfully persisted in seeking ways to compel this result. Efforts to provide federal aid for school construction were neatly checked by a coalition—conservative Republicans, conservative Democrats, and Northern liberals—which objected to such expenditures going to racially segregated facilities. The result of these programs, and the failure of Eisenhower to launch a massive rejection of New Deal reforms, was to place the seal of bipartisan approval on the "Roosevelt Revolution."

A Bipartisan Foreign Policy. Franklin D. Roosevelt had never forgotten the disastrous political lesson accorded Woodrow Wilson; he had taken care to give prominent Republicans a full and responsible role in the formulation of peace, and with the cooperation of Senator Arthur Vandenberg, Wendell Willkie, and John Foster Dulles, American foreign policy became bipartisan, a subject for private discussion and restrained public debate, but not for dispute. Both Truman and Eisenhower kept foreign policy generally out of partisan politics, in spite of Secretary of State John Foster Dulles's ability to alarm Democrats with verbal sallies that pledged liberation to the Soviet Union's satellites, and preached "brinkmanship," or the fine art of *almost* going to war. But Dulles's words were not matched by his actions, which were generally characterized by firm but cautious restraint.

Eisenhower's Asia Policy. Barely two weeks before the 1952 election, Eisenhower pledged if he were elected to go to Korea to settle the war. By his action he confirmed, rather than repudiated, Truman's policy of a war of limited results. In a series of protracted negotiations that terminated in an armistice on July 27, 1953, the Korean War was finally ended. The nation had sustained 137,530 casualties, of which 34,246 were dead—a high price not for victory but simply for a draw. Once launched, the policy of stabilizing the Asiatic situation went on apace. The American Seventh Fleet continued the task (assigned it by Truman) of patrolling the Formosa Strait, keeping the Chinese Communists from launching an assault on Formosa, and restraining Chiang Kai-shek from any adventures on the China mainland. When faced with the choice of aiding the French in crushing a Communist rebellion in Indochina or in bringing about a settlement, the administration settled for negotiation. The armistice of July 21, 1954, divided Indochina into the kingdoms of Cambodia and Laos, while Vietnam was divided along the 17th parallel, with the northern half passing under Communist authority and the southern half under the control of a government friendly to the United States. The administration refrained from participating in these negotiations, but subsequently underwrote the Laotian and South Vietnamese regimes with military aid. Both countries have since been plagued with Communistic subversion and guerrilla warfare, and the United States has become increasingly involved in lending not only material, but the assistance of troops as well.

Eisenhower and Defense. Nothing interested Eisenhower more than the prospect of balancing the budget, but three recessions during his eight years of office, and a steady increase in defense expenditures, prevented his achieving that goal. The harnessing of thermonuclear energy, and the launching by the Russians, on October 4, 1957, of an earth satellite, Sputnik I, provoked a national outcry for even greater defense expenditures. By the end of his administration, Eisenhower had launched a vast program of space exploration and rocket development which his successor, John F. Kennedy, would continue. For better or for worse, the nation and the world seemed committed to a policy of preparing for war with weapons which were, in the words of President Kennedy, "ten million times more powerful than anything the world has ever seen and only minutes away from any target on earth," in the hope that the existence of such weapons would prove a sufficient deterrent to their use.

The Rise in International Tensions. The death of Stalin on March 6, 1953, began a power struggle in the Kremlin that resulted in a shift of emphasis in both the domestic and foreign policy of the Soviet Union. The world watched with puzzlement and unease as Nikita S. Khrushchev elbowed aside such formidable rivals as Premier Georgi Malenkov, Foreign Minister V. M. Molotov, and General Gregory K. Zhukov. Evidence of discord in the Soviet satellite empire mounted, first in a series of riots and strikes throughout East Germany during June 1953; then in the coming to power in October, 1956 of Wladyslaw Gomulka, an anti-Stalinist Communist, in Poland; and finally in the wholesale rebellion in Hungary during October and November 1956. As the American public trooped to the polls on November 6 to give Eisenhower a second election triumph over Adlai Stevenson, the world was wracked by an international crisis of awesome proportions. Five hundred thousand Russian troops, aided by thousands of tanks, crushed the Hungarian uprising. Simultaneously a combined British, French, and Israeli invasion of Egypt began, only to be halted by a United Nations intervention backed by both the United States and the Soviet Union. Two results of this crisis were of lasting significance: the United Nations had proved itself an effective instrument for keeping the peace, and the United States, by its failure to intervene in Hungary, had confirmed the finality of Russian predominance in eastern Europe.

The Middle East Crisis. Since 1939, the American public has been subjected to an extended geography lesson, as one area after another has demanded national attention. Since the establishment of Israel in 1948 as an independent state in the Middle East by United Nations vote, the small country has been assailed by threats and actual attacks on the part of neighboring Arab states. Under the leadership of Egypt's Gamal Abdel Nasser a program of Arab unity and anti-Zionism has served to provide a focal point of Arab nationalism. The situation has been further complicated by a never-ceasing rivalry between the United States and the Soviet Union for dominance in the region. Nasser has shrewdly exploited these conflicting aspirations to obtain aid and military equipment. The vast oil resources of the region have also been of considerable interest to the western-controlled petroleum corporations. In an effort to stabilize the region, Eisenhower issued, on March 9, 1957, the "Eisenhower Doctrine," which pledged to uphold the integrity of all the Middle Eastern nations. When in the summer of 1958 a revolution broke out, first in Lebanon and then in Iraq, the United States and Britain, both responding to the appeals of the President of Lebanon and King Hussein of Jordan, sent military forces to stabilize the two countries. These forces were withdrawn in October after the General Assembly committed the United Nations to guaranteeing the security of Lebanon and Jordan. Middle Eastern politics were outwardly stabilized, but inwardly they remained in turmoil as Nasser struggled to extend Arab unity and as other Arab governments worked to maintain their sovereignty.

The Election of 1958. No aspect of the Eisenhower years was more peculiar than the inability of the President to transfer his personal popularity to the Republican party. Except for the Eighty-third Congress elected in 1952, the Democrats controlled both Houses of Congress for six years of Eisenhower's terms. A sharp recession in the first half of 1958, and revelations that the President's closest confidant, Sherman Adams, was guilty of accepting gifts from a New England textile manufacturer and of using his influence in behalf of the manufacturer with several federal agencies, did little to help the Republican image. The Democrats, gleefully recalling Republican exploitation of similar charges during the Truman administration, and ably assisted by conservative Republicans who suspected that Adams was too liberal, hounded the former Governor of New Hampshire from office. Eisenhower's plea, "I personally like Governor Adams. I admire his abilities. I respect him because of his personal and official integrity. *I need him . . .*" were ignored. When Vice-President Nixon launched freewheeling attacks upon the Democrats, those gentlemen, sharing a mutual distaste for their attacker, united as they rarely had previously. The presence of "right-to-work" referendums in several key industrial states brought hordes of union voters to the polls. The result was a landslide victory for the Democrats, who increased their strength to

62 in the Senate and 282 in the House, figures that resembled the salad days of the early New Deal.

The End of the Eisenhower Years. The death of John Foster Dulles in May 1959 and the earlier departure of Sherman Adams resulted in Eisenhower's taking an ever more forceful role in both domestic and diplomatic affairs. At home, he guided Alaska into the Union on January 3, 1959, as the forty-ninth state, and Hawaii on August 21, 1959, as the fiftieth. Through 1959 he vetoed ten bills, only one of which was subsequently overriden, largely to insure a conservative fiscal policy.

Abroad, Eisenhower returned to exploring the possibilities of a summit meeting—with disastrous results. Earlier efforts to reach an accord at Geneva in 1955 at a meeting of heads of state had ended without any measurable results. Some evidence of a warmer relationship between the United States and the Soviet Union seemed possible after the visit to America of Premier Khrushchev in September 1959. A summit meeting was scheduled for May 16 in Paris, but it never occurred, for on May 5, 1960, Khrushchev announced that an American U-2 spy plane had been shot down near the Siberian city of Sverdlovsk. At first American authorities denied the accuracy of this report; but when the Russians subsequently revealed that they held the American pilot prisoner, Washington admitted the flight and acknowledged that other similar flights had been made. On May 16, Khrushchev abruptly terminated the summit meeting, expressing his hope that a newly elected United States government might, the following year, be able to approach such a conference with an understanding of "the futility of pursuing aggressive policies." Eisenhower returned to America to await the 1960 elections.

JOHN F. KENNEDY AS PRESIDENT

The Election of 1960. The Democrats met in Los Angeles in July 1960 and defied tradition by nominating on their first ballot the senator from Massachusetts, John Fitzgerald Kennedy, then only forty-three years old, and a Roman Catholic. As his running mate, Senator Lyndon B. Johnson of Texas, the Democratic majority leader in the Senate who had shrewdly managed the Congress with Speaker Sam Rayburn for the previous six years, was chosen. Ten days later, the Republicans convened in Chicago to nominate Vice-President Richard M. Nixon and, as his running mate, Henry Cabot Lodge, the American Ambassador to the United Nations and the senator from Massachusetts whom

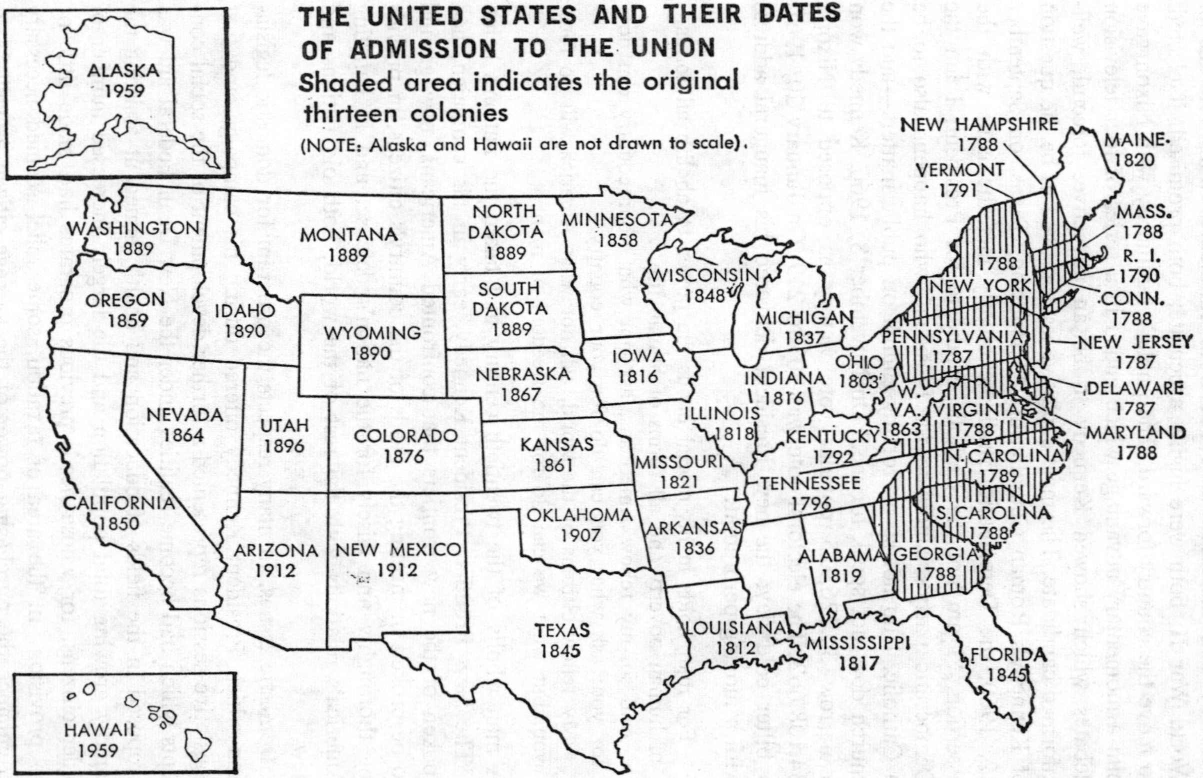

THE UNITED STATES AND THEIR DATES OF ADMISSION TO THE UNION

Shaded area indicates the original thirteen colonies

(NOTE: Alaska and Hawaii are not drawn to scale).

Kennedy had displaced in 1952. Both candidates were veterans of World War II; both were highly articulate; both promised, if elected, to move the country forward. The public's familiarity with Nixon gave him a momentary advantage which ended in a series of four television debates which showed Kennedy to be an attractive, forceful, well-informed candidate. The most explosive issue proved to be the question of Kennedy's Roman Catholicism. At Houston, Texas, on September 12, 1960, the Democratic candidate bluntly met the issue with the assertion, "I am not the Catholic candidate for President; I am the Democratic party's candidate for President, who happens also to be a Catholic. I do not speak for my church on public matters—and the church does not speak for me." On November 8, 1960, Kennedy won a narrow 34,226,925 popular vote victory as opposed to Nixon's 34,108,662. The electoral vote was 303 to 219. On January 20, 1961, a bitter cold day, the new President delivered his inaugural address with a moving peroration:

> For man holds in his mortal hands the power to abolish all forms of human poverty and all forms of human life. . . .
>
> And so, my fellow Americans, ask not what your country can do for you; ask what you can do for your country.
>
> My fellow citizens of the world, ask not what America will do for you, but what we can do for the freedom of man.

A man wholly of the twentieth century had taken the nation's helm.

The New Frontier. President Kennedy, early in his campaign, had spoken of the new frontiers that confronted Americans, new ground to be broken in meeting the needs of the country's citizens, in providing thoroughly and wisely for the nation's defense, and in handling America's relations with the rest of the world, both old nations and new.

Domestic Issues. In many respects the program for domestic legislation which President Kennedy offered during his campaign and first legislative sessions represented a further development of the social concepts which had become realities under the New Deal. Federal aid was proposed in the fields of education and health, aimed at assisting the rapidly growing total population and the largely increased number of older citizens, for whose needs previous programs had made little or no provision. In the area of taxation, some relief seemed necessary to enhance the purchasing power of the average citizen as well as to stimulate corporate investment and thus spur the economy as a whole.

The question of civil rights, which had come to the fore during the

Eisenhower administration, demanded new and vigorous action. In May 1954 the Supreme Court had decided that the doctrine of racially separate but equal facilities set forth in Plessy *v.* Ferguson in 1896 must be set aside, stating in Brown *v.* Board of Education of Topeka its conviction that inequality is inherent in separation, for such separation "solely because of their race generates a feeling of inferiority as to their status in the community that may affect their hearts and minds in a way unlikely ever to be undone."

Thus American law was at last uncompromisingly committed to fulfilling the rights of the Negro. But when President Eisenhower had to send federal troops into Little Rock, Arkansas, to insure the admission of a handful of Negro students to Central High School, when President Kennedy had to do the same to secure one admission to the University of Mississippi, when the centennial year of the Emancipation Proclamation saw the swelling of racial unrest throughout the country, it became inescapably clear to the nation as a whole that the moral issue of inequality had yet to be confronted.

The new administration sought to encourage congressional action which would bring about the necessary legislation for these and other basic domestic needs. But whether because of a conservative trend in congressional leadership, or because popular support of the proposed legislation was not vigorous enough, or because of rivalries between various groups in the administration and decreased cooperation between the various branches of the government, the President's program as a whole would face difficult and perhaps impassible obstacles in its way to enactment.

Defense Program. The harnessing of the atom as a source of power through nuclear fission and fusion brought with it the promise of vast benefits to mankind from the almost boundless energy which could be made available. But coupled with this power for good was the terrifying potential of this same nuclear force if used in weapons, as the first atomic bombs released at the end of World War II had demonstrated.

The Kennedy administration, like its postwar predecessors, continued the national commitment to a large, constantly on the alert military establishment and to the massive spending for this preparedness and the research and development of new systems of weaponry that the pressures of the Cold War seemed to demand.

Efforts were continued by the United States and the other western nations to work out with the Soviet Union some dependable formula for disarmament or, at least, for cessation of nuclear testing and its contamination of the earth's atmosphere. The signing, in August 1963, of an international agreement banning further atmospheric nuclear explosions for any purpose by the United States, Russia, England, and a host of other nations, may be regarded as a positive step forward. However, until further steps toward international peace and world order proved unquestionably successful, this country would be involved in a military effort that had no parallel in its history, even in wartime, and its people would have to learn to live in a world where the nation's historical alternatives, the quick use of force or turning away from the world scene, were no longer possible.

Foreign Affairs. The continuing division of the nations of the world essentially into two large groups representing opposed and, to a considerable degree, hostile conceptions of the true role of individuals and peoples required that the Kennedy administration foreign policy be directed at all times to strengthening the ties between the western allies, to enhancing the friendship of the nations uncommitted in their relations to the two large groups, and to seeking a means of arriving at a condition of peaceful coexistence with the opposing groups in the face of the nuclear alternative.

But problems on the international scene would grow more and more complex. In the Far East, Communist China, with no international allegiance, could present a danger equal to that of the Soviet Communist bloc, and despite fallings-out between these two Communist powers, there was no guarantee that their similarities would not in the long run bind them together. So the United States was obliged to demonstrate its global commitments even in those areas in Southeast Asia adjacent to China.

In addition to the unique problems presented by the militantly Communistic powers, the United States faced the task of making and maintaining friendship among the independent nations all around the world —in Latin America, the Middle East, and Africa. The Kennedy administration has made several new attempts in this direction. The Peace Corps, for example, has sent Americans of all ages into various underdeveloped lands in a person-to-person program of educational, medical, and technical aid. In Latin America, massive aid in solving its economic and social difficulties was begun through the Alliance for Progress. And America has increasingly relied upon and supported the United Nations work in the resolution of problems throughout the world.

The Cuban crisis of October 1962 demonstrated the urgency of fighting the conditions on which Communism feeds, as well as the immediacy of the United States' involvement in the world conflict.

When Fidel Castro led a revolution against the Batista dictatorship in 1953, few Americans realized that a Communist satellite would soon be on their doorstep or that Soviet missiles capable of striking all major American cities would be installed there, allegedly to protect Cuba from a repetition of such "attacks" as the ill-conceived, U.S.-supported Bay of Pigs invasion by Cuban counterrevolutionaries. Although the missiles threat was countered by the President's ultimatum for their removal, and Khrushchev's eventual acquiescence brought the world back from the brink of nuclear war, the Western Hemisphere could never consider itself removed from the ideological clashes of the rest of the world.

The role of the United Nations was less evident in later confrontations around the world than it had been a number of important times earlier in its existence. Yet there was strong conviction, particularly on the part of the smaller countries, that the international organization had a vital role to play in the development of peaceful years in the future.

The Assassination of President Kennedy. On Friday, November 22, 1963, while riding in an open car in a motorcade through Dallas, Texas, President Kennedy was struck down by an assassin's bullet. Within hours of the President's death, Lyndon B. Johnson, who was also in Texas at the time, took the oath of office, becoming the thirty-sixth man to assume the presidency. A shocked and grieving nation had reason to be grateful that Kennedy had throughout the three years of his administration taken his Vice-President fully into his confidence on all major matters of policy; and on assuming the presidency, Johnson pledged himself to the continuation and furtherance of the goals, both national and international, of the New Frontier.

The Exploration of Space. In the midst of uncertainties, one new development has excited all the peoples of the world—the successful missile-launched flights of astronauts and cosmonauts into space and back to earth with news of their experiences. The perfecting of these unprecedented skills, with the promise of future capabilities to follow, gives an entirely new dimension to life today.

So, amid the multitude of threatening and unimaginable dangers in other phases of world affairs, has come the dawn of a new age of exploration and discovery unequaled in its challenge, surpassing even the great days when Columbus and others first crossed the seas to the New World. We can only speculate on how man will use his conquest of space, and hope that future historians will record that he used the abilities which enabled him to reach other worlds to insure peace on his own earth.

TABLES OF PARTIES AND PRESIDENTS

MAJOR TRENDS IN THE DEVELOPMENT AND GROWTH OF AMERICAN POLITICAL PARTIES, 1864 to 1960

The name of each party is listed under the year in which it became an important factor. The horizontal line following each party name indicates the length of time the party actively functioned. A broken line indicates continued action at local levels

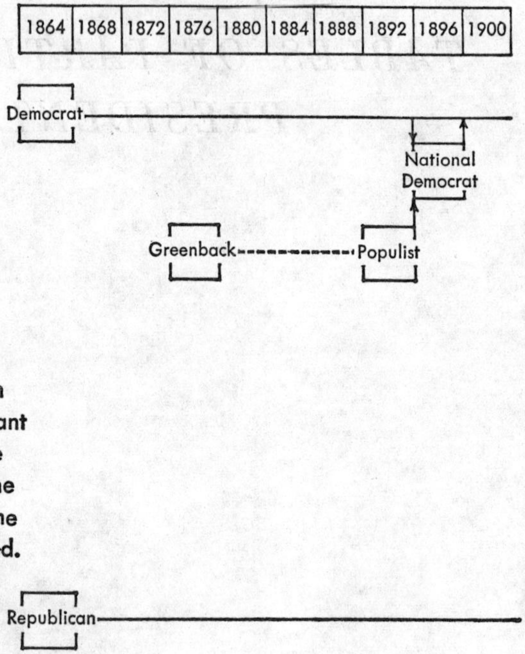

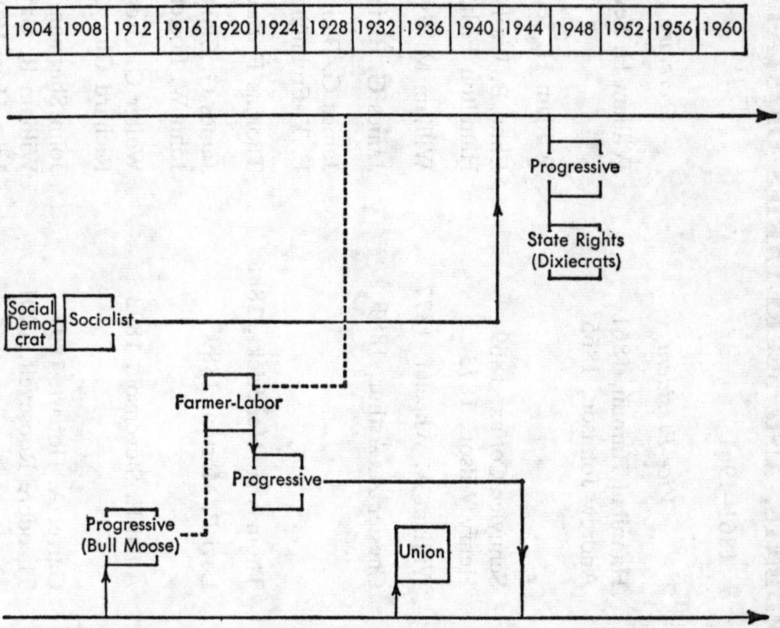
1904
1908
1912
1916
1920
1924
1928
1932
1936
1940
1944
1948
1952
1956
1960
Progressive
State Rights (Dixiecrats)
Social Democrat
Socialist
Farmer-Labor
Progressive
Progressive (Bull Moose)
Union

PRESIDENTS, VICE-PRESIDENTS, AND SECRETARIES OF STATE

1861–1961

President	*Vice-President*	*Secretary of State*
Abraham Lincoln, Republican, 1861	Hannibal Hamlin, 1861 Andrew Johnson, 1865	William H. Seward, 1861
Andrew Johnson, Republican, 1865		William H. Seward, 1865
Ulysses S. Grant, Republican, 1869	Schuyler Colfax, 1869 Henry Wilson, 1873	Elihu B. Washburne, 1869 Hamilton Fish, 1869
Rutherford B. Hayes, Republican, 1877	William A. Wheeler, 1877	William M. Evarts, 1877
James A. Garfield, Republican, 1881	Chester A. Arthur, 1881	James G. Blaine, 1881
Chester A. Arthur, Republican, 1881		James G. Blaine, 1881 F. T. Frelinghuysen, 1881
Grover Cleveland, Democrat, 1885	Thomas A. Hendricks, 1885	Thomas F. Bayard, 1885
Benjamin Harrison, Republican, 1889	Levi P. Morton, 1889	James G. Blaine, 1889 John W. Foster, 1892
Grover Cleveland, Democrat, 1893	Adlai E. Stevenson, 1893	Walter Q. Gresham, 1893 Richard Olney, 1895
William McKinley, Republican, 1897	Garret A. Hobart, 1897 Theodore Roosevelt, 1901	John Sherman, 1897 William R. Day, 1898 John Hay, 1898

Theodore Roosevelt, Republican, 1901	Charles W. Fairbanks, 1905	John Hay, 1901 Elihu Root, 1905 Robert Bacon, 1909
William H. Taft, Republican, 1909	James S. Sherman, 1909	Philander C. Knox, 1909
Woodrow Wilson, Democrat, 1913	Thomas R. Marshall, 1913	William J. Bryan, 1913 Robert Lansing, 1915 Bainbridge Colby, 1920
Warren G. Harding, Republican, 1921	Calvin Coolidge, 1921	Charles E. Hughes, 1921
Calvin Coolidge, Republican, 1923	Charles G. Dawes, 1925	Charles E. Hughes, 1923 Frank B. Kellogg, 1925
Herbert Hoover, Republican, 1929	Charles Curtis, 1929	Henry L. Stimson, 1929
Franklin D. Roosevelt, Democrat, 1933	John N. Garner, 1933 Henry A. Wallace, 1941 Harry S. Truman, 1945	Cordell Hull, 1933 E. R. Stettinius, 1945
Harry S. Truman, Democrat, 1945	Alben W. Barkley, 1949	E. R. Stettinius, 1945 James F. Byrnes, 1945 George C. Marshall, 1947 Dean Acheson, 1949
Dwight D. Eisenhower, Republican, 1953	Richard M. Nixon, 1953	John Foster Dulles, 1953 Christian A. Herter, 1959
John F. Kennedy, Democrat, 1961	Lyndon B. Johnson, 1961	Dean Rusk, 1961
Lyndon B. Johnson, Democrat, 1963		Dean Rusk, 1963

PRESIDENTIAL ELECTIONS

1864–1960

Year	*Candidates*	*Parties*	*Popular Vote*	*Electoral Vote*
1864	Abraham Lincoln	Republican	2,213,665	212
	George B. McClellan	Democrat	1,805,237	21
1868	Ulysses S. Grant	Republican	3,015,071	214
	Horatio Seymour	Democrat	2,709,615	80
1872	Ulysses S. Grant	Republican	3,597,070	286
	Horace Greeley	Democrat	2,834,079	—
1876	Rutherford B. Hayes	Republican	4,033,950	185
	Samuel J. Tilden	Democrat	4,284,757	184
1880	James A. Garfield	Republican	4,449,053	214
	Winfield S. Hancock	Democrat	4,442,030	155
1884	Grover Cleveland	Democrat	4,911,017	219
	James G. Blaine	Republican	4,848,334	182
1888	Benjamin Harrison	Republican	5,444,337	233
	Grover Cleveland	Democrat	5,540,050	168
1892	Grover Cleveland	Democrat	5,554,414	277
	Benjamin Harrison	Republican	5,190,802	145
	James Weaver	Populist	1,027,329	22
1896	William McKinley	Republican	7,035,638	271
	William J. Bryan	Democrat	6,467,946	176
1900	William McKinley	Republican	7,219,530	292
	William J. Bryan	Democrat	6,358,071	155
1904	Theodore Roosevelt	Republican	7,628,834	336
	Alton B. Parker	Democrat	5,084,491	140
1908	William H. Taft	Republican	7,679,006	321
	William J. Bryan	Democrat	6,409,106	162
1912	Woodrow Wilson	Democrat	6,286,214	435
	Theodore Roosevelt	Progressive	4,216,020	88
	William H. Taft	Republican	3,483,922	8

1916	Woodrow Wilson	Democrat	9,129,606	277
	Charles E. Hughes	Republican	8,538,221	254
1920	Warren G. Harding	Republican	16,152,200	404
	James M. Cox	Democrat	9,147,353	127
1924	Calvin Coolidge	Republican	15,725,016	382
	John W. Davis	Democrat	8,385,586	136
	Robert M. La Follette	Progressive	4,822,856	13
1928	Herbert Hoover	Republican	21,392,190	444
	Alfred E. Smith	Democrat	15,016,443	87
1932	Franklin D. Roosevelt	Democrat	22,821,857	472
	Herbert Hoover	Republican	15,761,841	59
1936	Franklin D. Roosevelt	Democrat	27,476,673	523
	Alfred M. Landon	Republican	16,679,583	8
1940	Franklin D. Roosevelt	Democrat	27,243,466	449
	Wendell Willkie	Republican	22,304,755	82
1944	Franklin D. Roosevelt	Democrat	25,602,505	432
	Thomas E. Dewey	Republican	22,006,278	99
1948	Harry S. Truman	Democrat	24,105,812	303
	Thomas E. Dewey	Republican	21,970,065	189
	J. Strom Thurmond	State Rights	1,169,021	39
	Henry A. Wallace	Progressive	1,157,172	—
1952	Dwight D. Eisenhower	Republican	33,936,252	442
	Adlai E. Stevenson	Democrat	27,314,992	89
1956	Dwight D. Eisenhower	Republican	35,585,316	457
	Adlai E. Stevenson	Democrat	26,031,322	74
1960	John F. Kennedy	Democrat	34,226,925	300
	Richard M. Nixon	Republican	34,108,662	223

Index